LEVITICUS
A Commentary in the Wesleyan Tradition

*New Beacon Bible Commentary

LEVITICUS
A Commentary in the Wesleyan Tradition

Thomas J. King

BEACON HILL PRESS
OF KANSAS CITY

Copyright 2013
by Beacon Hill Press of Kansas City

ISBN 978-0-8341-3157-6

Printed in the United States of America

Cover Design: J.R. Caines
Interior Design: Sharon Page

Portions of the Introduction have been adapted from the author's book, *The Realignment of the Priestly Literature*. Used by permission of Wipf and Stock Publishers. www.wipfandstock.com.

Unless otherwise indicated all Scripture quotations are from the *Holy Bible, New International Version®* (NIV®). Copyright © 1973, 1978, 1984 by Biblica, Inc.™ Used by permission of Zondervan. All rights reserved worldwide. www.zondervan.com.

The following versions of Scripture are in the public domain:

King James Version (KJV).

Young's Literal Translation (YLT).

The following copyrighted versions of the Bible are used by permission:

Good News Translation® (*Today's English Version*, Second Edition) (GNT). Copyright © 1992 American Bible Society. All rights reserved.

The *New American Bible* (NAB). Copyright © 1970 by the Confraternity of Christian Doctrine, 3211 4th St. N.E., Washington, DC 20017-1194. All rights reserved.

The *New American Standard Bible®* (NASB®), © copyright The Lockman Foundation 1960, 1962, 1963, 1968, 1971, 1972, 1973, 1975, 1977, 1995.

The *NET Bible®* (NET), copyright © 1996-2006 by Biblical Studies Press, L.L.C., http://bible.org. All rights reserved.

Hebrew-English Tanakh (NJPS), © 2000 by The Jewish Publication Society. All rights reserved.

The *New King James Version* (NKJV). Copyright © 1979, 1980, 1982 Thomas Nelson, Inc.

The *New Revised Standard Version* (NRSV) of the Bible, copyright 1989 by the Division of Christian Education of the National Council of the Churches of Christ in the USA. All rights reserved.

The *Revised Standard Version* (RSV) of the Bible, copyright 1946, 1952, 1971 by the Division of Christian Education of the National Council of the Churches of Christ in the USA. All rights reserved.

Library of Congress Control Number: 2013947523

DEDICATION

For my family, with gratitude:
John and Joanne King,
who raised their children in the holiness of the Lord;
Timothy and Michael King,
who forgive, love, and encourage their spoiled middle sibling;
Janine King,
who inspires and awakens the very best in her husband;
Charis, Crystal, and Cayla,
who enrich their father's life beyond measure

COMMENTARY EDITORS

General Editors

Alex Varughese
   Ph.D., Drew University
   Professor of Biblical Literature
   Mount Vernon Nazarene University
   Mount Vernon, Ohio

Roger Hahn
   Ph.D., Duke University
   Dean of the Faculty
   Professor of New Testament
   Nazarene Theological Seminary
   Kansas City, Missouri

George Lyons
   Ph.D., Emory University
   Professor of New Testament
   Northwest Nazarene University
   Nampa, Idaho

Section Editors

Joseph Coleson
   Ph.D., Brandeis University
   Professor of Old Testament
   Nazarene Theological Seminary
   Kansas City, Missouri

Robert Branson
   Ph.D., Boston University
   Professor of Biblical Literature
      Emeritus
   Olivet Nazarene University
   Bourbonnais, Illinois

Alex Varughese
   Ph.D., Drew University
   Professor of Biblical Literature
   Mount Vernon Nazarene University
   Mount Vernon, Ohio

Jim Edlin
   Ph.D., Southern Baptist Theological
      Seminary
   Professor of Biblical Literature and
      Languages
   Chair, Division of Religion and
      Philosophy
   MidAmerica Nazarene University
   Olathe, Kansas

Kent Brower
   Ph.D., The University of Manchester
   Vice Principal
   Senior Lecturer in Biblical Studies
   Nazarene Theological College
   Manchester, England

George Lyons
   Ph.D., Emory University
   Professor of New Testament
   Northwest Nazarene University
   Nampa, Idaho

CONTENTS

General Editors' Preface	11
Acknowledgments	13
Abbreviations	15
Bibliography	19
INTRODUCTION	25
A. Authorship	25
1. Mosaic Foundations	25
2. Source Critical Scholarship	27
B. Date	30
C. Composition	34
1. The Priestly Source	34
2. The Holiness Code	38
D. Theology	38
1. The Relational Purpose of the Sacrificial System	39
2. Reverence for Life in the Impurity Laws	40
3. Call to Holiness in the Holiness Code	41
COMMENTARY	45
I. The Sacrificial System (1:1—7:38)	45
A. Voluntary Sacrifices (1:1—3:17)	45
1. Burnt Offering (1:1-17)	47
2. Grain Offering (2:1-16)	53
3. Well-Being Offering (3:1-17)	58
B. Required Sacrifices (4:1—6:7 [4:1—5:26 HB])	64
1. Purification Offering (4:1—5:13)	65
2. Guilt Offering (5:14—6:7 [5:14-26 HB])	76
C. Allocation of the Sacrifices (6:8—7:38 [6:1—7:38 HB])	84
1. Allocation of the Burnt Offering (6:8-13 [6:1-6 HB])	84
2. Allocation of the Grain Offering (6:14-23 [6:7-16 HB])	86
3. Allocation of the Purification Offering (6:24-30 [6:17-23 HB])	87
4. Allocation of the Guilt Offering (7:1-10)	89
5. Allocation of the Well-Being Offering (7:11-38)	90
II. Ordination and First Sacrifices (8:1—10:20)	97
A. Ordination of the Priests (8:1-36)	98
1. Cleansing and Anointing (8:1-13)	98
2. Sacrificial Service (8:14-30)	100
3. Ordination Meal and Sanctuary Confinement (8:31-36)	102

	B.	Inauguration of the Sacrificial System (9:1-24)	103
		1. The First Sacrifices (9:1-21)	103
		2. Community Blessing and Divine Fire (9:22-24)	108
	C.	The Sons of Aaron and Priestly Portions (10:1-20)	109
		1. Nadab and Abihu (10:1-7)	109
		2. Priestly Duties and Priestly Portions (10:8-15)	113
		3. Eleazar and Ithamar (10:16-20)	114
III.	Impurity Laws (11:1—15:33)	121
	A.	Dietary Restrictions (11:1-47)	122
		1. Land, Water, and Sky Creatures (11:1-23)	122
		2. Unclean Animals and Purification Procedures (11:24-40)	125
		3. Land Swarmers (11:41-45)	127
		4. Summation (11:46-47)	128
	B.	Childbirth (12:1-8)	131
	C.	Skin Disease (13:1—14:57)	133
		1. Swellings, Spots, Boils, Burns, Sores (13:1-44)	133
		2. Conduct of Person with Skin Disease (13:45-46)	137
		3. Skin Disease in a Garment (13:47-59)	137
		4. Purification after Skin Disease (14:1-32)	138
		5. Skin Disease on a House (14:33-53)	143
		6. Summation (14:54-57)	147
	D.	Sexual Discharges (15:1-33)	148
		1. Male Discharges (15:1-18)	148
		2. Female Discharges (15:19-30)	150
		3. Summation (15:31-33)	152
IV.	The Day of Atonement (16:1-34)	155
	A.	Overview and Preparation (16:1-10)	157
		1. Introductory Warning (16:1-2)	157
		2. Priestly Garments and Assembly of Offerings (16:3-5)	158
		3. Designation of Bull and Goats (16:6-10)	159
	B.	The Ceremony (16:11-28)	161
		1. The Blood Rite (16:11-19)	161
		2. The Live Goat (16:20-22)	166
		3. Remaining Offerings and Closing Procedures (16:23-28)	167
	C.	Final Instructions (16:29-34)	168
		1. Designation of Date and Sabbath Instruction (16:29-31)	168
		2. Summation (16:32-34)	169
V.	The Holiness Code (17:1—27:34)	173
	A.	Slaughter and the Blood Prohibition (17:1-16)	173
		1. Ban on Common Slaughter of Sacrificial Animals (17:1-9)	174
		2. Prohibition against Ingesting Blood (17:10-12)	177
		3. Wild Game and Animals Found Dead (17:13-16)	178
	B.	Prohibited Sexual Relations (18:1-30)	181
		1. Introductory Exhortation (18:1-5)	181

	2. Sexual Prohibitions (18:6-23)	183
	3. Concluding Exhortation (18:24-30)	190
C.	Commands for Holiness (19:1-37)	193
	1. Parents, Sabbath, Idols, Well-Being Offering (19:1-8)	194
	2. Laws Regarding Treatment of Neighbor (19:9-18)	198
	3. Various Laws (19:19-37)	201
D.	Molech Worship and Sexual Prohibitions (20:1-27)	208
	1. Molech Worship Forbidden (20:1-5)	209
	2. Sorcery, Call to Holiness, Dishonoring Parents (20:6-9)	210
	3. Penalties for Sexual Transgressions (20:10-21)	211
	4. Concluding Exhortation, Distinguishing Clean and Unclean, Appendix on Sorcery (20:22-27)	214
E.	Priestly Holiness and Acceptable Sacrifices (21:1—22:33)	218
	1. Restrictions for the Priests (21:1-9)	218
	2. Restrictions for the High Priest (21:10-15)	222
	3. Priests with Physical Defects (21:16-24)	223
	4. Sacred Donations (22:1-16)	224
	5. Rules for Acceptable Offerings (22:17-33)	226
F.	Appointed Times of the Lord (23:1-44)	230
	1. Introduction and Sabbath (23:1-4)	232
	2. Passover and Festival of Unleavened Bread (23:5-8)	233
	3. Offering of the First Sheaf (23:9-14)	235
	4. Festival of Weeks (23:15-22)	236
	5. First Day of the Seventh Month (23:23-25)	238
	6. Day of Atonement (23:26-32)	240
	7. Festival of Tabernacles (23:33-36)	241
	8. Summation (23:37-38)	242
	9. Supplement Regarding Tabernacles (23:39-44)	242
G.	Oil and Bread for the Tabernacle; Blasphemy (24:1-23)	245
	1. Lamp and Bread of the Tabernacle (24:1-9)	247
	2. Case of the Blasphemer (24:10-23)	249
H.	Laws Regarding Sabbatical and Jubilee Years (25:1-55)	254
	1. The Sabbatical Year (25:1-7)	256
	2. The Year of Jubilee (25:8-55)	257
I.	Reward, Punishment, and Repentance (26:1-46)	268
	1. Blessings for Obedience (26:1-13)	269
	2. Punishments for Disobedience (26:14-39)	272
	3. Repentance and Remembrance of Covenant (26:40-46)	275
J.	Consecrations and Redemption (27:1-34)	278
	1. Vows Regarding Humans and Animals (27:1-13)	279
	2. Consecrations Regarding Houses and Fields (27:14-25)	281
	3. Firstborn, Devoted Things, and Tithes (27:26-34)	283

GENERAL EDITORS' PREFACE

The purpose of the New Beacon Bible Commentary is to make available to pastors and students in the twenty-first century a biblical commentary that reflects the best scholarship in the Wesleyan theological tradition. The commentary project aims to make this scholarship accessible to a wider audience to assist them in their understanding and proclamation of Scripture as God's Word.

Writers of the volumes in this series not only are scholars within the Wesleyan theological tradition and experts in their field but also have special interest in the books assigned to them. Their task is to communicate clearly the critical consensus and the full range of other credible voices who have commented on the Scriptures. Though scholarship and scholarly contribution to the understanding of the Scriptures are key concerns of this series, it is not intended as an academic dialogue within the scholarly community. Commentators of this series constantly aim to demonstrate in their work the significance of the Bible as the church's book and the contemporary relevance and application of the biblical message. The project's overall goal is to make available to the church and for her service the fruits of the labors of scholars who are committed to their Christian faith.

The *New International Version* (NIV) is the reference version of the Bible used in this series; however, the focus of exegetical study and comments is the biblical text in its original language. When the commentary uses the NIV, it is printed in bold. The text printed in bold italics is the translation of the author. Commentators also refer to other translations where the text may be difficult or ambiguous.

The structure and organization of the commentaries in this series seeks to facilitate the study of the biblical text in a systematic and methodical way. Study of each biblical book begins with an **Introduction** section that gives an overview of authorship, date, provenance, audience, occasion, purpose, sociological/cultural issues, textual history, literary features, hermeneutical issues, and theological themes necessary to understand the book. This section also includes a brief outline of the book and a list of general works and standard commentaries.

The commentary section for each biblical book follows the outline of the book presented in the introduction. In some volumes, readers will find section ***overviews*** of large portions of scripture with general comments on their overall literary structure and other literary features. A consistent feature of the commentary is the paragraph-by-paragraph study of biblical texts. This section has three parts: **Behind the Text**, **In the Text**, and **From the Text**.

The goal of the **Behind the Text** section is to provide the reader with all the relevant information necessary to understand the text. This includes specific historical situations reflected in the text, the literary context of the text, sociological and cultural issues, and literary features of the text.

In the Text explores what the text says, following its verse-by-verse structure. This section includes a discussion of grammatical details, word studies, and the connectedness of the text to other biblical books/passages or other parts of the book being studied (the canonical relationship). This section provides transliterations of key words in Hebrew and Greek and their literal meanings. The goal here is to explain what the author would have meant and/or what the audience would have understood as the meaning of the text. This is the largest section of the commentary.

The **From the Text** section examines the text in relation to the following areas: theological significance, intertextuality, the history of interpretation, use of the Old Testament scriptures in the New Testament, interpretation in later church history, actualization, and application.

The commentary provides **sidebars** on topics of interest that are important but not necessarily part of an explanation of the biblical text. These topics are informational items and may cover archaeological, historical, literary, cultural, and theological matters that have relevance to the biblical text. Occasionally, longer detailed discussions of special topics are included as **excurses**.

We offer this series with our hope and prayer that readers will find it a valuable resource for their understanding of God's Word and an indispensable tool for their critical engagement with the biblical texts.

Roger Hahn, Centennial Initiative General Editor
Alex Varughese, General Editor (Old Testament)
George Lyons, General Editor (New Testament)

ACKNOWLEDGMENTS

The influence of Jacob Milgrom is evident throughout this work. This is due only in part to his three-volume magnum opus on Leviticus in the Anchor Bible series. I was privileged beyond warrant to have spent a year in the Leviticus seminar at his home, and to benefit from his meticulous guidance through the following years of completing my doctoral exams and dissertation.

I give thanks to the personnel at Beacon Hill Press of Kansas City and the members of the commentary project editorial committee for the invitation to participate in the production of this series. The opportunity to walk through and become immersed in the lines of Leviticus has been a treasured experience for which I am truly grateful.

I wish to express appreciation to the administration, faculty, staff, and students of Nazarene Bible College for granting a sabbatical for this project, for graciously abiding my attempts at seclusion, and for showering me with encouragement and support. My thanks to librarian Ann Attig for working beyond the call of duty to track down sources. Special thanks to colleague and friend Alan Lyke for our lunchtime therapy sessions, and to Ron Attig for nearly daily inspiration from the office down the hall. I am especially grateful to Dan Powers, ally in biblical studies and treasured friend.

Ever present with love, patience, and affirmation throughout this project (and in life) has been my wife. Thank you, Janine—most precious gift of God.

Thanks be to God who provides for our atonement, empowers us for holiness, and sustains us with Sabbath *rest*.

—Thomas J. King

ABBREVIATIONS

With a few exceptions, these abbreviations follow those in *The SBL Handbook of Style* (Alexander 1999).

General

→	see the commentary at
11QT^a	*Temple Scroll^a* (Dead Sea Scrolls)
B.C.	before Christ
BHS	*Biblia Hebraica Stuttgartensia*
ch(s)	chapter(s)
D	Deuteronomist source (of the Pentateuch)
E	Elohist source (of the Pentateuch)
e.g.	*exempli gratia*, for example
H	Holiness Code
HB	Hebrew Bible
Heb.	Hebrew
idem	the same
i.e.	*id est*, that is
J	Jahwist or Yahwist source (of the Pentateuch)
lit.	literally
LXX	Septuagint (the Greek OT)
MT	Masoretic Text (of the OT)
n.	note
n.d.	no date
NT	New Testament
OT	Old Testament
P	Priestly source (of the Pentateuch)
P^N	Northern component of the priestly literature (P narrative in Genesis)
Sam.	Samaritan Pentateuch
v(v)	verse(s)

English Versions

GNT	Good News Translation (Today's English Version)
KJV	King James Version
NAB	New American Bible
NASB	New American Standard Bible
NET	NET Bible: New English Translation
NIV	New International Version (1984)
NJPS	Jewish Publication Society Tanakh: Jewish Bible (Torah, Nevi'im, Kethuvim)
NKJV	New King James Version
NRSV	New Revised Standard Version
RSV	Revised Standard Version
YLT	Young's Literal Translation

Print Conventions for Translations

Bold font	NIV (bold without quotation marks in the text under study; elsewhere in the regular font, with quotation marks and no further identification)
Bold italic font	Author's translation (without quotation marks)

Behind the Text: Literary or historical background information average readers might not know from reading the biblical text alone

In the Text: Comments on the biblical text, words, phrases, grammar, and so forth

From the Text: The use of the text by later interpreters, contemporary relevance, theological and ethical implications of the text, with particular emphasis on Wesleyan concerns

Old Testament

Gen	Genesis	Dan	Daniel		
Exod	Exodus	Hos	Hosea		
Lev	Leviticus	Joel	Joel		
Num	Numbers	Amos	Amos		
Deut	Deuteronomy	Obad	Obadiah		
Josh	Joshua	Jonah	Jonah		
Judg	Judges	Mic	Micah		
Ruth	Ruth	Nah	Nahum		
1—2 Sam	1—2 Samuel	Hab	Habakkuk		
1—2 Kgs	1—2 Kings	Zeph	Zephaniah		
1—2 Chr	1—2 Chronicles	Hag	Haggai		
Ezra	Ezra	Zech	Zechariah		
Neh	Nehemiah	Mal	Malachi		
Esth	Esther				
Job	Job				
Ps/Pss	Psalm/Psalms				
Prov	Proverbs				
Eccl	Ecclesiastes				
Song	Song of Songs/ Song of Solomon				
Isa	Isaiah				
Jer	Jeremiah				
Lam	Lamentations				
Ezek	Ezekiel				

New Testament

Matt	Matthew
Mark	Mark
Luke	Luke
John	John
Acts	Acts
Rom	Romans
1—2 Cor	1—2 Corinthians
Gal	Galatians
Eph	Ephesians
Phil	Philippians
Col	Colossians
1—2 Thess	1—2 Thessalonians
1—2 Tim	1—2 Timothy
Titus	Titus
Phlm	Philemon
Heb	Hebrews
Jas	James
1—2 Pet	1—2 Peter
1—2—3 John	1—2—3 John
Jude	Jude
Rev	Revelation

(Note: Chapter and verse numbering in the MT and LXX often differ compared to those in English Bibles. To avoid confusion, all biblical references follow the chapter and verse numbering in English translations, even when the text in the MT and LXX is under discussion.)

OT Pseudepigrapha
1 En.   *1 Enoch (Ethiopic Apocalypse)*

Targumic Texts (Aramaic)
Tg. Ps.-J.   *Targum Pseudo-Jonathan*
Tg. Neof.   *Targum Neofiti*

Josephus
Ag. Ap.   *Against Apion*
Ant.   *Jewish Antiquities*

Philo
Alleg. Interp. 1, 2, 3   *Allegorical Interpretation* 1, 2, 3
Dreams 1, 2   *On Dreams* 1, 2
Flight   *On Flight and Finding*
Heir   *Who Is the Heir?*
Moses 1, 2   *On the Life of Moses* 1, 2
Spec. Laws 1, 2, 3, 4   *On the Special Laws* 1, 2, 3, 4

Secondary Sources

ATLA	American *Theological Library Association*
BDAG	*A Greek-English Lexicon of the New Testament and Other Early Christian Literature* (see Bauer)
BDB	*A Hebrew and English Lexicon of the Old Testament* (see Brown)
GKC	*Gesenius' Hebrew Grammar*
JBL	*Journal of Biblical Literature*
JSOT	*Journal for the Study of the Old Testament*
JSOTSup	*Journal for* the *Study of the Old Testament: Supplemental Series*

Greek Transliteration			Hebrew Consonant Transliteration		
Greek	**Letter**	**English**	**Hebrew/Aramaic**	**Letter**	**English**
α	alpha	a	א	alef	ʾ
β	bēta	b	ב	bet	b
γ	gamma	g	ג	gimel	g
γ	gamma nasal	n (before γ, κ, ξ, χ)	ד	dalet	d
δ	delta	d	ה	he	h
ε	epsilon	e	ו	vav	v or w
ζ	zēta	z	ז	zayin	z
η	ēta	ē	ח	khet	ḥ
θ	thēta	th	ט	tet	ṭ
ι	iōta	i	י	yod	y
κ	kappa	k	כ/ך	kaf	k
λ	lambda	l	ל	lamed	l
μ	mu	m	מ/ם	mem	m
ν	nu	n	נ/ן	nun	n
ξ	xi	x	ס	samek	s̄
ο	omicron	o	ע	ayin	ʿ
π	pi	p	פ/ף	pe	p; f (spirant)
ρ	rhō	r	צ/ץ	tsade	ṣ
ρ	initial rhō	rh	ק	qof	q
σ/ς	sigma	s	ר	resh	r
τ	tau	t	שׂ	sin	ś
υ	upsilon	y	שׁ	shin	š
υ	upsilon	u (in diphthongs: au, eu, ēu, ou, ui)	ת	tav	t; th (spirant)
φ	phi	ph			
χ	chi	ch			
ψ	psi	ps			
ω	ōmega	ō			
ʼ	rough breathing	h (before initial vowels or diphthongs)			

BIBLIOGRAPHY

Early Church Fathers: Cyril of Jerusalem, Caesarius of Arles, Clement of Alexandria, Bede, Basil the Great, Gregory the Great (see Lienhard 2001).
Medieval Jewish Exegetes: Rashi, Rashbam, Ibn Ezra, Nahmanides, Kimhi, Hizkuni, Gersonides, Abarbanel (see Carasik 2009).
Balentine, Samuel E. 2002. *Leviticus*. Interpretation. Louisville, Ky.: John Knox.
Bauer, Walter, F. W. Danker, W. F. Arndt, and F. W. Gingrich. 2000. *A Greek-English Lexicon of the New Testament and Other Early Christian Literature*. 3d ed. Chicago: University of Chicago Press.
Biblia Hebraica Stuttgartensia. 1983. Edited by K. Elliger and W. Rudolph. Stuttgart: Deutsche Bibelgesellschaft.
Blenkinsopp, Joseph. 1992. *The Pentateuch: An Introduction to the First Five Books of the Bible*. Anchor Bible Reference Library. New York: Doubleday.
_____. 1994. Introduction to the Pentateuch. Pages 305-18 in *General & Old Testament Articles, Genesis, Exodus, Leviticus*. New Interpreter's Bible 1. Nashville: Abingdon.
Bonar, Andrew A. 1851. *A Commentary on the Book of Leviticus*. New York: Robert Carter & Brothers. Google e-book.
Brown, Francis, S. R. Driver, and Charles A. Briggs. 1952. *A Hebrew and English Lexicon of the Old Testament*. Oxford: Clarendon.
Browne, Stanley G. 1970. *Leprosy in the Bible*. London: Christian Medical Fellowship.
Brueggemann, Walter, and Hans Walter Wolff. 1982. *The Vitality of Old Testament Traditions*. 2d ed. Atlanta: John Knox.
Budd, Philip J. 1996. *Leviticus*. New Century Bible Commentary. Grand Rapids: Eerdmans.
Calvin, John. N.d. *Commentaries on the Last Four Books of Moses*. Vol. 2. Translated by Charles William Bingham. Grand Rapids: Eerdmans.
Campbell, Antony F. 1989. *The Study Companion to Old Testament Literature: An Approach to the Writings of Pre-exilic and Exilic Israel*. Old Testament Studies 2. Wilmington, Del.: Glazier.
_____, and Mark A. O'Brien. 1993. *Sources of the Pentateuch: Texts, Introductions, Annotations*. Minneapolis: Fortress.
Carasik, Michael, ed. 2009. *Leviticus*. The Commentators' Bible: The JPS Miqra'ot Gedolot. Philadelphia: Jewish Publication Society.
Carroll, Michael P. 1985. One More Time: Leviticus Revisited. Pages 117-26 in *Anthropological Approaches to the Old Testament*. Edited by Bernhard Lang. Philadelphia: Fortress.
Childs, Brevard S. 1974. *The Book of Exodus: A Critical, Theological Commentary*. The Old Testament Library. Philadelphia: Westminster.
Church of the Nazarene. 2009. *Manual/2009-2013 Church of the Nazarene*. Kansas City: Nazarene Publishing House.
Collins, John J. 2004. *Introduction to the Hebrew Bible*. Minneapolis: Fortress.
Coote, Robert B., and David Robert Ord. 1991. *In the Beginning: Creation and the Priestly History*. Minneapolis: Fortress.
Day, Alfred Ely. 1956. Sheep. Pages 2756-57 in vol. 4 of *International Standard Bible Encyclopaedia*. Edited by James Orr. 4 vols. Grand Rapids: Eerdmans.
Dillmann, A. 1897. *Die Bücher Exodus und Leviticus*. Leipzig: S. Mirzel; Chicago: ATLA monograph preservation program, fiche 1986-3460, 1986.
Douglas, Mary. 1966. *Purity and Danger: An Analysis of Concepts of Pollution and Taboo*. New York: Praeger.
_____. 1999. *Leviticus as Literature*. Oxford: University Press.
_____. 2003. The Go-Away Goat. Pages 121-41 in *The Book of Leviticus: Composition and Reception*. Edited by Rolf Rendtorff and Robert A. Kugler. Atlanta: Society of Biblical Literature.
_____. 2004. *Jacob's Tears: The Priestly Work of Reconciliation*. Oxford: University Press.
Driver, S. R. 1910. *An Introduction to the Literature of the Old Testament*. International Theological Library. New York: Charles Scribner's Sons.
Ehrlich, Arnold B. 1968. *Leviticus, Numeri, Deuteronomium*. Vol. 2 of *Randglossen zur hebräischen Bibel*. Hildesheim: George Olms.

Elliger, Karl. 1966. *Leviticus.* Handbuch zum Alten Testament 4. Tübingen: J.C.B. Mohr (Paul Siebeck).
Feinberg, Charles L. 1958. The Scapegoat of Leviticus Sixteen. *Bibliotheca Sacra* 115:320-33.
Firmage, Edwin. 1990. The Biblical Dietary Laws and the Concept of Holiness. Pages 177-208 in *Studies in the Pentateuch.* Edited by J. A. Emerton. Vol. 41 of *Supplements to Vetus Testamentum.* Edited by J. A. Emerton et al. Leiden: Brill.
Fohrer, Georg. 1968. *Introduction to the Old Testament.* Translated by David E. Green. Nashville: Abingdon.
Fretheim, Terence E. 1996. *The Pentateuch.* Interpreting Biblical Texts. Nashville: Abingdon.
Friedman, Richard Elliott. 1981. *The Exile and Biblical Narrative: The Formation of the Deuteronomistic and Priestly Works.* Chico: Scholars Press.
Frymer-Kensky, Tikva. 1983. Pollution, Purification, and Purgation in Biblical Israel. Pages 399-414 in *The Word of the Lord Shall Go Forth: Essays in Honor of David Noel Freedman in Celebration of His Sixtieth Birthday.* Edited by Carol L. Meyers and M. O'Connor. Winona Lake, Ind.: Eisenbrauns.
_____. 1989. Law and Philosophy: The Case of Sex in the Bible. *Semeia* 45:89-102.
Füglister, Notker. 1977. Sühne durch Blut—Zur Bedeutung von Leviticus 17, 11. Pages 143-64 in *Studien zum Pentateuch.* Edited by Georg Braulik. Wien: Herder.
Gall, August. 1918. Der hebräische Pentateuch der Samaritaner. *The McMaster Collection.* Paper 163. http://digitalcommons.mcmaster.ca/mcmastercollection/163.
Gane, Roy E. 2004. *Leviticus, Numbers.* The NIV Application Commentary. Grand Rapids: Zondervan.
_____. 2005. *Cult and Character: Purification Offerings, Day of Atonement, and Theodicy.* Winona Lake, Ind.: Eisenbrauns.
_____. 2008. Privative Preposition *mn* in Purification Offering Pericopes and the Changing Face of "Dorian Gray." *Journal of Biblical Literature* 127.2:209-22.
Gaster, Theodor H. 1953. *Festivals of the Jewish Year: A Modern Interpretation and Guide.* New York: William Sloane.
_____. 1962. Sacrifices and Offerings, OT. Pages 147-59 in vol. 4 of *Interpreter's Dictionary of the Bible.* Edited by G. A. Buttrick. 4 vols. New York: Abingdon.
Gerstenberger, Erhard S. 1996. *Leviticus: A Commentary.* The Old Testament Library. Translated by Douglas W. Stott. Louisville, Ky.: Westminster John Knox.
Gesenius, W. 1910. *Gesenius' Hebrew Grammar.* Edited by E. Kautzsch. Translated by A. E. Cowley. 2d ed. Oxford: Clarendon.
Ginsberg, H. L. 1946. *The Legend of King Keret: A Canaanite Epic of the Bronze Age.* New Haven, Conn.: American Schools of Oriental Research.
_____. 1982. *The Israelian Heritage of Judaism.* New York: Jewish Theological Seminary of America.
Gorman, Frank H., Jr. 1997. *Divine Presence and Community: A Commentary on the Book of Leviticus.* International Theological Commentary. Grand Rapids: Eerdmans.
_____. 2009. Sacrifices and Offerings. Pages 20-32 in vol. 5 of *The New Interpreter's Dictionary of the Bible.* Edited by Katherine Doob Sakenfeld. 5 vols. Nashville: Abingdon, 2006-9.
Gottwald, Norman K. 1985. *The Hebrew Bible: A Socio-Literary Introduction.* Philadelphia: Fortress.
Grabbe, Lester L. 2003. The Priests in Leviticus—Is the Medium the Message? Pages 207-24 in *The Book of Leviticus: Composition and Reception.* Edited by Rolf Rendtorff and Robert A. Kugler. Atlanta: Society of Biblical Literature.
Graf, Karl Heinrich. 1866. *Die Geschichtlichen Bücher des Alten Testaments.* Leipzig: T. O. Weigel.
Grintz, Jehoshua M. 1972. "Do Not Eat on the Blood": Reconsiderations in Setting and Dating of the Priestly Code. *Annual of the Swedish Theological Institute in Jerusalem* 8:78-105.
Haran, Menahem. 1971. *ărākîm.* Pages 391-94 in vol. 6 of *Encyclopaedia Miqra'it.* Edited by Umberto Cassuto et al. 8 vols. Jerusalem: Bialik Institute, 1954-76.
_____. 1981. Behind the Scenes of History: Determining the Date of the Priestly Source. *Journal of Biblical Literature* 100: 321-33.
_____. 1985. *Temples and Temple-Service in Ancient Israel.* Winona Lake, Ind.: Eisenbrauns.
Harrison, R. K. 1962. Leprosy. Pages 111-13 in vol. 3 of *Interpreter's Dictionary of the Bible.* Edited by G. A. Buttrick. 4 vols. New York: Abingdon.
_____. 1980. *Leviticus: An Introduction and Commentary.* Tyndale Old Testament Commentaries 3. Downers Grove, Ill.: InterVarsity.
Hartley, John E. 1992. *Leviticus.* Word Biblical Commentary 4. Dallas: Word Books.
Heller, Jan. 1970. Die Symbolik des Fettes im A.T. *Vetus Testamentum* 20:106-8.

Herczeg, Yisrael Isser Zvi, trans. 1999. *Leviticus*. Vol. 3 of *The Torah: With Rashi's Commentary Translated, Annotated, and Elucidated*. Sapirstein ed. Artscroll Series. Brooklyn: Mesorah Publications.
Hertz, J. H., ed. 1960. *The Pentateuch and Haftorahs: Hebrew Text, English Translation, and Commentary*. 2d ed. London: Soncino.
Hertzberg, Hans Wilhelm. 1976. *I & II Samuel*. The Old Testament Library. Translated by J. S. Bowden. Philadelphia: Westminster.
Hildebrand, David R. 1986. A Summary of Recent Findings in Support of an Early Date for the So-called Priestly Material of the Pentateuch. *Journal of the Evangelical Theological Society* 29:129-38.
Hoffmann, D. 1906. *Das Buch Leviticus*. Vol. 2. Berlin: M. Poppelauer. Google e-book.
Houston, Walter J. 2003. Towards an Integrated Reading of the Dietary Laws of Leviticus. Pages 142-61 in *The Book of Leviticus: Composition and Reception*. Edited by Rolf Rendtorff and Robert A. Kugler. Atlanta: Society of Biblical Literature.
Hulse, E. V. 1975. The Nature of Biblical Leprosy and the Use of Alternative Medical Terms in Modern Translations of the Bible. *Palestine Exploration Quarterly* 107:87-105.
Hurvitz, Avi. 1974. The Evidence of Language in Dating the Priestly Code. *Revue Biblique* 81:24-56.
_____. 1981. The Language of the Priestly Source and Its Historical Setting—The Case for an Early Date. In *Proceedings of the Eighth World Congress of Jewish Studies* 5:83-94. Jerusalem: World Union of Jewish Studies, 1983.
ICN Online. 2011. Human Sexuality. Official Site of the Board of General Superintendents Church of the Nazarene. http://nazarene.org/ministries/superintendents/statements/sexuality/display.html.
Isaac, E. 1983. 1 (Ethiopic Apocalypse of) Enoch: A New Translation and Introduction. Pages 5-89 in *Apocalyptic Literature and Testaments*. Vol. 1 of *The Old Testament Pseudepigrapha*. Edited by James H. Charlesworth. Garden City: Doubleday.
Josephus, Flavius. 1974. *The Works of Flavius Josephus*. Translated by William Whiston. 4 vols. Grand Rapids: Baker.
Judisch, Douglas McC. L. 1984. Propitiation in the Language and Typology of the Old Testament. *Concordia Theological Quarterly* 48:221-43.
Kaiser, Walter C., Jr. 1994. *Leviticus*. New Interpreter's Bible 1. Nashville: Abingdon.
Kalisch, M. M. 1872. *Leviticus, Part II*. A Historical and Critical Commentary on the Old Testament. London: Longmans, Green, Reader, and Dyer. Google e-book.
Kaufmann, Yehezkel. 1960. *The Religion of Israel: From Its Beginnings to the Babylonian Exile*. Translated by Moshe Greenberg. Chicago: University of Chicago Press.
Keil, C. F., and F. Delitzsch. N.d. *The Pentateuch*. Vol. 2. Biblical Commentary on the Old Testament. Translated by James Martin. Grand Rapids: Eerdmans.
King, Thomas J. 2009. *The Realignment of the Priestly Literature: The Priestly Narrative in Genesis and Its Relation to Priestly Legislation and the Holiness School*. Princeton Theological Monograph Series 102. Eugene, Ore.: Pickwick.
Kiuchi, Nobuyoshi. 1987. *The Purification Offering in the Priestly Literature: Its Meaning and Function*. Journal for the Study of the Old Testament Supplemental Series 56. Sheffield: JSOT Press.
_____. 1999. Spirituality in Offering a Peace Offering. *Tyndale Bulletin* 50:23-31.
Klawans, Jonathan. 2000. *Impurity and Sin in Ancient Judaism*. Oxford: University Press.
Klostermann, August. 1893. *Der Pentateuch: Beiträge zu seinem Verständnis und seiner Entstehungsgeschichte*. Leipzig: A. Deichert [Georg Böhme].
Knohl, Israel. 1987. The Priestly Torah Versus the Holiness School: Sabbath and the Festivals. *Hebrew Union College Annual* 58:65-117.
_____. 1995. *The Sanctuary of Silence: The Priestly Torah and the Holiness School*. Minneapolis: Fortress.
Kuenen, Abraham. 1886. *An Historico-Critical Inquiry into the Origin and Composition of the Hexateuch*. Translated by Philip H. Wicksteed. London: Macmillan.
Laughlin, John H. 1976. The "Strange Fire" of Nadab and Abihu. *Journal of Biblical Literature* 95:559-65.
Lee, Bernon P. 2006. Leviticus 24:15b-16: A Crux Revisited. *Bulletin for Biblical Research* 16.2:345-49.
Levine, Baruch A. 1989. *Leviticus*. JPS Torah Commentary. Philadelphia: Jewish Publication Society.
Lewis, C. S. 1952. *Mere Christianity*. Westwood, N.J.: Barbour and Company.

Lienhard, Joseph T., ed. 2001. *Exodus, Leviticus, Numbers, Deuteronomy*. Ancient Christian Commentary on Scripture: Old Testament 3. Downers Grove, Ill.: InterVarsity.

Lockshin, Martin I., ed. 2001. *Rashbam's Commentary on Leviticus and Numbers*. Translated by Martin I. Lockshin. Providence, R.I.: Brown University.

MacRae, George W. 1960. The Meaning and Evolution of the Feast of Tabernacles. *Catholic Biblical Quarterly* 22:251-76.

Magonet, Jonathan. 1996. "But If It Is a Girl She Is Unclean for Twice Seven Days . . ." The Riddle of Leviticus 12.5. Pages 144-52 in *Reading Leviticus: A Conversation with Mary Douglas*. JSOTSup 227. Edited by John F. A. Sawyer. Sheffield: Academic Press.

Maher, Michael. 1994. Introduction to Pseudo-Jonathan: Leviticus. Pages 115-19 in vol. 3 of The Aramaic Bible. Edited by Kevin Cathcart, Michael Maher, and Martin McNamara. Collegeville, Md.: Liturgical Press.

Martínez, Florentino García. 1996. *The Dead Sea Scrolls Translated: The Qumran Texts in English*. 2d ed. Leiden: Brill; Grand Rapids: Eerdmans.

_____, and Eibert J. C. Tigchelaar, eds. 1997-98. *The Dead Sea Scrolls Study Edition*. 2 vols. Leiden: Brill; Grand Rapids: Eerdmans.

Marx, Alfred. 2003. The Theology of Sacrifice According to Leviticus 1-7. Pages 103-20 in *The Book of Leviticus: Composition and Reception*. Edited by Rolf Rendtorff and Robert A. Kugler. Atlanta: Society of Biblical Literature.

Masterman, E. W. G. 1956. Frankincense. Pages 1144-45 in vol. 2 of *The International Standard Bible Encyclopaedia*. Edited by James Orr. 4 vols. Grand Rapids: Eerdmans.

Mays, James Luther. 1969. *Hosea*. The Old Testament Library. Philadelphia: Westminster.

Mazar, Amihai. 1990. *Archaeology of the Land of the Bible: 10,000-586 B.C.E.* Anchor Bible Reference Library. New York: Doubleday.

McEvenue, Seán. 1971. *The Narrative Style of the Priestly Writer*. Analecta Biblica 50. Rome: Biblical Institute.

_____. 1990. *Interpreting the Pentateuch*. Collegeville, Md.: Liturgical Press.

Meyer, Nicholas, and Denny Martin Flinn. 1991. Klingon Justice. Scene 7 in *Star Trek VI*. Directed by Nicholas Meyer. Hollywood: Paramount Pictures.

Milgrom, Jacob. 1990. *Numbers*. JPS Torah Commentary. Philadelphia: Jewish Publication Society.

_____. 1991. *Leviticus 1—16: A New Translation with Introduction and Commentary*. Anchor Bible 3. New York: Doubleday.

_____. 1992. Priestly ("P") Source. Pages 454-61 in vol. 5 of *Anchor Bible Dictionary*. Edited by David Noel Freedman. 6 vols. New York: Doubleday.

_____. 2000. *Leviticus 17—22: A New Translation with Introduction and Commentary*. Anchor Bible 3A. New York: Doubleday.

_____. 2001. *Leviticus 23—27: A New Translation with Introduction and Commentary*. Anchor Bible 3B. New York: Doubleday.

_____. 2004. *Leviticus: A Book of Ritual and Ethics*. Continental Commentaries. Minneapolis: Fortress.

_____. 2007. The Preposition *mn* in the *ḥṭ't* Pericopes. *Journal of Biblical Literature* 126.1:161-63.

Möller, Wilhelm. 1956. Atonement, Day of. Pages 324-28 in vol. 1 of *International Standard Bible Encyclopaedia*. Edited by James Orr. 4 vols. Grand Rapids: Eerdmans.

Moorehead, William G. 1956. Priest. Pages 2439-41 in vol. 4 of *International Standard Bible Encyclopaedia*. Rev. ed. Edited by James Orr. 4 vols. Grand Rapids: Eerdmans.

Nicholson, Ernest. 1998. *The Pentateuch in the Twentieth Century: The Legacy of Julius Wellhausen*. Oxford: University Press.

Noordtzij, A. 1982. *Leviticus*. Bible Student's Commentary. Translated by R. Togtman. Grand Rapids: Zondervan.

North, Robert. 1954. *Sociology of the Biblical Jubilee*. Analecta Biblica 4. Rome: Pontifical Biblical Institute.

Noth, Martin. 1972. *A History of Pentateuchal Traditions*. Translated by Bernhard W. Anderson. Englewood Cliffs, N.J.: Prentice-Hall.

_____. 1977. *Leviticus*. Translated by J. E. Anderson. The Old Testament Library. Rev. ed. Philadelphia: Westminster. Translation of *Das dritte Buch Mose, Leviticus*. Das Alte Testament Deutsch 6. Göttingen: Vandenhoeck & Ruprecht, 1962.

Paran, M. 1983. Literary Features of the Priestly Code: Stylistic Patterns, Idioms and Structures. Ph.D. diss., Hebrew University of Jerusalem.

Patch, James A. 1956. Honey. Page 1418 in vol. 3 of *International Standard Bible Encyclopaedia*. Rev. ed. Edited by James Orr. 4 vols. Grand Rapids: Eerdmans.
Pedersen, Johs. 1926. *Israel: Its Life and Culture*. Vols. 1 and 2. London: Oxford University Press.
_____. 1940. *Israel: Its Life and Culture*. Vols. 3 and 4. London: Oxford University Press.
Péter, René. 1977. L'imposition des mains dans l'Ancien Testament. *Vetus Testamentum* 27:48-55.
Philo. 1929-62. Translated by F. H. Colson and G. H. Whitaker. 10 vols. Loeb Classical Library. Cambridge: Harvard University Press.
Porter, J. R. 1976. *Leviticus*. Cambridge Bible Commentary. Cambridge: University Press.
Queen-Sutherland, Kandy. 1991. Cultic Calendars in the Old Testament. *Faith and Mission* 8:76-87.
Rad, Gerhard von. 1962. *The Theology of Israel's Historical Traditions*. Vol. 1 of *Old Testament Theology*. Translated by D.M.G. Stalker. New York: Harper & Row. Translation of *Die Theologie der geschichtlichen Überlieferungen Israels*. Vol. 1 of *Theologie des Alten Testaments*. Munich: Chr. Kaiser Verlag, 1957.
_____. 1966. *Deuteronomy*. Translated by Dorothea Barton. The Old Testament Library. Philadelphia: Westminster. Translation of *Das fünfte Buch Mose: Deuteronomium*. Das Alte Testament Deutsch 8. Göttingen: Vandenhoeck & Ruprecht, 1964.
Rainey, Anson. 1972. Sacrifice, in the Bible, in Biblical Tradition and History. Pages 600-607 in vol. 14 of *Encylopaedia Judaica*. Edited by Cecil Roth. 16 vols. Jerusalem: Keter, 1972.
Rattray, Susan. 1987. Marriage Rules, Kinship Terms and Family Structure in the Bible. Pages 537-44 in the *SBL Seminar Papers, 1987*. Society of Biblical Literature Seminar Papers 26. Atlanta: Scholars Press.
_____. 1996. Worship. Pages 1222-26 in *HarperCollins Bible Dictionary*. Rev. ed. Edited by Paul J. Achtemeier. New York: HarperCollins.
Reeve, J. J. 1956. Sacrifice (OT). Pages 2638-51 in vol. 4 of *International Standard Bible Encyclopaedia*. Rev. ed. Edited by James Orr. 4 vols. Grand Rapids: Eerdmans.
Rendsburg, Gary A. 1980. Late Biblical Hebrew and the Date of "P." *Journal of the Ancient Near Eastern Society of Columbia University* 12:65-80.
Rendtorff, Rolf. 1990. *The Problem of the Process of Transmission in the Pentateuch*. Translated by John J. Scullion. JSOTSup 89. Sheffield: JSOT Press.
_____. 1993. Two Kinds of P? Some Reflections on the Occasion of the Publishing of Jacob Milgrom's Commentary on Leviticus 1-16. *Journal for the Study of the Old Testament* 60:75-81.
Reuss, Eduard. 1890. *Die Geschichte der Heiligen Schriften Alten Testaments*. Zweite Ausgabe. Braunschweig: C. A. Schwetschke und Sohn.
Robinson, H. Wheeler. 1942. Hebrew Sacrifice and Prophetic Symbolism. *The Journal of Theological Studies* 43:129-39.
Rowley, Harold H. 1950-51. The Meaning of Sacrifice in the Old Testament. *Bulletin of the John Rylands Library* 33:74-110.
Rylaarsdam, J. C. 1962. Atonement, Day of. Pages 313-16 in vol. 1 of *Interpreter's Dictionary of the Bible*. Edited by G. A. Buttrick. 4 vols. New York: Abingdon.
Saalschütz, J. L. 1853. *Das Mosaische Recht nebst den vervollständigenden thalmudisch-rabbinischen Bestimmungen*. 2d ed. Vol. 2. Berlin: Heymann. Google e-book.
Sanderson, Judith E. 2001. Exodus. Pages 82-141 Hebrew Bible in *The New Oxford Annotated Bible*. 3d ed. Edited by Michael D. Coogan. Oxford: University Press.
Schenker, Adrian. 2003. What Connects the Incest Prohibitions with the Other Prohibitions Listed in Leviticus 18 and 20? Pages 162-85 in *The Book of Leviticus: Composition and Reception*. Edited by Rolf Rendtorff and Robert A. Kugler. Atlanta: Society of Biblical Literature.
Schwartz, Baruch J. 1991. The Prohibitions Concerning the "Eating" of Blood in Leviticus 17. Pages 34-66 in *Priesthood and Cult in Ancient Israel*. Edited by Gary A. Anderson and Saul M. Olyan. Sheffield: JSOT Press.
Sklar, Jay. 2008. Sin and Impurity: Atoned or Purified? Yes! Pages 18-31 in *Perspectives on Purity and Purification in the Bible*. Edited by Baruch J. Schwartz et al. New York: T&T Clark.
Soler, Jean. 1979. The Dietary Prohibitions of the Hebrews. *The New York Review of Books*, June 14, 24-30.
Targum Neofiti 1: Leviticus. 1994. Translated with Apparatus by Martin McNamara. The Aramaic Bible 3. Collegeville, Md.: Liturgical Press.
Targum Pseudo-Jonathan: Leviticus. 1994. Translated with notes by Michael Maher. The Aramaic Bible 3. Collegeville, Md.: Liturgical Press.
Toombs, L. E. 1962. Clean and Unclean. Pages 641-48 in vol. 1 of *Interpreter's Dictionary of the Bible*. Edited by G. A. Buttrick. 4 vols. New York: Abingdon.

Trevaskis, Leigh M. 2009. The Purpose of Leviticus 24 within its Literary Context. *Vetus Testamentum* 59:295-312.
Vainstub, Daniel. 2011. *Molech:* Human Sacrifices in Canaan and Israel Reconsidered. Paper presented at the annual meeting of the SBL. San Francisco, November 20.
Vaux, Roland de. 1997. *Ancient Israel: Its Life and Institutions.* Translated by John McHugh. Biblical Resource Series. Grand Rapids: Eerdmans.
Vink, J. G. 1969. *The Priestly Code and Seven Other Studies.* Old Testament Studies 15. Leiden: Brill.
Walsh, Jerome T. 1977. From Egypt to Moab: A Source Critical Analysis of the Wilderness Itinerary. *Catholic Biblical Quarterly* 39:20-33.
Walton, John H., and Victor H. Matthews. 1997. *Genesis—Deuteronomy.* IVP Bible Background Commentary. Downers Grove, Ill.: InterVarsity.
Watts, James W. 2006. *'ōlāh:* The Rhetoric of Burnt Offerings. *Vetus Testamentum* 56:125-37.
Wegner, Judith Romney. 1992. Leviticus. Pages 36-44 in *The Women's Bible Commentary.* Edited by Carol A. Newsom and Sharon H. Ringe. Louisville, Ky.: Westminster/John Knox.
Wellhausen, Julius. 1885. *Prolegomena to the History of Israel.* Translated by J. Sutherland Black and Allan Menzies. ATLA. Edinburgh: Adam and Charles Black. Text-fiche.
Wenham, Gordon J. 1979. *The Book of Leviticus.* New International Commentary on the Old Testament. Grand Rapids: Eerdmans.
Wesley, John. 1765. *Explanatory Notes upon the Old Testament.* Vol. 1. Bristol: William Pine.
Wette, Wilhelm Martin Leberecht de. 1971. *Kritischer Versuch über die Glaubwürdigkeit der Bücher der Chronik mit Hinsicht auf die Geschichte der Mosaischen Bücher und Gesetzgebung.* Vol. 1 of *Beiträge zur Einleitung in das Alte Testament.* Halle: Schimmelpfennig und Compagnie, 1806. Repr., Hildesheim: Georg Olms Verlag.
_____. 1971. *Kritik der Israelitischen Geschichte.* Vol. 2 of *Beiträge zur Einleitung in das Alte Testament.* Halle: Schimmelpfennig und Compagnie, 1807. Repr., Hildesheim: Georg Olms Verlag.
Whybray, R. Norman. 1987. *The Making of the Pentateuch.* JSOTSup 53. Sheffield: JSOT Press.
Wolff, Hans Walter. 1974. *Anthropology of the Old Testament.* Translated by Margaret Kohl. Philadelphia: Fortress.
Wright, Christopher J. H. 1992. Jubilee, Year of. Pages 1025-30 in vol. 3 of *The Anchor Bible Dictionary.* Edited by David Noel Freedman. 6 vols. New York: Doubleday, 1992.
Wright, David P. 1986. The Gesture of Hand Placement in the Hebrew Bible and in Hittite Literature. *Journal of the American Oriental Society* 106:433-46.
_____. 1999. Holiness in Leviticus and Beyond: Differing Perspectives. *Interpretation* 53:351-64.
_____, and Richard N. Jones. 1992. Leprosy. Pages 277-82 in vol. 4 of *The Anchor Bible Dictionary.* Edited by David Noel Freedman. 6 vols. New York: Doubleday.
Zevit, Ziony. 1982. Converging Lines of Evidence Bearing on the Date of P. *Zeitschrift für die Alttestamentliche Wissenschaft* 94:481-511.
Ziskind, Jonathan R. 1996. The Missing Daughter in Leviticus XVIII. *Vetus Testamentum* 46:125-30. *ATLA Religion Database with ATLASerials,* EBSCOhost. http://search.ebscohost.com.

INTRODUCTION

A. Authorship

1. Mosaic Foundations

The discussion of the authorship of Leviticus is inseparable from that of the Pentateuch as a whole. Leviticus is clearly integral to the wilderness traditions reflected in Exodus through Deuteronomy. Tradition reaching back to biblical times attributes the writing of the Pentateuch to Moses. This tradition initially derives from passages within the Pentateuch itself that indicate Moses was involved in the writing of certain texts. In each case, however, it is clear that the composition does not involve the entire Pentateuch. For example, Exod 17:14 relates that Moses was directed to simply record a statement intended to serve as a reminder. Another passage describes Moses writing what is referred to as the Book of the Covenant (Exod 24:4, 7), which is normally identified with God's speech in Exod 20:22—23:33. In a similar manner, at Exod 34:27 God instructs Moses to write down the words of the covenant recounted in Exod 34:10-26 (Exod 34:28 refers to God writing the Ten Commandments on the tablets; see Exod 34:1; Childs 1974, 615). Numbers 33:2 indicates that Moses recorded the wilderness itinerary contained in Num 33:3-49. Deuteronomy refers to a book of the Law written by Moses (Deut 31:9, 24) that can be identified with Moses' speech in Deut 4:44—28:68 (the following speeches from Moses include additional references to this book of the Law [see Deut 29:21; 31:26]). Finally, the Pentateuch testifies that Moses wrote, as commanded (Deut 31:19, 22), the song recorded in Deut 32:1-43.

Beyond the Pentateuch, yet still within the OT, Josh 8:32 describes Joshua writing a copy of the Law that Moses had written. In this reference it is unclear exactly what the author understood to be the Law that Moses had written and Joshua copied onto *stones*. The immediate context concerning the building of an altar at Mount Ebal suggests a connection with material in Deuteronomy (Josh 8:30-31 cites Deut 27:4-5).

The tradition of Mosaic authorship is further reflected in a number of NT passages that mention Moses speaking, commanding, permitting, or giving information pertaining to the Law (e.g., Matt 8:4; 19:7-8; 22:24; Mark 1:44; 7:10; 10:3-4; Luke 5:14; John 1:17; 7:19, 22; 8:5; Acts 3:22; Rom 10:19; Heb 7:14; 9:19). Technically, such references do not provide evidence of Moses *writing* anything, and should not be cited as proof of Mosaic authorship of the Pentateuch. More substantial evidence of a NT view that attributes the *writing* of the Pentateuch to Moses comes from texts that actually mention Moses writing information pertaining to the Law (Mark 12:19; Luke 20:28; John 1:45; 5:46; Rom 10:5). Even these passages, however, do not provide conclusive evidence that Moses wrote the entire Pentateuch, or was perceived to have done so by NT writers. We move closer to such a perception in the NT with texts that treat the name of Moses (sometimes in parallel with the Prophets), not so much as a person, but as a recognized division of Scripture (Luke 16:29, 31; 24:27; Acts 15:21; 21:21; 2 Cor 3:15).

The traditional association of Moses with the writing of the Pentateuch is further driven by the phrases "Law of Moses" and "Book of Moses" found in both the OT and the NT. The phrase "Book of Moses" appears in 2 Chr 25:4; 35:12; Ezra 6:18; Neh 13:1; and Mark 12:26. The phrase "Law of Moses" is more common and appears in Josh 8:31, 32; 23:6; 1 Kgs 2:3; 2 Kgs 14:6; 23:25; 2 Chr 23:18; 30:16; Ezra 3:2; 7:6; Neh 8:1; Dan 9:11, 13; Mal 4:4 (Mal 3:22 HB); Luke 2:22; 24:44; John 7:23; Acts 13:39 (for some English versions, v 38); 15:5; 28:23; 1 Cor 9:9; and Heb 10:28. These phrases clearly link Moses with the Law of the OT. However, in themselves, they do not necessarily indicate authorship. They can just as easily be taken to simply signify that Moses was recognized as the main character in the Pentateuch with whom the Law can be identified. Though such common identification resulted in a tradition that holds that Moses actually recorded all of the Law, these phrases in themselves do not constitute conclusive evidence of Mosaic authorship of the Pentateuch.

The words of Jesus, as recorded in some of the passages listed above, are sometimes cited to support the argument that Jesus believed Moses wrote the Pentateuch, thereby providing, especially for Christian readers, divine sanction of Mosaic authorship. However, within such passages it is clear that Jesus is more concerned about addressing certain matters related to the Law, than about debating its authorship. In the context of communicating to an audience who recognized the Law by its Mosaic authority, Jesus would obviously follow the tradition of referencing the Law in relation to Moses. Thus, Jesus' words as recorded in the Gospels should not be understood as divine claims supporting the Mosaic authorship of the Pentateuch.

It can be seen that the direct claims of biblical texts do not verify Mosaic authorship of the Pentateuch. However, the Scriptures do testify to some written materials originating from the hand of Moses. This supports the conviction that at least portions of the Pentateuch may be traced to compositions as early as the time of Moses.

2. Source Critical Scholarship

The perception that Moses wrote the Pentateuch was commonly held until the rise of critical scholarship. Among the earliest observations that raised doubt about Mosaic authorship were those of medieval Jewish scholar Abraham Ibn Ezra (1089-1164). Ibn Ezra alluded to references in the Pentateuch that identified circumstances belonging to times much later than Moses, such as Canaanites in the land during the days of Abraham (Gen 12:6), and mention of the iron bed of King Og of Bashan (Deut 3:11; in Blenkinsopp 1994, 308). In the centuries that followed, additional incongruities were discovered in the text of the Pentateuch that led critical scholarship to recognize the Pentateuch as a product of sources. These complexities derive mainly from diverse terminology, duplicate accounts, and blended stories.

The most commonly recognized division in terminology within the Pentateuch involves the names used for God. Some passages refer to God as *Yahweh* (YHWH), while others identify God with the term *Elohim*. The division of texts becomes more apparent in relation to the question of when the name YHWH became known. The words of God to Moses in Exod 3:15 and 6:3 imply that God was not known as YHWH until these revelations to Moses in Exodus (Sanderson 2001, 87 Hebrew Bible). In contrast, YHWH is mentioned throughout Genesis in relation to the patriarchs and others (see especially Gen 4:26; 13:4). This suggests the existence of a source that represented that the name YHWH was known from the beginning, and another source that claimed that the name YHWH was not known until it was revealed to Moses. Other examples of the diverse use of terminology in the Pentateuch include two different names used to refer to the covenant mountain (Sinai and Horeb), and two different names used to refer to the native inhabitants of Palestine (Canaanites and Amorites).

Duplicate accounts add to the evidence that led to the theory of sources in the Pentateuch. Examples of such repetition include: two creation accounts (Gen 1:1—2:4a and Gen 2:4b-25), two accounts of God's covenant with Abraham (Gen 15:7-21 and 17:1-22), three accounts of a patriarch who contrives to have his wife recognized as his sister (Gen 12:10-13; 20:1-2; and 26:6-7), two accounts of Moses being called to deliver the children of Israel (Exod 3:4-10 and 6:2-9), two versions of the Ten Commandments (Exod 20:1-17 and Deut 5:6-21), and two versions of the dietary restrictions for Israel (Lev 11:1-23 and Deut 14:3-21). It has been claimed that there are more than one hundred such duplications in the Pentateuch (Fretheim 1996, 25).

Related to duplicate accounts are blended stories, in which two renditions of an event appear to have been combined into one. The flood account provides a significant example of a blended story. One version of the story calls for Noah to bring into the ark two of every kind of animal (Gen 6:19-20). A second version distinguishes between clean and unclean animals and requires Noah to bring seven pairs of all clean animals and seven pairs of the birds (Gen 7:2-3). The two versions are again evident when it appears that Noah and company all enter the ark twice: once at Gen 7:7-9 and again at Gen 7:13-16. One version describes the deluge as the result of rain that falls for forty days (Gen 7:4, 12; 8:6), while the second version describes the deluge as the result of fountains from below and windows from above flooding the earth for one hundred and fifty days (Gen 7:11, 24; 8:2a, 3).

Another example of a blended account is evident in the story of Joseph and his brothers. In one rendition of the story Reuben seeks to rescue Joseph by persuading the brothers to throw him in a pit without killing him, and Joseph ends up being sold to *Midianites* who in turn sell him to Potiphar (Gen 37:20-24, 28a, 29-36). The second rendition of the story describes Judah as the one who persuades the brothers not to kill Joseph, and Joseph is sold to *Ishmaelites* who in turn sell him to Potiphar (Gen 37:25-27; 39:1).

The pervasiveness throughout the Pentateuch of such divergence, as that illustrated above, resulted in the recognition that the Pentateuch must be the product of a long and complex history involving more than one source. Consequently, modern discussions of the composition of the Pentateuch have taken place predominantly under the influence of source critical studies. The central product of source criticism in relation to the Pentateuch is the Documentary Hypothesis. The classic synthesis of the arguments that culminated in the Documentary Hypothesis is attributed to Julius Wellhausen (1844—1918). The hypothesis suggests four sources make up the Pentateuch. Each source is assigned a letter for the sake of identification: J (Yahwist), E (Elohist), D (Deuteronomist), P (Priestly writer). The following is a simple outline of the sources identified by the hypothesis and their general makeup:

1. J is considered the earliest work. It begins with Gen 2:4*b* and is found in Genesis, Exodus, Numbers, and a few passages in Deuteronomy.
2. E begins with the story of Abraham (Gen 15) and follows the same general course as J.
3. JE is formed by a redactor through the combination of J and E. This process involved the omission of parts of each, but mostly omission of parts of E.
4. D consists mainly of the book of Deuteronomy.
5. JED is formed by a second redactor who basically appended D to JE. This process included, however, the insertion of a few passages into JE by the redactor, and the incorporation of a few JE passages into D.
6. P is the final work. It begins with Gen 1:1 and follows the same chronological scheme as J. P material predominates in Exodus and Numbers. P is the sole source of Exod 25—31; 35—40; and of Leviticus.
7. JEDP constitutes the combination of JED and P by a third redactor, to form the Pentateuch.
8. A few passages are considered as independent fragments that do not derive from any of the four main sources. (Whybray 1987, 20-21)

Despite the significant revisions, challenges, and in some cases outright rejection of the Documentary Hypothesis, source critical dialogue remains the dominant base on which discussions of the composition of the Pentateuch take place. In a book that surveys the varied history of arguments following Wellhausen, including more recent developments and suggestions, Nicholson rightly affirms the proper foundation for further investigation. He writes at the close of the twentieth century that "the Documentary Hypothesis should remain our primary point of reference, and it alone provides the true perspective from which to approach this most difficult of areas in the study of the Old Testament" (1998, vi).

It is important to note that recognizing sources in the composition of the Pentateuch need not threaten the authority or inspiration of the Scriptures. The Lord God can inspire God's revelation through a single individual all at once, or through a number of writers and editors over time. The evidence of the biblical text suggests that the Pentateuch certainly includes material that dates back to the time of Moses. That material appears to have been included and encased within a long history of composition reflecting a number of sources.

B. Date

As identified in the outline above, the book of Leviticus is made up entirely of material included within the Priestly source (P). The date for the composition of the priestly literature remains subject to a wide range of viewpoints. Arguments regarding the date of the Priestly source have shifted from early within the history of ancient Israel, to a much later period, and back to an early date, depending on how one evaluates the evidence related to the source.

Kuenen (1828-91) described the dominant theory among the critical scholars of his day as one in which the priestly material was viewed as among the earliest of the pentateuchal components. The J source (Yahwist) was dated to around the eighth century B.C., and the priestly material (identified as the *Grundschrift*) was considered even earlier.

> To this Yahwist we owe the first four books of the Pentateuch and the earlier (præ-deuteronomic) recension of Joshua. His work was in its turn based upon a still earlier composition—the "Grundschrift" or "Book of Origins"—which came from the pen of a priest or Levite and might be referred to the century of Solomon. Embedded in this "Grundschrift" were still more ancient fragments, some of them Mosaic. (1886, xi)

The shift from an early view of P to the later date reflected in the Documentary Hypothesis was not brought about by Wellhausen alone. Wellhausen pointed to de Wette (1780—1849) as the first to clearly perceive the historical disjunction that suggested a later date for the priestly literature (Wellhausen 1885, 3-5).

De Wette argued that the picture of the hierarchical priesthood as described in the Mosaic legislation could not have belonged to the Mosaic age or the following age of the monarchy, because such an established priesthood would never have allowed the state of freedom and anarchy apparent in the worship practices depicted in Kings (1971, 1:102, 115-16, 255-58, 263-64). De Wette believed that much of the Mosaic legislation (including sacrificial and ritual laws) must have developed gradually. He reasoned that such legislation was refined over time by the priests and was put to writing late in the process (1971, 2:279-81, 288-89). Reuss (1804-91) observed an absence of priestly influence in the prophetic books and pointed to the postexilic period of Ezra as that which most reflected the impact of the priestly legislation (1890, 86, 485, 487). Reuss pushed the date of some of the priestly material to possibly the latest component of the Pentateuch rather than the earliest. Graf (1815-69) contributed a detailed argument defending the idea that the legislation of Leviticus and related laws in Exodus and Numbers comprised the latest part of the Pentateuch. He concluded that the Yahwist's document (J) had been reworked and extended through the addition of the priestly laws in the period associated with Ezra (1866, 2, 4-95, 112). Graf's arguments confirmed Kuenen's later investigations and convinced him that the priestly material should be assigned a late date (postexilic), in contrast to the dominant theory among other critical scholars of his day (Kuenen 1886, xxii-xxiii). On the basis of such work, and that of others, Wellhausen produced the synthesis and refinement of source investigation that has come to be known as the Documentary Hypothesis. Wellhausen's view on the date of the Priestly source echoed and supplemented the arguments claiming it was a postexilic (late) composition.

Wellhausen viewed the composition of the Pentateuch as a progression of religious development, with P at its latest stage. The acceptable place of sacrifice moved from multiple locations in Samuel's time, to exclusively at the Jerusalem temple in Josiah's day, and then exclusively at the tabernacle in Leviticus (which was understood as a retrojection of the Jerusalem temple back into the Mosaic period). Sacrifices evolved from a joyous fellowship meal to a complicated priestly ceremony. The festivals were originally held as agricultural celebrations that took place at varying times in accordance with the harvest in a particular area; while later, worship became centralized, and the festivals were put on a fixed timetable. In earlier times priests were not required for offering sacrifices; while later, priests were required for sacrificial acts, and divisions of rank emerged among the priesthood (high priest, priest, Levite). Finally, it was perceived that in the early stages of Israel's religion, gifts to the priests were voluntary; while in later times, the priesthood required tithes, firstfruits, and portions of sacrifices (Hildebrand 1986, 129-30; Wellhausen 1885, 28-38 [locations of sacrifice], 59-71 [character of sacrifices], 83-107 [character of festivals], 141-52 [priestly divisions], 153-58 [priestly tithes]). The more advanced forms of worship were seen as being reflected in P and 1 and 2 Chronicles, as opposed to 1 and 2 Kings. Thus, P was assigned a postexilic date, closer to the time of the Chronicler.

More recent arguments defending a late date for P typically understand the program of P as a response to the situation of the postexilic community and Persian rule. For example, Vink contends that the dispersion of Israel was the catalyst for an emphasis on the purity of the worshiping community, with Palestine as its central focus. Behind the program of P, and the related mission of Ezra, was the influential Persian policy to make Palestine a stronghold of its empire (based on religious cohesion; Vink 1969, 143-44). Gottwald explains that a restored and functioning Jewish community in Palestine following the exile required civil order and a legitimate system of worship. The Law under Persian imperial administration provided civil order, and a system of sacrificial and ritual holiness established worship (Gottwald 1985, 461-62, 479).

In contrast to the above, *the shift back to an early date for P* was led by Kaufmann, who countered Wellhausen's arguments. Part of Wellhausen's scheme understood the priestly tabernacle as a retrojection of the Second Temple into the earlier wilderness setting. Kaufmann objected that the priestly tabernacle could not be representative of the Second Temple because the ark, cherubim, and urim and thummim of the tabernacle are all missing from Second Temple accounts. In addition, Kaufmann understood the issue of centralization in terms that required an early date for P. He explained that Deuteronomy required ritual slaughter to be performed at the central place of worship chosen by God. However, nonritual slaughter for food could take place anywhere (Deut 12:15-16). In contrast, P makes no such allowance. Therefore, if P and its tabernacle reflected the Second Temple period, those outside of Jerusalem could not have eaten meat without great difficulty (Kaufmann 1960, 180-84). Friedman clarifies: "Rather, in Kaufmann's view, the Priestly Tabernacle must correspond to the local sanctuaries of numerous Israelite towns, it reflects the opposite of centralization, and P therefore was composed prior to Josianic reform" (Friedman 1981, 45). Kaufmann countered a number of other arguments put forth by Wellhausen regarding the date of the priestly literature.

In response to more recent arguments, it is understandable that the Persians would not want to grant political sovereignty to the returning exiles but would lend stability to the area by promoting unity based on religious practice. However, it is entirely likely that existing and previously documented traditions in Israel, rather than newly generated writings, would have provided the impetus for unity within the restored Jewish community in Palestine.

A growing number of scholars have followed Kaufmann's lead and contributed further evidence that the composition of P stems from an early period, that is, preexilic with some material dating to the time of Moses. Zevit asserts that P derives from a time prior to Josiah's reform on the basis of the priestly tithe laws (1982, 485-92). Hildebrand describes similarities between P and other early biblical sources and discusses the antiquity of the tabernacle depicted in P (1986, 131; see Ginsberg 1946, 23). Hildebrand also cites evidence suggesting that early biblical books reference, or allude to, passages in Numbers and Leviticus, implying that such early texts as those in Samuel and Kings had access to P accounts that must have been extant even earlier (1986, 137). In a similar manner, Milgrom demonstrates that Deuteronomy reflects dependence on, and therefore the prior existence of, P (1991, 9-10; see also Zevit 1982, 503-10). Finally, when comparing P to other biblical texts, Klostermann argued that Ezekiel demonstrates dependence on the Holiness Code (Lev 17—26) included within the priestly literature (1893, 385). Friedman adds further evidence that P must have been earlier than Ezekiel (1981, 61, 63-64; see also Hildebrand 1986, 136; and Haran 1981, 327).

The strongest arguments for recognizing the early date of P stem from the linguistic evidence. Milgrom's argument regarding the use of the term *ăbōdâ* in the OT refutes accusations of archaizing on the part of P and demonstrates the early composition of P. This term denotes "physical labor" in P, but in postexilic texts its meaning changes to "cultic service." The term *ăbōdâ* is applied in P to the Levites. Their *ăbōdâ* is confined to the physical transport of the tabernacle. The Levites, however, are forbidden on pain of death to officiate in the sacrificial services of the tabernacle (Num 18:3). In contrast, postexilic texts confine the application of the term *ăbōdâ* to priests alone. This is because for postexilic texts the term now means "cultic service." Thus, if P were late and guilty of archaizing, it would never apply *ăbōdâ* to Levites as it does, for Levites are forbidden to officiate in cultic service (1991, 7). Milgrom sums up the contradiction as follows: "No postexilic writer could have used *ăbōdâ* in its earlier sense of 'physical labor' when it flatly contradicted the meaning it had in his own time. His readers would have been confused, nay shocked, to learn that 'cultic service,' exclusively the prerogative of priests and fatal to non-priests, had been assigned to the Levites" (1991, 8).

A cursory look at the distinct terminology in P and its distribution in the Hebrew Bible consolidates the argument for an early date of composition. Rendsburg points to three linguistic features that suggest an early date for the priestly literature: use of the third person common dual suffix, use of the epicene third person common singular independent pronoun (*hw'*, pointed *hiw'* when used for the feminine pronoun), and the absence of Persian loan words (1980, 77-80).

Hurvitz contributes a study of nine terms or word pairs that distinguish P from the late works of 1 and 2 Chronicles, Ezra, Nehemiah, and Ezekiel (1974, 26-45). In another article Hurvitz adds the evidence of the priestly term *ēdâ* ("congregation"), which appears in biblical texts indicative of the preexilic period (1981, 87). Hurvitz's work demonstrates a linguistic distinction between P and the works of Ezekiel, 1 and 2 Chronicles, Ezra, and Nehemiah. Though Ezekiel, 1 and 2 Chronicles, Ezra, and Nehemiah may use terminology from earlier times as well as later terms, P exclusively prefers the earlier terminology. Thus, P is independent of the later literature and is unaware of the "special priestly terminology characteristic of the exilic and post-exilic writings" (1974, 47). Milgrom reinforces Hurvitz's arguments with additional priestly terms that either fall out of use, or are replaced by synonyms, in postexilic Hebrew. Milgrom concludes that "the replacement of P terms by others indicates not only that the former belong to an earlier age but also that their cumulative effect—twenty-two attestations in all—makes it unlikely that their absence in late Hebrew is purely an accident" (1991, 5).

C. Composition

I. The Priestly Source

The entire book of Leviticus is commonly attributed to the Priestly source (of which H was initially considered an early component, see below). Therefore, a discussion of the composition of Leviticus is subsumed within a discussion of the composition of the priestly writings. The investigation of the sources of the Pentateuch has advanced to the point at which reasonably standard and accepted indexes of the contents of the sources of the Pentateuch (J, E, D, P) have been produced. A good illustration of this is evident in the work of Campbell and O'Brien, who present a helpful synthesis, with slight refinement, of Martin Noth's source critical analysis. They provide an index listing the passages that are assigned to the sources J, E, and P (Campbell and O'Brien 1993, 259-63).

To a great extent, the discussion of the composition of P has focused on narrative material, to the exclusion of the legislation in P. Scholars often begin their work by pointing to the two types of material in P (narrative and legal). Then, they make a brief statement regarding the antiquity of the legal material, label the legal material as later additions to P, and ultimately proceed to discuss the significance of P based on investigation of the narrative material alone (e.g., Noth 1972, 8; McEvenue 1971, 19; idem, 1990, 116; Whybray 1987, 10). Noth's reasoning for this procedure is that the legal sections are additions to P that originally had no direct relation to the narrative in P. The legal material was inserted into what he considers an originally independent P source. Noth concludes that the legislation in P should be given a neutral sign as simply additional legal material that should be disregarded in the consideration of P narrative (1972, 8-10; see also Campbell 1989, 67).

P narrative is normally identified with certain passages in Genesis, Exodus, a small portion of Leviticus (mainly chs 8—10), Numbers, and a small portion of Deuteronomy. The characteristic style of P is defined predominantly by these narratives, especially those in Genesis. The *narratives* are seen as the definitive portion of P, while the legal material is pushed aside as mere additions and supplements. In contrast to this approach, Milgrom's work characterizes P almost exclusively in relation to the *legal* material. These diverse approaches reflect an impasse among scholars in regard to the primary identification of the priestly literature. The resolution to this dilemma calls for a reevaluation of the divisions and relationships evident within the composition of the priestly writings.

The disjunction between the P narratives (especially in Genesis) and the P legal material in Exodus—Numbers suggests that perhaps these two sets of material are actually not portions of the same source. Noth rejected the legal portions of Exodus—Numbers affiliated with P, while Milgrom has isolated much of the same material as if it is the only significant focus of P (see this disjunction illustrated further in Rendtorff 1993, 75-78). Rendtorff's discussion of P further drives apart the narrative and legal portions of P. In relation to P, Rendtorff sees no continuous narrative but notes that a small group of theological texts attributed to P stand out in Genesis, along with several chronological notes from P. The theological texts attributable to P, along with links or cross-references between these texts, are found in the primeval story (Gen 1—11), the patriarchal story (Gen 12—50), and as far as Exod 6. However, no evidence of these priestly theological texts appears beyond Exod 6. Similarly, some connections appear between the chronological notes attributed to P within the larger units of tradition in the Pentateuch. These notes appear to make connections between the primeval story, the patriarchal story, and the Moses story. Again, however, the chronological notes, like the theological texts, do not reach beyond the Moses account. Rendtorff concludes that the priestly texts are a layer of reworking that places emphasis on specific key themes, such as covenant and a unique concept of creation with its significant pronouncements (1990, 136-70, 192-94). This priestly layer of reworking does not extend beyond the Moses account: "After this there is no further sign of the priestly layer in the Pentateuch" (Rendtorff 1990, 194). Rendtorff asserts that the pentateuchal strata associated with P does not appear in any form beyond Exod 6 (see Blenkinsopp 1992, 24). This affirms the proposition that a significant line of division appears between materials associated with the P narrative in Genesis (up to Exod 6) and materials normally attributed to P in Exodus—Numbers.

The viewpoints of Noth and Rendtorff, and the ongoing debate regarding the relationship between narrative and legal material in P, suggest that these two sets of material are not actually part of the same original source. That is, the narratives in Genesis (up to Exod 6) commonly assigned to P, and the P legal material in Exodus—Numbers should simply be recognized as originally two distinct sources. As Milgrom does, it seems most appropriate to label the predominantly legal component (in Exodus—Numbers) as "P" due to its focus on specifically priestly concerns, namely the tabernacle and its related sacrificial system. The narrative material normally attributed to P in Genesis (up to Exod 6) should be assigned a separate designation. For the sake of convenience, I have identified this material with the sign "P^N" (re a discussion of the composition and character of this separate material, see King 2009, 77-122). P itself should be identified with the predominantly legal material found in Exodus—Numbers.

A more explicit identification of the content of P can begin with that which Brueggemann and Wolff designate as P legal material. This includes: Exod 25—31; 35—40; Leviticus; and Num 1—10 (1982, 102). It can be seen that this core of P focuses on the sanctuary and its related sacrificial system. The definitive element of P is the legislation in Exodus, Leviticus, and Numbers, with some brief surrounding narrative providing the appropriate frame and historical backdrop. This material is set within the Sinai account. The core of P can be outlined as follows:

> Exodus 25—31 = instructions concerning the tabernacle, tabernacle furniture, priestly garments, and priestly consecration
>
> Exodus 35—40 = execution of the instructions regarding the tabernacle, tabernacle furniture, and priestly garments
>
> Leviticus 1—7 = sacrificial laws
>
> Leviticus 8—10 = execution of the instructions regarding priestly consecration, and the first sacrifices
>
> Leviticus 11—15 = purity laws
>
> Leviticus 16 = the Day of Atonement
>
> Numbers 1—10 = instructions including the roles of priests and Levites, and ordering of the camp around the tabernacle

The priestly characteristic of command-fulfillment is illustrated in much of this material. For example, the instructions in Exod 25—31 are carried out in Exod 35—40 (the instructions regarding the consecration of the priests are carried out in Lev 8 in conjunction with the first sacrifices). Similarly, the instructions regarding sacrificial laws (Lev 1—7) are initially carried out in the description of the first sacrifices (Lev 8—9). The remaining P material (beyond the above outline) from Exod 6 through Num 36 consists mostly of brief narratives that serve to frame the legal material and depict the appropriate historical setting, namely, that of the wilderness period, and specifically, the giving of the Law at Sinai.

Wilderness itineraries found in Exodus and Numbers serve to frame the P material, and add flow to the limited narrative. Eight wilderness itinerary notices appear in P as a framing device and are identified mainly by the formula *wayyisʿû . . . wayyaḥănû* ("they set out from . . . and encamped at . . ."; some of the notices only include the first verb of the formula). Though there are additional wilderness itinerary notices, these eight have been identified as a chain forming a consistent series of linked movements through the wilderness: Exod 12:37; 13:20; 17:1; 19:2*a*; Num 10:12; 12:16*b*; 21:10-11; 22:1 (King 2009, 21-23; see Walsh 1977, 20-29; this list of notices constitutes Walsh's "chain-I"). This list of eight wilderness stations frames the central portion of P legislation. The placement of the notices highlights the Sinai account as the heart of the priestly concern. Four notices appear on the way to Sinai, and four notices appear following the stay at Sinai. The vast majority of priestly legislation is placed within the setting of the Sinai wilderness station (the Israelites arrive at Sinai at Exod 19:2*a* and depart Sinai at Num 10:12). This corresponds to the core of P as outlined above, all of which is set within the Sinai wilderness station.

The parameter of P is clearly identified through the placement of the phrase *wayĕdabbēr YHWH ʾel-mōšeh* (lit. "and the LORD spoke to Moses"), which occurs ninety-one times in the OT, all within the priestly literature. This characteristic formula of P can be considered P's "command formula." The formula first appears at Exod 6:10, and recurs throughout the P material until its next to the last occurrence at Num 35:9 (the final occurrence identifies Moses' death notice at Deut 32:48; see King 2009, 23 n. 59, 163-64). Thus, the main parameter of P extends from the deliverance from Egypt through the final instructions on the Plains of Moab.

The command formula that introduces God's instruction to Moses is complemented by the "execution formula" in P, which marks the fulfillment of commands from God. The execution formula can be identified with the phrase *kaʾăšer ṣiwwâ YHWH ʾet-mōšeh* (lit. "according as the Lord commanded Moses"). This formula appears consistently forty-one times in P without variation (see King 2009, 23-25; see also Gottwald 1985, 472).

This fulfillment formula affirms the basic parameter of P as defined by its complement, the command formula. Accordingly, the parameter of P ranges from Exod 6 to Num 36 (as with the final instance of the command formula, the final four instances of the execution formula are extensions of P attributable to H; see King 2009, 25 n. 65, 163-65). The book of Leviticus is wholly contained within this priestly material.

2. The Holiness Code

Leviticus 17—26 has long been recognized as a unique component of the priestly literature. Klostermann seems to have coined the phrase "das Heiligkeitsgesetz," which is often translated "The Holiness Code" (1893, 368-85, esp. 385). The label "Holiness Code" stems from the emphasis on holiness evident in Lev 17—26 (→ Behind the Text for ch 17). As with the other sources of the Pentateuch, this subunit of the priestly literature has been assigned an abbreviation, the letter "H." H is traditionally understood to have been an earlier independent law collection that was incorporated into P (Fohrer 1968, 144-45). However, Knohl and Milgrom have demonstrated that H is actually later than P and is the editor (redactor) of P material (Knohl 1995, 6; Milgrom 1991, 13). Knohl goes so far as to assert that H edited and compiled the Torah (Pentateuch) itself (1995, 6, 101-3). His work prompted the realization that H appears to have incorporated P^N (the independent priestly material in Genesis, up to Exod 6) into the larger body of priestly writings (King 2009, 125-51, 157-69). A number of phrases and themes characterize H, some of which are unique to Lev 17—26; for example: "be holy," "I am the LORD your God," "cut off from his people," inclusion of the "alien," and emphasis on Sabbath (for these and more, see Kuenen 1886, 87-91, 275-87; Driver 1910, 47-50; Fohrer 1968, 137-42; Knohl 1995, 1-2 n. 3, 108-10; Milgrom 1991, 35-42; idem 2000, 1325-32). The presence of such characteristically H terminology outside of Lev 17—26 has also long been recognized (Klostermann 1893, 377; Driver 1910, 49-50). In some cases, this may indicate borrowing from H; but in other cases, especially within the Pentateuch, it may indicate the editorial hand of H. H should also be considered preexilic, except for a few passages stemming from a later exilic or postexilic strand (see Knohl 1995, 204-20, 224; Milgrom 2000, 1361-64).

D. Theology

Kaiser expresses the foundational theological theme of the book of Leviticus with these words: "Indeed, the word *sacrifice* comes from a Latin word meaning 'to make something holy.' As such, sacrificing is fully in accord with the main theme of holiness stressed in Leviticus" (1994, 1005).

I. The Relational Purpose of the Sacrificial System

Sin as a general disposition in humanity seems foreign to the legislation in Leviticus. Even *unintentional* sins are addressed with the added qualification of *doing* "what is forbidden in any of the LORD's commands" (4:2, 13, 22, 27). The need for atonement in Leviticus underscores the violation of a known law of God (as opposed to a general sinful disposition). Sin disrupts relations with God. In Leviticus, this disruption becomes evident on two fronts: the defiling impact of sin on persons, and the defiling impact of sin on the sanctuary of God's presence. God who is holy cannot abide sin and its defiling effects. God's presence is especially associated with the holy of holies within the tabernacle (Exod 40:34-35; Lev 16:2). The effects of sin and impurity are represented in Leviticus as defiling the tabernacle, the place of God's presence (Lev 15:31; 20:3; Num 19:13, 20). If such corruption becomes too great, God will abandon the sanctuary and thereby the community. This is pictured in Ezekiel's vision (Ezek 10:18-19; 11:22-23) and mourned in Lamentations (Lam 2:7). A major source of the defilement is human sin. A primary function of the sacrificial system is to cleanse the sanctuary (Milgrom 1991, 256-61) and cleanse persons whose waywardness generated the defilement. The purpose of this cleansing is atonement, that is, the restoration of right relationships between God and people.

In addition to atonement, the sacrificial system provides for the expression of other significant *relational* concerns. For example, the functions of the burnt offering include the invocation of God's presence, a declaration of devotion to God, and a means of celebration in response to significant events. The dedication of firstfruits to the Lord also reflects devotion to God (Lev 2:12, 14; Exod 13:11-13; 22:29-30; 34:19-20; Num 8:17; 2 Chr 31:5). The faithful worshiper acknowledges that everything comes from God and is therefore dedicated back to God by means of a token or representative "firstfruit." The grain offering and the well-being offerings specifically demonstrate cherished relationship with God (2—3; 6:14-18; 7:11-21). Both bread shared between God and priests (grain offerings) and meat shared between God and offerers (well-being offerings) represent a theme of communion uniting God and humanity in intimate fellowship. Finally, the motivations for the various types of well-being offerings further reflect positive relationship with God. The thanksgiving offering provides for expressions of gratitude to the Lord. The votive offering depicts celebration upon the accomplishment of a vow, and the freewill offering represents spontaneous praise to God.

The sacrificial system serves to keep relationship with God constantly before God's children. The daily morning and evening burnt offerings (*continual* burnt offerings) are a perpetual reminder that the community lives in relation to God. Keeping the evening burnt offering smoldering all night suggests that petition on behalf of Israel continued through the night (Walton and Matthews 1997, 149). The pleasing aroma of burnt offerings (1:9, 13, 17) ascended continually and calls to mind the burning incense associated with the prayers of the saints in the NT (Rev 5:8; 8:3-4).

The sacrificial system reflects an inclusive concern for relationship to God. This is evident by the active participation of laypersons in the sacrificial rites in cooperation with the priests. Both the offerer and the priest had alternating roles in offering a sacrifice such as the burnt offering. This partnership allows the layperson to be directly involved in meaningful interaction with God (Milgrom 2004, 17, 22). The tabernacle is not an isolated sacred space for the exclusive activity of the priests. It is a center for the community's expression of its walk with the Lord.

The addition of the burnt offering of birds and the grain offering, for the sake of those who cannot afford a large animal, reinforces the relational and inclusive foundation of the sacrificial system. Such provisions make it possible for every member of the community to participate in the sacrificial expressions of genuine relationship with God.

The sacrificial system also facilitates right relationships between humans themselves. For example, the guilt offering includes atonement for wrongs committed against one's neighbor. Such atonement only follows upon appropriate acts of reparation and reconciliation.

2. Reverence for Life in the Impurity Laws

The theological principle behind the impurity laws becomes evident upon consideration of the sources of impurity identified in the priestly legislation. The priests limited impurity to only three main sources: a corpse or carcass, genital discharges, and scale disease. This narrow inventory excludes a number of known contagious diseases in the ancient world and bodily secretions. The specificity of the sources of impurity in Leviticus reveals the common denominator they share, that is, death in some manner. Clearly, a corpse/carcass reflects death. Genital discharges (semen and vaginal blood) represent forces of life, and therefore their loss represents death. The wasting away of the body is the common characteristic of the highly visible form of scale disease labeled impure in the Bible. It symbolizes the process of death. When scale disease (often translated "leprosy") afflicted Miriam, Moses prayed, "Oh, do not let her be like one dead, whose flesh is half eaten away when he comes from his mother's womb!" (Num 12:12 NASB). Leviticus 13—14 includes moldy fabrics and fungous houses as impure, not because they have scale disease but because they *look* like they have it. The impurity laws symbolically call Israel to *choose life* by means of obedience to these commands of God (Milgrom 1991, 45-47). Impurity, associated with death, stands in opposition to holiness that represents life. Consequently, in this symbolic system, holiness and life overcome impurity and death. The system represents the victory of life over death! The impurity laws provide an expression of God's commitment to resurrection and life!

The impurity legislation also serves as a constant reminder of relationship with God. Even the most private, mundane, irritating, and embarrassing aspects of being human, such as seminal emissions and menstrual cycles, are subject to relationship with God. The impurity laws remind God's people to stop in the midst of the most tedious elements of life, acknowledge God, and recognize God's grace even in places where, and at times when, one would rather be left alone.

3. Call to Holiness in the Holiness Code

The Holiness Code (chs 17—26) extends the call to holiness beyond the tabernacle and the priests, to all Israel. For H, the land is holy, and all who dwell in it must be holy (Milgrom 1992, 457). H extends P's conception of God's presence in the tabernacle to a broader image of God dwelling among the people. The Lord proclaims, "I will put my dwelling place among you, and I will not abhor you. I will walk among you and be your God, and you will be my people" (26:11-12). In the pursuit of holiness, Israel is called to reflect God's holiness: "Be holy because I, the LORD your God, am holy" (19:2).

One expression of the call to holiness in Leviticus appears in the form of separation from the immoral practices of the nations. Holiness is advanced, in part, by abstaining from incest, adultery, homosexuality, and bestiality. The pursuit of holiness and purity is pictured as critical to the sustenance of life. Just as the defilement of the tabernacle through sin and impurity threatens the presence of God in the community, so also the defilement of the land through sexual immorality threatens the presence of the people in the promised land (18:24-28).

The call to holiness is a call to close relationship with God and others by means of emulating God (see Levine 1989, 125). Genuine loving relationships are what truly define God's desire for humanity. The Ten Commandments, including their "priestly" expression in Lev 19, are readily encapsulated within the two categories of loving God and loving neighbor. Christ makes this explicit by stating that "all the Law and the Prophets hang on these two commandments" (Matt 22:40; see Gerstenberger 1996, 267).

The call to holiness expressed in Leviticus is expounded through ethical and ritual regulations intended to promote right relationships with God and neighbor. Hartley observes that the laws of Lev 19 cluster around three topics: faithfulness in worship (vv 3-8, 21-22, 27-28, 30-31), love and respect in interpersonal relationships (vv 11, 13-14, 17-18, 19-20, 29, 32-34), and justice in business and at court (vv 15-16, 35-36). "All these laws reveal God's desire that Israel bring every area of her life into conformity with his holy character" (1992, 308). Leviticus expands the concept of holiness beyond just a quality or power of God and defines it in relational and experiential terms. Holiness is enacted and actualized through the life of the community. It is "manifest in relationships characterized by integrity, honesty, faithfulness, and love" (Gorman 1997, 111-12). Kaiser adds, "In Leviticus, if you want to be holy, don't pass out a tract; love your neighbor, show hospitality to the stranger, and be a person of justice" (1994, 1136). Leviticus 19 expresses the approach to holiness consistent throughout the Holiness Code:

> Holiness is thus not so much an abstract or a mystic idea, as a regulative principle in the everyday lives of men and women. The words, "ye shall be holy," are the keynote of the *whole* chapter, and must be read in connection with its various precepts; reverence for parents, consideration for the needy, prompt wages for reasonable hours, honourable dealing, no talebearing or malice, love of one's neighbor and cordiality to the alien, equal justice to rich and poor, just measures and balances—together with abhorrence of everything unclean, irrational, or heathen. Holiness is thus attained not by flight from the world, nor by monk-like renunciation of human relationships of family or station, but by the spirit in which we fulfil the obligations of life in its simplest and commonest details: in this way—by doing justly, loving mercy, and walking humbly with our God—is everyday life transfigured. (Hertz 1960, 497-98)

For Leviticus, even *time* becomes a vehicle for extending holiness. The festivals and related occasions are presented as liturgical events and are fixed within a regular annual cycle (ch 23). As a result, the list of community agricultural celebrations becomes an enumeration of *mô'ădê YHWH* (lit. "the appointed times of the Lord"). Kalisch describes the focus of the priestly calendar as an upgrading of the ordinary calendar to the ethical sphere.

An advance had been made from the cosmic and historical to the ethical sphere: the festivals were no longer understood merely as days of thanksgiving for the bounty of *nature*, nor as occasions for tracing, with awe and reverence, in past and present events, the rule of a *Divine Providence*, but as seasons for self-examination and contrition, for the improvement and purification of the *soul* and the *heart*. (1872, 487)

COMMENTARY

I. THE SACRIFICIAL SYSTEM (1:1—7:38)

A. Voluntary Sacrifices (1:1—3:17)

BEHIND THE TEXT

Following the heading for the book of Leviticus (1:1), the section regarding voluntary sacrifices is introduced in v 2. The term *kî* ("when") designates the general category of a legal instruction, following which specific instances are identified by the term *'im* ("if"). In this case, the general heading regarding voluntary animal offerings (1:2) governs the burnt offering in ch 1, which is subdivided into specific instructions related to whether/"if" (*'im*) the burnt offering is "from the herd" (1:3), or "if" the burnt offering is "from the flock" (1:10). This same general heading (1:2) also governs the well-being offering in ch 3, which is likewise subdivided in relation to whether/"if" (*'im*) the well-being offering is "from the herd" (3:1), or "if" the well-being offering is "from the flock" (3:6). The well-being offering from the flock is further subdivided into an offering of a lamb (3:7) or a goat (3:12). Accordingly, chs 1 and 3 appear to reflect a literary unity (Milgrom 1991, 144-46, 178, 203; Kaiser 1994, 1009).

The instructions regarding a burnt offering of birds (1:14-17) appears out of place because birds do not fit under the general heading of livestock (*běhēmâ*) that introduces the voluntary offerings (1:2). Nevertheless, this section does begin with *'im* ("if"), as though the bird offering was intended to be a specific case under the general heading of livestock offerings. Due to this seeming misclassification, and because the well-being offerings (ch 3) do not include a case involving birds, Lev 1:14-17 may be a later addition. The purpose of this addition is to provide a means for the poor to participate in presenting burnt offerings to the Lord. This rationale is explicit elsewhere in relation to bird offerings (5:7; 12:8; 14:21-22, 30-31; Milgrom 1991, 166-67).

Similarly, ch 2 (grain offering) appears to interrupt the unity between chs 1 and 3, which deal with the livestock offerings governed by the general heading at 1:2. Chapter 2 not only deals with grain as opposed to animals but is further set off by the presence of its own general heading beginning with *kî* ("when," v 1), followed by specific types of grain offerings introduced by *'im* ("if . . . on a griddle," v 5; "if . . . cooked in a pan," v 7; "if" as "firstfruits," v 14). One would also expect v 4 to begin with *'im* as implied by the NIV's use of "if" at the head of that verse; however, v 4 actually begins with *kî* ("when"). Perhaps this is because the baked grain offering introduced in v 4 can be made into one of two varieties. Thus, the *kî* of v 4 introduces the general category of baked grain offerings, which can be subdivided into baked "cakes" or baked "wafers." Accordingly, the structure of the discussion in ch 2 reveals five types of grain offerings. Rashi clarifies that the first grain offering discussed is that of raw fine flour (vv 1-3). Next, the two types of baked grain offerings are identified (cakes or wafers, v 4), followed by grain offerings "prepared on a griddle" (v 5) and those "cooked in a pan" (v 7; in Herczeg 1999, 18-19, see 19 n. 5). A sixth type of grain offering is discussed in vv 14-16 in the form of a firstfruits offering.

The grain offering may have been placed between the burnt offering and well-being offering because, like the offering of birds, it is designated as an offering that can be presented by the poor (5:11; Milgrom 1991, 167). In addition, the grain offering often functions as an accompanying sacrifice to burnt offerings and well-being offerings. This too may account for its position in the center of the voluntary sacrifices (Kaiser 1994, 1016).

IN THE TEXT

1. Burnt Offering (1:1-17)

■ 1 The opening verse of Leviticus serves as a heading for the entire book. The particular phrase, **called to Moses** (*wayyiqrā' 'el-mōšeh*), with **the LORD** (YHWH) as subject, occurs only here and Exod 24:16 in the Hebrew Bible (in the MT of Exod 24:16 YHWH is implied as subject from the first half of the sentence, while the LXX explicitly names the Lord as subject). In the Exodus passage, the glory of the Lord had settled on Mount Sinai and the Lord called to Moses "from within the cloud." At the opening of Leviticus, the Lord calls to Moses **from the Tent of Meeting.** The transfer of the presence of the Lord from cloud to tent is communicated at the end of the book of Exodus, which explains that "the cloud covered the Tent of Meeting, and the glory of the LORD filled the tabernacle" (Exod 40:34). This final passage of Exodus is linked to the beginning of Leviticus by means of the tent of meeting, which the Lord enters at the end of Exodus and from which the Lord calls Moses at the beginning of Leviticus (Marx 2003, 105; see also Milgrom 1991, 134).

Two other texts in Exodus reflect similar terminology in relation to God calling Moses. At Exod 3:4 God called to Moses from the midst of the burning bush (here the MT specifies the subject as *'ĕlōhîm*, though again the LXX names the Lord, *kyrios*, as subject). Finally, Exod 19:3 relates that the Lord called to Moses from the mountain (here, as with Exod 3:4, the proper name, Moses, does not appear as the object of the verb, but rather the masculine pronoun is used). While the phrase *wayĕdabbēr YHWH 'el-mōšeh* (lit. "and the LORD spoke to Moses") appears numerous times throughout the priestly literature, the unique heading that opens Leviticus (**The LORD called to Moses**) is considered a "rare, special revelatory formula" (Hartley 1992, 8). The formula reveals a progression of the Lord/God calling Moses from the burning bush (Exod 3:4), the mountain (Exod 19:3), the cloud (Exod 24:16), and finally the tent of meeting (Lev 1:1).

Two traditions appear in the Pentateuch regarding the **Tent of Meeting.** The nonpriestly tradition sees the tent as a place located outside the camp, upon which the Lord descends in the cloud, and where anyone may inquire of the Lord (Exod 33:7-10; Num 11:24-27; 12:4-5). This tent is guarded by Joshua (Exod 33:11). In contrast, the priestly tradition regarding the tent sees it located in the center of the camp and guarded by Levites (Num 2:17; 3:5-10). While the cloud of God's presence descends periodically in relation to the nonpriestly tent, God's cloud is always present in the holy of holies according to the priestly tradition. In terms of function, the nonpriestly tent serves mainly for the purpose of inquiring from the Lord, while the priestly tent includes the additional function of serving as the center of the sacrificial system (Childs 1974, 590; Milgrom 1991, 139-40). In the priestly tradition, the tent of meeting (*'ōhel mô'ēd*) is also called the tabernacle (*miškān*; Exod 39:32; 40:2, 6, 29, 34-35; Lev 17:4; Num 3:7-8, 38; see Haran 1985, 179 n. 8, 272).

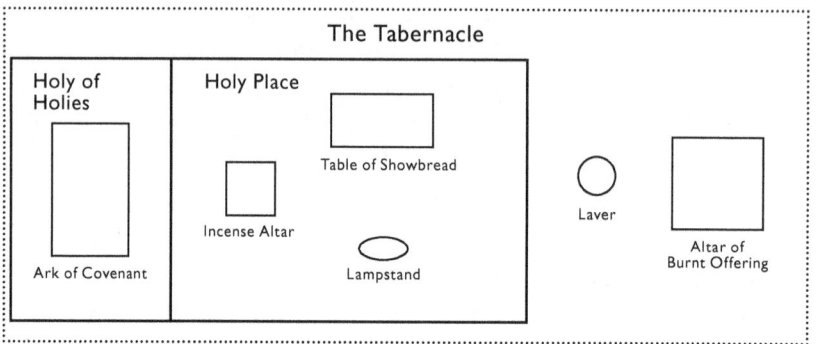

■ **2** This general introduction stipulates that **when** an **offering** of livestock is presented **to the Lord,** it should be chosen **from either the herd or the flock** (→ Behind the Text above).

■ **3** The first offering detailed in Leviticus is the **burnt offering** (*'ōlâ*). This offering is characterized by being entirely consumed upon the altar (vv 9, 13), except for the skin, which is the property of the priests (7:8). Consequently, it is sometimes known as the *whole* burnt offering.

The following four functions stand out among the purposes of the burnt offering: invocation, devotion, celebration, and atonement. The burnt offering is consistently mentioned first in lists of sacrifices and in order of ritual practice. This suggests its function as a means of attracting God's attention and invoking God's presence (Levine 1989, 5-6). The **aroma pleasing to the Lord** (vv 9, 13, 17) further depicts the attention-seeking character of the burnt offering (Budd 1996, 43). Such invocation serves to provide opportunity to entreat a response from the Lord regarding whatever plea concerns the offerer (Kaiser 1994, 1010; Walton and Matthews 1997, 144).

Gerstenberger explains the burnt offering as a sacrifice of complete devotion to God in terms of its economic impact on the offerer: "Giving up to God a healthy ox as a burnt offering, without even partaking of it in a meal (as is presupposed for the sacrifices in chap. 3), would represent something like opening a vein for the person presenting the offering, comparable today only to the surrender of a portion of one's wealth" (1996, 27, see also pp. 33-34). The "ideal of self-less devotion to God" is profoundly illustrated in Abraham's sacrifice of Isaac (intended as a burnt offering), a typology for Christian theology that, when combined with Christ's sacrifice on the cross, turns the crucifixion into the ultimate burnt offering (Watts 2006, 133, 136). In being fully consumed on the altar and ascending in smoke, the burnt offering stands out as the embodiment of complete surrender to the Lord (see Keil and Delitzsch n.d., 291).

The burnt offering shares with the well-being offering the distinction of serving for joyful expressions of celebration and thanksgiving. Great events such as the end of the flood, the return of the stolen ark of the covenant, and bringing the ark into Jerusalem were celebrated with burnt offerings (Gerstenberger 1996, 23). Elsewhere, legislation associates the burnt offering with the joyful occasion of the fulfillment of a vow or as a freewill offering (Lev 22:17-19; Num 15:3; see Kaiser 1994, 1010).

The atoning function of the burnt offering seems unusual since the purification and guilt offerings specialize in addressing atonement. Nevertheless, the burnt offering appears to participate in atonement (Lev 1:4; Ezek 45:15, 17), is associated with the purification offering (Lev 9:7; 14:19-20; 16:24-25), and is offered in case of possible wrongdoing (Job 1:5).

The burnt offering is to be presented **at the entrance to the Tent of Meeting.** This refers to the courtyard where the outer altar is located, between the opening to the gate and the opening to the tent (see Milgrom 1991, 147-48).

Love: The Motive for Atonement

Hartley speculates that since no specific sins are stipulated in relation to the burnt offering, it must serve to atone for the general sinful disposition of the offerer (1992, 19). However, such concern seems foreign to the priestly legislation. Even unintentional sins are qualified by the action of *doing* "what is forbidden in any of the LORD's commands" (4:2, 13, 22, 27), placing the emphasis regarding the need for atonement on violating a known law of God.

Levine, acknowledging that the burnt offering was not occasioned by any offense needing expiation, claims the need here is for redemption from God's wrath. He argues that proximity to God was inherently dangerous even when no violation had occurred to anger the Lord (1989, 6-7). This identifies the motivation for atonement as God's wrath rather than love. Christians make the same mistake by asserting that appeasing God's wrath is the motivation behind the crucifixion and the atonement it offers. Such thought would require the revision of John 3:16 so that it should read, "For God was so *angry* with the world, that he sent his only begotten Son . . ." In contrast, it is God's love and grace that provide the means of atonement for ancient Israel through the sacrificial system, which is brought to fulfillment through the life, death, and resurrection of Christ.

■ **4** The offerer is instructed to **lay his hand on the head** of the offering. This same instruction for laying a single hand on the head of a sacrifice is given in the case of the well-being offering from the herd (3:1-2) or flock (lamb, 3:7-8; goat, 3:12-13), and for the various instances of the purification offering (priest, 4:3-6; community, 4:13-15; leader, 4:22-24; layperson, 4:27-29, 32-33). In the case of the community purification offering, the term for hand is plural (4:15). Nevertheless, the assumption is that the plural noun refers to the combined hands of the elders, each of whom extends one hand to the head of the animal. This same assumption applies to other instances of animal sacrifice in which laying hands (plural) on an offering involves a group (consecration of Aaron and sons, Exod 29:10, 15, 19; Lev 8:14, 18, 22; consecration of Levites, Num 8:12; king and assembly, 2 Chr 29:23). There is one instance in the Hebrew Bible that explicitly calls for "both" (*štê*) hands to be laid on the head of an animal, that is, the case of the live goat on the Day of Atonement (Lev 16:21). This points to the key for understanding the meaning of the rite of hand laying (Milgrom 1991, 151; Péter 1977, 51-52; Wright 1986, 434).

A common view is to interpret the laying of hands on a sacrifice as a transference of sin so that the sacrifice becomes a substitute for the offerer. The offerer is thus excused by substituting the death of the animal for his or her own death (Kaiser 1994, 1011; Reeve 1956, 2643). However, the concept of substitution in relation to the sacrificial system lacks support from other biblical texts (Budd 1996, 47).

The transference of sin does apply in the case of the live goat ritual on the Day of Atonement (two-hand laying), in which the priest explicitly places the sins of the people on the head of the goat that then carries those sins to a solitary place in the wilderness (16:21-22). However, substitution is not pictured here; rather, the image is that of removing sin out of the community to a remote location. Consequently, two-hand laying represents transference, but not substitution. This is affirmed by the other cases of two-hand laying (not involving animals). When Moses lays his hands on Joshua, he transfers authority to him, as Joshua is commissioned to be Israel's new leader (Num 27:22-23 [plural hands]; God's instruction in Num 27:18 should also be read as plural [hands], with the LXX; Wright 1986, 435; Milgrom 1990, 235). Also, in the case of the witnesses laying hands on the blasphemer (Lev 24:14), there is a transference of pollution from those who heard the blasphemy back onto the blasphemer whose words defiled them (Péter 1977, 53; Milgrom 2001, 2113-14).

In the case of one-hand laying, the transference of sin is not possible because it is used for the burnt offering, which is completely offered to

God on the altar and therefore cannot be defiled by the transfer of sins to it. In addition, one-hand laying is prescribed for the well-being offering, which does not involve sin or the need for atonement (Hartley 1992, 20-21; see de Vaux 1997, 416). When the Israelites lay hands on the Levites, it is clear that no sin is being transferred onto them (for the Levites are being set apart for service to God), and no authority or power is being transferred (for *laypersons,* or their representatives, are laying hands on those who will "do the work *of the* LORD" [Num 8:10-11, emphasis added]). Thus, it is held that this must be a one-hand imposition, and it serves to identify the Levites as Israel's sacrifice by which the Levites represent the people in doing the work of the Lord. By this, the service of the Levites accrues to all Israel (Wright 1986, 439; Milgrom 1990, 62).

In a similar manner, one-hand laying on animal sacrifices designates the offering as representative of the offerer and as accruing to the offerer (de Vaux 1997, 416). However, the significance of this rite should not be denigrated to mere substitution. Rather, it marks sacrifice in general as a giving of oneself (Noth 1977, 22). *One-hand laying conveys representation and participation by which offerers designate the animals through which they consecrate themselves to God in relation to acts of praise, thanksgiving, dedication, and purification.* Though Wesley held that laying hands on the sacrifice signified that the offerer was worthy of the death that the animal "suffered in his stead," he also affirmed the representative character of the sacrifice by stating that "together with it he [the offerer] did freely offer up himself to God" (1765, 345).

■ **5-9** The offering is to be presented **before the** LORD (*lipnê YHWH*). This was already stipulated in relation to God's reception of the offerer at v 3, which literally reads "for his acceptance before the LORD." For the priestly legislation, since the presence of God is associated with the tabernacle (specifically the holy of holies), the phrase **before the** LORD generally refers to the area of the courtyard at the entrance to the tent of meeting (see Milgrom 1991, 150, 155). This is evident from texts, such as v 3, that directly associate "before the LORD" with the "entrance to the tent of meeting" (Exod 29:11, 42; Lev 4:4; 14:11, 23; 15:14; 16:7; see also Lev 9:5). "Before the LORD" can, however, refer more specifically to areas closer to God's presence in the holy of holies; for example, the holy place inside the tent of meeting (4:6, 7, 18), or the holy of holies itself (16:13).

The rites involved in relation to the burnt offering are shared by the layperson and the priest. The wording of the text alternates the action of the sacrifice between the offerer and the priest (i.e., sons of Aaron). The offerer designates the sacrifice by laying a hand on its head, and then slaughters the bull. The priest sprinkles the blood against the altar. The offerer skins the animal and cuts it into pieces (the skin is given to the priest, 7:8). The priest arranges the pieces of the sacrifice on the fire and the wood, on the altar. The offerer washes the inner parts and the legs. Finally the priest burns all of the animal on the altar. This partnership allows the layperson to be directly involved in meaningful interaction with God. The priest, who alone is permitted to carry out the work of the altar, acts on behalf of the offerer (Milgrom 2004, 17, 22; see also idem 1991, 155, 163).

The blood rite for the burnt offering calls for the priest to **toss** or **throw/dash** (*wĕzārĕqû*) the blood of the sacrifice **on all sides** of (lit. "round about") the altar. In contrast to the NIV and other common translations, the verb is not "to sprinkle" (*hizzâ*, from *nzh*) as found in the blood rite for other offerings. The blood rite for the burnt offering signifies returning the life of the animal back to God (Milgrom 1991, 156; Hartley 1992, 21). Ancient Israel was to understand that blood represented life (Gen 9:4; Lev 17:11), and life belongs to the Creator who gave it. Therefore when a life is taken in sacrifice, its blood (life) must be returned to God. In the sacrificial system, this is accomplished by pouring out the blood at the altar.

The offerer must **wash the inner parts and the legs** so that no excrement or dirt defiles the altar (Milgrom 1991, 159; Hartley 1992, 22).

■ **10-13** The instructions for **a burnt offering from the flock** basically repeat the rites described for the offering of a bull from the herd. Again, the action alternates between the offerer and the priest (→ 1:5-9; also Gerstenberger 1996, 29).

In dealing with the smaller animal from the flock, the ritual details are abbreviated. It is understood that the ritual should follow the same procedure as that for a sacrifice from the herd (Noth 1977, 24).

■ **14-17** The instructions for **a burnt offering of birds** varies somewhat from the routine described in relation to offerings from the herd or flock, presumably due to the size of the animal. In the previous sets of instructions (for herd and flock), the alternation of action between offerer and priest was marked by specific references to the priest or the sons of Aaron, contrasted by third person singular verbs (designating the offerer). The same pattern appears to be reflected in the instructions for the birds. Thus, the priest wrings off the head of the bird, burns it on the altar, and drains the blood on the side of the altar. The offerer removes the crop with its contents, throws it on the ashes, and tears the bird without completely severing it. Finally, the priest burns the bird on the altar (Harrison 1980, 48; in contrast to the view that the priest performs all the rites related to offering birds, Hartley 1992, 23; Gerstenberger 1996, 28).

In regard to the removal of the **crop with its contents,** Rashbam identifies the concern here as that of cleaning the bird for sacrifice. He associates the crop with filth, like feces or manure (in Lockshin 2001, 17). The common translation, "crop," for the term *mur'â* has been taken to refer to a pocket in the throat of birds where food is retained during digestion. This pocket with its contents of undigested food was unfit for the altar and therefore had to be removed before sacrifice (Levine 1989, 8-9). However, Milgrom has clarified that *mur'â* should be understood as a reference to the lower digestive organs that contain the excrement of the bird. In addition, the term *nōṣâ*, which is commonly translated "plumage" or "feathers" (NIV = **contents**), specifically refers to the tail wing. Accordingly, the procedure is to remove the entrails by means of the tail wing (1991, 170-71). This rendering is reflected clearly in the New English Translation of the Bible: "remove its entrails by cutting off its tail feathers." The removal of the entrails of a bird is consistent with washing the inner parts and the legs of the larger animals in order to remove any excrement, which would defile the altar (→ 1:5-9).

The offerer **shall tear it open by the wings, not severing it completely,** in correlation with the procedure of cutting up the pieces of the sacrifices from the herd or the flock, and in order to make the offering appear as large as possible (Milgrom 1991, 171-72).

2. Grain Offering (2:1-16)

■ 1 The general use of *minḥâ* (**grain offering**) points to the basic meaning of the term as gift or tribute (de Vaux 1997, 421; Kaiser 1994, 1017; Marx 2003, 114). Such gifts serve to honor God and seek God's favor, fulfill hospitality requirements for divine visitations (Judg 6:18; 13:19), secure general appeasement (1 Sam 26:19), or implement regular sanctuary procedure (1 Kgs 18:29, 36; 2 Kgs 3:20; 16:15; Ps 141:2; Budd 1996, 55). In at least two instances, the *minḥâ* appears to participate in the function of atonement (Lev 14:20; 1 Sam 3:14; Milgrom 1991, 197; Budd 1996, 55).

In the priestly legislation, *minḥâ* refers exclusively to the **grain offering** (Keil and Delitzsch n.d., 291; Rainey 1972, 602; Milgrom 1991, 179). The grain offering can serve as an independent offering (Lev 2; Num 5:15; 18:9) or is often used in accompaniment with other sacrifices (especially evident by the phrase, "with its/their grain offering"; Lev 23:18; Num 6:15; 7:87; 8:8; 15:4, 6, 9, 24; Ezek 46:5, 7, 14). Grain offerings may accompany sacrifices related to joyous occasions, such as well-being offerings and burnt offerings. On more somber occasions, such as those calling for the jealousy offering (Num 5:15, 18, 25-26) and the poor person's purification offering (Lev 5:11-13), no oil or frankincense was added to the grain offering (Rainey 1972, 602-3).

The grain offering of the priestly literature carries a similar range of applications as that of the burnt offering. In fact, it is held that the grain offering serves as a replacement for the burnt offering for the sake of the poor who cannot afford to sacrifice an animal or a bird (Milgrom 1991, 195-96). More than a surrogate, however, the grain offering adds a unique dimension to the sacrificial system. As food shared by God and the priest, the grain offering expresses intimate communion between God and humans (Gerstenberger 1996, 45; Marx 2003, 114).

The grain offering is to be made up of **fine flour** (*sōlet*). Rashi asserts that *sōlet* always denotes wheat (in Herczeg 1999, 19). Rabbinic tradition specifies that *sōlet* refers to the inner kernels of wheat that are left in the sieve after the flour has fallen through (Milgrom 1991, 179; Kaiser 1994, 1017). This is the choice part of the wheat, representing a gift of the best to God (Levine 1989, 9; Kaiser 1994, 1017). **Oil** and **incense** are to be applied to the grain. The oil is olive oil, and the term the NIV translates "incense" here specifically denotes frankincense; the former used commonly for cooking and the latter costly (see Milgrom 1991, 180-81). Frankincense is derived from certain trees of the genus Boswellia, which grow in southern Arabia and Somaliland (Masterman 1956, 1144). While some state that frankincense enhances flavor (Levine 1989, 9), others claim it has a nauseous taste (Masterman 1956, 1145).

■ **2** The priest separates a portion of the grain offering by removing **a handful of the fine flour and oil, together with all the incense.** The handful that the priest scoops is identified as the **memorial portion** (*'azkārâ*) of the grain offering. Some prefer the rendering "token portion" (NAB; see NJPS), because the handful serves to represent the whole offering (Levine 1989, 10; Milgrom 1991, 181-82; Budd 1996, 58). However, *'azkārâ* is commonly understood to derive from *zākar*, meaning "remember." Accordingly, the memorial portion burnt on the altar is said to remind God of the offerer and his or her goodness and consecrations (Ps 20:3; so Rashi in Herczeg 1999, 21-22; Keil and Delitzsch n.d., 292). In addition, the burnt portion of the offering serves to remind the offerer of God's grace and provision (Hartley 1992, 30; Kaiser 1994, 1020-21). The memorial portion is also described as **an aroma pleasing to the LORD.** This attention-seeking aspect of the offerings reflects a type of invocation (→ 1:3; see also Rainey 1972, 602; Gerstenberger 1996, 42). The idea is to symbolically attract God's attention by means of the pleasing odor of the sacrifice.

■ **3** The remainder of the grain offering, after the memorial portion is burnt on the altar, **belongs to Aaron and his sons.** The priests have no tribal inheritance of land and are dependent on their allotted portions of the sacrifices for their meat and daily bread (Kaiser 1994, 1020). This portion assigned to the priests is designated **most holy** (*qōdeš qodāšîm*). The designation most holy is applied to: the holy of holies (Exod 26:33); altar of burnt offering (Exod 29:37; 30:29; 40:10); incense altar (Exod 30:10, 29); tent of meeting, ark, table, lamp, and basin of the tabernacle (Exod 30:29); incense for the tabernacle (Exod 30:36); grain offering (Lev 6:17 [6:10 HB]; 10:12; Num 18:9); purification offering (Lev 6:17 [6:10 HB]; 6:25, 29 [6:18, 22 HB]; 10:17; Num 18:9); guilt offering (Lev 6:17 [6:10 HB]; 7:1, 6; 14:13; Num 18:9); the bread of the tabernacle (Lev 24:9); and things devoted to the Lord (Lev 27:28).

■ **4-9** The cooked grain offerings may be presented in any of four varieties: baked **cakes,** baked **wafers, prepared on a griddle,** or **cooked in a pan.** The instructions for the cooked grain offerings are essentially the same as those for the raw grain offering (vv 1-3). However, the cooked grain offerings do not include frankincense. This may be another concession to the poor, for whom frankincense would be too costly (Milgrom 1991, 183).

■ **10** Belongs to Aaron and his sons (→ 2:3).

■ **11** Grain offerings **must be made without yeast** (lit. "shall not be made leavened" [*ḥāmēṣ*]), **for you are not to burn any yeast** (*śĕ'ōr*) **on the altar.** The requirement that the bread of the grain offering be unleavened calls to mind the similar prohibitions against yeast in the instructions regarding Passover and the Festival of Unleavened Bread commemorating the exodus from Egypt (Exod 12:8, 15, 17-20). In relation to the annual pilgrimage festivals, similar legislation forbids that which is leavened to be included with blood sacrifices (Exod 23:18; 34:25). In contrast, the thanksgiving offering is to be presented with bread that is leavened (Lev 7:13), and the wave offering for the Festival of Weeks includes loaves that are leavened (23:17); both, however, are not burned on the altar. Thus, the prohibition only excludes leaven from being included **in an offering made to the Lord by fire.**

Honey (*dĕbaš*) is also excluded from the altar. Rashi clarifies that *dĕbaš* refers to anything sweet that comes from fruit, such as grapes, dates, or figs (in Herczeg 1999, 26; see also Noth 1977, 29; Milgrom 1991, 189-90). The Hebrew term *dĕbaš* is cognate to Arabic *dibs*, which refers to the sweet syrup made from grapes, raisins, carob beans, or dates (Patch 1956, 1418). It is uncertain whether the OT references to *dĕbaš* denote such fruit honey or honey from bees. Judges 14:8 clearly refers to bee honey as evidenced by the mention of a "swarm of bees" in proximity to the honey.

Other OT passages include *děbaš* in the context of agricultural products, implying that *děbaš* designates a sweet substance from the fruit of the field (Gen 43:11; Deut 8:8; 2 Kgs 18:32; 2 Chr 31:5; Ezek 16:13; Milgrom 1991, 189; Hartley 1992, 31). Consequently, the evidence leaves room for the probability that the prohibition in Lev 2:11 refers to both bee honey and fruit nectars (Levine 1989, 12).

It is commonly held that the reason for the prohibition of leaven and honey from the altar is due to association of these products with heathen worship. Ancient Near Eastern cults are known for their use of leaven and honey in sacrifices as indicated in ritual texts. Thus, the prohibition for Israel was intended to dissociate Israel's sacrificial system from pagan practices (Levine 1989, 12; Hartley 1992, 33; Kaiser 1994, 1018). Others argue that the fermentive action of leaven and honey is considered the basis for their rejection. The character of fermentation is associated with deterioration, corruption, and death and is therefore rejected from use on the altar (Keil and Delitzsch n.d., 294-95; Noth 1977, 28-29; Milgrom 1991, 188-90). In contrast, the fermentation of leaven and honey can also be understood as representative of a life force, like blood, which cannot be burnt on the altar (Porter 1976, 26; Budd 1996, 61-62; re blood as life, see Lev 17:11 and Milgrom 1991, 156). This is more consistent with the focus on life evident within the sacrificial system for Israel (→ 1:5-9; 3:16-17; also → 11:46-47 sidebar, "Rationale for the Dietary Restrictions," and From the Text for chs 11—15). This also clarifies why honey and leaven, though forbidden from being burned on the altar, are still acceptable as part of the firstfruits offering discussed in 2:12.

■ **12** The prohibition from v 11 is repeated with the words **they [yeast and honey] are not to be offered on the altar as a pleasing aroma.** Nevertheless, yeast and honey are allowed **as an offering of the firstfruits.** The term translated **firstfruits** here in v 12 (*rēʾšît*) is different from the term also translated firstfruits in v 14 (*bikkûrîm*). The former (*rēʾšît*) generally means first or foremost, while the latter (*bikkûrîm*) more specifically refers to first ripened fruits or crops of the soil. Milgrom argues that, in the priestly legislation, *rēʾšît* should be translated "first-processed" in relation to grain, wine, oil, fruit syrup, and bread, which are processed from crops; while *bikkûrîm* should be understood as "first-ripe" crops (1991, 190-91). The two terms appear together in relation to the Feast of Harvest as "best [first/foremost] of the firstfruits" (*rēʾšît bikkûrê*; Exod 23:19; 34:26). The dedication of firstfruits to God is reflected in the law of the firstborn, in which the firstborn of livestock, and even the firstborn of one's body, are to be committed to God (Exod 13:11-13; 22:29-30; 34:19-20; Num 8:17; see Budd 1996, 63).

Similarly, the firstfruits of the produce of the land are to be offered to the Lord. In the case of those that include honey or leaven, they are to be "placed before God rather than burned on the altar" (Levine 1989, 13). The *rēʾšît* of this verse is often associated with the *ʿōmer rēʾšît qĕṣîrĕkem* (lit. "sheaf of the first of your harvest") of the barley harvest (23:10). However, the instruction here is more directly reflected in the "wave offering of firstfruits" (*bikkûrîm*) of the wheat harvest, which is "baked with yeast" (23:17), and the Chronicler's description of the offering of firstfruits (*rēʾšît*) in the days of Hezekiah, which included "honey" (2 Chr 31:5).

■ 13 The offerer is instructed to **add salt to all your offerings**. The rationale for the addition of salt is vaguely expressed by the command, **Do not leave the salt of the covenant of your God out of your grain offerings**. The rare phrase "covenant of salt" appears only twice in the Hebrew Bible (Num 18:19; 2 Chr 13:5). In both cases, the meaning of the phrase seems to draw upon the character of salt as a preservative, highlighting the enduring quality of the covenant. Both texts include the term *ʿôlām* (forever, eternal, everlasting) in relation to the covenant under consideration in each passage. Arabs and Greeks establish covenant and mark the bond of community by eating salt together (Noth 1977, 29; Hartley 1992, 32). Accordingly, Israel likely recognized salt as a sign of the permanence and communal character of the covenant relationship reflected in the sacrificial system.

■ 14-16 The final form of grain offering treated in ch 2 appears to be appended, due to its separation from the other grain offerings by the interruption created by the instructions regarding leaven, honey, and salt (vv 11-13). The addition of vv 14-16 could be in response to the prohibition in v 12 (Gerstenberger 1996, 41). Thus, this legislation clarifies that, though yeast and honey are only acceptable in relation to firstfruits offerings that are *not* burnt on the altar, regular offerings of firstfruits are acceptable on the altar as grain offerings (without yeast or honey).

2:13-16

The **grain offering of firstfruits** (*bikkûrîm*) here cannot refer to the *wheat* offering of firstfruits attached to the Feast of Weeks, because that offering includes yeast and is not burned on the altar (23:17). Thus, perhaps the grain offering of firstfruits here relates to the *ʿōmer* and the firstfruits of *barley* (23:10-11; with Rashi in Herczeg 1999, 27). Yet, the *ʿōmer* is described as a sheaf presented to the Lord as a wave or elevation offering, and "lacks oil and incense" (Milgrom 2001, 1985). Thus, the grain offering of firstfruits here in 2:14 appears distinct from both the wheat offering of firstfruits at the Feast of Weeks, and the *ʿōmer* associated with the barley harvest. Nevertheless, there is a connection between the three. The distinct form of the grain offering of firstfruits, **crushed heads of new grain**

roasted including **oil and incense**, may denote a voluntary "form" of the firstfruits offerings, consistent with the other grain offerings in ch 2 (in contrast with Milgrom, 1991, 192-93, and 2001, 1985; see Levine 1989, 14). That is, though it is required that all firstfruits must be offered to the Lord (Milgrom 1991, 193), the grain offering of firstfruits as described in 2:14 constitutes an optional form for such an offering, which may be presented in addition to the forms mandated at 23:10-11 (the *'ōmer* of barley) and 23:16-17 (the wave offering of firstfruits at the Feast of Weeks, wheat harvest). Therefore, the grain offering of firstfruits described here at 2:14, which is not specified as *sōlet* (wheat flour), may refer to either a firstfruits offering of wheat *or* barley (see Hartley 1992, 32).

The rest of the instructions for this grain offering (vv 15-16) follow those of the previous grain offerings (vv 1-2, 9).

3. Well-Being Offering (3:1-17)

■ **1** This verse includes a dual heading in which the first "if" (*'im*) clause introduces the instructions for the well-being offering as a whole, and the second "if" (*'im*) clause designates the first section of those instructions, which pertains to whether/"if" (*'im*) the offering is from the herd (Hartley 1992, 34; → Behind the Text above). Accordingly, a literal rendition of the verse reads, "*if* his offering is a sacrifice of well-being; *if* he offers it from the herd . . ."

The designation for the **well-being offering** is made up of two terms: *zebaḥ* and *šĕlāmîm*. The use of these terms in the Hebrew Bible suggests that the well-being offering is identified by the full phrase, *zebaḥ šĕlāmîm*, or by either term alone (*zebaḥ* or *šĕlāmîm*). The priestly material prefers using the full phrase, while other biblical texts normally use one of the single terms (Hartley 1992, 38; see Budd 1996, 68). It must be added that *zebaḥ* (sacrifice) is the broader term in relation to which *šĕlāmîm* (well-being) appears as a type (Milgrom 1991, 218; Levine 1989, 14).

The distinguishing feature of a well-being offering is that it constitutes a shared meal between God, the worshiper, and the priests. The clearest depiction of such a meal is recorded in relation to the sacrifice (*zebaḥ*) shared by Samuel, Saul, and the people of the town (1 Sam 9:12-25; see Levine 1989, 14-15).

The priestly literature presents three types of well-being offerings: thanksgiving (*tôdâ*), votive (*neder*), and freewill (*nĕdābâ*). The thanksgiving offering serves to express thanks and praise to God; the votive offering celebrates the successful completion of a vow; and the freewill offering reflects the spontaneous response of a worshiper (Milgrom 2004, 28; see

Kiuchi 1999, 25). These three categories of the well-being offering are identified in ch 7 in relation to the instructions regarding the disbursement of the offering.

It is evident that the common foundation for the well-being offerings is joy (Deut 27:7). Milgrom claims that all joyous celebrations would have included well-being offerings (2004, 29). Gerstenberger describes the meals associated with the well-being offering as occasions of "unrestrained joy" with "sumptuous food and drink, and the experience of the divine presence and of blessing" (1996, 46).

In contrast to the burnt offering, the well-being offering may consist of either a **male or female** animal. The authorization to use either a male or female animal may reflect the concern for greater choice, since the offering serves to provide a meal for the worshiper's family (Kaiser 1994, 1025; Milgrom 1991, 204). Such liberty of choice may also allow the poor to participate more readily in the well-being offering (Kaiser 1994, 1025).

Before the LORD (→ 1:5-9).

■ **2-4** Lay his hand on the head of his offering (→ 1:4).

Tent of Meeting (→ 1:1).

Sprinkle the blood against the altar on all sides (→ 1:5-9).

The instructions call for *the fat which covers the inward part and all the fat which is upon the inward part* to be burned on the altar to the LORD. The fat (*ḥēleb*) was regarded as a choice portion reserved for God (Harrison 1980, 57-58). The term *ḥēleb* is associated with "the best," as indicated by its metaphorical use in relation to land, oil, wine, grain, and wheat ("*ḥēleb* of the land," Gen 45:18; "*ḥēleb* of the oil, wine, and grain," Num 18:12; and "*ḥēleb* of the wheat," Deut 32:14; Milgrom 1991, 207, 210). The inward part (*qereb*) refers to the entrails (intestines) of the animal. Also, *the two kidneys and the fat which is upon them which is beside the loins, and the appendage upon the liver, in addition to the kidneys,* are to be removed in order to be burned on the altar, for the Lord. The portions given to the priests are outlined in ch 7. The remaining meat from the well-being offering goes to the worshiper and his or her family.

■ **5** The NIV clearly portrays the sharing of tasks within the ritual, as the singular references refer to the offerer and the plural references (sons of Aaron) indicate the priests. Verses 1-5 record alternate action between the offerer and the priests, in a manner similar to that of the burnt offering (→ 1:5-9). The worshiper is to "present before the LORD" the animal for sacrifice (v 1), and "lay his hand on the head of his offering and slaughter it" (v 2). Then "the priests shall sprinkle the blood against the altar" (v 2). Next, the worshiper removes the fat and the elements to be presented

3:2-5

as the Lord's portion. Finally, the priests are to **burn it on the altar** (see Hartley 1992, 36). As in the case of the burnt offering, the ritual of the well-being offering demonstrates that the layperson actively participates in meaningful interaction in relationship to God.

The priests are instructed to burn the Lord's portions of the well-being offering **on top of the burnt offering**. The preposition *'al* in this context can be translated "on top," "over," "beside," or "with." In any case, as Rashi points out, it seems evident that the implication here is that the regular morning burnt offering (Exod 29:38-39; Num 28:3-4) precedes any other offering for the day (in Herczeg 1999, 30; see Levine 1989, 16; Milgrom 1991, 208). Accordingly, the portions of the well-being offering are arranged "on," "beside," or "with" the remains of the burnt offering presumably still smoldering on the altar.

■ **6-10** The instructions for a well-being offering from the flock are virtually identical to the instructions for the well-being offering from the herd (vv 1-5). There are only two noticeable differences. In the case of the offering from the herd, the animal is to be presented "before the LORD" (*lipnê YHWH*) and slaughtered "at the entrance to the Tent of Meeting" (*petaḥ 'ōhel mô'ēd*). The instructions for a well-being offering from the flock, however, stipulate that the animal should be presented **before the LORD** (*lipnê YHWH*) and slaughtered **in front of [*before*] the Tent of Meeting** (*lipnê 'ōhel mô'ēd*). This new phrase likely refers to the same location as "at the entrance to the Tent of Meeting" (parallel with "before the LORD"; → 1:5-9). **In front of the Tent of Meeting** may be an abbreviated form of the more complete expression **in front of [*before* the Lord at the entrance to] the Tent of Meeting** (*lipnê YHWH petaḥ 'ōhel mô'ēd*), which appears in other passages (Exod 29:11; Lev 14:11; 16:7; Josh 19:51). This understanding of Lev 3:8 is also suggested by the LXX, which reads "at the entrance to (the Tent of Meeting)," and more so by the Peshitta, which inserts *YHWH petaḥ* in order to render the full expression "**in front of (*before*)** the Lord at the entrance to **the Tent of Meeting**" (see Milgrom 1991, 210).

The second distinction regarding the instructions for the well-being offering from the flock concerns the elements that make up the portions burned on the altar for the Lord. In the case of the **lamb**, its **fat tail** must be **cut off** and included among the fat portions burnt on the altar. Sheep from Palestine and Syria are known for having a large, fat tail that can weigh many pounds. It is considered a delicacy (Day 1956, 2756). The rest of the portions to be burnt on the altar are the same as those stipulated for an offering from the herd.

Rashi explains that separate instructions for lamb and goat (vv 12-16) are required in the case of the well-being offering (though they are treated together in the instructions for the burnt offering), because the well-being offering specifies that the fat tail of the sheep must be burnt on the altar. This is the only difference in the regulations for the offering of the lamb versus the goat, and prompts the need for separate instructions (in Herczeg 1999, 30; see Noth 1977, 31).

■ 11 The portions burnt on the altar to the Lord are designated **as food**. This may simply serve to indicate the nature of the well-being offering as a shared meal between God and the worshiper. As such, God's participation in the meal reflects the desire for fellowship with humanity and in no way indicates God's need for sustenance from animal sacrifices (Hartley 1992, 41). The designation of sacrifices on the altar as food, however, is not limited to the well-being offering (see also Lev 21:6, 8, 17, 21-22; 22:25; Num 28:24; Mal 1:7). Thus, the designation of sacrifices as food for the Lord appears to be a general reflection of the understanding that portions burnt on the altar are committed to God. Nevertheless, the Lord's sacrifices are not intended to feed God. Rashi considers the term for **food** (*leḥem*) to be in construct with *'iššeh* (**offering made . . . by fire**), and therefore should be rendered "food of the fire" for the Lord. This is because God does not need food (in Herczeg 1999, 31 n. 2). Levine affirms that God required sacrifices, not for sustenance, but for fellowship with worshipers (1989, 17). This distinguishes Israel from pagan conceptions that do consider sacrificial food as necessary to nourish the gods. Psalm 50:12-13 rejects such pagan thinking in the context of relationship to the Lord (Walton and Matthews 1997, 147). References to sacrificial portions as food for God contribute to the recognition that much of the biblical sacrificial system reflects the influence of the larger ancient context within which Israel emerged (see Haran 1985, 17). Nevertheless, God's revelation clearly transforms pagan understanding and practice, and invests it with God's own meaning and purpose (→ 16:8 sidebar, "Azazel: Wilderness Satyr," and From the Text for ch 16).

■ 12-15 The instructions for the well-being offering that consists of a goat are the same as those for the lamb, except for the fat tail in the case of the lamb, which is added to the portions burnt on the altar (→ 3:6-10).

■ 16-17 As food (→ 3:11).

Verse 17 serves to conclude the instructions, not only for the well-being offering, but also for all the voluntary offerings (chs 1—3). Throughout these instructions, references to the offerer have been in third person singular form (except for much of ch 2 regarding the grain offering; recall ch 2 interrupts the unity evident in chs 1 and 3; → Behind the Text above). However, this final verse of ch 3 switches to second person. This forms an inclusio with 1:2 that begins the instructions for the voluntary offerings, also in the second person (Milgrom 1991, 216).

Culminating these regulations is the declaration that **all the fat is the Lord's** and the prohibition that **you must not eat any fat or any blood**. Consequently, fat is added to blood as that which belongs to the Lord (re blood, → 1:5-9). Like blood, fat may be restricted from human consumption because it represents life (de Vaux 1997, 418; Porter 1976, 31). Alternatively, as blood denotes "life," fat may denote its own quality of "strength" (2 Sam 1:22; Isa 34:6; Deut 32:15; Jer 17:4[5]; Heller 1970, 107).

Rashbam held that the stipulation **wherever you live** was added to the prohibition against fat and blood in order to clarify that the prohibition extended to common slaughter as well as to meat offered on the altar (in Lockshin 2001, 24). This means that the restriction applies in the homes of the Israelites as well as at the tabernacle (Levine 1989, 17). In fact, the application of "in all your dwelling places" (RSV) only seems sensible in a context that allows common slaughter (Gerstenberger 1996, 49-50). In contrast, based on the requirement that the fat of the well-being offering must be burnt on the altar, the prohibition against consuming fat may reflect the innovative concern of the Holiness School (HS) to actually prohibit common slaughter by requiring that all animals fit for the altar must be brought to the altar and made a well-being offering before they may be eaten (Knohl 1995, 49-51; Milgrom 1991, 28-29, 216; → Behind the Text for ch 17; and 17:3-7 sidebar, "Question of Common Slaughter and Centralization").

FROM THE TEXT

The opening instructions in the book of Leviticus begin to reveal important themes and theological concerns imbedded in the sacrificial system. The sacrificial scheme serves to address much more than the expiation of sin. In addition to atonement, it provides a means of invoking God's presence, declaring one's devotion to God, and celebrating significant events with joy and thanksgiving. In providing for such expressions, it is evident that God's love and grace (not anger) motivate the sacrificial system, including its demand for atonement (→ 1:3 sidebar, "Love: The Motive for Atonement"). Accordingly, the sacrificial system reflects a foundational concern for right relationships.

Devotion to God is reflected in the dedication of firstfruits to the Lord. The first of the crop, the first of that which is processed from the crop, the first of the livestock, and even the firstborn of one's body, are all to be committed to God. Thereby the faithful worshiper acknowledges that all comes from God, and everything is dedicated back to God by means of a token or representative "firstfruit."

The rite of laying a hand on the head of one's offering provides initial insight into the profound connection intended between an offerer and the sacrifice he or she brings. Too often this is understood only symbolically, in terms of substitution, such that the worshiper offers himself or herself only through the victim (Péter 1977, 52). In contrast, identification with the sacrifice is intended to compel the offerer to truly consecrate his or her own "life and labour to the Lord" (Keil and Delitzsch n.d., 283). The idea is not for the sacrifice to replace the offerer, but rather for the offerer to take on the representative consecration reflected in the sacrifice. Therefore, in order for the intent of an offering to be fulfilled, the offerer must follow up the act of sacrifice with behavior that is consistent with an authentic relationship to God. As Harrison states, "The sacrifice consecrated to God by the donor must be matched by an intent to live an equally holy and consecrated life" (1980, 53). The prophetic critique of the sacrificial system reinforces this very concept. The eighth-century prophets do not reject sacrifices but rather reject the hypocritical abuse of the sacrificial system by which Israelites present their offerings to God while behaving in ways that deny their intent. The prophets proclaim that proper fulfillment of the sacrificial system should result in justice, care for the needy, loyalty, knowledge of God, righteousness, kindness, and a humble walk with the Lord (Isa 1:11-19; Hos 6:6; Amos 5:21-24; Mic 6:6-8). Kaiser implies more than mere substitution when he writes, "At the core of Leviticus is a conviction that human life is most rich, beautiful, and free when, amid the confusion of life, people fashion themselves into offerings to God" (1994, 1014). This is surely the intention of the Apostle Paul, by the words, "I urge you, brothers, in view of God's mercy, to offer your bodies as *living sacrifices*, holy and pleasing to God" (Rom 12:1, emphasis added).

The sacrificial system further reflects an emphasis on relationship as evidenced by the active participation of laypersons in the sacrificial rites, in cooperation with the priests. The tabernacle is not an isolated sacred space for the exclusive activity of the priests. It is a center for the community's expression of its walk with God.

The addition of the burnt offering of birds, and the grain offering, for the sake of those who cannot afford a large animal, reinforces the relational foundation of the sacrificial system. Provision is made so that economic limitations should not prevent any member of the community from participating in the sacrificial expressions of genuine relationship with God.

The relational foundation of the sacrificial system is also evident in the divine-human fellowship reflected in the grain offerings and well-being offerings. Bread shared between God and priests (grain offerings) and meat shared between God and offerers (well-being offerings) represent a theme of communion uniting God and humanity in intimate fellowship.

Too often the sacrificial system of the Bible is considered messy and morose, with a sole focus on sin and impurity. However, the voluntary sacrifices, particularly the well-being offering, demonstrate that the sacrificial system includes expressions of praise, thanksgiving, and joyful celebration. Accordingly, in relation to the well-being offerings, Milgrom states, "Thus the freewill sacrifice makes a link between individual/communal joy and thanksgiving: in our moments of greatest happiness, the sacrificial system teaches us, we pause to appreciate the blessings in our lives and say thanks" (2004, 29). Wesley acknowledges this range of functions when he described the sacrifices with these words: "Some by way of acknowledgment to God for mercies either desired or received; others by way of satisfaction to God for men's sins; others were mere exercises of devotion" (1765, 344).

B. Required Sacrifices (4:1—6:7 [4:1—5:26 HB])

BEHIND THE TEXT

The voluntary sacrifices (chs 1—3) are introduced by the phrase *'ādām kî* ("*When any* of you brings an offering . . . ," 1:2, emphasis added). In contrast, the required sacrifices are introduced with *nepeš kî* ("*When anyone* sins . . . ," 4:2, emphasis added; see 5:1, 15; 6:2 [5:21 HB]; see Marx 2003, 109). The voluntary sacrifices serve to invoke God's presence, express devotion to God, and celebrate occasions of joy and thanksgiving (→ From the Text for 1:1—3:17). The required sacrifices serve to secure atonement for sin.

The required sacrifices are the *ḥaṭṭā't* (purification offering) and the *'āšām* (guilt offering). The purification offering is treated in 4:1—5:13, and the guilt offering is prescribed in 5:14—6:7 (5:14-26 HB).

As with the voluntary sacrifices (→ 1:1—3:17 Behind the Text), the organization of the purification offering is evident through the use of the terms *kî* ("when") and *'im* ("if"). In this case, the general heading regarding "when [*kî*] anyone sins unintentionally" (4:2) governs the purification offerings in ch 4, which are subdivided into specific instructions related to whether/"if [*'im*] the anointed priest sins" (4:3) or "if the whole Israelite community sins" (4:13) or "when a leader sins" (4:22; in this verse *'ăšer* appears in place of *'im;* see Milgrom 1991, 228) or "if any member of the community sins" (4:27).

The general heading *when [kî]* ***anyone sins*** appears again at 5:1 (in contrast to the NIV change in wording between 4:2 and 5:1), introducing four specific cases of sin structured in parallel through the use of the term *'ô* (***or when anyone*** [*'ô nepeš 'ăšer,* 5:2]; ***or when*** [*'ô kî,* v 3]; ***or when anyone*** [*'ô nepeš kî,* v 4]). These four specific cases are followed by two subsections marked by whether/"if" (*'im*) a person cannot afford a lamb (v 7), and "if" (*'im*) a person cannot afford two birds (v 11) for their purification offering (see Kaiser 1994, 1032, re structure of chs 4—5). Leviticus 5:1-13 continues the instructions for the purification offering, but this section is distinguished from the previous section by the following: ch 4 deals with the transgression of prohibitive commands ("what is forbidden in any of the LORD's commands," vv 2, 13, 22, 27), while 5:1-13 lacks such a stipulation; and ch 4 speaks in general terms, while 5:1-13 addresses four specific cases (Milgrom 1991, 307-8; see Marx 2003, 109). The discussion in Lev 5:1-13 is also distinguished by the inclusion of alternative offerings (birds or flour) that may be presented in place of a goat or lamb.

The instructions regarding the guilt offering begin with the general heading "when [*kî*] ***anyone*** commits a violation and sins" (v 15) and are divided into two sections. The first addresses offenses against the property of God (vv 14-19), and the second deals with transgressions against the property of a fellow Israelite (6:1-7 [5:20-26 HB]; Marx 2003, 110). The first section is subdivided into two parts: 5:15-16, which addresses offenses against the property of God, and vv 17-19, which extend such offenses to include those committed even "if" (*'im*) done unknowingly. The second section also begins with the general heading "*when* [*kî*] anyone sins" (6:2 [5:21 HB]) and is subdivided by a series of offenses against a fellow Israelite, including deceiving a neighbor "or" (*'ô*) defrauding a neighbor "or" (*'ô*) lying about finding lost property. These offenses are bound together with the overall sin of swearing falsely about them.

IN THE TEXT

1. Purification Offering (4:1—5:13)

■ **1-2** This general introduction indicates that the purification offering is required **when anyone sins**. The verb used for sin (*ḥāṭā'*) is commonly understood to mean "missing the mark," "committing error," or "doing wrong" (see BDB 1952, 306-7). Sin that requires a purification offering is qualified as that which is committed **unintentionally** or inadvertently (*bišĕgāgâ*).

Accordingly, the sins addressed by this sacrifice are "offenses committed out of ignorance or human frailty" (Hartley 1992, 55, 58-59; for an opposing view, see Kaiser 1994, 1033-34). It is striking that the sacrificial system provides purification for inadvertent sins, but, at first glance, not for willful sins. Numbers 15:30-31 states that the person who "sins defiantly" (*ta'ăśeh běyād rāmâ*, lit. "acts with a high hand") cannot be atoned! This refers to one who brazenly reviles the Lord, with seemingly no intention of repenting (see Milgrom 1991, 369). In contrast, a means of atonement is made possible for *deliberate* sins, through genuine repentance (→ 5:5-6; 6:4-7 [5:23-26 HB]).

Sins that require a purification offering are further qualified as doing **what is forbidden in any of the LORD's commands.** Thus, the purification offering addresses the violation of prohibitive commands. Acts that violate prohibitive commands generate impurity that defiles the sanctuary of God (Lev 15:31; 20:3; Num 19:13, 20; see Milgrom 1991, 229-30). Accordingly, the purification offering serves to cleanse the defilement generated by acts of sin, as well as the person who commits such acts (→ 4:20).

■ **3** The instructions for the purification offering begin by addressing what should be done **if the anointed priest** [*hakkōhēn hammāšîaḥ*] **sins.** This is commonly understood to refer to the high priest, the one among his brothers upon whom is poured the anointing oil (Lev 21:10; see 6:22 [6:15 HB]; 16:32; Num 35:25; Levine 1989, 20; Kaiser 1994, 1034; Gerstenberger 1996, 73). The use and distribution in the Hebrew Bible of "anointed priest" in comparison with the synonymous terms "chief priest" (*kōhēn hārō'š*) and "high priest" (*hakkōhēn haggādôl*) suggest that the phrase "anointed priest" reflects early (preexilic) times (Milgrom 1991, 231; see Hartley 1992, 53-54).

The sin of the anointed priest results in **bringing guilt on the people.** This reflects the great spiritual responsibility of the priest as a representative of the entire community (Harrison 1980, 61). Accordingly, the priest must be diligent to properly execute all the rites on behalf of the people, and avoid wrongful decisions that may lead people to sin (see Milgrom 1991, 231-32). A similar concern is reflected in the NT warning that teachers incur a stricter judgment (Jas 3:1).

For his sin, the priest must bring a young bull **as a *purification* offering** (*ḥaṭṭā't*). The noun *ḥaṭṭā't* is commonly translated "sin offering," but Milgrom has conclusively demonstrated that the term should be rendered "purification offering." Though the basic *qal* form of the related verb does mean "to sin, do wrong," the noun *ḥaṭṭā't* derives from the intensive *piel* verb form, which means "to cleanse, expurgate, decontaminate" (1991,

232, 253-54; see Kaiser 1994, 1032-33). The use of *ḥaṭṭā't* in the sacrificial system affirms this rendering. For example, the *ḥaṭṭā't* is required after childbirth (12:6, 8), when recovering from a hemorrhage (15:25-30), upon completion of a Nazirite vow (Num 6:13-14), and at the dedication of a new altar (Lev 8:15). These cases clearly do not involve acts of sin (Milgrom 1991, 253; Kaiser 1994, 1033). Thus, the *ḥaṭṭā't* serves "to cleanse or purify" persons and objects from sin and impurity and should be translated "purification offering."

■ **4 Tent of Meeting** (→ 1:1). It should be added that the "tent of meeting" may also refer to the holy place, which is the main room of the sanctuary (thereby bearing the name of the whole tent; Dillmann 1897, 579; Keil and Delitzsch n.d., 400).

Before the LORD (→ 1:5-9).

Lay his hand on its head (→ 1:4).

■ **5-7** The priest is required to take the blood of the bull and **sprinkle some of it** before the Lord. In relation to the burnt offering, the priest was instructed to *"toss* or *throw/dash"* (*wĕzārĕqû*) the blood of the sacrifice "on all sides" of (lit. "round about") the altar (→ 1:5-9). Here, in the case of the purification offering, the priest is instructed to **sprinkle** (*hizzâ*) the blood **in front of the curtain of the sanctuary.** The blood, which acts as a cleansing agent, serves to purify the entire room (the holy place) as represented by this act of sprinkling (Milgrom 1991, 233; Walton and Matthews 1997, 148). Rabbinic literature indicates that the blood does not touch the curtain but is merely sprinkled "before or toward" the curtain (see Milgrom 1991, 234). The sprinkling is carried out **seven times.** Seven is a sacred number, not only in the Bible, but throughout the ancient Near East (Porter 1976, 38). Seven is also commonly understood to represent wholeness or totality. Thus, the sevenfold sprinkling signifies completeness in relation to purifying the holy place (Hartley 1992, 60).

The priest is also instructed to **put some of the blood on the horns of the altar of fragrant incense.** This introduces a third form of blood manipulation, that is, "to put or smear" (*nātan*), in contrast to "toss/throw/dash" or "sprinkle." As sprinkling blood toward the curtain signified cleansing the entire holy place, so also putting blood on the horns of the altar denotes purifying the entire altar (Milgrom 1991, 236; Hartley 1992, 60).

In addition to representing the purification of the holy place and the altar, the sprinkling and smearing of blood signifies an offering of life to God from the worshiper. Gane points out that the application of blood on the horns of an altar "makes the blood prominent in a vertical direction," toward God in heaven (2005, 62; see Ps 11:4). Furthermore, the sevenfold sprinkling toward the curtain extends the blood manipulation "in a horizontal direction to within the tent, closer to the place of YHWH's enthronement in the holy of holies" (88). The concept of life in the blood (17:11; see Gane 2005, 63-65) suggests that this ritual represents the worshiper's offering of life to God (in contrast to Gane, who sees this only as representative of the purgation of the offerer). This offering of life is foundational to understanding the prophetic critique of the sacrificial system, aimed against the hypocritical abuse of the system. That is, for the prophets, fulfillment of sacrificial acts is most evident through righteous and holy living, dedicated/offered to God (→ sidebars "The Offering of Life in the Sacrificial System" at 4:32-35 and "The Representative Nature of Sacrifice" at From the Text for 4:1—6:7; also From the Text for 1:1—3:17).

The priest is instructed to **pour out** the remainder of the blood **at the base of the altar of burnt offering.** This act serves to return life (represented in the blood, 17:11) back to God (see Noth 1977, 39). This reflects an underlying theme in the Hebrew Bible that communicates that life belongs to God (→ 1:5-9).

■ **8-10** The priest is instructed to **remove all the fat from the bull of the *purification* offering.** The description of the fat to be removed, in relation to the **kidneys** and the **liver,** is the same as that indicated for the well-being offering (→ 3:2-4). The priest must **burn** the fat portions **on the altar of burnt offering.** Accordingly, as with the well-being offering, the portion of the purification offering that is offered up to the Lord on the altar consists of the fat portions.

Noticeably missing is the statement that "in this way the priest will make atonement" for his sin, "and he will be forgiven." Such a statement appears in the parallel instructions for the purification offerings for the community, leader, individual, and the following four specific cases (4:20, 26, 31, 35; 5:6, 10, 13). The absence of this statement in regard to the high priest suggests that the purification offerings of the high priest and the community may actually constitute a single case. The ritual instructions for the two procedures are virtually parallel, and it has already been noted that the priest's sin brings guilt on the people (see v 3). When both parties are guilty in this way, the priest must be cleansed first through the offering of his own bull, in order to effectively facilitate the cleansing of the community by means of its offering. Thus, the statement of atonement and forgiveness in v 20 may be applied to both the community and the priest (in regard to "their" sin), as a culmination of the two procedures (Milgrom 1991, 241).

■ **11-12** After burning the fat on the altar, **all the rest of the bull** must be taken **outside the camp.** Priestly legislation stipulates that any purification offering whose blood is brought into the holy place must not be eaten (6:30 [6:23 HB]). The offerings from which blood is brought into the holy place only include those for the inadvertent sins of the priest and whole community (4:3-21) and the rebellious sins of the community on the Day of Atonement (→ 16:15 and 16:16). In each of these cases, the priest must not eat the meat of the sacrifice, because priests are not allowed to benefit from an offering related to their own sins or those of the community of which they are a part (Milgrom 1991, 264; Hartley 1992, 58, 61; Gane 2005, 89-90, 97-98).

Milgrom argues that the impurity transferred to the purification offering for the priest (or the whole community) likely penetrates the carcass of the animal, is too dangerous to be eaten, and therefore must be burned (1991, 263). However, if the carcass is penetrated by impurity, it would seem the fat of the animal would also be compromised. Yet, the fat is acceptable (pure) enough to be burned on the altar to the Lord. In addition, transference of impurity to the carcass contradicts Milgrom's argument elsewhere that the priests eat other purification offerings in order to refute the superstitious belief that the remains of the sacrifice carry magical power (based on the potency of the dangerous impurity; Milgrom 1991, 637, 639; also 239-40; → From the Text below). The transference of impurity to the carcass is further contradicted by the instruction requiring that the flesh of the bull is to be taken **to a place ceremonially clean.** Accordingly, Hartley contends that it is inconceivable that flesh that has absorbed uncleanness can be eaten in a holy place (6:24-26 [6:17-19 HB]) or burned in a clean place (4:12; 6:30 [6:23 HB]), and he concludes that the flesh of the purification offerings is not contaminated by sin (1992, 61, 136, 276).

■ **13-14** The instructions for the purification offering for the **whole Israelite community** closely follow those for the high priest (vv 3-12). Some details are assumed so that this section appears as a shorthand version of the previous section (Noth 1977, 40). It may be that the purification offering for the high priest and for the entire congregation form a single case (→ 4:8-10). The parallel between the congregation of Israel and the high priest is grounded in the community's calling to be "a kingdom of priests and a holy nation" (Exod 19:5-6; Harrison 1980, 64).

Sins unintentionally (→ 4:1-2).

The community must present a purification offering **even though the matter is concealed from their eyes.** The term *wě'āšēmû* (**they are guilty**) suggests that a state of guilt exists, regardless of whether or not the offender is aware of it (see Levine 1989, 22). However, the term may also be translated "and they feel guilt." Accordingly, the following phrase in the text (v 14a) can be taken as preceding in time. Thus, "they feel guilt" **when they become aware of the sin they committed.** That is, after the sin becomes known to the members of the congregation, they feel guilty (Milgrom 1991, 243-44).

■ **15** **The elders of the community** serve as representatives for the whole congregation (*ziqnê hāʿēdâ* appears only here and at Judg 21:16; for *ziqnê yiśrāʾēl*, "elders of Israel," see Exod 3:16, 18; 12:21; 17:5-6; 18:12; 24:1, 9; Lev 9:1; Num 11:16, 30; 16:25; Deut 27:1; 31:9).

On behalf of the community, the elders were to **lay their hands on the bull's head.** This likely meant that each elder placed one hand on the bull's head (→ 1:4).

■ **16-19** The instructions for the manipulation of the blood, the burning of the fat, and the disposal of the flesh of the purification offering for the community are the same as those for the high priest (→ 4:5-12). In v 18, though the location is described (**before the L**ORD **in the Tent of Meeting**), the altar is not specified as it was for the offering of the high priest (v 7). However, the LXX and Sam. add clarification by specifying the "altar of incense." Verse 19 abbreviates the instructions for removing and burning the fat of the offering (see vv 8-10).

■ **20** The parallel between the ritual for the high priest's purification offering and that of the community is further affirmed by the stipulation that he must **do with this bull just as he did with the bull for the** *purification* **offering** (that is, the bull for the high priest's offering).

The priest **will make atonement** for the community, **and they will be forgiven.** The central verb regarding atonement is *kipper*. Judisch has provided a helpful overview of the etymology of *kipper*. The term is traditionally understood as a cognate of the Arabic root *kaphara*, meaning "cover" or "conceal." This is supported by the use of Hebrew *kāsâ/kissâ* ("cover," "conceal") in ways that appear parallel to the use of *kipper* (Pss 32:1; 85:2 [v 3 HB]). The term *kipper* has also been associated with the Syriac term *kephar/kappar* ("wipe," "wipe away") and the Akkadian term *kuppuru* ("wash away" or "erase"; also "to purify"). In this sense, *kipper* can be found in parallel with *māḥâ* ("wipe off," "wipe away"; Jer 18:23; Judisch 1984, 222). In correspondence with the Syriac and Akkadian cognates, Milgrom asserts that *kipper* should be translated "purge" (especially in the context of the *ḥaṭṭāʾt*, "purification offering"). This is further supported by the use of *ṭihar* ("purify") and *ḥiṭṭēʾ* ("decontaminate"), which appear as synonyms for, and in parallel with, *kipper* (Ezek 43:20, 26; Milgrom 1991, 255, 1079).

Gane has revived the debate regarding whether the purification offering purges only the sanctuary (see Milgrom 1991, 254-58; idem 2007,

161-63), or whether it also purges the offerer (see Gane 2005, 106-43; idem 2008, 209-22) from the effects of sin and impurity. Given the emphasis on restoring relationships between God and humans, it would seem that purification would certainly be accomplished for both the offerer and the place of God's presence. Thus, Gorman's definition for *kipper*, at the most general level, may be the most useful: "to deal with disruptions in the divine-human relations" (1997, 16). The purpose of the purification offering is not judicial, but is relational. The offerer seeks, not pardon from punishment, but rather reconciliation with God (Walton and Matthews 1997, 148; see Milgrom's discussion of *sālaḥ* ["to forgive"], 1991, 245).

■ 21 The instructions for the disposal of the bull are abbreviated by simply requiring that this bull be burned **as he burned the first bull** (→ 4:8-10 and 11-12).

■ 22-23 This verse opens with *'ăšer* in place of the expected *'im* (→ Behind the Text above), to introduce the instructions for **when [if] a leader sins unintentionally** (re unintentional sins, → 4:1-2). The distinctive use of *'ăšer* marks a turning point in the text. The previous two purification offerings (for priest and congregation) require blood to be applied in the holy place and the remains of the sacrifice to be burned outside the camp. In contrast the remaining two purification offerings (for leader and common person) require the blood to be applied on the outer altar in the courtyard and the meat to be consumed by the priests. The use of *'ăšer* brings attention to this important transition from one type of purification offering to the other (Milgrom 1991, 246).

The term *nāśî'* (**leader**) refers to a secular leader of a tribe, or clan leader within a tribe (Noth 1977, 42; Levine 1989, 24; Hartley 1992, 66; Milgrom 1991, 246-47).

When he is made aware of the sin he committed, the leader is required to bring **a male goat** for an offering. The shift from a bull for the previous purification offerings (priest and congregation) to a male goat for the leader and a female goat for the common person (v 28) depicts the diminishing value of the sacrifice in correspondence with the lesser position of accountability related to the offerer (see Gerstenberger 1996, 74).

■ 24-26 Lay his hand on the goat's head (→ 1:4).

The blood of the offering for the leader is to be applied to **the horns of the altar of burnt offering** in the outer courtyard of the sanctuary. This represents the purification of the outer altar, and the offering of life in relation to the leader (→ 4:5-7).

The priest is directed to **burn all the fat on the altar**. This refers to the altar of burnt offering, and the fat portions to be burned are the same as those indicated for the purification offerings for the priest and the congregation (vv 8-10, 19-20) and **the fat of the *well-being* offering** (→ 3:2-4).

This offering serves to **make atonement for** the sin of the leader, and **he will be forgiven** (→ 4:20).

Further legislation regarding the purification offering stipulates that the priest shall eat the meat of the offering (6:26, 29 [6:19, 22 HB]). The requirement that this offering be eaten by the priests serves to refute the superstitious belief that the sacrifice bears magical power stemming from the potency of the impurity it has supposedly absorbed. The priests prove there is no such threat by ingesting the meat with no harm to themselves (Milgrom 1991, 637, 639; → vv 11-12 and From the Text below).

■ **27-31** The instructions for the purification offering for **a member of the community** (common person) are nearly identical to those for the leader (vv 22-26; re unintentional sins, → vv 1-2). However, in the case of the common person, the offering is **a female goat** or a female lamb (v 32). The female goat represents a lower status of offering in comparison to the bull for the priest and congregation, and the male goat for the leader (Budd 1996, 91; → vv 22-23).

Lay his hand on the head of the *purification* offering (→ 1:4).

The blood of the offering is to be applied to **the horns of the altar of burnt offering** in the outer courtyard of the sanctuary. This parallels the application of blood to the horns of the incense altar in the case of the priest and congregation (4:7, 18) and to the altar of burnt offering in the case of the leader (v 25). This represents the purification of the outer altar, and the offering of life in relation to the common person (→ vv 5-7).

The fat of the offering is to be removed and burned on the altar of burnt offering, in the same manner as instructed regarding the well-being offering (→ 3:2-4). The instructions for the purification offering of the common person uniquely add that the fat shall be burned **as an aroma pleasing to the Lord** (compare vv 10, 19, 26). This phrase may be implied for the other purification offerings, while explicitly stated only in the case of the common person. This may be intended to communicate comfort to common persons by assuring them that the hope, mercy, and grace of God is available to them, even though their sacrifices are less costly and glamorous (Kaiser 1994, 1036).

This offering serves to **make atonement for** the sin of the common person, and **he will be forgiven** (→ v 20).

■ **32-35** The common person is allowed the alternative of offering a female lamb for a purification offering (→ vv 27-31). This reflects the concessions made in the sacrificial system to accommodate the economic ability of the offerer (Keil and Delitzsch n.d., 302).

The Offering of Life in the Sacrificial System

The horns of the altar are recognized as symbols of "strength and force" or "power and might" (Milgrom 1991, 236; Keil and Delitzsch n.d., 304). Harrison indicates that the horns have been interpreted as directing the thoughts of worshipers upward (1980, 62). Keil and Delitzsch oppose this thought and see the altar as the place of the manifestation of God's grace and salvation ultimately reflected in the power and might represented by the horns. The blood of the sacrifices for the priest and for the congregation (called as a kingdom of priests) was applied to the incense altar, because the priest and congregation maintained communion with God in the holy place. In contrast, the blood of the sacrifice for an individual was applied to the outer altar, because, for the individual, the outer court was the place of communion with God (n.d., 304-5).

Despite the fact that the congregation was not allowed into the holy place, the focus on relationship with God is a legitimate emphasis in relation to the sacrificial system. Gane does not see a conflict between the upward movement symbolized by the horns and the manifestation of divine grace and salvation, but rather sees the two concepts as complementary (2005, 62 n. 70). Add to this the foundational association of blood as life (17:11), and a significant feature of the purification offering is revealed. The application of the blood to the altar signifies the offering of *life* (not a substitutionary *death*) to God as the worshiper's thoughts are directed upward, and the worshiper renews fellowship with God by means of divine grace and salvation; all of which finds expression through a life committed/offered to God through the pursuit of holiness and righteousness (→ 4:5-7).

■ **5:1-4** Verses 1-4 identify four specific cases in which a person may incur guilt and therefore must present a purification offering. The first case (v 1) involves a person who **sins because he does not speak up when he hears a public charge to testify regarding something he has seen or learned about.** That is, the person hears a proclamation calling those who have information regarding a certain case to testify, but the person refuses to comply by withholding evidence (Levine 1989, 26). Such an act cannot be classified as unintentional or inadvertent, and therefore Budd stipulates that this first case cannot be atoned with a purification offering, but rather the person must **be held responsible** ("subject to punishment," NRSV, or "bear his iniquity," RSV; 1996, 93-94; → 4:1-2). However, the use of the term *'ô* ("or") places 5:1-4 in parallel, so that each of the cases identified are eligible for the purification offering indicated in v 5 (→ Behind the Text above). This clearly intentional sin is made eligible for atonement through genuine repentance expressed through confession (v 5) and feeling remorse (Milgrom explains that the term *'āšēm* [vv 2, 3, 4, 5] should be understood in relation to feeling guilt).

Such expressions of repentance serve to downgrade intentional sins to inadvertent sins, thereby making them eligible for atonement (Milgrom 1991, 295; → 5:5-6; 6:4-7 [5:23-26 HB]).

The second case (5:2) implicates a person who **touches anything ceremonially unclean.** The references to guilt and sin in vv 5-6, in relation to these four cases, suggest that contact with impurity is a sin (see Gerstenberger 1996, 69). Rashi clarifies, however, that touching impurity is not a sin. He reasons that the person involved must have forgotten about touching an impurity and, while unclean, ate sacred food or entered the temple (in Herczeg 1999, 44). Accordingly, the sin lies in neglecting to purify oneself within the prescribed time limit and thereby risking defilement of the sanctuary and its sancta (Keil and Delitzsch n.d., 310-11; Milgrom 1991, 298). The third case (v 3) is an extension of the second. While the second case refers to contact with impurity related to unclean animals, the third case involves touching **human uncleanness.**

The fourth case (v 4) concerns a person who **thoughtlessly takes an oath.** The concern here is not a false oath, which requires the guilt offering (6:1-7 [5:20-26 HB]), but rather an impulsive oath that is neglected and left unfulfilled (see Deut 23:21-23; Milgrom 1991, 299-300; Hartley 1992, 68-69).

■ **5-6** The person who **is guilty in any of these ways** (i.e., the four cases of vv 1-4) **must confess** the sin. For the inadvertent sins of ch 4, confession is not necessary, for they reflect a lack of intention in breaking prohibitive commands. In contrast, the four cases of sin in 5:1-4 may or may not be intentional (the case in v 1 is certainly intentional). Confession, when expressed genuinely in repentance, signifies the sinner's wish that such sin had never occurred. Thus, it is an expression that reverses intention ("I wish I had not done that"). Accordingly, confession serves to downgrade intentional sin to inadvertent sin, thereby making it eligible for atonement (otherwise *defiant* sins cannot be atoned, Num 15:30-31 [→ Lev 4:1-2]; see Milgrom 1991, 301-2, 308; also → 6:4-7 [5:23-26 HB]).

The phrase **as his** penalty (*'ăšāmô*; here and in v 7) should not be confused with "a guilt offering" (*'āšām*). The use of the term here (and in vv 7, 15; 6:6 [5:25 HB]) is parallel to "as **his** offering" (*qorbānô*) in v 11 (Milgrom 1991, 303).

Like a member of the community who sins unintentionally (4:27-35), the person who commits any of the sins specified here (5:1-4; intentional or unintentional) **must bring to the LORD a female lamb or goat** as a purification offering.

■ **7-10** Verses 7 and 11 introduce two options for the purification offering required for the four cases of vv 1-4, which are acceptable **if the offerer cannot afford a lamb** (v 7) or birds (v 11). These concessions for the poor reinforce the concern to allow everyone to participate in the sacrificial system (→ 2:1, 4-9; 3:1; and From the Text for 1:1—3:17).

For those who cannot afford a lamb or goat, **two doves or two young pigeons** can be presented for sacrifice. Normally the meat of a purification offering is eaten by the priests (6:24-30 [6:17-23 HB]), while the fat of the offering is burned on the altar for the Lord (4:26, 31). Birds, however, are too small to provide enough meat and fat for priest and altar. Therefore, as Ibn Ezra explains, two birds are necessary in order to compensate for the fatty portions of a purification offering that would normally be burned on the altar (in Levine 1989, 29). The first bird serves as the required purification offering. The second bird becomes a burnt offering to substitute for the fatty portions of a regular purification offering that are normally burned on the altar to the Lord (see Hartley 1992, 69; Budd 1996, 96).

As *his* **penalty** (→ vv 5-6).

The priest is instructed to **sprinkle some of the blood of the *purification* offering against the side of the altar,** while **the rest of the blood must be drained out at the base of the altar.** This corresponds to the smearing of blood on the horns of the altar and draining the blood at the base of the altar as described for the regular purification offering (4:25, 30; → 4:5-7). The second bird (the one for the burnt offering) is to be treated **in the prescribed way.** This refers the reader back to the instructions for "a burnt offering of birds" in 1:14-17.

This offering serves to **make atonement for** the sinner, **and he will be forgiven** (→ 4:20).

■ **11-13** The person who is too poor to even afford birds may bring **a tenth of an ephah of fine flour for a *purification* offering.** The allowance of flour for a purification offering is striking. Obviously it lacks the blood that is so foundational to the atoning function of purification offerings. Nevertheless, for the sake of the poor, the allowance of flour for atonement (v 13) reinforces the recognition that the power for cleansing and forgiveness does not reside in blood but rather in the grace and mercy of almighty God (→ From the Text below).

The offerer **must not put oil or incense** on this offering. This distinguishes this *purification* offering from a regular *grain* offering. Oil and incense may be associated with joyous occasions; thus, their absence here denotes the more somber circumstance of the purification offering (Milgrom 1991, 306; see Porter 1976, 42).

The **memorial portion** of flour burnt on the altar parallels the burning of the fat of the animal purification offerings and the bird for the burnt offering (v 10; Milgrom 1991, 306; Budd 1996, 97).

2. Guilt Offering (5:14—6:7 [5:14-26 HB])

■ **14-16** The **guilt offering** (*'āšām*) is required when one **commits a violation** (*ma'al*) against property, whether the Lord's property (5:14-19) or the property of a fellow Israelite (6:1-7 [5:20-26 HB]; see Marx 2003, 109-10, 118). The offense requiring a guilt offering is specified by the term *ma'al*, in distinction from *ḥaṭṭā't*. One who commits *ḥaṭṭā't* ("sin") must offer a *ḥaṭṭā't* ("purification offering"), while one who commits *ma'al* must offer the *'āšām* ("guilt offering"; Marx 2003, 109). The term *ma'al* refers to acts of unfaithfulness. It appears in the context of marital infidelity (Num 5:12-13) but finds its greatest expression in relation to breaking faith with God, including the violation of holy things belonging to God (Lev 5:15; 6:2 [5:21 HB]; 26:40; Num 5:6; Deut 32:51; Josh 7:1; 1 Chr 5:25; 10:13; 2 Chr 26:16; Ezra 10:2; Ezek 14:13; Dan 9:7).

Sins unintentionally (→ 4:1-2).

Acting unfaithfully **in regard to any of the Lord's holy things** may include unlawfully eating sacrificial meat assigned to the altar or the priests; failing to present a required offering; presenting an offering of inferior value; or misuse/abuse of any dedicated or sacred property, such as land, clothing, temple furniture, tithes, or precious metal or artifacts owed to the temple treasury (see Pedersen 1940, 371-72; Noth 1977, 46; Gorman 1997, 42; Hartley 1992, 80; Marx 2003, 118).

As *his* penalty (→ vv 5-6).

In contrast to the bull or goat or lamb stipulated for the purification offering, the guilt offering calls for a **ram, which is of the proper value in silver** (*bĕ'erkĕkā kesep*). The focus on monetary value (*bĕ'erkĕkā*) throughout this passage (5:15, 18; 6:6 [5:25 HB]) suggests that the offender may bring money in place of an actual ram for sacrifice. This is reinforced by the absence of any ritual instructions for the offering. In addition, there is some confusion regarding whether the ram must be appraised at a value equivalent to the offense (see Budd 1996, 102), or whether money is to be provided equivalent to the value of a ram **without defect**. Milgrom asserts that the former cannot be the case, because it would not always be possible to find an animal equivalent to the loss. "What if the amount [of the loss] turned out to be less than the value of the most emaciated beast or more than the pride of Bashan?" (1991, 330, 326). It appears that the offender is to be charged the amount of the loss to **make restitution,** plus a fine of **a fifth of the value** of the loss, plus the amount needed to purchase the animal for sacrifice. After the animal is purchased, then the priest is to carry out the proper sacrificial procedure as outlined in the guilt offering instructions specifically addressed to the priests in 7:1-6 (Milgrom 1991, 327, 409). Thereby, the priest **will make atonement** for the offender **with the ram as a guilt offering, and he will be forgiven.**

■ **17-19** The phrase **if a person sins and does what is forbidden in any of the LORD's commands** mimics the formula introducing the cases requiring a *purification* offering (4:2, 13, 22, 27). In addition, the offense requiring a *guilt* offering (i.e., *ma'al*) is not specified in this subunit (see Milgrom 1991, 331). This has led some to conclude that 5:17-19 is a later insertion (re a revised *purification* offering) that disrupts the instructions regarding the *guilt* offering in 5:14-16 and 6:1-7 (5:20-26 HB; Noth 1977, 47-48).

Rashi suggests that these verses refer to a *conditional* guilt offering. If a person is unsure about whether he or she has sinned, he or she must present a guilt offering "just in case." If the person later learns that he or she did indeed sin, then the person must bring a purification offering as well (in Carasik 2009, 31-32). This prompts recognition of the significant distinction between the wording here and the instructions for the purification offering. The purification offering stipulates subsequent knowledge of sin ("when they become aware of the sin they committed," 4:14, 23, 28). In contrast, the sin here remains unknown to the offender (**even though he does not know it**). The phrase **he does not know** (*wĕlō' yāda'*) is different than the term used throughout the purification offering instructions ("unintentionally," *bišĕgāgâ*, 4:2, 22, 27). For the purification offering the sin is unintentional, but the offender becomes aware of the sin; while for this guilt offering, the sin is committed without the offender knowing it (see Milgrom 1991, 331, 333). The distinction is even more apparent in v 18, which states that the offender will be atoned **for the wrong he has committed unintentionally** [*šigĕgātô 'ăšer-šāgāg*] **and he did not know** (*wĕhû' lō'-yāda'*). Unfortunately, the NIV misses the all-important phrase depicting lack of awareness, by collapsing the translation into just the term **unintentionally** and dropping **he did not know.**

These verses appear to introduce the category of *suspected* violations. To address all possible contingencies, a guilt offering is required for the person who may have sinned but is not sure about the matter (Harrison 1980, 72). The guilt offering in this case is preventative and may be referred to as the "contingent" *'āšām* (Levine 1989, 32). It recalls Job's presentation of burnt offerings in case his children may have sinned (Job 1:5). Milgrom ties this argument back to the original focus of the guilt offering by explaining that since any of the Lord's commands could have been violated, but the sin is not known, it is possible that the sin was actually a *ma'al*, thereby requiring a guilt offering (1991, 332).

Of the proper value (→ vv 14-16).

■ **6:1-3** (5:20-22 HB) The phrase **unfaithful to the LORD** (*ûmāʿălâ maʿal baYHWH*) clearly places this passage within the realm of the guilt offering (required for acts of *maʿal*; → 5:14-16). In this case the violation (*maʿal*, "unfaithful act") is against the property of a fellow Israelite. It is commonly recognized that a sin against a fellow human is also a sin against God. Wesley noted that it is a violation against God because God is the author and defender of human society, God alone is witness and judge of such secret sin, and God's name is abused by swearing falsely about the sin (1765, 360). In addition, God is considered the ultimate owner of all property (Marx 2003, 118). Furthermore, offenses against humans are violations against God because humans bear the image of God (1 John 4:20; Hartley 1992, 85).

The text delineates three offenses and then includes the general statement, **any such sin that people may do.** The first offense is identified by the verb *kiḥēš* ("deceive"; see BDB 1952, 471), which is followed by three nouns, each linked to the verb by the prefixed preposition *bĕ*. Accordingly, this first offense involves a person **deceiving his neighbor in regard to a deposit or investment or robbery** (re translation of the three nouns, see Milgrom 1991, 335). The second offense is identified by the verb *ʿāšaq* ("oppress," "extort"; see BDB 1952, 798). Thus, **if he cheats him** carries the idea of withholding something due a neighbor or forcing something from the neighbor (Keil and Delitzsch n.d., 315). The third offense includes the verb *kiḥēš* again, but this time the deception is specifically through lying. Thus, the offender is one who **finds lost property and lies about it.**

The NIV treats the phrase **swears falsely** as if it were a fourth offense by translating the conjunction *wĕ* (*and*) as if it were another in the preceding series of *ʾô* (*or*) statements. However, the false swearing should be understood not as a separate offense but rather as applying to all the previous wrongs. Invoking the Lord's name to swear falsely about these crimes against fellow humans reinforces the recognition that the offenses are also against God (Keil and Delitzsch n.d., 315; see Milgrom 1991, 337-38).

■ **4-7** (5:23-26 HB) The offender must make restitution by returning whatever was wrongly taken or by compensating for the loss with a monetary equivalent (Milgrom 1991, 338). The offender must also pay an additional 20 percent of the value of what was lost, to the owner/victim.

As *his* penalty (→ 5:5-6).

After reparation is made, the offender must present a guilt offering **of the proper value** to the priest (→ 5:14-16). Thereby, **the priest will make atonement** on behalf of the offender. It is clear that the sins being atoned here are intentional and deliberate. As such, they can only be atoned through genuine remorse and confession. Numbers 5:6-8 is a parallel passage to Lev 6:1-7 (5:20-26 HB) and stipulates that the offender "must confess the sin he has committed" (Num 5:7) before making restitution. Sincere remorse and confession serve to reduce deliberate sins to unintentional sins, which can thereby be atoned by sacrifice (Milgrom 1991, 365-78; → Lev 5:5-6). Milgrom cites the early rabbis as already acknowledging this principle: "'R. Simeon b. Lakish said: Great is repentance, which converts intentional sins into unintentional ones' (*b. Yoma* 86b)" (Milgrom 1991, 373).

FROM THE TEXT

The article of faith regarding sin in the *Manual* for the Church of the Nazarene provides a helpful distinction between intentional sin and inadvertent sin. Paragraph 5.3 begins, "We believe that actual or personal sin is a voluntary violation of a known law of God by a morally responsible person. It is therefore not to be confused with involuntary and inescapable shortcomings, infirmities, faults, mistakes, failures, or other deviations from a standard of perfect conduct that are the residual effects of the Fall" (2009, 30). The sins addressed in ch 4, which are committed *unintentionally* and are specified as violations of prohibitive commands of God, would be included among the "shortcomings, infirmities, faults, mistakes, failures, or other deviations," which should not be confused with "actual or personal sin." Lest one conclude that such "infirmities" should not be reckoned as sin, the sacrificial system proclaims otherwise. Though they are unintentional, such sins still interfere with healthy righteous relationships and must be atoned. Willful, rebellious sins can only be atoned by means of genuine confession and repentance. Thereby, such deliberate sins are reduced to unintentional sins and are made eligible for atonement (→ 4:1-2; 5:5-6; 6:4-7 [5:23-26 HB]). Accordingly, the sacrificial system calls God's people to be attentive and diligent even with respect to weaknesses and infirmities. In addition, God graciously provides a means to atone even rebellious acts, if one turns to God with sincere repentance. Finally, for those with sensitive personalities, anxious about even "suspected" sins, God's love provides a means of easing the tender conscience through the guilt offering for unknown sins (Harrison 1980, 72; → 5:17-19).

The following chart summarizes the distinctive elements of the purification offerings described in ch 4:

	Anointed Priest	Israelite Community	Leader	Member of Community
Type of Animal	young bull	young bull	male goat	female goat or lamb
Blood Application	inside holy place: • in front of curtain • on horns of incense altar	inside holy place: • in front of curtain • on horns of incense altar	outer court: • on horns of altar of burnt offering	outer court: • on horns of altar of burnt offering
Disposal of Animal Flesh	burn outside camp in a clean place	burn outside camp in a clean place	eaten by priests	eaten by priests

The type of animal, the application of blood, and the means by which the animal flesh is disposed reflect the degree of impurity that a particular purification offering purges. The *inadvertent* sins of the anointed priest and the whole community generate impurity that penetrates as far as the holy place (see Milgrom 1991, 263). Thus, a young bull is required, blood must be sprinkled in front of the curtain in the holy place and on the horns of the incense altar within the holy place, and the flesh of the animal must be burned outside the camp. In contrast, the *inadvertent* sins of a leader or a common member of the community generate impurity that only penetrates as far as the outer altar in the courtyard of the sanctuary. Accordingly, a male goat (in the case of a leader) or a female goat or lamb (in the case of the common person) is required for the purification offering. In addition, the blood is applied to the outer altar, and the animal flesh is eaten by the priests. *Deliberate* sins penetrate all the way into the holy of holies. These are dealt with once a year on the Day of Atonement, when the high priest enters the holy of holies to apply the blood of a bull and a goat inside the holy of holies (→ 16:14, 15, 16, 17).

The gradation of animals required (from bull to female lamb) reflects the greater or lesser sense of consequence attached to the sins of the offerer. The sins of the priest and the whole community represent more serious offenses that require a sacrifice of greater value, while the sins of a leader or common person represent lesser offenses that require sacrifices of lesser value. Accordingly, the sacrificial system applies greater accountability to those in leadership positions, especially those exercising spiritual and moral influence (see Jas 3:1).

The application of blood in relation to the purification offering signifies the cleansing of the sanctuary from the impurity generated by sin. The sins of the leader or common person only require the cleansing of the outer altar, while the sins of the priest and whole community require the cleansing of the incense altar and the holy place. The defilement of the sanctuary as a result of uncleanness and sin is clearly expressed in the Pentateuch:

> Thus you shall keep the people of Israel separate from their uncleanness, so that they do not die in their uncleanness *by defiling my tabernacle* that is in their midst. (15:31 NRSV, emphasis added)
>
> I will set my face against that man and I will cut him off from his people; for by giving his children to Molech, *he has defiled my sanctuary* and profaned my holy name. (20:3, emphasis added)
>
> Whoever touches the dead body of anyone and fails to purify himself *defiles the LORD's tabernacle*. (Num 19:13, emphasis added)
>
> But if a person who is unclean does not purify himself, he must be cut off from the community, because *he has defiled the sanctuary of the LORD*. (Num 19:20, emphasis added)

The defilement of the sanctuary is a vital concern, because God, who is holy, cannot abide impurity. For the priestly legislation, the place of God's presence is understood to be the holy of holies within the sanctuary (Exod 40:34-35; Lev 16:2). When impurity begins to penetrate the sanctuary (from courtyard, to holy place, and even into the holy of holies itself; → 16:16-17) a growing fear arises that God may abandon the sanctuary and the presence of God may be removed from the midst of the community. Such a devastating event is reflected in Ezekiel's vision (10:18-19; 11:22-23) and mourned in Lamentations: "The LORD has rejected his altar and abandoned his sanctuary" (2:7). Consequently, a primary function of the purification offering is to keep the sanctuary free of defilement from sin and impurity (see Milgrom 1991, 256-61).

Abiding in a clean sanctuary, however, is not God's foremost concern. God's greatest desire is right and holy relationships with the covenant community in whose midst God has placed the sanctuary of God's presence. The defilement generated by sin and impurity pollutes the sacred space (the sanctuary), which represents the meeting place for relationship with God. Such defilement represents the brokenness and alienation that sin inflicts upon relationships and drives away the presence of God. In addition to cleansing the sanctuary, the purification offering also serves to purge the unclean and the sinner, with the goal of restoring relationship to God. That is, even though the cleansing agent of blood is not applied to persons, the goal of reconciling humans in relationship to God, expressed through purification and forgiveness, indicates that the purification offering also cleanses the offerer (see Gane 2005, 129).

The foundational concern for relationship, represented through ritual in the priestly legislation, becomes most evident in subsequent judgments against the abuse of ritual acts (1 Sam 15:22; → From the Text for 1:1—3:17). God's passion for right relations with his creatures is most dramatically expressed through incarnation in Christ. This God, who cannot abide sin and impurity, for whom the elaborate sacrificial system provides a means of cleansing in order to maintain God's presence among people, is made manifest in Christ, through whom God reaches for humanity even to the point of *defiling himself* by touching the unclean (Matt 8:1-3; 26:6; Mark 5:25-27) and associating with sinners (Matt 9:10-11; 11:19)! When the sacrificial system fails, contrary to the threat of abandoning his creatures, God breaks God's own rules in relation to avoiding impurity, and sacrifices himself in Christ in order to restore relations with his creatures!

The disposal of the flesh of the animal also reflects a form of gradation in relation to the purification offering. The flesh of the sacrifice for the priest and the whole community must be burned outside the camp, while that for the leader or common person is to be eaten by the priests. The meat from the offerings for the priest and community cannot be eaten by the priests, because the priests are not allowed to benefit from an offering related to their own sins or those of the community of which they are a part (Milgrom 1991, 264; Hartley 1992, 58, 61; Gane 2005, 89-90, 98). The meat from the offerings for a leader or common person, however, are to be eaten by the priests. Milgrom points out that this act conveys a significant theological message in the context of the ancient Near East. In the ancient Near East, sacrifices were destroyed after being used, in order to avert the exploitation of their remaining power for the purposes of sorcery. By eating the flesh of the purification offering, the priests of Israel proclaim that there is no magical power (dangerous for ingestion) in the ritual or sacrifice itself. Rather, the power to cleanse and purify are completely dependent on the will of God (1991, 637). Consequently, despite the tendency to recognize "power in the blood," the sacrificial system asserts that the power of atonement rests in the grace and mercy of almighty God alone (see Rylaarsdam 1962, 316).

Similarly, the priests' consumption of the sacrifice as something "most holy" (6:29 [6:22 HB]) refutes the notion that the sacrifice takes on the sin of the offerer or becomes sin. Rather, in accepting portions of the same sacrifice on the altar as *pleasing* unto God, it is clear that God is the One who has removed (forgiven) the sin (see de Vaux 1997, 419).

The ingestion of the meat of the purification offering also conveys a message of hope. The priest, who represents holiness and life, swallows up the sacrifice that evokes impurity and death (not that the sacrifice has absorbed sin or impurity, but rather sin and impurity prompted the need for a purification offering in the first place). Thereby, the rite of the purification offering reflects the powerful theological theme of resurrection by portraying that "holiness has swallowed impurity" and "life can defeat death" (Milgrom 1991, 638).

It must be added that the sacrificial system seeks to enable right relationships, not only with God, but also among humans. The guilt offering atones for wrongs committed against one's neighbor. However, such atonement only follows upon appropriate acts of reparation and reconciliation. Accordingly, the primary concern of the sacrificial system is to restore and maintain right relationships with God and among humans.

The Representative Nature of Sacrifice

The sacrificial system is representative. The laying of a single hand upon a sacrifice identifies the offering and designates it as representative of the offerer (→ 1:4 and From the Text for 1:1—3:17). The offerer indicates that the sacrifice belongs to the offerer, and he or she is the one who presents it. This does *not* indicate that the offerer intends for the sacrifice to suffer in his or her place. The OT never suggests that a sacrificial victim is meant to suffer a penalty (Robinson 1942, 130). Rather, in relation to the offerer, "the death of the victim symbolized his death to his sin, or to whatever stood between him and God, or his surrender of himself to God in thankfulness and humility" (Rowley 1950-51, 88). In parallel with gestures of primitive prayer and acts of prophetic symbolism, the sacrificial act can be described as representative realism. Accordingly, the act of sacrifice effects change in the offerer's relationship to God, by representing the devotion and commitment of the worshiper (Robinson 1942, 135). Such commitment must be expressed through righteous behavior, or the sacrifice is invalidated. That is precisely the message of the eighth-century prophets in relation to sacrifice (Isa 1:11-19; Hos 6:6; Amos 5:21-24; Mic 6:6-8; see Robinson 1942, 137; Rowley 1950-51, 88-93).

Wesley affirms that the sacrificial system called worshipers to offer themselves entirely to God: "The sacrifices signified that the whole man, in whose stead the sacrifice was offered, was to be intirely [sic] offered or devoted to God's service; and that the whole man did deserve to be utterly consumed, if God should deal severely with him; and directed us to serve the Lord with all singleness of heart, and to be ready to offer to God even such sacrifices or services wherein we ourselves should have no part or benefit" (1765, 344-45). Further, Wesley wrote "that man, represented by these sacrifices, should aim at all perfection of heart and life, and that Christians should one day attain to it, *Eph.* v. 27" (1765, 345). Thus, when referring to fulfilling the intent of the sacrificial system, it must be recognized that the system calls one to holy and righteous living.

C. Allocation of the Sacrifices (6:8—7:38 [6:1—7:38 HB])

BEHIND THE TEXT

Leviticus 1—5 (through 6:7 English text) describes the general steps for offering each type of sacrifice and is addressed "to the Israelites" (1:2; 4:2). Chapters 6—7 (starting at 6:8 English text) deal mainly with the distribution and disposal of the sacrificial portions and are addressed to the priests ("Aaron and his sons," 6:9 [6:2 HB]; note the exceptions of 7:22-27 and 7:28-34, which are addressed "to the Israelites"). The material in chs 1—5 is revealed "from the Tent of Meeting" (1:1), while the instructions in chs 6—7 are revealed to Moses "on Mount Sinai" (7:38*a*), and later related to the Israelites "in the Desert of Sinai" (7:38*b*; understood to be from the tent of meeting "in the Desert"; see Milgrom 1991, 437-38).

Nahmanides observed that the organization of chs 1—5 begins with the voluntary offerings (burnt, grain, well-being), followed by the required sacrifices (purification, guilt). In contrast, chs 6—7 begin with the "most holy" offerings (burnt, grain, purification, guilt; see 6:17 [6:10 HB]), and conclude with the offerings of lesser holiness (i.e., well-being offering; in Carasik 2009, 39). Marx suggests that the order of chs 6—7 reflects three divisions that parallel the floor plan of the tabernacle. First, the burnt offering devoted entirely to God corresponds to the holy of holies where God alone is present (except for the high priest once a year). Second, the offerings shared by God and the priests (grain, purification, guilt) correspond to the holy place in which both God and priests are present. Finally, the well-being offering shared by God, priests, and people corresponds to the outer courtyard that allows the presence of God, priests, and people (2003, 107-8).

The formula *zō't tôrat* ("these are the regulations for") links this section of instructions and identifies it with laws directed to the priests (Driver 1910, 44; see Milgrom 1991, 382-83). The formula introduces five sets of instructions for the priests in relation to the five major offerings: burnt, 6:9 [6:2 HB]; grain, 6:14 [6:7 HB]; purification, 6:25 [6:18 HB]; guilt, 7:1; and well-being, 7:11.

IN THE TEXT

1. Allocation of the Burnt Offering (6:8-13 [6:1-6 HB])

■ **8-9** (1-2 HB) The formula **these are the regulations for** introduces the instructions for the priests regarding the **burnt offering** (→ Behind the

Text above). Wesley recognized that this pericope refers to the daily morning and evening burnt offerings (1765, 361). These constitute the first and last offerings for each day (Exod 29:38-42; Num 28:3-8) and are known as the *tāmîd* ("continual" [NIV = "regular"] burnt offering [Exod 29:42; Num 28:3, 6]). The evening burnt offering was to **remain on the altar hearth throughout the night.** The *tāmîd* was a public version of the individual (private) burnt offerings described in ch 1 (Budd 1996, 109).

■ **10-11** (3-4 HB) Each morning the priest was required to **remove the ashes of the burnt offering.** This refers to the daily burnt offering from the evening before, along with all the ashes that were formed from the previous day's sacrifices. To do this the priest must put on the **linen clothes,** which were required whenever a priest ministered in the sanctuary or at the altar (Exod 28:39-43). Removing the ashes involved two steps. First, the ashes were removed and placed **beside the altar.** Then, the priest had to change clothes in order to **carry the ashes outside the camp to a place that is ceremonially clean.** This process reflects the strict concern for maintaining separation between the sacred and the profane (clean and unclean). The priest had to wear the sacred garments while functioning in the sanctuary grounds, but change into regular clothes for going outside the camp. Also, the sacred ashes from the altar must be removed to a clean place in order not to mix with the profane.

■ **12-13** (5-6 HB) Even while cleaning the ashes from the altar (vv 10-11), the priests must keep the altar fire burning (Gorman 1997, 45). It is stated repeatedly that **the fire on the altar must be kept burning; it must not go out.** Wesley noted that the various sacrifices would keep the fire burning during the day, but the priests must be diligent to manage the fire through the night (1765, 361). A number of related explanations have been given for why the altar fire must be kept burning. One rationale focuses not on the fire itself, but on the burnt offering that must be kept smoldering because it represented uninterrupted worship, which must never be suspended (Keil and Delitzsch n.d., 318-19). The flame itself can be seen as representative of the continual presence of God among his people (see Exod 13:21-22; Harrison 1980, 75). Alternatively, the perpetual flame may express the devotion of the people of God as they are attendant upon God at all times in the sanctuary (Levine 1989, 36). Most significantly, the fire on the altar must be maintained because it originated miraculously from the divine fire that consumed the inaugural public sacrifices of the tabernacle (Lev 9:24; Porter 1976, 49; Milgrom 1991, 389). Accordingly, all subsequent offerings would be consumed by the original divine flame (see Calvin n.d., 364).

2. Allocation of the Grain Offering (6:14-23 [6:7-16 HB])

■ **14-15** (7-8 HB) The formula **these are the regulations for** introduces the instructions for the priests regarding the **grain offering** (→ Behind the Text above). These instructions parallel those in 2:1-2 regarding the grain offering. However, the focus here is on the actions of the priest. The actions of the offerer (2:1) are assumed in this text (see Gerstenberger 1996, 84).

■ **16-18** (9-11 HB) After the memorial portion of the grain offering is burned on the altar to the Lord (→ 2:2), the priests **shall eat the rest of it**. It must be eaten **without yeast** because it is a **share of the offerings made to me [the Lord] by fire**. Since yeast is prohibited from being burned on the altar (2:11), the priestly portion of the offering made to God remains unleavened (Milgrom 1991, 392, 394).

The priests' portion must be eaten **in a holy place** specified here as **the courtyard of the Tent of Meeting**. The grain offering, like the ***purification* offering and guilt offering**, is designated **most holy**. "Most holy" status signifies that the offering can be eaten only by priests in the tabernacle precincts (see Wenham 1979, 120; Harrison 1980, 76).

Most holy offerings appear to be contagious, for **whatever touches them will become holy**. This seems to contradict Hag 2:12, which implies that holiness is not transmittable. Levine contends that this phrase should be translated, "Anyone who is to touch these must be in a holy state." Thus, only consecrated persons were allowed to contact **most holy** sacrificial materials (1989, 37-38). However, Milgrom provides a detailed discussion that supports the NIV rendering. He demonstrates that in the priestly literature, holiness is contagious, but its transmission is reduced to *direct* contact with *objects*, not persons (thus **whatever** as opposed to "whoever" as found in some translations). The Haggai passage is not contradicted because it addresses secondary contact (through the "fold" of a garment) as opposed to direct contact (1991, 443-56).

The concern over contracting holiness may reflect the fear that contact with the divine or that which is most holy is dangerous (Exod 19:10-12; Lev 16:2; 1 Sam 6:19; 2 Sam 6:6-7; see Budd 1996, 111). Alternatively, the concern may simply reflect the requirement to maintain strict separation between the sacred and the profane (→ Lev 6:10-11 [vv 3-4 HB]). This implies a warning that whatever becomes holy must be kept from common use so that holiness does not become defiled (Budd 1996, 116). Such must be cleansed from the contagion of holiness before it can be put to ordinary use (Porter 1976, 50).

■ **19-23** (12-16 HB) This pericope introduces the high priest's daily grain offering. It is appropriately added here, and not mentioned in ch 2, because it pertains specifically to priests (→ Behind the Text above; Keil and Delitzsch n.d., 319-20). Verse 22 (15 HB) specifies the high priest with the phrase, **the son who is to succeed him as anointed priest.**

On the day he is anointed should be understood to indicate the day *from which* the sacrifice began to be offered on a daily basis (Wenham 1979, 122). Rashbam states that "on" the day of his anointing was read by many as "from," indicating that the high priest was to bring the grain offering each day following his anointing (in Carasik 2009, 38). Milgrom demonstrates through lexical and comparative evidence that *bĕyôm* should be translated here as "from the time" (of his anointing; 1991, 397-98). This is affirmed by the identification of this grain offering as *tāmîd* (**regular** or **continual**). The perpetual character of this offering serves to emphasize that the high priest must maintain constant fellowship with the Lord (Hartley 1992, 102).

Every grain offering of a priest shall be burned completely in accordance with the principle that a priest cannot benefit (eat) from his own offering (→ 4:11-12). This applies to any grain offering brought by a priest, as well as the high priest's daily grain offering (Porter 1976, 51).

3. Allocation of the Purification Offering (6:24-30 [6:17-23 HB])

■ **24-26** (17-19 HB) The formula **these are the regulations for** introduces the instructions for the priests regarding the ***purification* offering** (→ Behind the Text above). The offering must be slaughtered **before the LORD** (→ 1:5-9). More specifically, the text stipulates the offering is to be slaughtered **in the place the burnt offering is slaughtered.** The same stipulation is made in the broader discussion regarding the purification offering in ch 4. However, slaughtering at the same place as the burnt offering is only indicated in relation to the leader or common individual who sins (4:24, 29, 33). Likewise, this pericope, addressed to the priests, relates to a goat or a lamb, not a bull as in the purification offering for a priest or for the Israelite community (4:3, 13-14). This is affirmed by the command that any offering whose blood is brought into the tent of meeting "must not be eaten" (6:30 [6:23 HB]). The blood from the offerings for the priest or for the community is brought into the tent of meeting. Since this pericope specifically relates to what may be eaten by the priest, it only addresses the purification offerings from the flock (Milgrom 1991, 401; → From the Text for 4:1—6:7 [4:1—5:26 HB]).

The priest who offers it shall eat it (→ 4:11-12 and 4:24-26 and From the Text for 4:1—6:7 [4:1—5:26 HB]).

The purification offering is **most holy** and **is to be eaten in a holy place, in the courtyard of the Tent of Meeting** (→ 6:16-18 [6:9-11 HB]). Since no other restrictions are stipulated, it seems that the priestly portions that could be eaten include all the meat, with the blood and fat excluded (Gaster 1962, 155).

■ **27-28 (20-21 HB)** These verses further reflect the concern to maintain strict separation between the holy and the profane. **Whatever touches any of the flesh will become holy.** Consequently, anything that touches the meat of the offering must be cleansed in order to keep the holy from being defiled or exposed to common use (→ 6:16-18 [6:9-11 HB]). If the **meat is cooked in a clay pot**, the pot must be broken. This is likely because the clay material is too porous to be fully cleansed (Wesley 1765, 363). However, if the meat **is cooked in a bronze pot, the pot is to be scoured and rinsed with water.** Similarly, **if any of the blood** from the offering **is spattered on a garment,** the priest **must wash it in a holy place.**

The "most holy" character of the purification offering suggests that it does not absorb/carry sin and impurity, which would defile it, but rather the purification offering serves to protect and purify holy objects by transmitting holiness to them (Budd 1996, 116-17; in contrast to Milgrom 1991, 403-6).

■ **29-30 (22-23 HB) Any male in a priest's family may eat it.** This statement appears to contradict v 26 (v 19 HB), which assigns the meat of the offering to the individual priest who offered the sacrifice. Milgrom suggests that the meat is assigned to the officiating priest who is then allowed to share it with fellow priests (1991, 407).

An alternative view recognizes v 29 (v 22 HB) as a later addition reflecting actual practice, because a single priest could not consume all the meat of an entire purification offering (Noth 1977, 58). A variant of this explanation proposes that two traditions are reflected in this pericope. Verse 26 (v 19 HB) represents the small sanctuary with a single priest (such as Eli at Shiloh, 1 Sam 1—3), while Lev 6:29 (v 22 HB) represents the larger Jerusalem temple with a priestly staff. This proposal also serves to explain the same contradiction at 7:6-7, and the differences between priestly allocations in 7:9-10 and 7:31-33 (Milgrom 1991, 407; see King 2009, 55-57).

It is most holy (→ 6:16-18 [6:9-11 HB]).

Any *purification* offering whose blood is brought into the Tent of Meeting refers to the purification offerings for the priest (4:3-12) and for the whole Israelite community (4:13-21), as well as the purification offerings on the Day of Atonement (ch 16; Rashbam in Lockshin 2001, 39-40).

These purification offerings **must not be eaten**, but rather they **must be burned** outside the camp after the fat portions are offered on the altar (see 4:11-12). This is because these offerings serve to atone the priest and the community of which he is a part. The priest is not allowed to benefit (through eating) from such an offering related to his own sins (→ 4:11-12).

4. Allocation of the Guilt Offering (7:1-10)

■ **1-2** The formula **these are the regulations for** introduces the instructions for the priests regarding the **guilt offering** (→ Behind the Text above). The guilt offering **is most holy,** like the grain offering and the purification offering (see 6:17, 25 [6:10, 18 HB]). This designation indicates that the offering belongs to the priests and must be eaten in a holy place (see 7:6; Budd 1996, 117). It **is to be slaughtered in the place where the burnt offering is slaughtered** (→ 6:25 [6:18 HB]).

Its blood is to be sprinkled against the altar on all sides. The blood manipulation was not described in the broader instructions regarding the guilt offering (5:14—6:7 [5:14-26 HB]) but is included here. The reverse is true for the purification offering (blood manipulation is detailed in ch 4 and left out in 6:24-30 [6:17-23 HB]). In the case of the guilt offering, it was possible for the individual to bring a monetary equivalent in place of the animal itself. Consequently, the instructions for the blood manipulation would only be included here for the priest who subsequently performs the sacrificial rite after the animal is purchased (→ 5:14-16; Milgrom 1991, 408-9).

The terminology here regarding blood manipulation is the same as that for the burnt offering, in which the priest was instructed to *"toss* or *throw/dash"* (*wĕzārĕqû*) the blood of the sacrifice "on all sides" of (lit. "round about") the altar (1:5). This is in contrast to the blood manipulation for the purification offering, which calls for the priest "to sprinkle" (*hizzâ*) the blood ("in front of the curtain of the sanctuary") or "to put or smear" (*nātan*) the blood ("on the horns of the altar"; → 4:5-7). The guilt offering is not as concerned with cleansing the altar, as it is with expressing invocation and devotion (reflecting the functions of the burnt offering; → 1:3) in relation to seeking restitution (the primary concern of the guilt offering; Budd 1996, 117).

■ **3-6 All its fat shall be offered.** The description of the fat to be removed and burned **as an offering made to the LORD** is the same as that for the well-being offering and the purification offering (→ 3:2-4; 4:8-10).

As required for **most holy** offerings, the meat of the guilt offering **must be eaten in a holy place** (→ 6:16 [6:9 HB]).

■ **7-10** At this point, the priestly portions for all the "most holy" offerings are summarized (see Milgrom 1991, 410-11). In regard to **both the *purification* offering and the guilt offering,** the priestly portion includes all the meat, with the blood and fat removed (Gaster 1962, 155). The portions **belong to the priest who makes atonement with them.** This contradicts v 6, which indicates that "any male in a priest's family may eat it." The contrast may be the result of two different traditions reflecting distinct periods in the history of the tabernacle and temple (→ 6:29-30 [6:22-23 HB]).

The priestly portion of the **burnt offering** includes only the **hide,** for all the meat and fat must be burned on the altar to the Lord (that the burnt offering is also most holy, see Milgrom 1991, 394-95). The valuable hide may have been used as a mattress by night and a carpet for sitting by day (Kaiser 1994, 1049).

Every grain offering baked . . . or cooked belongs entirely **to the priest who offers it,** after the memorial portion was separated and burned on the altar to the Lord (see 2:2; 6:15 [6:8 HB]). This appears to contradict 7:10, which indicates that **every grain offering . . . belongs equally to all the sons of Aaron.** The distinction may derive from two traditions reflecting two different periods in the history of the tabernacle and temple (→ 6:29-30 [6:22-23 HB]; also Milgrom 1991, 411-12). Grain offerings **mixed with oil** include all those baked and cooked as described in 2:1-10. The only **dry** grain offerings appear to be that of the poor person's purification offering (→ 5:11-13) and that of the suspected adulteress (Num 5:15; Milgrom 1991, 412).

5. Allocation of the Well-Being Offering (7:11-38)

■ **11** The formula **these are the regulations for** introduces the instructions for the priests regarding the ***well-being*** offering (→ Behind the Text above). Three types of sacrifices are subsumed under the category of the well-being offering: the *tôdâ* (thanksgiving offering, v 12), the *neder* (votive offering, v 16), and the *nĕdābâ* (freewill offering, v 16).

■ **12-15** These verses address the well-being offering when it is offered **as an expression of thankfulness.** Four types of breads are required **along with this thank offering.** Three of the breads must be **without yeast** (unleavened), but with **oil (cakes of bread, wafers, cakes of fine flour).** The fourth bread stands out, as it is to be made **with yeast** (leavened). No yeast may be burned upon the altar (→ 2:11). These breads are not burned on the altar but are eaten by the offerer (Milgrom 1991, 414; but Levine states the leavened bread is eaten, while the unleavened cakes *are* offered on the altar, 1989, 42-43). However, **one of each kind** of the four types of bread is set apart as a **contribution to the** LORD and **belongs to the priest** (the Lord assigns his contribution to the priest). As a result, the breads (in addition to the animal sacrifice) contribute to the feast shared by the Lord, priests, and the offerer (with family and friends) in relation to the well-being offering.

The meat from the **thanksgiving** offering **must be eaten on the day it is offered.** Abarbanel comments that this practically forces the offerer to invite others to share the thanksgiving meal, in order that it may be completely consumed in one evening (in Carasik 2009, 44). The thanksgiving offering, and its accompanying meal, served to express gratitude and praise to God for such mercies as recovery from illness, safety on a journey, or rescue from captivity (Ps 107:22; Kaiser 1994, 1051).

■ **16-18** Additional instructions, in the case of a well-being offering that **is the result of a vow or is a freewill offering,** have to do with how quickly the sacrifice shall be eaten. A votive offering is presented upon the successful fulfillment of a vow, while a freewill offering is a spontaneous expression of joy for whatever reason (Milgrom 1991, 419-20). In the case of the votive and freewill versions of the well-being offering, any food left over from the sacrifice **may be eaten on the next day.** However, meat **eaten on the third day** prompts negative consequences. Presumably, the same applies to meat eaten beyond the *first* day in relation to the thanksgiving offering (v 15). Such meat **will not be accepted** and **will not be credited to the one who offered it.** This negation of the offering results from the meat becoming *piggûl* (NIV = **impure**). Milgrom clarifies that this refers to sacred or holy meat that has been *desecrated* by being eaten beyond its prescribed time limit (1991, 422).

■ **19-21** Once again, the concern to maintain strict separation between the holy and the profane (clean and unclean) is expressed (→ 6:10-11 [6:3-4 HB]; 6:16-18 [6:9-11 HB]; and 6:27-28 [6:20-21 HB]). In relation to the well-being offering, **meat that touches anything ceremonially unclean must not be eaten,** and **anyone who is unclean** should not eat **any meat of the *well-being* offering.** Verse 20 refers to the person who is directly unclean due to a condition such as a "bodily discharge" (15:1-17). Verse 21 refers to a person who becomes secondarily unclean by touching **something unclean** (Milgrom 1991, 423). Such a person must not eat **any of the meat of the *well-being* offering** or that person must be **cut off from his people.** The phrase *wĕnikrĕtâ mēʾamměhā* (**cut off from his people**) involves excommunication and suggests disinheritance and being deprived of family and property rights (Budd 1996, 122). Alternatively, the focus may not be on the individual's exclusion from the community, but the termination of the person's line (descendants) resulting in the person's name being "blotted out from the next generation" (Ps 109:13; Milgrom 1991, 424, 426, 457-60).

■ **22-27** This pericope and the next (vv 28-34) interrupt this larger section of instructions addressed to the priests, because they begin with the command to Moses, **say to the Israelites** (→ Behind the Text above). The instructions related to the priests regarding the well-being offering continue at vv 31-34, which identify the portions of the offering assigned to the priests (the main focus of the regulations in 6:8—7:38 [6:1—7:38 HB]). This pericope is addressed to the laity in order to ensure that they bring all the fat of the sacrifice to the altar, and thereby **do not eat any of the fat of cattle, sheep or goats** (see Milgrom 1991, 426-27).

The context here relates to domestic animals eligible for sacrifice. The fat of such animals belongs to God (3:16-17). If the animal is **found dead or torn by wild animals,** its fat must not be eaten. Such fat **may be used for any other purpose,** such as greasing equipment or instruments, lighting, polish, or other household purposes (Noth 1977, 64; Wenham 1979, 125). Those who eat **the fat of an animal from which an offering by fire may be made to the** LORD are subject to being **cut off** from their people (→ vv 19-21). In contrast, the fat of clean animals that are not eligible for sacrifice on the altar, such as wild game, may be eaten (Keil and Delitzsch n.d., 326). However, in regard to the **blood of any bird or animal** (as opposed to the *fat*), it is forbidden to eat it regardless of location or type of animal (→ 1:5-9; 3:17).

■ **28-34 Say to the Israelites** (→ vv 22-27). This pericope is addressed to the laity in order to ensure that they appropriately apportion the offering to the Lord (on the altar) and to the priests, since this is the only type of offering that is also eaten by the offerers themselves. Accordingly, **with his own hands,** the offerer is instructed **to bring the fat, together with the breast** of the well-being offering.

The breast of the sacrifice undergoes the rite of the *těnûpâ*. The term *těnûpâ* is commonly translated **wave offering** and is believed to indicate a rite in which the offering is waved back and forth in a horizontal motion (Kaiser 1994, 1054). Levine describes the rite as carrying the offering to and fro in a raised or elevated position in order to show the offering to God for acceptance (1989, 46). Milgrom demonstrates that the term should be translated "elevation offering," and the rite should be understood as raising or lifting the offering **before the** LORD as a means of dedicating it to God (1991, 461-73). The **fat** is burned **on the altar,** and the breast is given **to Aaron and his sons.**

In addition, **the right thigh of** the ***well-being*** **offerings is given to the priest as a** *tĕrûmâ*. This term is commonly translated "heave offering" and is believed to indicate a rite in which the offering is moved up and down in a vertical motion (Kaiser 1994, 1054; see Keil and Delitzsch n.d., 329). Milgrom demonstrates that *tĕrûmâ* should be recognized as a "gift" (NIV = **contribution**) presented to the officiating priest **who offers the blood and the fat of the** ***well-being*** **offering** (1991, 473-81). Though the breast and the thigh are dedicated to God, the Lord gives them over **to Aaron the priest and his sons as their regular share from the Israelites.**

In sum, the fat is burned on the altar as the Lord's, the breast is given to all the priests, the right thigh is presented to the individual priest who officiates over the sacrifice, and the rest of the meat is eaten by the offerer and family in a meal of love and joy (see Keil and Delitzsch n.d., 330).

■ **35-36** These verses and the following two are often identified as dual summary statements for the instructions to the priests in chs 6—7. Verses 35-36 emphasize the priestly provisions, while vv 37-38 refer to the rituals as a whole (see Noth 1977, 65; Hartley 1992, 95; Gerstenberger 1996, 83). However, the phrase **this is the portion of the offerings** may refer only to the immediately preceding instructions regarding the well-being offerings, thereby summarizing only vv 11-34 (Milgrom 1991, 433).

The priestly portions were allocated **to Aaron and his sons on the day they were presented to serve the** LORD **as priests.** From the time of their ordination, the priests receive the designated portions of the well-being offerings **as their regular share for the generations to come.**

■ **37-38** These verses clearly summarize the instructions to the priests in chs 6—7. **These . . . are the regulations for** (*zō't hattôrâ*) echoes and concludes the five *tôrôt* ("regulations") headings that make up this section of instructions to the priests (6:9 [6:2 HB]; 6:14 [6:7 HB]; 6:25 [6:18 HB]; 7:1; 7:11; → Behind the Text above). The offerings are listed here in the same order as discussed in chs 6—7: **the burnt offering, the grain offering, the** *purification* **offering, the guilt offering, the ordination offering and the** *well-being* **offering** (as opposed to chs 1—5: burnt, grain, well-being, purification, guilt). The reference to a different setting, that is **on Mount Sinai** as opposed to "from the Tent of Meeting" (1:1) further suggests that 6:8—7:38 is a self-contained unit (Porter 1976, 59).

Though the order of offerings listed is the same as those treated in chs 6—7, the **ordination offering** is added to this summation list. It is possible that the priestly allocations for the ordination offering were originally listed between the guilt offering and the well-being offering within chs 6—7 but were later omitted because they are repeated in the following chapter, which details the ordination service itself (Milgrom 1991, 436-37).

FROM THE TEXT

The sacrificial system serves to keep relationship with God constantly before God's children. The daily morning and evening burnt offerings (***continual*** burnt offering) are a perpetual reminder that the community lives in relation to God. Keeping the evening burnt offering smoldering all night suggests that petition on behalf of Israel continued through the night (Walton and Matthews 1997, 149). The pleasing aroma of burnt offerings (1:9, 13, 17) ascended continually and calls to mind the burning incense associated with the prayers of the saints as related in the NT (Rev 5:8; 8:3-4).

The holiness of God is emphasized by the strict separation between the sacred and the profane depicted in the sacrificial system. This is reflected in the priest's change of clothes when entering or leaving the tabernacle, the placing of the ashes from the burnt offering in a clean place (6:11 [6:4 HB]), eating the most holy offerings in a holy place, the warning against touching most holy offerings (6:16-18, 26-27 [6:9-11, 19-20 HB]), and breaking the clay pot or scouring the bronze pot in which meat from a most holy offering is cooked (6:28 [6:21 HB]). The concern to maintain a resolute boundary between that which is holy and that which is common is further manifested in the purification features of the sacrificial system. Despite this fastidious commitment to holiness, God reveals an even greater devotion to loving his children. The pursuit of holiness is intended to enrich relationship to God, and therefore is to be meticulously pursued. Nevertheless, even when idolatry and apostasy compromise holiness, the love of God is not overthrown, as expressed so passionately in the words of Hosea:

> How can I give you up, Ephraim?
> How can I hand you over, Israel?
> How can I treat you like Admah?
> How can I make you like Zeboiim?
> My heart is changed within me;
> all my compassion is aroused.
> I will not carry out my fierce anger,
> nor will I turn and devastate Ephraim.
> For I am God, and not man—
> the *Holy One* among you. (Hos 11:8-9, emphasis added)

God's overwhelming love is further evident in Christ, through whom God's holiness touches the unclean and mingles with sinners (→ From the Text for 4:1—6:7 [4:1—5:26 HB]).

Relations with God are not expressed solely through somber ceremony and meticulous ritual. Once again, the well-being offering serves to illustrate the aspects of joy and celebration that also characterize the sacrificial system. The three types of well-being offerings (thanksgiving, votive, and freewill) express gratitude, achievement, and adoration through ritual (→ From the Text for 1:1—3:17).

II. ORDINATION AND FIRST SACRIFICES (8:1—10:20)

BEHIND THE TEXT

Chapters 8—10 comprise a narrative section in the midst of the legislation of Leviticus. This narrative links Leviticus to the account of Israel's history that provides the setting for Israel's laws (Wenham 1979, 129; Kaiser 1994, 1056).

The priestly writings are known for exhibiting a characteristic of command and fulfillment, resulting in a sense of repetition. For example, the instructions concerning the construction of the tabernacle, its furniture, and the priestly garments, along with how to carry out the priestly consecration are detailed in Exod 25—31 (command). Much of this same information is repeated in Exod 35—40, which describes the implementation of these instructions (fulfillment). The instructions in Exod 25—31 are carried out in Exod 35—40 except for the priestly consecration. The fulfillment of the priestly consecration is delayed until Lev 8. Nahmanides explains that the consecration of the priests involved sacrifices for which the instructions had not yet been revealed. Accordingly, the instructions concerning the sacrifices (Lev 1—7) must precede the ordination of the priests in Lev 8 (in Carasik 2009, 49).

The narrative continues in Lev 9 with a description of the inauguration of the sacrificial system. The historic first sacrifices are performed by the newly ordained priests (thus Lev 9 brings initial fulfillment to the instructions in Lev 1—7; see King 2009, 21). It should be clarified, however, that the initial sacrifices performed in ch 9 do not simply represent the commencement of the regular sacrificial system practiced throughout the year. Rather, the ceremony related in ch 9 is a unique event completing the ordination of the priest, and sanctioning the tabernacle and sacrificial system for the worship practices of Israel. The inaugural ceremony calls for purification offerings and burnt offerings for the priest and the congregation respectively and culminates with a fellowship meal centered around a well-being offering. The event is brought to a dramatic conclusion with the appearance of "the glory of the LORD" (9:23).

Leviticus 10 culminates this narrative section with the account of two of Aaron's sons violating the instructions regarding their priestly duties, and the consequent judgment resulting from their actions.

IN THE TEXT

A. Ordination of the Priests (8:1-36)

1. Cleansing and Anointing (8:1-13)

■ **1-4** The priestly ordination begins with the command to gather the essential ingredients for the ceremony. This includes the priests to be ordained, **their garments, the anointing oil, the bull for the *purification* offering, the two rams and the basket containing bread made without yeast.** The definite articles preceding each item presume prior knowledge of these materials and highlight the dependence of this chapter on the instructions originally presented in Exod 29 (Milgrom 1991, 498). In addition, Moses was instructed to **gather the entire assembly.** Cyril of Jerusalem associates the later "church" with this original assembly for the inauguration of tabernacle worship by observing that the term "assemble" is used here for the first time in Scripture (the LXX uses a verb form related to *ekklēsia* ["church"] for the first time here; Lienhard 2001, 172-73).

The phrase **as the LORD commanded** (*ka'ăšer ṣiwwâ YHWH*) appears throughout this chapter (vv 4, 9, 13, 17, 21, 29 [vv 5, 36 without the initial preposition *ka*]), not only pointing back to the instructions in Exod 29, but also emphasizing Moses' obedience to the Lord and highlighting that the ceremony is carried out just as God intended.

■ **5-6 Moses brought . . . forward** Aaron and his sons. The term *wayyaqrēb* ("present," "bring near"; BDB 1952, 897-98) is commonly used for presenting an offering. In this case, **Aaron and his sons** are offered to God for service at the tabernacle (Hartley 1992, 111).

Moses **washed them with water.** The washing does not serve to cleanse Aaron and his sons from sin (contrary to Keil and Delitzsch n.d., 335; and Kaiser 1994, 1060). Instructions regarding atonement for sin do not include washing (see ch 4). Rather, washing is required to cleanse one from impurity (different from sin; see chs 12—15). The impurity regulations constitute "a symbolic system reminding Israel of its imperative to cleave to life and reject death" (Milgrom 1991, 1003).

■ **7-9** The garments of the high priest serve to draw attention to the mission and function of the position, rather than to the person. The elaborate clothing represents the significance of the office (Wenham 1979, 138-39).

The high priest's **robe** is described in Exod 28:31-35 (also Exod 39:22-26); it included cloth representations of pomegranates alternating with golden bells around its hem. Pomegranates are associated with fertility and abundance (Milgrom 1991, 504), and the bells serve to communicate the high priest's entrance and exit in relation to the place of God's presence (Exod 28:35).

The **ephod** was a type of apron fastened by shoulder pieces and a waistband (Haran 1985, 166). An onyx stone was attached to each shoulder piece of the ephod, engraved with the names of the twelve tribes of Israel (six on each stone; Exod 28:9-12).

The **breastpiece** was attached to and supported by the ephod (Exod 28:22-28). Twelve precious stones were mounted on the breastpiece, each with the name of one of the twelve tribes of Israel engraved upon it (Exod 28:17-21). Accordingly, the high priest "will bear the names of the sons of Israel *over his heart* on the breastpiece of decision as a continuing memorial before the LORD" (Exod 28:29, emphasis added).

The breastpiece is "folded double" (Exod 28:16) in order to form a pouch into which the **Urim and Thummim** are placed. The Urim and Thummim appear to have been used to inquire of the Lord (Num 27:21; 1 Sam 14:41 [LXX]; 28:6) in a manner similar to casting lots or throwing dice (Wenham 1979, 139). The function of seeking God's will is reflected in the references to the breastpiece as a "breastpiece for making decisions" (Exod 28:15; see 28:29-30).

The **gold plate** on the front of the high priest's **turban** is engraved with the words "HOLY TO THE LORD" (Exod 28:36).

■ **10-11** The sacred **anointing oil** is made up of "liquid myrrh," "cinnamon," "cane," "cassia," and "olive oil" (Exod 30:23-25). Moses **anointed the tabernacle and everything in it**. This included "the ark of the Testimony, the table [of showbread] and all its articles, the lampstand and its accessories, [and] the altar of incense" (Exod 30:26-27). These items are located inside the holy of holies and the holy place. Moses then moved outside and **sprinkled some of the oil on the altar seven times**. Also anointed were **all its** [the altar's] **utensils and the basin with its stand**.

The purpose of anointing the components of the tabernacle is **to consecrate them** (*lĕqaddĕšām*). Thereby, they are made holy (*qiddaš*) and set apart for the Lord's service in relation to the sacrificial system.

■ **12-13** Moses **poured some of the anointing oil on Aaron's head . . . to consecrate him** (*lĕqaddĕšô*). Accordingly, the high priest is made holy (*qiddaš*) and set apart for the Lord's service. As Moses **anointed him** (*wayyimšaḥ*), Aaron was elevated to a new status enabling him to function in the realm of the sacred (see Milgrom 1991, 553-54). To anoint (*māšaḥ*) someone is to render the person an anointed one (*māšîaḥ*), commonly known in English as "messiah." Kings and priests were anointed in Israel to serve as God's instruments. Messianic expectation included hope for an ideal priest as well as an ideal king (Collins 2004, 143). Christians recognize Jesus Christ as the ultimate fulfillment of God's Messiah.

Moses **put tunics . . . tied sashes . . . and put headbands** on Aaron's sons. It can be seen that the ordinary priest's garments were not as elaborate as the garments of the high priest (vv 7-9). The consecration of Aaron's sons occurs in v 30.

2. Sacrificial Service (8:14-30)

■ **14-17** A **bull for the** *purification* **offering** is the required animal for either a priest or the whole community (see 4:3, 13-14). Obviously here, the offering serves for **Aaron and his sons** as priests, not to atone them in this case, but to purify the altar on their behalf (see below; and Milgrom 1991, 522). **Aaron and his sons laid their hands on its head** (→ 1:4).

Blood is applied to **all the horns of the altar to purify the altar**. Rashi explains that the simple form of the verb *ḥṭ'* means "to sin," while the intensive (*piel*) form means "to cleanse from sin." Thus, **purify the altar** here literally means to "de-sin" the altar (in Herczeg 1999, 88 n. 1; Carasik 2009, 51).

The text does not indicate that this offering atones for Aaron or his sons (see Gane 2005, 130-31). Rather, in relation to the altar, Moses **consecrated it to make atonement for it**. Rashi and Ibn Ezra clarify that the altar was sanctified in order to atone *upon* it, from this point forward (in

Herczeg 1999, 88; Carasik 2009, 51). This explains why this particular purification offering does not atone for Aaron and sons; that is, because the altar must first be consecrated for that task. Subsequently, Aaron sacrifices a purification offering for himself in the following account of the first sacrifices (9:2, 7-8). Presumably, the sons of Aaron would have sacrificed a purification offering for themselves when they first officiated at the altar.

The **fat** portions are **burned . . . on the altar** consistent with the instructions for a purification offering of the priests (4:8-10). Likewise, the rest of the **bull** is **burned up outside the camp** (see 4:11-12).

■ **18-21** The second sacrifice of the ordination ceremony consists of a **ram for the burnt offering**. Wesley rightly identifies the burnt offering as a representation of the priests devoting themselves and all their service to God (1765, 368; re functions of the burnt offering, → 1:3).

Laid their hands on its head (→ 1:4).

Moses **sprinkled the blood against the altar**. The blood is "tossed or thrown/dashed" (*wayyizrōq*) in a manner consistent with the instructions for the burnt offering and the guilt offering, thereby signifying invocation and devotion (→ 7:1-2).

The cutting of the **ram into pieces**, washing **the inner parts and the legs**, and burning it **on the altar** all correspond with the instructions for a burnt offering (1:6-9).

■ **22-24** The second ram (see v 2) constitutes the third sacrifice of the ceremony and is called **the ram for the ordination**. The term *millu'îm* ("ordination") derives from a root meaning "to fill" or "be full." It reflects the expression "filling the hand" (*millē' yad*), which is used in reference to ordaining persons to divine service (Exod 28:41; 29:29; 32:29). The expression stems from the moment of the ordination ceremony in which the hands of the priests are filled with all the elements of the wave offering (Exod 29:22-24; Lev 8:25-27; de Vaux 1997, 346). The same term (*millu'îm*) is also used in relation to "settings" of precious stones (Exod 25:7; 35:9, 27; 1 Chr 29:2). This prompts the translation "installation," or in this context, "ordination" (Rainey 1972, 605).

Laid their hands on its head (→ 1:4).

The blood from the ram is applied to Aaron and his sons **on the lobes of their right ears, on the thumbs of their right hands and on the big toes of their right feet**. The priests' extremities represent the whole person, and these particular appendages suggest that the priest is dedicated to carefully listen to the word of God (ear), diligently perform priestly functions (hand), and walk rightly before the Lord (foot; Keil and Delitzsch n.d., 340). The use of *nātan* ("to put or smear") in relation to the application of blood upon Aaron and his sons implies that an element of purification is also in view here (→ 7:1-2; Milgrom 1991, 528-29; also Exod 29:33).

Moses also **sprinkled blood against the altar** (*wayyizrōq*; → vv 18-21).

■ **25-29** The **hands of Aaron and his sons are filled** (→ vv 22-24) with all the **fat** portions, **the right thigh**, and the breads (**a cake of bread, and one made with oil, and a wafer**). These are waved before the Lord, **as a wave offering** (*těnûpâ*; → 7:28-34). Thereby having been dedicated to God, Moses **burned them on the altar . . . as an ordination offering**. Normally, following the apportionment of a well-being offering, the **right thigh** is given to the priest as a "contribution" (*těrûmâ*; → 7:28-34). As acting priest for the ceremony, Moses might have received the right thigh, as he does the **breast** (also assigned to the priests; see 7:31). However, the right thigh is given to the Lord on the altar, suggesting that both Moses and God served as officiants at this inaugural ordination ceremony (Wenham 1979, 142).

■ **30** The use of **anointing oil** in combination with **blood** suggests both consecration and purification. This is affirmed by the use of *hizzâ* ("to sprinkle") in relation to the application of the mixture (particularly the blood), which implies purification (→ 4:5-7 and 7:1-2). As in 8:10-12, the anointing oil serves to consecrate. Accordingly, Moses **consecrated Aaron and his garments and his sons and their garments**. Aaron himself was already consecrated earlier (v 12). Consecrating Aaron at this later stage (with his sons) corresponds with Exod 29, which does not explicitly indicate that his earlier anointing resulted in consecration (Exod 29:7), though it does stipulate that Aaron is consecrated at this later stage of the ceremony with his sons (Exod 29:21; see Milgrom 1991, 519, 532-33). This stage of the ceremony highlights the consecration of the priestly **garments** in addition to that of Aaron and his sons. This focuses attention on the position and function of the priests, as opposed to the individuals (Keil and Delitzsch n.d., 341; → Lev 8:7-9).

3. Ordination Meal and Sanctuary Confinement (8:31-36)

■ **31-32** Aaron and his sons partake of the **meat** and the **bread** allotted to them from the ordination offering, as offerers; while Moses, as the officiant, partakes of the breast from the offering (v 29). The food is to be eaten **at the entrance to the Tent of Meeting** (→ 1:1, 3, 5-9). Similar to the well-being offering, the ordination offering establishes community and fellowship between God and the sacrificial participants; in this case, the newly ordained priests (Noth 1977, 71; Hartley 1992, 31-32).

They must **burn up the rest of the meat and the bread**. Exodus 29:34 stipulates that any meat or bread from the ordination offering that is left till morning must be burned. This resembles the thanksgiving offering among the well-being offerings (7:15). Votive and freewill offerings (also among the well-being offerings) may be eaten over two days (7:16-17).

■ **33-36** The ordination continues for **seven days** (re significance of "seven," → 4:5-7), during which time Aaron and his sons must remain at **the entrance to the Tent of Meeting** (→ 1:1, 3, 5-9). This represents the time required for the important rite of passage from layperson to priest (Hartley 1992, 115).

Exodus 29:36-37 specifies that a purification offering must be offered each of the seven days, to purify the altar. In addition, the altar must be anointed to consecrate it. Thereby, the altar will become most holy. Moses tells Aaron and his sons, **your ordination will last seven days.** This phrase literally reads *for seven days he will fill your hand* (*kî šib'at yāmîm yĕmallē' 'et-yedkem*; re "filling the hand," → 8:22-24). This suggests that perhaps the ordination offering was also repeated for each of the seven days (some argue the entire ceremony was repeated all seven days; Wesley 1765, 368; Milgrom 1991, 537-40).

The priests are informed that the ordination is carried out **to make atonement for you.** Elements of purification for the priests are evident in relation to the ordination offering (→ vv 22-24) and the sprinkling of oil and blood (→ v 30). The use of *kipper* ("to atone") in the priestly literature normally refers to purification ("to purge"; → 4:20). In this instance, the term is used in a general sense in relation to "being cleansed of all impurities and sins so that the offerer is reconciled and 'at one' with God" (Milgrom 1991, 541).

B. Inauguration of the Sacrificial System (9:1-24)

1. The First Sacrifices (9:1-21)

■ **1** The inauguration ceremony takes place **on the eighth day.** This refers to the eighth day of the priestly ordination ceremony (see 8:33, 35). Assuming the narrative (Lev 8—10) picks up from the completion of the tabernacle (Exod 40:17), this would be the eighth day of the month of Nisan (Milgrom 1991, 571). Distinguishing an eighth day following a seven-day event also occurs in relation to the Festival of Tabernacles (Lev 23:34-36, 39; for more on this pattern, see Milgrom 1991, 571). This eighth day serves to inaugurate the sacrificial system with a unique ceremony featuring the first sacrifices performed on behalf of the congregation and conducted by the newly ordained priests.

It is commonly held that **the elders of Israel** were **summoned** to witness this day as representatives of the people. However, it is clear that the people themselves were present and active in the ceremony ("Israelites," v 3; "the entire assembly," v 5; "all the people," v 23). Rashi suggests that the elders were specified so that they would witness that Aaron assumes priestly office by the command of God (in Carasik 2009, 56). Such a thought anticipates and counteracts the rebellions against Aaron and the priesthood that occur later in the narrative history (Num 16:10-11, 40; 17:5-10).

■ **2-6** As with the priestly ordination ceremony, the inauguration of the sacrificial system begins by gathering the essential ingredients for the ceremony and assembling the people (→ 8:1-4).

Aaron is instructed to present a **calf** (*'ēgel*) for his ***purification* offering**. The normal purification offering for a priest is a bull (*par*; 4:3). The Aramaic Bible adds the explanation that a calf was required for Aaron in order to compensate for making the golden *calf* at Horeb (Sinai; Exod 32:2-4), lest Satan accuse him (*Tg. Ps.-J.*, Lev 9:2). Similarly, Rashi claims the calf offering serves to absolve Aaron for his part in the sin of the golden calf (in Carasik 2009, 56).

The inventory of offerings for this ceremony includes: for the priest, a **calf** for his ***purification* offering**, and a **ram for his burnt offering;** and for the people, **a male goat for a *purification* offering, a calf and a lamb . . . for a burnt offering, and an ox and a ram for a *well-being* offering, . . . together with a grain offering mixed with oil**. Consequently, for this unique inauguration day of the sacrificial system, Aaron offers every type of sacrifice (except for the guilt offering, which is meant as a private offering for specific offenses). In addition, most kinds of sacrificial animals are involved, except for birds, which were considered alternative offerings for the poor (Wenham 1979, 149; see Milgrom 1991, 572). Accordingly, the focus of this day is not as much on purification from sin as it is on launching the sacrificial system with every variety of sacrifice.

The anticipated climax of the ceremony is proclaimed twice; first with the promise that **today the LORD will appear to you** (v 4), and second with the result clause, **so that the glory of the LORD may appear to you** (v 6). This highlights the goal of worship as an encounter with God (Hartley 1992, 123). The **glory of the LORD** (*kĕbôd YHWH*) is a technical phrase in the priestly literature, used to describe theophanies. Exodus 24:15-17 describes the glory of the Lord in relation to cloud and fire (von Rad 1962, 240). This is associated with the "pillar of cloud" that led the Israelites through the wilderness by day and the "pillar of fire" that led them by night (Exod 13:21). This manifestation of God's presence that led the Israelites through the wilderness will now be present with them in the tabernacle (Kaiser 1994, 1065). In Lev 9:4 the verb **will appear** is actually in the perfect form (denoting completed action; "appeared"). Wesley explains this as similar to what some call a "prophetic perfect," which reflects such certainty for the occurrence of an event that the text uses a form that is translated in the past (1765, 371; see Harrison 1980, 104).

■ **7** This verse provides a summary outline of the action to take place in vv 8-21. Aaron is instructed to sacrifice the offerings for himself (vv 8-14), and then the offerings for the people (vv 15-21). The sequence reflects the important rule that the priest must atone for himself before he can atone for others (Milgrom 1991, 578; see Wenham 1979, 149).

Aaron is told, by means of *his* offerings, to **make atonement for yourself [Aaron] and the people.** The term *hā'ām* (the people) should be read as *bêtěkā* (your household), which corresponds with the LXX (Greek OT) and with the parallel expressions in 16:6, 11, 17 (Milgrom 1991, 578). Accordingly, Aaron's offering atones for himself and his household, while **the offering that is for the people** serves to **make atonement for them.** On the other hand, in keeping with the Hebrew reading, Wesley's comment here recalls the principle that the priest's sins, and his offerings, have an impact on the congregation (1765, 372; → 4:3; and Keil and Delitzsch n.d., 346).

Since atonement here is linked to *purification* and **burnt** offerings (and one might add the well-being and grain offerings for the people; see 9:4, 17-18), *wěkappēr* (**make atonement**) should be understood in the general sense of reconciliation in order to "become 'at-one'" with God (Milgrom 1991, 578; → 8:33-36 and 4:20). This is reinforced by the recognition that purification itself is not the focus here. The people are already presumed to be clean (since they "stood before the LORD," v 5), and the priests were both clean and holy based on the consecration ceremony they have just undergone (Kiuchi 1987, 43).

■ **8** Noticeably missing throughout this eighth day ceremony is the rite of laying a hand on the head of the offerings (→ 1:4). This omission is often understood as a result of intentional abbreviation on the part of the writer in order to focus attention on the distinctive features of the ceremony (see Budd 1996, 145), or more specifically on the rites involving the altar (Milgrom 1991, 579). Consequently, it is assumed that the hand-laying did take place. Abbreviation in the record of the ceremony is clearly illustrated in 9:16, which *details* the sacrifice of the people's burnt offering by merely stating that Aaron "offered it in the prescribed way." In contrast, Gane contends that hand-laying is not required for "calendric sacrifices" (offered in conjunction with annual festivals and ceremonies). This is because in such cases there would be no ambiguity in relation to identifying the animals with their respective offerers. Though it is a one-time event, the inauguration ceremony is included as *calendric* because it took place at a specific time set by the Lord (2005, 54 n. 34).

Aaron offered the **calf as a *purification* offering for himself** (→ 8:14-17). Though it seems that all of the offerings for this day participate in atonement (→ 9:7), the purification offering in particular highlights the cleansing of the priest. Since this ceremony constitutes the beginning of official sacrificial practice for Israel, this first purification offering for the priest himself serves to purge him of sins committed and impurities acquired prior to this inauguration of the sacrificial system.

■ **9-11** The blood of the priest's purification offering is applied **on the horns of the altar.** The text does not specify whether this refers to the "altar of fragrant incense" or the "altar of burnt offering" (see 4:7). Given the tendency to abbreviate the details of this ceremony (→ 9:8), perhaps it is assumed that the blood was put on the horns of the *incense* altar, while the rest was poured out at the base of the altar *of burnt offering*, which would parallel the description for the application of blood for the priest's purification offering in 4:7 (see Budd 1996, 145). The meat of this offering would not be eaten but must be **burned up outside the camp** (see 4:11-12; 6:30).

Alternatively, many scholars presume that the blood is only applied to the outer altar of burnt offering and is not brought into the holy place (conflicting with the instructions in 4:7). This is because of the unique standing of this inaugural ceremony. Aaron has not yet fully entered into his office (Wesley 1765, 372) and only enters the holy place for the first time in 9:23 (Porter 1976, 73). Kiuchi adds that the eighth day ceremony continues the consecration period (ch 8), and therefore Aaron and his sons are not yet entitled to enter the holy place until its completion. Accordingly, the rituals of chs 8—9 must take place on the outer altar and serve to enable the priests to subsequently work in the tent of meeting (1987, 45). Similarly, Gorman explains that the rituals of chs 8—9 do not reflect the repeated and regular sacrificial acts in Israel. Rather, these ceremonies reflect one-time "ritual acts of founding" that will not be performed in this particular way again (1997, 55, 62). Thus, the difference regarding the application of blood between the purification offering here and that for the priest in 4:3-12 likely stems from a difference in ritual function (see Gane 2005, 45 n. 3).

Poured out at the base of the altar (→ 4:5-7).

The **fat** portions are burned on the altar to the Lord, consistent with the instructions for a purification offering of the priests (4:8-10; 8:16).

■ 12-14 Sprinkled it [the blood] against the altar on all sides (→ 1:5-9; 4:5-7; and 7:1-2).

The burnt offering expresses surrender and complete devotion to God (→ 1:3).

■ 15 Aaron sacrifices the people's *purification* offering . . . as he did with the first one. Thus, this offering was carried out in the same manner as Aaron's purification offering (9:8-11), without taking the blood into the holy place (Keil and Delitzsch n.d., 347). That the blood was not taken into the holy place is affirmed in 10:16-18 (see Budd 1996, 146). This adds weight to the argument that neither the blood from the priest's purification offering nor that of the people's was applied within the holy place (→ 9:9-11).

Since this ceremony constitutes the beginning of official sacrificial practice for Israel, this first purification offering for the people serves to purge them of sins committed and impurities acquired prior to this inauguration of the sacrificial system (→ v 8).

■ 16-17 Aaron offered the people's burnt offering . . . in the prescribed way. As opposed to the purification offerings in this ceremony (→ vv 9-11, 15), the burnt offerings follow standard procedure as described in ch 1.

The instructions for the grain offering are also abbreviated. Aaron took a handful of it to serve as the memorial portion (Harrison 1980, 106; → 2:2). It was burned on the altar in addition to the morning's burnt offering. This refers to the *tāmîd* ("continual" [NIV = "regular"] burnt offering [Exod 29:42; Num 28:3, 6]), which is sacrificed each morning and evening (→ 6:8-9 [6:1-2 HB]). Since the regular practice of the sacrificial system is not yet underway (before the conclusion of the consecration and inauguration ceremonies), this statement is commonly considered a later addition harmonizing this ceremony with the instructions regarding the daily morning offering (Exod 29:38-41; Num 28:3-8; Levine 1989, 57). Knohl attributes this editorial addition to the Holiness School, which sought to promote the popular and public aspects of the sacrificial system. In this case, the daily burnt offering is depicted as having been sacrificed before the completion of the priestly ordination ceremonies of the eighth day (1995, 56, 194-95).

■ 18-21 The final sacrifice of the inauguration ceremony is the *well-being* offering for the people. Accordingly, the inauguration of the sacrificial system culminates with a joyous celebration (→ 3:1). The use of both an ox and a ram amplify the significance of this particular occasion (see Levine 1989, 57). Communion and unity are emphasized as God, priests, and people share a common meal (Keil and Delitzsch n.d., 345; → 7:28-34).

Sprinkled it [the blood] **against the altar on all sides** (→ 1:5-9; 4:5-7; and 7:1-2).

The **fat portions** of the offering were **burned . . . on the altar** in accordance with the instructions for well-being offerings (3:3-5; re **the fat tail**, → 3:6-10). **The breasts and the right thigh** were waved as a **wave offering** (*těnûpâ*). Normally, the breast undergoes the rite of *těnûpâ* (dedicated to God, but given to the priests), while the right thigh is given as a *těrûmâ* ("contribution" for the officiating priest; → 7:28-34). Milgrom suggests that designating the right thigh as a *těnûpâ* (thereby assigning it to all the priests, as opposed to just the one officiating) is a later development based on the need for equitable distribution of portions for the priests, at a time when the number of priests serving at the single sanctuary grew, such as during the reforms of Hezekiah and Josiah (1991, 476-81).

2. Community Blessing and Divine Fire (9:22-24)

■ **22 Aaron lifted his hands toward the people.** Milgrom clarifies that Aaron faced the people, but his hands were lifted to heaven (Exod 9:29, 33; Milgrom 1991, 587). Rashi claims that Aaron **blessed them** (the people) with the priestly blessing of Num 6:24-26 (in Carasik 2009, 60). Wesley contends it could only have been *something similar* to the blessing of Num 6, because that priestly blessing had not yet been given by God (1765, 373). Nevertheless, it is noteworthy that immediately following the revelation of the priestly blessing, the text describes Moses completing the setup of the tabernacle and its anointing and consecration, following which the tribal leaders bring gifts (Num 7:1-3). Accordingly, like Rashi, Ibn Ezra associates the priestly blessing of Num 6:24-26 with Aaron's blessing here and adds that immediately following Aaron's blessing, the tribal leaders brought their gifts (in Milgrom 1990, 53).

■ **23** With the completion of his ordination, Aaron **went into the Tent of Meeting** (re tent of meeting, → 1:1) for the first time (Porter 1976, 74). Rashi suggests what appear to be the two most common explanations for why Moses and Aaron entered the tabernacle at this time. Moses may have taken this opportunity to teach Aaron the ritual related to the incense altar. Alternatively, Moses and Aaron may have entered the tent in order to pray (in Carasik 2009, 60; see also Rashbam here). Wesley expands the first thought to include Moses teaching Aaron and overseeing him perform all the duties of the holy place, involving the lamps, table of showbread, and the incense altar (1765, 373-74).

Upon emerging from the tabernacle, Moses and Aaron **blessed the people** a second time (→ v 22).

As anticipated in vv 4 and 6, **the glory of the LORD appeared to all the people** (→ vv 2-6).

■ **24** God's glory is manifested through the **fire** that **came out from the presence of the LORD**. The precise phrase is repeated in 10:2 (*wattēṣē' 'ēš millipnê YHWH wattō'kal;* "fire came out from the presence of the LORD and consumed . . ."), though the object changes from **the burnt offering** (9:24) to "them" (10:2, referring to Nadab and Abihu). Rashbam conflates the two occurrences and claims that the fire came out from the holy of holies, lit the incense altar in the holy place, encountered Nadab and Abihu next to the incense altar and burned them, and then came forth to the outer altar and consumed the offering there (in Carasik 2009, 60-61).

Hizkuni asserts that the fire that came forth was not extinguished from the altar until the time of the temple, and then that which came down upon the altar of Solomon's temple (2 Chr 7:1-3) was not extinguished until the time of Manasseh (2 Kgs 21:1-18; in Carasik 2009, 60-61). This reflects the admonition that the altar fire, now of divine origin, must be kept burning indefinitely (→ Lev 6:12-13 [6:5-6 HB]).

The sacrifices on the altar were originally set on fire by natural means (9:10, 13-17, 20). The slow burning process would normally take hours to fully incinerate the offerings. However, the divine fire consumed them suddenly (see Keil and Delitzsch n.d., 348-50; Wenham 1979, 150).

The appearance of God's glory and the divine fire on the altar demonstrate that God has confirmed the ordination of the priests, accepted the offerings of the priests and the people, and taken up residence in the newly inaugurated tabernacle. The sacrificial system is now officially in operation, and the Lord dwells in the midst of the community (Gorman 1997, 63).

In response, **all the people . . . shouted for joy and fell facedown.** Clearly, praise and humble adoration mark this final scene of worship and celebration.

C. The Sons of Aaron and Priestly Portions (10:1-20)

1. Nadab and Abihu (10:1-7)

■ **1 Nadab and Abihu** were the eldest sons of Aaron (Num 3:2; see Exod 6:23; 28:1; Num 26:60; 1 Chr 6:3; 24:1). They were among the privileged group who, with Moses and Aaron, "ate and drank" together, and worshiped the Lord on Mount Sinai (Exod 24:1, 11). Most significantly, the text indicates twice that they "saw" God, though God "did not raise his hand against" them (Exod 24:9-11).

In relation to an **incense** offering, Nadab and Abihu presented **unauthorized fire** (*'ēš zārâ*; see also Num 3:4; 26:61; and LXX of Lev 16:1). The instructions for the daily morning and evening incense offering are found in Exod 30:7-9, according to which *"unauthorized* incense" (*qĕṭōret zārâ*; NIV = "other incense") is forbidden (the recipe for the Lord's incense is described in Exod 30:34-38). Accordingly, some argue that the sin of Nadab and Abihu was offering "strange" or "foreign" fire or incense, reflecting pagan and idolatrous practice (see Porter 1976, 77; Hartley 1992, 132; Milgrom notes that the incense of Nadab and Abihu must have been a different composition than that specified in Exod 30 [1991, 597]). Keil and Delitzsch suggest that their sin was bringing an incense offering at a *time other than* the regular daily incense offering (n.d., 351).

Rashbam and Ibn Ezra point to the most commonly accepted explanation for Nadab and Abihu's sin; that is, they brought fire from a *common* source other than the outer altar that held the divine fire (in Lockshin 2001, 50; Carasik 2009, 61; see Wesley 1765, 374). In relation to Korah's rebellion, it appears that fire is also taken from a profane source. Moses commands Korah and his followers to bring censers with fire but does not tell them from where they should obtain the fire (Num 16:6-7, 17). In contrast, when the community grumbles the next day, Moses specifically tells Aaron to obtain fire for his incense offering "from the altar" (Num 16:46 [17:11 HB]). Accordingly, in both accounts (rebels in Num 16, and Nadab and Abihu in Lev 10), it appears that fire was taken from the wrong source, and in both accounts the wrongdoers suffer the same fate (Num 16:35; see Lev 10:2; Laughlin 1976, 561).

In a later comment on 16:1, Ibn Ezra states that Nadab and Abihu must have actually entered the holy of holies with their incense offering, for this passage states "they drew too close" (in Carasik 2009, 117). Indeed, the opening statement to ch 16 implies that their sin may have been entering the holy of holies in the wrong manner and encroaching upon a task restricted to the high priest alone (Kiuchi 1987, 81). Consequently, the proper way to approach the Lord with incense is specified in 16:12-13, including the requirement of taking coals (fire) "from the altar" (see Laughlin 1976, 560-61).

■ **2** As a result of Nadab and Abihu's sin, **fire came out from the presence of the LORD and consumed them.** This precise wording is also used for the consumption of the sacrifices at the end of the inauguration service

(→ 9:24). Similar terminology indicates the same fate for Korah and the others who rebelled against Moses and Aaron (Num 16:35; → Lev 10:1).

Nadab and Abihu died **before the LORD** (→ 1:5-9 and 10:4).

■ **3** Moses explains, **This is what the LORD spoke of** . . . The implicit quote that follows is not found explicitly anywhere in the Bible, though it may be an allusion to such texts as Exod 19:22 or 29:43 (Kaiser 1994, 1070). **Those who approach me** refers especially to the priests in relation to their service before the Lord in the tabernacle (see Noth 1977, 85).

The Lord's words are commonly understood in reference to the punishment of Nadab and Abihu. The Lord shows himself **holy** by impartial judgment against sinners even though they are close to God. **In the sight of all the people** the Lord **will be honored** so that all will learn to respect God's authority and obey his commands (see Wesley 1765, 375; Levine 1989, 59). The harsh judgment against the priests highlights the high standard and expectation placed on those in positions of leadership and influence. Kiuchi suggests the following translation for the sense of this verse: "When I am sanctified in those who are close to me, then I am honoured before all the people" (1987, 70). Emphasis is placed on the heavy responsibility carried by the priests. When they fail to show God as holy through their right actions, they mar the glory of God before others (Kiuchi 1987, 70; see also Wenham 1979, 155-56; Harrison 1980, 112). This recalls the warning that a priest's actions may bring guilt upon the people and perhaps lead others to sin (→ 4:3).

Milgrom discovered a unique positive rendering of this event. Philo interpreted Nadab and Abihu's deaths as a translation to heaven through God's holy fire.

> It is thus that the priests Nadab and Abihu die in order that they may live, receiving an incorruptible life in exchange for mortal existence, and being translated from the created to the uncreate. Over them a proclamation is uttered betokening immortality, "They died before the Lord" (Lev. X. 2), that is "They came to life," for a corpse may not come into God's presence. And again, "This is that which the Lord hath said, 'I will be sanctified in them that draw nigh unto me'" (Lev. X. 3), "But dead men," as we hear in the Psalms, "shall not praise the Lord" (Psalm cxiii. 25): for that is the work of living men. (*Flight* 59; see also, *Alleg. Interp.* 2.57-58; *Heir* 309; *Dreams* 2.67, 186 + n.)

Milgrom suggests that Philo's interpretation may have also been reflected in the Gospel writers' understanding of the deaths of Nadab and Abihu. The same terminology in this verse (10:3) for God being *sanctified* (shown **holy**) and *glorified* (**honored**) is found in the Lord's prayer ("hallowed [*sanctified*] be your name," Matt 6:9), and Christ's prayer regarding his death ("Father, *glorify* [honor] your name," John 12:28, emphasis added). God's response to Christ, "I have glorified it, and will glorify it again," may refer back to the only other scriptural case in which God had been glorified through the death of his "intimates" (Milgrom 1991, 603-4). Accordingly, God is glorified through the death and resurrection (translation) of his faithful servants. This would require an understanding of Nadab and Abihu's actions as righteous (at least in intent), as reflected in a minor tradition within the rabbinic literature. This tradition claims Nadab and Abihu zealously sought to hasten the appearance of God by offering incense with impure fire. "God rewarded them by consuming them with his pure fire" (635).

■ **4-7** Great-cousins of Nadab and Abihu were summoned to remove their corpses **from the front of the sanctuary.** This suggests that Nadab and Abihu died in front of the tent and not inside (Keil and Delitzsch n.d., 352). However, their attempt to offer incense implies they may have entered the holy place or even the holy of holies (→ v 1). If so, the Levites **Mishael and Elzaphan** would not have been allowed to enter the tent in order to retrieve the bodies. Nahmanides refers to an old rabbinic story that claims that Mishael and Elzaphan cast metal hooks into the holy place in order to snag the bodies and drag them out (in Carasik 2009, 63). Levine offers the simple solution that the two (Nadab and Abihu) were probably struck down as they exited the tent (1989, 60).

The priests Eleazar and Ithamar were not allowed to remove their brothers' bodies because they could not defile themselves by contact with the corpses (see Nahmanides in Carasik 2009, 63). Normally, ordinary priests could become unclean for the sake of a "close relative" (21:1-3), while only the high priest was completely restricted from defiling himself even for "his father or mother" (21:10-11). The high priest is identified as one with **the LORD's anointing oil** on him. Milgrom contends that Aaron's sons were anointed with Aaron (Exod 40:15*a*; see Exod 30:30; Num 3:3), in contrast to successive ordinary priests who were not anointed (Exod 40:15*b*). Accordingly, Aaron's sons uniquely held a status similar to their father (1991, 607, 610-11; see Nahmanides in Carasik 2009, 64; and Porter 1976, 78). In fact, all the restrictions placed on Aaron and his sons in these verses (**do not let your hair become unkempt, do not tear your clothes,** and **do not leave the entrance to the Tent of Meeting**) reflect the regulations imposed upon the high priest, "because he has been dedicated by the anointing oil" (21:10-12).

Tearing one's clothing is commonly associated with mourning (Gen 37:34; Josh 7:6; Judg 11:35; 2 Sam 1:11-12), while it appears that only in Leviticus is **unkempt** hair added as a custom of mourning (Gerstenberger 1996, 122; see Noth 1977, 86). In relation to this particular event, the priests were not allowed to mourn, lest they **die** and **the LORD** become **angry with the whole community.** Mourning for their brothers could be construed as opposition to God's judgment and disregarding their brothers' sin (Wenham 1979, 157; see Gane 2004, 191). Rashbam suggests that God is honored when Aaron exhibits priority upon the service of God above mourning over family (in Lockshin 2001, 54; see Kaiser 1994, 1071). Such radical allegiance to God is reflected in Christ's words, "Anyone who loves his father or mother more than me is not worthy of me; anyone who loves his son or daughter more than me is not worthy of me" (Matt 10:37).

2. Priestly Duties and Priestly Portions (10:8-15)

■ **8-11** This section abruptly changes the subject and interrupts the account regarding the death of Aaron's two sons and the concluding acts of the inauguration of the sacrificial system (see Driver 1910, 45). Rashi points to a possible connection with the previous verses by suggesting that Nadab and Abihu's sin may have been that they were intoxicated when they entered the sanctuary. Therefore, the general instruction is given here to the priests that they **are not to drink wine or other fermented drink** (in Herczeg 1999, 101). However, the sin of Aaron's sons centers on "unauthorized fire" in relation to offering incense. The unusual shift from the Lord speaking through Moses, to the Lord speaking directly to Aaron (only here in all of Leviticus; Wenham 1979, 154), reinforces the recognition of this passage as secondary. The phrase *an everlasting statute for your generations* (*ḥuqqat 'ôlām lĕdōrōtêkem*) is one of the characteristic indicators of the editing activity of the Holiness School. Accordingly, this pericope may have been added to vv 6-7 (see 21:10-12) in order to create a small collection of laws for the priests when on duty (Knohl 1995, 51-52).

Rashi ties the prohibition against drinking to the priestly duties that are subsequently addressed. That is, a priest must not drink anything fermented because it would impair his ability to **distinguish between the holy and the common, between the unclean and the clean,** and to **teach the Israelites.** Similarly Gersonides adds that priests particularly should not teach while drunk, for if they make a mistake while teaching, it may cause much more damage than an ordinary Israelite who teaches (in Carasik 2009, 66).

A person or object may be **holy** (sacred, *qōdeš*) or **common** (*ḥōl*), and **clean** (pure, *ṭāhôr*) or **unclean** (impure, *ṭāmē'*). Thus, it is possible to be holy and clean, or common and clean, or common and unclean. The one combination that is forbidden in the priestly system is holy and unclean. The task of the priests is not only to **distinguish between** these realms but more significantly to enlarge the realms of the holy and the clean while diminishing the spheres of the common and the unclean. This conversion facilitates God's call for Israel to become "a kingdom of priests and a holy nation" (Exod 19:6). This concern is a characteristic feature of the Holiness School, adding to the evidence that these verses may stem from H (Milgrom 1991, 616-17).

■ **12-15** This section initiates the final stage of the inauguration ceremony of the eighth day (ch 9), that is, the eating of the priestly portions. The **grain offering** refers to that which "was for the people" (9:15-17). That it was to be eaten by the "male" descendants of Aaron, **prepared without yeast,** recognized as **most holy,** and eaten **in a holy place,** follows the regulations in 6:16-18 (6:9-11 HB).

In contrast, both the **sons** *and* **daughters** of the priest may eat the priestly portions from the Israelites' ***well-being*** offerings. The **breast that was waved** (*těnûpâ*) and the **thigh that was presented** (*těrûmâ*) refer to the priestly portions of the people's *well-being* offering from the inauguration ceremony (9:18-21). The two types of priestly portions are confused when both the presented thigh (*těrûmâ*) and the waved breast (*těnûpâ*) are to be **waved,** with the fat portions, **as a wave offering** (*těnûpâ*; re the distinction between *těnûpâ* and *těrûmâ*, → 7:28-34). The same confusion of these portions is expressed in the inauguration ceremony in which both the "breasts and the right thigh" are treated "as a wave offering" (9:21; → 9:18-21).

3. Eleazar and Ithamar (10:16-20)

■ **16-18** The **goat of the *purification*** **offering** refers to "the goat for the people's ***purification*** offering" from the inauguration service (9:15). The flesh from the calf that served as a purification offering for the priest was burnt outside the camp, and not eaten, because a priest may not benefit from a sacrifice offered on his own behalf (→ 4:11-12 and 6:29-30 [6:22-23 HB]). However, it seems that the goat for the people's purification offering should have been eaten by the priests **since its blood was not taken into the Holy Place** (see 6:24-26, 30 [6:17-19, 23 HB]; re why the blood from this offering was not taken into the holy place, → 9:9-11, 15).

Aaron treated the people's offering "as he did the first one" (9:15; i.e., the calf for the priest). As a result, Moses **was angry with Eleazar and Ithamar** because they did not **eat the *purification*** **offering** for the people. Moses explains to the priests, **it was given to you to take away the guilt of**

the community. This is often understood to mean that by eating the flesh of the sacrifice, to which sin or impurity has been transferred, the priest effectively removes the iniquity (see von Rad 1962, 248; Levine 1989, 62-63; Milgrom 1991, 624-25; Gane 2005, 91-99). However, as held herein, sin and impurity are not transferred to the carcass or flesh of the sacrifice (→ 4:11-12 and sidebar, "Why Priests Eat the Meat of the Purification Offering," below).

This particular phrase (**it was given to you to take away the guilt of the community**) does not refer to eating the flesh of the sacrifice. Rather, it refers to the whole ritual, especially the blood manipulation, through which the **guilt of the community** is removed **by making atonement for them.** Thus, eating the purification offering is not part of the atoning process. This is affirmed by the fact that the atonement for the people was not invalidated by the priests' failure to eat the meat of the sacrifice (Kiuchi 1987, 51-52, 72). The priest does serve to remove the iniquity of Israel, but he does so by "purging the sanctuary with the blood of the purification offering, in reward for which he receives its meat" (Milgrom 1991, 625; Milgrom's original view as opposed to his later stance). The reason for needing to eat the purification offering is given in v 18 (i.e., **since its blood was not taken into the Holy Place**).

Why Priests Eat the Meat of the Purification Offering 10:16-18

Milgrom argues that the blood of the purification offering removes impurities that are then transferred to the carcass of the animal. The meat of the animal is eaten by the priests in order to refute the ancient world's superstitious belief that ritual detergents and the impurities they bear were powerful and harmful. By eating the meat of the sacrificial animal without harm, the priests of Israel demonstrated that the real power to purge and forgive sin and impurity depends completely on the will of God, and not on the ritual itself. Furthermore, this profound act on the part of the priests provides an object lesson that proclaims that holiness and life (represented by the priests) swallows/defeats impurity and death (1991, 625, 637-38). This message is so significant that Moses became angry when it was omitted on the occasion of the inauguration ceremony, because the priests did not eat the meat of the people's purification offering. Milgrom explains that Moses "was afraid that the priests would thereby engender the suspicion that they were indeed afraid of the harm that might befall them if they ate the impurity-laden meat of the purification offering, a belief that was current in Israel's contemporary world but which P assiduously attempted to eradicate" (1991, 639).

Up to this point, Milgrom provides a powerful explanation consistent with the priestly material. However, he compromises, and practically overturns, his point when discussing the difference between the purification offering that must be eaten, and that which must be burned. He argues that the purification offering whose blood is taken into the holy place represents a higher degree of impurity and is indeed too dangerous to be ingested by the priests, and therefore must be burned (263, 637). If this proves true, then the superstitious belief "which P assiduously attempted to eradicate" would only be reaffirmed (furthermore, → 4:11-12)!

A key to understanding this aspect of the sacrificial system (a representative system) lies in recognizing that indeed the blood serves to purge and remove sins and impurities; however, there is no transfer of defilement to the carcass or flesh of the sacrificial animal. The fact that the fat of the purification offering is burnt on the altar to the Lord, and that the priests eat its flesh as a most holy thing, contradicts the theory that the sacrifice is loaded with sin or impurity (de Vaux 1997, 419). Having the priests eat the flesh of the sacrifice without harm to themselves is intended to demonstrate this very point. That is, there is in actuality no sin or impurity with its inherent danger present in the carcass or flesh of the sacrifice, because it was simply removed by the blood rite. This may suggest that the power of the blood has absorbed and overcome the threat of sin and impurity. However, as with the priest who administers atonement through sacrifice, the blood is only representative of the power of God who is the actual source of cleansing, forgiveness, holiness, and life!

In the case of the purification offerings from which blood is taken into the holy place, and of which flesh is not eaten by the priests (6:30 [6:23 HB]), it must be remembered that they serve to atone for the priest (4:3-12) and the community of which the priest is a part (4:13-21). In such cases, the priest is not allowed to benefit (by eating) from a sacrifice offered on his own behalf (→ 4:11-12; 6:29-30 [6:22-23 HB]). As back-to-back purification offerings are presented separately for priest and congregation on the Day of Atonement, it appears that the priest is doubly atoned. First, he and his household are atoned by a bull for the priest, and second he is atoned with a goat for the congregation of which he and his family are a part. This serves to maintain the principle that, in his role as priest, the priest must be cleansed first, before he can effectively facilitate the cleansing of the community. At the same time, the priest is recognized as a member of the larger community that is called to be a "kingdom of priests and a holy nation" (Exod 19:6).

■ **19-20** Aaron's response to Moses begins with a reminder that his sons (including Nadab and Abihu) had **sacrificed their sin offering and their burnt offering before the Lord**. What was supposed to be a joyous occasion (9:24) had turned to sorrow because in Aaron's words, **such things as this have happened to me.** Hizkuni understands Aaron as saying that the priests (his own sons) who were to help him eat the purification offering have died (10:2), and therefore he cannot be expected to carry on as usual this day (in Carasik 2009, 68). Wesley notes an additional concern for the acceptability of eating the offering, expressed by Aaron's inquiry, **would the Lord have been pleased if I had eaten the sin offering today?** That is, it may have been inappropriate to eat the offering in a state of sorrow, when the occasion was intended to convey joy and thanksgiving (1765, 377).

Levine suggests that Aaron's response recognizes that the priests were not allowed to eat the meat of sacrifices while in mourning (Deut 26:14; see Ibn Ezra in Carasik 2009, 69). While Moses approves in this case, he nevertheless reassures Aaron that priestly duties take precedence over personal bereavement. Therefore, priests are forbidden to mourn (Lev 10:6; Levine 1989, 63).

Others contend that behind Aaron's inquiry is a concern that, as officiating priest for the day, he too bears guilt for the sin of his sons (Noth 1977, 88); or due to the incorrect ritual of his sons, it would be too dangerous to proceed with sacrificial acts (Porter 1976, 81); or due to the pollution of the sanctuary from the corpses of Nadab and Abihu, the purification offering changed status from an edible offering to one that must be burned and not eaten (Milgrom 1991, 639). According to the instructions for purification offerings, this offering should already have been recognized as one that must be burned and not eaten. It was a purification offering for the community, the blood from which should have been brought into the holy place, and therefore not allowed to be eaten (4:13-21; 6:30 [6:23 HB]). However, confusion ensued because this particular occasion of the "founding" of the sacrificial system could not follow standard protocol for the application of the blood from the sacrifices (→ 9:9-11). In the end, **when Moses heard this, he was satisfied.**

FROM THE TEXT

The ordination ceremony further reflects the foundational theme of relationship. The ordination offering culminates in a meal of fellowship and community between God and the priests (8:31). The themes of separation and holiness are also reflected in the priestly ordination rite. The tabernacle, and everything in it, is consecrated (lit. "made holy") for service unto the Lord. The altar is purified (separated from sin and impurity; lit. "de-sinned") and also consecrated. Likewise Aaron and his sons are purified and consecrated for service unto the Lord. The stringent concern to separate the unclean from the clean remains evident throughout the rite.

The ordination of the priests assigned them to a new status. They transitioned from the common world into the sacred realm (de Vaux 1997, 347-48; Grabbe 2003, 213). In light of the tradition of "the priesthood of all believers," reflected in Israel's call to become "a kingdom of priests and a holy nation" (Exod 19:6), the conversion from common to holy should be the pursuit of all those who fear the Lord. One's task may not involve service in the sanctuary, or the sacrifice of animals; nevertheless, daily routines should reflect the purification of one's being and the consecration of life in relationship to God. The ordination ceremony of the priests highlights God's concern for separation *from* all that which is profane and separation *to* holiness (being "set apart") in the service of the Lord.

In tension with the common call to priesthood (kingdom of priests), the particular sense of accountability and responsibility held by the designated priests continues to be evident in the sacrificial system. The seven-day ordination period serves to set the priests apart. In addition, the order of sacrifices in the inauguration ceremony requires the priest to make atonement for himself before doing so for the people (9:7; see Wenham 1979, 149). This calls to mind the present-day instructions repeated before every commercial flight that require you to "secure your own mask before trying to help another." The priest himself must first be right with God before he is able to serve and intercede on behalf of the people. This principle compels God's children, especially those in positions of leadership and influence, to diligently maintain their own right relationship with God.

The inauguration ceremony of the eighth day of ordination extends the sense of fellowship and communion to the laity as it culminates with a well-being offering. God, priest, and people celebrate together through a shared meal. The dramatic appearance of the glory of the Lord completes the ceremony with an emphasis on joy and worship (9:23-24).

With ordination and inauguration, the tabernacle and the sacrificial system are officially launched for service and worship. The dramatic manifestation of God's glory before all the people, and the Lord's indwelling of the holy of holies, center the presence of God in the midst of the community. Through this representative system, God has provided a means for enriching relationship through devotion, thanksgiving, atonement, and reparation; all worthy of a response of joyful celebration.

The account of the deaths of Nadab and Abihu (ch 10) is a sober reminder of the biblical tension between guarded holiness and sacrificial mercy. The death of the priests reminds contemporary servants of the Lord of the exhortation to be above reproach (1 Tim 3:2-13). The account also serves to invoke the warning regarding the stricter judgment directed against those who teach, due to their influence over others (Kaiser 1994, 1073). The restriction from mourning over Nadab and Abihu in deference to the priority of priestly service evokes Christ's call to absolute allegiance (Matt 8:21-22; Wenham 1979, 160). Among his instructions to his disciples, Jesus states, "Anyone who loves his father or mother more than me is not worthy of me; anyone who loves his son or daughter more than me is not worthy of me" (Matt 10:37).

Gane reminds us that stories such as Nadab and Abihu, and the death of Uzzah for touching the ark when trying to steady it (2 Sam 6:6-7), are difficult and shocking in light of other accounts emphasizing God's wondrous grace and mercy. Even the "meek and mild" Jesus burst into messianic rage when driving the money changers out of the temple area (2004, 194). Such accounts reflect a profound tension between the sovereignty, holiness, and majesty of almighty God, which is stringently guarded in some texts; and the grace, mercy, and sacrificial love that is overwhelmingly evident in other passages. This God, who so fiercely defends purity, rejecting all encroachments of defilement, is the same God who, in Christ, *defiles* himself by associating with sinners (Matt 9:11), touching lepers (Matt 8:2-3), and ultimately dying on a tree (Gal 3:13; Deut 21:23) in order to reconcile relationships with his creatures!

III. IMPURITY LAWS (11:1—15:33)

BEHIND THE TEXT

At first glance chs 11—15 seem to interrupt the treatment of the sacrificial system in chs 1—10 culminating in the annual Day of Atonement ceremony in ch 16. However, the discussion of the impurity laws (chs 11—15) is rightly placed as evidenced by two connections that link back to the previous material and forward to ch 16 respectively. A central concern of the impurity laws is to distinguish between the clean and the unclean, a task assigned to the priests in 10:10. The cleansing at the heart of the Day of Atonement includes purging impurities such as those detailed in chs 11—15 (see 16:16; Kaiser 1994, 1074). Leviticus 15:31 in particular anticipates the cleansing of the tabernacle in ch 16.

Opening and closing formulas appear to organize chs 11—15 into six sections. The "command formula" *wayĕdabbēr YHWH 'el-mōšeh* ("**And** the Lord **spoke** to Moses"), which defines the parameters of the priestly legislation as a whole (King 2009, 23-26), appears at 11:1; 12:1; 13:1; 14:1, 33; and 15:1. The concluding formula *zō't tôrat* ("these are the regulations"; → Behind the Text for 6:8—7:38 [6:1—7:38 HB], where this phrase serves as an introductory formula) appears at 11:46; 12:7; 13:59; 14:32, 57; and 15:32 (Gerstenberger 1996, 129). In the discussion below, however, the divisions beginning at 14:1 and 14:33 will be treated as subsections of 13:1, because chs 13—14 are united by their common treatment of forms or appearances of *ṣāra'at* ("skin disease"). The impurity laws involve dietary restrictions, childbirth, skin disease, and sexual discharges.

IN THE TEXT

A. Dietary Restrictions (11:1-47)

1. Land, Water, and Sky Creatures (11:1-23)

■ **1-3** Land animals that the Israelites may eat are identified by two criteria: **any animal that has a split hoof completely divided and that chews the cud.** Leviticus 11 presumes that sacrificial animals (cattle, sheep, goats) are recognized as permissible to eat. Therefore, they are not specifically listed here (Milgrom 1991, 647). In fact, the criteria may derive from using sacrificial animals as the model for identifying all animals that may be eaten (Firmage 1990, 188).

■ **4-7** Animals that **only chew the cud or only have a split hoof** must not be eaten. Edible animals include only those exhibiting both criteria. Those animals that do not qualify by either lacking both criteria or displaying only one are designated **unclean** (*ṭāmē'*). Calvin is correct in affirming that no animal is unclean/impure in itself. Animals are designated unclean only in relation to whether or not they may be eaten. God declared all animals "good," as part of a "very good" creation (Gen 1:25, 31; Calvin n.d., 63). The **rabbit** and **coney** (rock badger) are not true ruminants (chew cud), but they appear to be due to the movement of their jaws when eating (Harrison 1980, 121; Milgrom 1991, 648).

■ **8** The statement **you must not eat their meat** repeats the prohibition in v 4, forming an inclusio emphasizing the rejection of these animals (see vv 4-7) as food (Milgrom 1991, 653; for a detailed discussion re the rejection of the pig, see 649-53).

It is also forbidden to **touch their carcasses, for they are unclean** (*ṭāmē'*). This adds to the mainly dietary focus of this passage, the general prohibition against touching death (dead bodies of humans or animals). Nahmanides clarifies that the prohibition is not strictly concerned with *touching* a corpse, but rather with warning that doing so will make one unclean. An unclean person must wash before doing anything that requires purity, such as approaching the sanctuary or eating consecrated food (in Carasik 2009, 72; see Rashbam in Lockshin 2001, 60-61). Touching an *animal* corpse requires washing and waiting until evening in order to become clean again (vv 24-25, 27-28, 31, 39-40; 22:4-8). Touching a *human* corpse requires washing and waiting *seven days* to become pure again (Num 19:11-13). Defilement from contact with corpses is not limited to animals that are unclean for food, but also applies to edible animals when they die naturally (Lev 11:39; Keil and Delitzsch n.d., 360). This affirms that the regulation reflects the general concern to avoid impurity from touching death in the form of any corpse.

■ **9-12** Water creatures that may be eaten are identified by two criteria (→ vv 1-3): **any that have fins and scales.** Water creatures are divided into those **among all the swarming things** and those **among all the other living creatures in the water.** In either category, if the water creature **does not have fins and scales,** it is to be detested. Kaiser proposes that the detestable fish are scavengers that dwell in mud bottoms and may carry parasites (1994, 1081).

The term *šereṣ* (**swarming things**) is applied to certain water creatures (v 10), flying creatures (vv 20-21, 23), and land creatures (vv 29, 31, 41-44). The concept of "swarming" may refer to their tendency to creep or crawl (e.g., eels and reptiles; Budd 1996, 165-66) or reflect how they dart to and fro in an unpredictable, haphazard fashion (Wenham 1979, 175, 178). Alternatively, swarming may signify that such creatures normally appear in a multitude (Keil and Delitzsch n.d., 366). Douglas suggests that swarming should be understood as "teeming" in relation to life and reproduction (1999, 159-63).

In conjunction with the focus on dietary restrictions, Israelites **must not eat their meat** (i.e., that of water creatures without fins and scales). In conjunction with the general prohibition against touching corpses (→ v 8), Israel also **must detest their carcasses.** Water creatures (vv 9-12), flying creatures (vv 13-23), and swarming land creatures (vv 41-42) are designated *šeqeṣ* (**detestable**); as opposed to *ṭāmē'* ("unclean"), the designation for impure land animals (vv 4-8). Nevertheless, animals that are *šeqeṣ* ("detestable") still cause one to become *ṭāmē'* ("unclean"), as indicated by the phrase *šeqeṣ ṭāmē'* ("unclean, detestable thing," 7:21) and by the warning against making oneself *ṭāmē'* ("unclean") by means of creatures that are *šeqeṣ* ("detestable," 11:41-43; in contrast to Milgrom 1991, 656-59, also 425-26). Douglas contends that *šeqeṣ* ("abomination") should be understood as "shun" or "avoid." In relation to the "teeming" ("swarming") creatures representing life and fertility, God instructs Israel to stay out of their way, and not harm them, much less eat them (1999, 166-67; also re "abomination" as "shun," see Noth 1977, 93).

■ **13-19 These are the birds** introduces the list of sky creatures that Israel is **to detest and not eat.** No criteria is given to identify edible birds (→ vv 1-3 and vv 9-12). Rather, a specific list of inedible birds is recorded. All other birds are permissible to eat (see Milgrom 1991, 657). The list of prohibited birds and reptiles is difficult to identify with accuracy (Wenham 1979, 164). It is complicated by the rare occurrence of some of the Hebrew terms for the creatures. Eight of the twenty-four names for birds occur only here and in Deut 14 (two of the terms occur only in Lev 11). Five additional names occur only three times in the entire OT (Gerstenberger 1996, 137; nevertheless, for a discussion of each named bird in ch 11, see Milgrom 1991, 662-64).

Nahmanides explains that the rabbis determined characteristics shared by the forbidden birds. They hunt, seize living prey with their claws, and eat as carnivores (in Carasik 2009, 73-74). Wesley adds that forbidden birds are ravenous and cruel, or delight in darkness. Thus, the prohibitions serve to teach people to shun all cruelty, oppression, and the works of darkness (1765, 379-80). The forbidden birds are also considered unclean because they are scavengers that eat carrion (Toombs 1962, 645; Wenham 1979, 170).

■ **20-23 Flying insects that walk on all fours** are added to the list of creatures considered **to be detestable** (*šeqeṣ*, → vv 9-12). These are the "swarming things" (*šereṣ*) among the flying creatures (→ vv 9-12; **flying insects** [v 20] translates what is literally *winged swarming things*, see NET, NJPS). An exception is made for *flying swarming creatures* that **have jointed legs for hopping.** Thus, insects that have the ability to hop as opposed to simply crawling when **on the ground** are permissible to eat (Wenham 1979, 175). Four such insects are listed, which are varieties of the **locust** (BDB describes each of the four Hebrew terms as a kind of locust/grasshopper [1952, 290, 353, 701, 916]). The third term in the Greek Bible (LXX, v 22) is the same as that used in Matt 3:4 and Mark 1:6 where the diet of John the Baptist is described as "*locusts* and wild honey" (emphasis added).

2. Unclean Animals and Purification Procedures (11:24-40)

■ **24-25** Israel is instructed that **you will make yourselves unclean by these.** Noth contends that this refers to, not only the most recently mentioned creatures, but also to all previously mentioned animals in ch 11 (1977, 94). It particularly applies to the creatures designated *šeqeṣ* ("detestable," vv 9-23; → vv 9-12; in contrast to Milgrom 1991, 667). The inedible land animals have already been identified as *ṭāmē'* ("unclean," vv 4-8). Here, all inedible creatures are designated *ṭāmē'* ("unclean"), and abbreviated instructions are included regarding the remedy for uncleanness. **Whoever touches their carcasses will be unclean till evening.** Ibn Ezra adds that it is understood that such a person must also bathe in water (in Carasik 2009, 76; see also Milgrom 1991, 667-68; see Lev 17:15; 22:6; and → 11:8). In addition, **whoever picks up one of their carcasses must wash his clothes, and he will be unclean till evening.** Evidently *carrying* a carcass makes one's *clothing* unclean, as opposed to simple contact with a carcass.

■ **26-28** These verses extend the instructions related to land animals (vv 2-8). Reinforcing the criteria of "a split hoof completely divided" and "chews the cud"; the text now addresses animals that may have **a split hoof, but it is not completely divided.** This is distinct from the discussion in vv 4-8 that dealt with animals with a completely divided split hoof (v 7) or no split hoof at all (vv 4-6; see Milgrom 1991, 647-48).

Whoever touches the carcass of any of them will be unclean. The NIV follows the Greek Bible (LXX) by adding **the carcass of** to the Hebrew text. This makes the regulation consistent with the rest of the chapter (see vv 8, 24, 27, 36, 39). In addition, it corrects the wrong impression that merely touching an inedible *live* animal makes one unclean (see Hartley 1992, 161).

Another category of unclean land animals is introduced as **those that walk on their paws.** These might include dogs, monkeys, bears, lions, and wolves (Budd 1996, 175). Anyone who touches the carcasses of these, or of the previously mentioned animals, **will be unclean till evening;** that is, if they bathe first (Nahmanides in Carasik 2009, 77; → vv 8, 24-25). **Anyone who picks up their carcasses must wash his clothes.** Carrying an animal carcass requires not only bathing one's body but also washing one's clothing (→ vv 24-25).

■ **29-38** The phrase **animals that move about on the ground** renders what might literally be translated *swarmers that swarm upon the earth*. This section introduces "swarming things" (*šereṣ*) of the land (→ vv 9-12). Among such creatures, eight are listed as **unclean for you.** In light of the concern that such creatures might fall on or into pots, ovens, or seeds; it is commonly held that these eight are small rodents and reptiles that might regularly be found in the kitchen (e.g., mice and lizards; see Toombs 1962, 645; Wenham 1979, 178; Milgrom 1991, 671). **Whoever touches them when they are dead will be unclean till evening.** This presumes that the person must also bathe (→ v 8 and vv 24-25; also Milgrom 1991, 672).

When one of them dies and falls on something, that thing **will be unclean.** However, **put it in water; it will be unclean till evening, and then it will be clean.** This reflects the general regulation to avoid impurity from touching death in the form of a corpse (→ v 8). In this case, the impurity stemming from a carcass is transmitted to articles upon which it may fall. Just like a person who touches a carcass, the article upon which a carcass falls may become clean through washing ("put it in water") and waiting until evening. If one of these creatures **falls into a clay pot,** any food or liquid from the pot **will be unclean.** Even allowable food that **has water on it from such a pot is unclean.** The pot itself "must be broken" (→ 6:27-28 [6:20-21 HB]). Similarly, an **oven or *stove* must be broken up** (NIV renders *kîrayim* as **cooking pot**; however, it is commonly translated "stove"; see NASB, NET, NJPS, NKJV, NRSV; Kimhi explains the dual form of the term refers to a stove made to hold two pots [in Carasik 2009, 79]). Like the clay pot, an oven or stove would be made of earthenware (Milgrom 1991, 679).

A spring, however, or a cistern for collecting water remains clean, even if one of these creatures dies and falls into them. Keil and Delitzsch reason that springs and wells would not be defiled because the fresh supply of water would continually wash away uncleanness (n.d., 371). Gane clarifies that a spring or cistern is a source of purity and cannot be defiled (2004, 216).

If a carcass falls on any seeds . . . they remain clean; unless water has been put on the seed, then **it is unclean.** This reverses the usual understanding that water cleanses impurity. In this case, water becomes a means of transmitting impurity, or at least creating conditions that bring about impurity. Nahmanides explains that wetness causes uncleanness to stick to food that would otherwise be dry and clean (in Carasik 2009, 80). More specifically in relation to seed, the regulation may reflect the concern that impurity would penetrate the softened grains of wet seed (Keil and Delitzsch n.d., 371).

■ **39-40** If an animal that you are allowed to eat dies, anyone who touches the carcass will be unclean. Up to this point, the restriction regarding touching a carcass has been expressed in relation to animals that should not be eaten (vv 8, 11, 24, 26-27, 31). Here, the same restriction is applied to animals that are permissible to eat. Though they are clean for eating, their carcasses will impart impurity. This affirms the general regulation that contact with death causes impurity (→ vv 8, 29-38). Touching the carcass will make a person unclean **till evening**. The person is also required to bathe (→ vv 8, 24-25).

Anyone who eats some of the carcass must wash his clothes, and he will be unclean till evening. Wesley rightly notes that this pericope applies to animals that die naturally or are killed by other wild animals. In such cases, the blood would not be properly drained (1765, 382). This is made explicit in 17:15, which states that anyone "who eats anything found dead or torn by wild animals must wash his clothes and bathe with water, and he will be ceremonially unclean till evening." Notice that 17:15 clearly stipulates all three components for becoming clean again: bathing, washing clothes, and waiting till evening. Normally, washing clothes is only required when someone **picks up the carcass.** In this case, however, the concern includes *eating* from a permissible animal, though one that has died. As with *carrying* a carcass, *eating* from an animal that has died causes greater impurity than merely touching the carcass (→ vv 24-25).

This regulation does not apply to animals that are slaughtered for sacrifice or hunted as game. In such cases, even the carcasses do not convey impurity, for they are eligible for the altar or designated for human consumption. Sacrificial animals are dedicated to the Lord, and their blood is properly poured out at the altar. The only requirement that remains for permissible hunted animals is that a person "must drain out the blood and cover it with earth" (17:13).

3. Land Swarmers (11:41-45)

■ **41-43** Every creature that moves about on the ground (*swarmers that swarm upon the earth*) constitutes the entire category of animals *from which* the eight rodents and lizards specified in vv 29-30 are designated as unclean. The eight creatures discussed in vv 29-38 are distinguished as small "kitchen" creatures that might fall into kitchen utensils (→ vv 29-38). Here, the entire set of **swarming things** (*šereṣ*) of the land are designated **detestable** (*šeqeṣ*). This corresponds with the detestable character of inedible water and flying creatures (→ vv 9-12). As such, they are **not to be eaten.** This is the case for any **land swarmer,** whether it moves on its belly or walks on all fours or on many feet.

Verse 43 emphatically stipulates that this category of animal conveys uncleanness (*ṭāmēʾ*; → vv 9-12). The detestable (*šeqeṣ*) character of these animals is reflected in the imperative statement, **do not defile yourselves** (lit. **make yourselves detestable** [*tĕšaqqĕṣû*]; see NRSV) **by any of these** creatures. This is followed by the seemingly repetitive statement, **do not make yourselves unclean** [*tiṭṭammě'û*] **by means of them or be made unclean** [*niṭmētem;* with alef missing; see Milgrom 1991, 685] **by them.**

■ **44-45** Knohl identifies the phrase **I am the LORD your God** (*'ănî YHWH 'ĕlōhêkem*) as "the characteristic signature of HS" (Holiness School); and the shortened version, "I am the LORD" (*'ănî YHWH*), as "the distinguishing concluding formula of HS" (1995, 38, 16, also 9, 54; see also Kuenen 1886, 88-89; Driver 1910, 49; King 2009, 126-27). God's call to **be holy, because I am holy** is also representative of the Holiness Code (19:2; 20:26; 21:8). Accordingly, these verses reflect the editorial hands of the Holiness School (→ Behind the Text for ch 17).

Do not make yourselves unclean by any creature that moves about on the ground. Synonymous with **swarmers that swarm upon the earth** (→ vv 29-38), the phrase here is literally "*swarmers* (*šereṣ*) that move about upon the earth" (*rōmēś* in place of *šōrēṣ;* see BDB 1952, 942-43; Milgrom 1991, 687).

The Holiness School grounds the dietary restrictions in the call to be holy. Wesley affirms that God's creatures are not unclean in themselves; rather, the legislation serves to provide lessons in holiness through diligent obedience (1765, 382; → vv 4-7).

4. Summation (11:46-47)

■ **46-47** The formula **these are the regulations** (*zō't tôrat*) links the dietary restrictions to laws directed to the priests (→ Behind the Text for 6:8—7:38 [6:1—7:38 HB]). In this case, the regulations are for the priests to teach to the people (11:1-2; see 10:10-11; Milgrom 1991, 688).

The regulations are summarized as those **concerning animals, birds, every living thing that moves** [*rōmeśet*] **in the water and every creature that moves about** [lit. "swarms"; *šōreṣet*] **on the ground.** Israel is instructed to **distinguish between the unclean and the clean** (see 10:10-11). Accordingly, they will differentiate **between living creatures that may be eaten and those that may not be eaten.** Separating the pure and the impure reflects Israel's call to separate itself from the nations in order to be holy to the Lord as stated explicitly in 20:25-26 (Milgrom 1991, 689).

Rationale for the Dietary Restrictions

A common rationale applied to the food laws emphasizes their health benefits. Gersonides suggests that God wished for Israel to avoid foods that "block the intellect from operation" (in Carasik 2009, 72). Rashbam argues that the prohibited foods "damage and heat up the body," a contention with which he claimed physicians concur (in Lockshin 2001, 59-60). Some modern scholars have adopted this same view, claiming that medical studies confirm that the impure animals are shown to be unhealthy. The unclean animals are most susceptible to carrying infection and disease, stimulating allergic reactions, and hosting parasitic infestations. The related requirement to wash after contact with a corpse or carcass reflects the need to eliminate germs, viruses, and harmful organisms (Harrison 1980, 124-27, 130-33).

Calvin opposes such a view, claiming that God had in mind more important concerns than physical health (n.d., 65). Even earlier, Abarbanel asserts that the dietary laws should not be understood as health regulations. He reasons that the Torah does not prohibit toxic plants, and other nations eat that which is forbidden to Israel while remaining perfectly healthy. Thus, these rules deal with the welfare of the soul, and not the body (in Carasik 2009, 82).

Douglas explains the dietary restrictions on the basis of anthropological studies. She claims that the dietary laws of Lev 11 represent cultural provisions for dealing with anomalous creatures. That is, creatures that do not fit the basic categorical norms set forth in the creation account defy the created order and are therefore unclean and unfit for consumption (1966, 38-57; see also Soler 1979, 24-30). Following this approach, Coote and Ord recognize that acceptable animals are those that portray the characteristics that are normative for a creature in its prescribed environment (i.e., land, air, or water). Any creature that deviates from its intended realm was considered unclean. Correspondence with a particular venue was determined mainly by means of locomotion. Thus, edible land animals are identified by hooves for walking, sea creatures by fins for swimming, and sky creatures by wings for flying. Animals that do not abide by such characteristics represent anomalies and are therefore unclean. For example, shellfish do not swim with fins through water; and the ostrich, though a feathered bird, walks on land but does not fly (1991, 63-65; see also Porter 1976, 84). Linking the rationale for the dietary laws to an intended order of creation insinuates that the anomalous prohibited creatures are somehow defective or inadequate. This contradicts God's judgment that all creatures are "good," and indeed the entire creation is "very good" (Gen 1:20-21, 24-25, 31; for a more detailed critique of Douglas's argument, see Carroll 1985, 118-20).

11:46-47

Douglas has since shifted her argument so that the dietary laws serve to promote honor to God and loyalty to God's covenant. Permissible foods are restricted to those that can be offered to God upon the altar. As a feudal lord, God is honored when his subjects consume a diet restricted to that which God has decreed acceptable. Douglas understands Israel's diet to be limited to the domestic flocks and herds of the people (1999, 134-51, 174). This argument appears to exclude the hunting of wild animals for food. However, hunting animals for food is permissible, so long as the blood is properly drained (17:13).

The only explicit rationale expressed in the text of Lev 11 connects the dietary restrictions to Israel's call to be a holy people (vv 44-45). Firmage argues that the identification of clean creatures begins with domestic animals common to the ordinary human diet and customary as sacrificial animals. This socioeconomic preference was transformed into the key element for Israel's religious dietary scheme. This served to distinguish Israel from the nations and thereby advance Israel's call to holiness. Sacrificial animals served as the model for what is clean and acceptable to eat. Accordingly, the criteria of cloven-hoof and rumination characterized land animals that resemble the sacrificial model. In the case of fish (no sacrificial model to follow) and birds (no criteria listed), the notion of using *sacrificial* animals as a model for permissible foods begins to break down (1990, 184-90).

Nevertheless, the theme of holiness and separation from the nations seems to be a foundational concern undergirding the dietary restrictions. Calvin asserts that the focus of the dietary laws is to "set apart" Israel as holy, distinct from her neighbors (n.d., 60). A number of scholars argue that the animals labeled unclean for Israel were used for idolatrous sacrifice, or considered holy, by foreign cults (von Rad 1962, 27, 208-9; Toombs 1962, 643; Noth 1977, 92). Clearly, Israel was called to distance itself from such practices.

Kaiser extends Israel's call to holiness beyond just the religious sphere, to include separation in relation to every aspect of life, even the mundane act of eating (Kaiser 1994, 1074, 1082). The creation account implies an original intention that all creatures eat as vegetarians/herbivores (Gen 1:29-30). Following the flood, however, God expanded the human diet to include animal meat, so long as the blood was drained (Gen 9:2-4). Thus, humanity is allowed to eat all animals. Israel, however, is restricted to only those animals that are designated pure (Lev 11). A still more limited number of animals are eligible to be sacrificed upon the altar as holy to the Lord (22:17-25). The sphere of permissible animals for consumption shrinks when moving from humanity (all), to Israel (clean animals), to the altar for the Lord (domestic and unblemished, clean animals). This serves to distinguish and separate Israel from the nations (rest of humanity). This is made explicit in 20:24b-26: "I am the LORD your God, who has set you apart from the nations. You must therefore make a distinction between clean and unclean animals and between unclean and clean birds. Do not defile yourselves by any animal or bird or anything that moves along the ground—those which I have set apart as unclean for you. You are to be holy to me because I, the LORD, am holy, and I have set you apart from the nations to be my own" (see Milgrom 1991, 721-25).

Wesley affirms that every creature is good and pure in itself, but that God was pleased to distinguish between clean and unclean animals for a number of reasons. Among them, Wesley includes the separation of Israel from other nations. He also suggests that restraining Israel's appetite in things lawful (eating meat) might better enable the children of Israel to deny themselves in things grossly sinful (1765, 378). While this speaks directly to promoting self-discipline, it also contributes to the broader concept of restraint for the sake of some higher concern. Levine points to a socioreligious intent that alludes to denigrating that which is carnivorous, or threatening to humanity. He contends that ideally humans should be sustained from the produce of the earth. When living creatures are consumed for food, they should be restricted to those that sustain themselves from that which grows on the earth. Animals that prey on other living creatures or attack humans should be rejected as unclean. As a result, Israel is separated from the beasts, and their humaneness is enhanced (1989, 248). Similarly, Keil and Delitzsch assert that the prohibited animals (beasts of prey, snakelike fishes, slimy shellfish, crawlers that feed in mire and filth) exhibit a dark type of sin, death, and corruption. Thus, the dietary restrictions represent an ethical foundation, rather than sanitary concerns (n.d., 372).

In the midst of an extensive discussion detailing the ethical foundations of the dietary restrictions, Milgrom reveals the central rationale of Israel's diet as "reverence for life" (1991, 704-42). The dietary laws limit the choice of meat to only a few animals, restrict the slaughter of such animals to the most humane means, and prohibit the eating of blood as "acknowledgment that bringing death to living things is a concession of God's grace and not a privilege of man's whim" (1991, 735). Douglas argues that the "swarming" creatures should be understood as "teeming" in relation to life and reproduction. She defines "abominating" such creatures as "shunning" or "avoiding" them. She concludes that God requires Israel to avoid such creatures, stay out of their way, and not harm them (much less eat them). This reflects God's protection for these creatures, which represent life and fertility (1999, 152-75). Houston maintains that the dietary laws are part of a larger structure of moral and cosmological thought serving to maintain Israel's holiness. Within such, the priestly writers recognized that eating cannot be separated from morality, human appetites must be restrained, and God's creatures should be treated with respect (2003, 160). He concludes that "perhaps the most important moral lesson we need to learn is that to preserve the 'integrity of creation' we must discipline our appetites, place limits upon our desires, even more now that there appears to be no limit to our power to satisfy them" (2003, 161).

B. Childbirth (12:1-8)

■ 1-2 When a woman **gives birth to a son, she will be ceremonially unclean.** The adverb **ceremonially** is added by the NIV and the NRSV, presumably to clarify that childbirth is not a sin or *moral* impurity, but simply a ritual state. The birth itself is not what makes the woman unclean, but rather the flow of blood associated with childbirth creates the state of impurity. Though life is brought forth in birth, the flow of blood represents the loss of life (Gorman 1997, 78; see Wenham 1979, 188). Designating the loss of blood as impurity aligns with the assertion that Israel's impurity laws are intended to promote reverence for life (→ From the Text below).

The period of uncleanness for giving birth to a **son is seven days, just as she is unclean during her monthly period** (see 15:19). The connection to menstruation affirms that the source of impurity is loss of blood. **Seven days** marks the period of *severe* impurity during which time contact with the common is avoided. Thus, a woman in this state is a source of impurity (15:19-24; see Wenham 1979, 186; and Milgrom 1991, 749). This period of severe impurity terminates with bathing in water. Though it is not explicit in the text, bathing in water is assumed (→ 11:8). Milgrom argues that such washing takes place after this first seven-day period (1991, 746,

749), while Keil and Delitzsch attach the implication of bathing and washing to the end of the entire purification period (12:6; n.d., 377).

■ **3 On the eighth day the boy is to be circumcised.** This is not a rite of purification. Rather, circumcision is the sign of the covenant with Abraham (Gen 17:9-14). Other nations in the ancient world practiced circumcision as a puberty rite preparing a young man for marriage. However, God transformed the rite, making it a symbol of covenant relationship (Kaiser 1994, 1084; see Milgrom 1991, 747).

■ **4** Following the circumcision of the boy (Lev 12:3), **the woman must wait** an additional **thirty-three days to be purified from her bleeding.** The total forty days of impurity (see vv 2-3) reflects the relative period of bleeding following childbirth (see 15:25; Porter 1976, 94; Milgrom 1991, 749). During the thirty-three-day stage of *lesser* impurity (→ 12:1-2), the woman must refrain from contact with the sacred (Milgrom 1991, 749). **She must not touch anything sacred or go to the sanctuary.** This includes abstaining from eating peace offerings, or if she is the wife of a priest, abstaining from eating the priestly portions of sacrifices (Wesley 1765, 383). This further illustrates the strong concern to maintain a separation between the holy and the common (Wenham 1979, 186; → 6:27-28 [6:20-21 HB]).

■ **5** A woman who **gives birth to a daughter** will be unclean **for two weeks.** This corresponds to the "seven days" of uncleanness for the birth of a "son" (12:2). This initial stage of *severe* impurity is associated with the impurity of **her period** and will conclude with bathing (→ vv 1-2). The woman **must wait** an additional **sixty-six days to be purified from her bleeding.** This corresponds to the "thirty-three days" of *lesser* impurity after the birth of a son (→ v 4).

Some presume that the longer period of uncleanness attached to the birth of a daughter (as opposed to a son) stems from ancient patriarchal bias that places women in a lower social standing (Hartley 1992, 168). In contrast, Klawans suggests that the capacity to defile actually reflects greater value. Animal corpses defile for a single day (11:24-28), while human corpses defile for an entire week (Num 19:11). Humans are certainly more highly valued than animals! Thus, a longer period for purification does not necessarily reflect a negative bias against women (2000, 39). Magonet adds that some vaginal bleeding may occur on the part of a newborn girl. Thus, the longer purification period may be based on the potential bleeding of both females (1996, 152).

■ **6-7a** Upon completion of **the days of her purification** after giving birth to **a son or daughter,** a woman must present the appropriate sacrifice. She is to bring her offerings **to the priest at the entrance to the Tent of Meeting.**

This locates the woman in the courtyard where the outer altar is located (→ 1:3, 5-9), affirming the participation of women in tabernacle ritual (Gorman 1997, 77). Later discrimination forced women out of this sphere of holiness (Gerstenberger 1996, 150).

The sacrifice consists of **a year-old lamb for a burnt offering and a young pigeon or a dove for a *purification* offering.** The burnt offering serves to express celebration and devotion to God in gratitude for the gift of a child (Hartley 1992, 169; Kaiser 1994, 1085; re functions of the burnt offering, → 1:3). The purification offering serves to remove ritual impurity from the woman. There is no moral fault involved here, for there is no sin in childbirth itself (re ***purification*** offering in place of "sin offering," → 4:3). Accordingly, there is no statement regarding forgiveness (in contrast to 4:20, 26, 31, 35 where moral faults are involved; Gane 2004, 221). Instead the priest will **make atonement for her** so that **she will be ceremonially clean.** Atonement (*kipper*) here refers to the general sense of cleansing from impurity (re meaning of *kipper*, → 4:20; also → 8:33-36). The impurity stems **from her flow of blood,** not from childbirth itself (→ 12:1-2).

■ **7b-8** This passage closes with the summary statement, **these are the regulations** [*zō't tôrat*] **for the woman who gives birth to a boy or a girl** (→ Behind the Text above). Provision is made for the poor woman who **cannot afford a lamb** (→ Behind the Text for 1:1—3:17; and → 2:1, 4-9; 3:1; 5:7-10, 11-13). Instead, she may present **two doves or two young pigeons, one for a burnt offering and the other for a *purification* offering. In this way the priest will make atonement for her, and she will be clean** (→ 12:6-7a).

This option for the poor woman's purification offering is illustrated in the case of Mary in relation to the birth of Jesus: "When the time of their purification according to the Law of Moses had been completed, Joseph and Mary took him to Jerusalem to present him to the Lord (as it is written in the Law of the Lord, 'Every firstborn male is to be consecrated to the Lord'), and to offer a sacrifice in keeping with what is said in the Law of the Lord: 'a pair of doves or two young pigeons'" (Luke 2:22-24; see Milgrom 1991, 762).

C. Skin Disease (13:1—14:57)

1. Swellings, Spots, Boils, Burns, Sores (13:1-44)

■ **1-2** Some of the Hebrew terms translated as symptoms of unclean skin diseases (e.g., **swelling, rash, bright spot**) appear only in these two chapters (13—14) of the Hebrew Bible. As a result, the symptoms cannot be identified with certainty, making it equally difficult to classify the disease(s) to which they point (Gerstenberger 1996, 161; see Browne 1970, 5). The concern is whether such symptoms **may become an infectious skin disease.** The term *ṣāraʿat* has been commonly translated "leprosy." However, what can be recognized from the symptoms described in ch 13 does not seem to correspond with clinical leprosy (de Vaux 1997, 462). In fact, some argue that the use of *ṣāraʿat* does not seem to reflect leprosy anywhere in the OT (Browne 1970, 5-8). Literary records outside the Bible and investigations of skeletal remains reveal no conclusive evidence that leprosy existed in ancient Egypt or Palestine during OT times (Browne 1970, 8-11; see Wenham 1979, 195). Hulse asserts that medical, historical, and palaeopathological evidence clearly affirms that "biblical leprosy" (*ṣāraʿat*) is not the same as modern clinical leprosy (1975, 91). The LXX (Greek Bible) renders *ṣāraʿat* with *lepra*, which signifies a rough, scaly skin condition, in contrast to the Greek term *elephantiasis*, which does correspond with leprosy (Harrison 1962, 111-12; Hulse 1975, 88, 90).

A related verb form of *ṣāraʿat* is described metaphorically as "snow" (Exod 4:6; Num 12:10; 2 Kgs 5:27). Translators often insert the adjective "white" in these passages, though the term for "white" does not appear in the Hebrew text of these verses (contrast Isa 1:18, which does draw on the "whiteness" of snow in a separate metaphor). In relation to *ṣāraʿat*, snow likely refers to the characteristic of flakiness, reflecting ailments in which the skin flakes off and falls like snow (Hulse 1975, 92-93; Wright and Jones 1992, 278; for snow as a metaphor of scattering, see Pss 68:14 [68:15 HB]; 147:16 [Wenham 1979, 195]). Hulse suggests that a suitable translation for *ṣāraʿat* might be "a repulsive scaly skin disease" (1975, 103; Milgrom suggests "scale disease" [1991, 775, 817]). Each of the cases described in this chapter seem to reflect forms of psoriasis, except for the "clean" condition in vv 38-39, which reflects vitiligo, and the condition described in vv 29-37, which reflects favus (Hulse 1975, 95, 97-99).

■ **3** The two primary indicators of **an infectious skin disease** are whether **the hair in the sore has turned white** and **the sore appears to be more than skin deep** (see vv 20-21, 25-26). If these conditions are found **when the priest examines** a person, then the priest **shall pronounce him ceremonially unclean.** It should be clarified that this impurity is not the result of any sin. Like the woman who gives birth to a child, the person with a skin disease becomes impure, but not because of any moral failure (→ 12:1-2).

■ **4-8** If a person has a **spot on his skin** that **is white,** then that person may be suspected of having an "infectious skin disease." However, if it **does not appear to be more than skin deep and the hair in it has not turned white,** then the priest shall **put the infected person in isolation for seven**

days. The Hebrew text literally reads that the priest will *close off the affliction* seven days. Rashi clarifies that the person is to be quarantined, rather than merely marking off the sore spot (in Herczeg 1999, 140 n. 5; see also Milgrom 1991, 779). If after seven days **the sore is unchanged and has not spread,** then the person must be quarantined **another seven days.** This is intended to allow enough time for the affliction to either diminish or increase so that the priest may make an accurate determination regarding the degree of the impurity.

After the second period of isolation, **if the sore has faded and has not spread,** the person is pronounced **clean.** The person **must wash his *or her* clothes.** Bathing is likely assumed along with washing clothes (Wright and Jones 1992, 280). If the clothes have become impure, surely the person whose skin had the **rash** is also impure. To **be clean** the person merely has to bathe, and wash clothes, as opposed to suffering the consequences of an actual infectious disease (in which case the person would remain unclean, see vv 45-46). Of course, it is assumed that if the sore had spread, become more than skin deep, and the hair in it had become white, then the person has an infectious disease and would be pronounced unclean. Similarly, if the "rash" of the person pronounced clean (v 6) subsequently **does spread,** that person must report back to **the priest again. If the rash has spread,** the person is pronounced **unclean** with **an infectious disease.**

■ **9-11** Verse 9 introduces a new section by repeating instruction similar to that of the introduction at v 2: **when anyone has an infectious skin disease, he *or she* must be brought to the priest.** Of course, such a person is only *suspected* of having the disease due to some mark or sore upon his or her skin. The terminology here does not refer to the actual disease but rather to its symptoms (Milgrom 1991, 783-84). The priest looks for **a white swelling in the skin that has turned the hair white** (→ v 3). The priest must also observe whether **there is raw flesh in the swelling.** Levine explains that this case involves an *old* condition that never healed properly (1989, 78). Accordingly, **it is a chronic skin disease.** The term *nôšenet* ("chronic") derives from a verb meaning "sleep" (BDB 1952, 445). Perhaps this case refers to a disease in remission that has now erupted in **raw flesh.** The priest does not need **to put *the person* in isolation** because it is evident that **he *or she* is already unclean.**

■ **12-17** If the disease [continuing vv 9-11] **breaks out all over his *or her* skin** so that it covers **his *or her* whole body,** the priest **shall pronounce that person clean. Since it has all turned white, he *or she* is clean.** The determining factor here is the presence or absence of raw flesh. **Whenever raw flesh appears on *the person*, he *or she* will be unclean. . . . Should the raw** flesh change and turn white . . . then he *or she* will be clean. Ulcerated flesh that recedes and turns white indicates the growth of new skin and healing (Levine 1989, 78; Hartley 1992, 191).

■ **18-23** If a **white swelling or reddish-white spot appears** in the place where a **boil** has healed on the skin, it must be inspected by the priest. Rashi explains that the spot may be streaked with red, rather than solid white (in Herczeg 1999, 144). If the spot **appears to be more than skin deep and the hair in it has turned white,** the person shall be pronounced unclean due to **an infectious skin disease** (→ v 3). If however, the symptoms of white hair and a marking deeper than the skin are absent, and the spot **has faded,** then the person must be put **in isolation for seven days.** If after seven days, the marking shows **spreading in the skin,** then the person is **unclean.** If there is no change and no spreading, then **it is only a scar from the boil,** and the person is **clean.**

In this case, only a one-week quarantine is required, and the person is clean if no adverse symptoms appear. In contrast, the case involving a two-week quarantine reflects minor impurity and requires bathing and washing clothes before the person is completely clean (→ vv 4-8; also Milgrom 1991, 782).

■ **24-28** The instructions regarding a suspicious **spot** that appears in a **burn** are nearly identical to those for a spot that appears in a boil that has healed (→ vv 18-23).

■ **29-37** This section addresses infections **on the head or on the chin.** Most translations indicate "on the head or in the beard" (see NASB, NET, NJPS, NKJV, NRSV). The focus is on the hairy parts of the head (Milgrom 1991, 791). The text specifies **a man or woman** (as opposed to inclusive "anyone," vv 2, 9) to make clear that these rules apply also to women, though they do not have beards (Ibn Ezra in Carasik 2009, 93). The instructions here parallel those for a suspicious spot on a person's skin (→ vv 1-2, 3, 4-8). In the case of a **sore on the head or *in the beard,*** however, one of the two primary symptoms has changed from white hair in the sore, to **yellow** hair (→ v 3). This is a characteristic of favus and seems to be identified by the term *neteq* (itch; Hulse 1975, 99). A sign of healing is the presence of a normal **black hair** as opposed to the yellow hair.

Following the first week of **isolation,** if there is no evidence of the progression of the disease (spreading, yellow hair, or more than skin deep), the person **must be shaved except for the diseased area** and put **in isolation another seven days.** The Aramaic Bible adds that the shaving need only occur "round about" the diseased area (*Tg. Neof.; Tg. Ps.-J.,* v 33). Rashi explains that if the infection spreads into the shaved area, the person is unclean (in Carasik 2009, 94). Following the second week of **isolation,** if there is no evidence of the progression of the disease (spreading, or more than skin deep), the person shall be pronounced **clean.** As required for cases involving two weeks of isolation, the person must bathe and **wash his or her** clothes (→ vv 4-8 and 18-23).

If the infection does spread, even **after he *or she* is pronounced clean,** the person must be reexamined. If spreading is evident, **the priest does not need to look for yellow hair; the person is unclean.**

■ **38-39** White spots on the skin that are **dull white** likely indicate leukoderma or vitiligo (Hulse 1975, 95). This is identified in the text as *bōhaq* (**harmless rash**). Once again, **a man or woman** (as opposed to inclusive "anyone," vv 2, 9) is specified, perhaps simply due to the influence of the wording in the previous case (→ vv 29-37; Milgrom 1991, 799). This condition is considered **clean.**

■ **40-44** In this case related to being **bald,** the text specifies **a man** because women do not typically lose their hair (→ vv 29-37; Ibn Ezra in Carasik 2009, 95). Baldness itself is considered **clean.** However, if a **reddish-white sore** appears **on his bald head,** it is considered *ṣāraʻat* (**infectious disease**), and the man is **unclean** (→ vv 1-2).

2. Conduct of Person with Skin Disease (13:45-46)

■ **45-46** The person with such an infectious disease, who has been pronounced unclean (vv 3, 8, 10-11, 14-15, 20, 22, 24-25, 27, 29-30, 35-36, 42-44), **must wear torn clothes, let his *or her* hair be unkempt, cover the lower part of his *or her* face and cry out, "Unclean! Unclean!"** The first three requirements reflect a state of mourning (Gen 37:34; Lev 10:6; 2 Sam 1:11-12; Ezek 24:17, 22). The Aramaic Bible adds that the diseased person "shall go with the mourners" and "be dressed like a mourner" (*Tg. Ps.-J.*, v 45). The diseased person is symbolically dead to the community (Porter 1976, 102) and appears to mourn his own death (Frymer-Kensky 1983, 400). Gane states that "persons whose flesh was rotting away with scale disease looked like living dead persons!" (2004, 238). Milgrom demonstrates conclusively that, in relation to impurity, the scale diseased person was "treated like a corpse" (1991, 819; re description of disease as *scaly,* → vv 1-2). Such a person was separated from others by warning them of his or her unclean state and by the requirement to **live alone . . . outside the camp.**

3. Skin Disease in a Garment (13:47-59)

■ **47-58** The same term for an "infectious skin disease" (*ṣāraʻat*) is here applied to clothing (→ vv 1-2). The NIV relates the practical sense of the issue with the phrase, **if any clothing is contaminated with mildew** (compare the more literal NASB, "when a garment has a mark of leprosy in it"). Garments do not become infected with the disease, but mold, mildew, or fungus in clothing may produce flaking that gives the appearance of skin disease and thereby prompts the use of the term *ṣāra'at* (Wenham 1979, 201; Hartley 1992, 193). Once again reflecting the concept of death (→ vv 45-46), contaminated clothing portrays rot, decay, and disintegration (Gorman 1997, 84).

The evidence of contamination is a **greenish or reddish** color and **spreading.** The process of examining the article reflects the procedures for infectious skin diseases that require a two-week quarantine (see vv 2-8, 29-37). The priest must **isolate the affected article for seven days.** After seven days, **if the mildew has spread . . . the article is unclean** and **must be burned up.** If, however, there is no evidence of spreading, the article must **be washed** and isolated **for another seven days.** If washing (and isolation; see Milgrom 1991, 813) does not serve to change the **appearance** (*color*; see Milgrom 1991, 813) of the contamination, **even though it has not spread,** the article is **unclean** and must be burned. If washing causes the contamination to appear **faded,** then the part with mildew must be torn out of the garment. Gersonides explains that if the contamination does not recur at this point, the article can be patched and returned to use (in Carasik 2009, 99). However, **if it reappears in the clothing,** the contamination **is spreading,** and the article **must be burned.**

Articles that were **washed** in this process and became **rid of the mildew** (through washing alone; or through washing, fading, tearing, and patching [v 56]), **must be washed again** and then they **will be clean.** The first washing (v 54) was a physical act attempting to literally clean the mildew from the garment, while the second washing is a ritual act intended to make the garment *pure* (Milgrom 1991, 815).

■ **59** This verse serves as the concluding summary statement for **the regulations concerning contamination by mildew** in garments (vv 47-58). The larger discussion regarding infectious skin diseases continues in ch 14.

4. Purification after Skin Disease (14:1-32)

■ **1-3a** The opening instruction in the NIV, **these are the regulations,** seems the same as the *concluding* formula that appears at the end of each section of the impurity laws (*zō't tôrat;* → Behind the Text above). However, this *opening* instruction is not exactly the same as the concluding formula (*zō't tihyeh tôrat,* **this shall be the regulation;** see NASB, NRSV; see Milgrom 1991, 830).

When a person is healed from an "infectious skin disease," **the priest is to go outside the camp and examine him *or her*.** The previous statement, **when he *or she* is brought to the priest,** should be read, "when it is reported to the priest" (Milgrom 1991, 831). The **diseased person** would not be allowed back into the camp until the priest verifies that he or she has been healed (see 13:46). The healed person must undergo **ceremonial cleansing** in order to be readmitted into the community. This involves a two-stage process. The first ritual serves to readmit the person back into the fellowship of the covenant community (i.e., "the camp," vv 4-8). The second ritual allows a person renewed access to fellowship with God in relation to the tabernacle (vv 9-20; Keil and Delitzsch n.d., 384).

■ **3b-4** The rite of cleansing for a person who **has been healed** of an **infectious skin disease** involves **two live clean birds and some cedar wood, scarlet yarn and hyssop.** The same ingredients (excluding the birds) are used to make the purification waters to be used when a person is defiled by touching the dead (Num 19:6-12). This reinforces the recognition that a person with an infectious skin disease is considered virtually dead to the community (→ Lev 13:45-46; Hartley 1992, 194). The cleansing rite serves to restore the person to life and the community (Gorman 1997, 85). **Cedar** is considered resistant to decay with antiseptic qualities, symbolizing endurance and continuance of life (Keil and Delitzsch n.d., 386; Hartley 1992, 194). Both **scarlet yarn** and **cedar wood** are red and thereby enhance the life-giving symbolism of the blood into which they are dipped (14:6; Milgrom 1991, 832, 835; Gane 2004, 251). **Hyssop** was used to absorb liquid and transfer it by sprinkling (Exod 12:22; Num 19:18; Heb 9:19) and is associated with purification (Ps 51:7 [v 9 HB]).

■ **5** One of the birds is to **be killed over fresh water in a clay pot.** The adjective modifying **water** literally means "living" (*ḥayyîm*; in relation to water, "fresh, flowing"; BDB 1952, 311-12). Accordingly, the water cannot be stagnant, but must be from a spring or stream, representing life-giving power (similar to blood [→ vv 3b-4]; Hartley 1992, 195).

Gerstenberger proposes that the ceremony must take place near flowing water such as a brook. The liquids may have been kept separate, requiring a sequence of dipping and sprinkling (first in blood, then in water; 1996, 176). Levine prompts the thought that only blood was used for dipping and sprinkling. The blood was collected in the vessel while being held **over** (above) flowing water. Thus, any blood that "was not collected in the vessel would flow down into the earth" (1989, 84, 86). However, the more common explanation is that water from a flowing source is placed into a vessel, and the blood from the bird is mixed into the vessel with the water (Rashi in Herczeg 1999, 161-62; Kaiser 1994, 1098; see v 51). Hizkuni explains that the blood had to be mixed with water because a small bird would not supply enough blood to provide for the ritual (in Carasik 2009, 101).

■ **6-7** The **live bird,** along with the **cedar wood, scarlet yarn and the hyssop,** is to be dipped **into the blood of the bird that was killed.** Rashi explains that the wood and hyssop are bound together by the scarlet yarn. The bird is held separately and all the elements are dipped in the blood (in Carasik 2009, 101; re the significance of each element, → vv 3*b*-4). The priest **shall sprinkle the one to be cleansed** with the blood, and he shall **be clean** (re significance of **seven times,** → 4:5-7). Though the altar is not involved, and therefore this is not a sacrifice, the blood still serves as a cleansing agent to purify the person healed of skin disease. The priest will **sprinkle** (*hizzâ*) the blood on the person in a manner similar to that which is done for purifying the sanctuary (→ 4:5-7).

It has long been noted that the **release** of the **live bird** is comparable to the sending out of the live goat on the Day of Atonement (16:20-22; see Nahmanides in Carasik 2009, 102). It is held that the bird carries away the impurity into **the open fields,** as to demons in the wilderness (Porter 1976, 108). However, there is no indication here of transferring impurity from the person to the bird, such as is done by means of two-hand laying in cases of sin, authority, or pollution (→ 1:4). Neither is the impurity transferred to the bird simply by means of the blood rite (→ 4:11-12; 10:16-18). The significance of this rite lies in the contrast between the live and the dead bird. Bekhor Shor rightly asserts that the dead bird symbolizes death in skin disease (→ 13:45-46), while the live bird represents the diseased person's return to freedom of movement. The live bird is not released to the wilderness, but rather to open fields, which are places of life and growth (in Carasik 2009, 102). "The 'death' of the individual is concretized and actualized in the slaughtered bird, whereas the 'life' toward which the recovered individual is ritually moving is concretized and actualized in the living bird" (Gorman 1997, 86; see also Frymer-Kensky 1983, 400).

■ **8-9** To **bathe** in water and **wash** clothes is commonly associated with cleansing from impurity (→ 13:4-8, 29-37). In this case, the person must also **shave off all his hair.** Washing and shaving serves to remove all surface impurity, reflecting a complete separation from the pollution of skin disease (Hartley 1992, 195; Gerstenberger 1996, 176). Clearly, the process of cleansing for the diseased person occurs in stages, as evident by the multiple declarations of being clean (vv 7, 8, 9, 20; → vv 1-3*a*). At this stage, the person **may come into the camp** but is not allowed to enter **his or her tent for seven days.** Thus, the person may associate once again with members of the community but must avoid direct contact with others

(Milgrom 1991, 842). Staying outside the tent protects the person's family from defilement (Hartley 1992, 195). Milgrom adds that a person at this stage can also defile "the sacred by overhang" (being under the same roof). Thus a person must remain outside his or her tent to avoid defiling any sacred object (meat of well-being offering, or sanctuary donations) that might be in the home (1991, 842-43).

Waiting (in this case, seven days) is also a common component of cleansing from impurity (→ 11:8, 39-40; 12:1-2). **On the seventh day** the person again **must shave . . . wash his *or her* clothes and bathe.** This brings the diseased person to the next level of purity, allowing the person to enter his or her tent.

■ **10-11** **On the eighth day** the formerly diseased person begins the final stage of purification, which will enable the person to approach the tabernacle once again (→ vv 1-3*a*). The rite here includes **two male lambs and one ewe lamb . . . a grain offering, and one log of oil.**

■ **12-13** One of the male lambs is to be offered **as a guilt offering** (*'āšām*; → 5:14—6:7 [5:14-26 HB]). The lamb and the **log of oil** are to be presented **as a wave offering** (*těnûpâ*; → 7:28-34). The guilt offering is designated **most holy** (*qōdeš qodāšîm*; → 2:3; 6:16-18 [6:9-11 HB]; 7:1-2).

The reason for the guilt offering is unclear. Normally a guilt offering is required due to unfaithfulness or a violation in relation to the Lord's property or that of a fellow Israelite (→ 5:14-16). Perhaps it is offered for a "suspected violation" (→ 5:17-19). The person may fear having been struck with skin disease as a punishment for some trespass, but he or she does not know what the trespass was. Alternatively, the guilt offering may serve as a token compensation for sacrifices and offerings that were missed while the person was unclean and restricted to living outside the camp. This corresponds with the function of the guilt offering as reparation for failing to present the Lord's offerings (Wenham 1979, 210). Hartley suggests another possible violation in relation to the property of God. The skin disease marred a human who bears the holy image of God (Gen 1:27; Ps 8:5 [8:6 HB]). Therefore, the guilt offering acknowledges the violation caused by the disease and participates in the full restoration of the person to fellowship with God (1992, 197). Similarly, Budd suggests that the priest (sacred property dedicated to the Lord) may be the one who has been endangered/violated by examining the diseased person and being exposed to uncleanness (1996, 206).

■ **14** The application of **some of the blood of the guilt offering** to the **ear, thumb,** and **big toe** of the formerly diseased person recalls the application of blood from the ram of ordination to the same extremities of the priests (8:22-

24). In each case, the rite serves to move persons from one state to another (Gorman 1997, 87; see Hartley 1992, 194). The priests move from common to sacred as they are consecrated for service in the house of the Lord. The diseased person moves from unclean outcast to one who is restored to purity and fellowship in the covenant community (see Milgrom 1991, 853). Both are symbolically committed to hearing the word of the Lord, acting according to God's commands, and walking rightly before the Lord (Keil and Delitzsch n.d., 387-88; Harrison 1980, 151). Also, in each case, the rite participates in purification (Wenham 1979, 210-11; → 8:22-24).

■ **15-18** Before applying **oil** to the diseased person in the same way as the blood of the guilt offering (→ v 14), the priest must **sprinkle some of it before the LORD seven times** (re **before the LORD**, → 1:5-9; re **seven times**, → 4:5-7). This served to consecrate the oil (Noth 1977, 109). In contrast to the *sacred* anointing oil of the priests (→ 8:10-11), the oil here is common and must be dedicated to the Lord before its use (Milgrom 1991, 853). The application of oil to the formerly diseased person again recalls the ordination of the priests (8:12, 30; → 14:14). The diseased person's anointing consecrates the person to fulfill his or her vocation as a member of the priestly nation of God (Keil and Delitzsch n.d., 388). Oil is viewed as having "life-renewing" effects (Noth 1977, 109). It symbolizes vigor, prosperity, and wholeness and serves to convey life to the person healed of skin disease (Porter 1976, 112; → 13:45-46).

As a result of this rite involving **the blood of the guilt offering** and the **oil** (14:12-18), the priest shall **make atonement for** the formerly diseased person. Skin disease sometimes appears as a divine sanction against wrongs (Num 12:9-15; 2 Kgs 5:27; 2 Chr 26:19-21). Such instances prompt the tradition that *all* diseased persons must be guilty of some sin. However, this is clearly "folk suspicion" (Frymer-Kensky 1983, 403-4). The book of Job challenges such faulty assumptions and reverses the condemnation of righteous persons afflicted with disease (Hartley 1992, 200). Skin diseased persons are not necessarily guilty of a moral fault; they are only subject to ritual impurity that must be cleansed. Consequently, **atonement** here refers to the general sense of cleansing from impurity that restores the person to fellowship with God (→ 4:20; 8:33-36; 9:7). The diseased person is reconciled to God so that he or she may freely participate in the life of the community and in worship events centered around the tabernacle (Milgrom 1991, 856; Gorman 1997, 87).

■ **19-20** The *purification* **offering** participates in cleansing the diseased person; it purifies the sanctuary from impurity caused by the disease and represents a renewed offering of life to God on the part of the formerly diseased person (→ 4:3, 5-7, 20; 16:14, 15, 16; and From the Text for 4:1—6:7 [4:1—5:26 HB]). This offering more than any other serves to **make atonement** [*kipper*] **for the one to be cleansed** (→ 14:15-18). Nahmanides clarifies that the "ewe lamb" (14:10) must be the animal chosen for this offering, because 4:28 (see also 4:30) stipulates that the common person's purification offering is to be female. Thus, the remaining male lamb (see 14:12) serves for the burnt offering, in accordance with 1:10 (in Carasik 2009, 103).

The **burnt offering** signifies the diseased person's complete devotion to God (→ 1:3). The accompanying **grain offering** expresses tribute and gratitude to God for healing and restoration (Kaiser 1994, 1099; Harrison 1980, 152; → 2:1). As with the guilt offering, these remaining offerings participate in general **atonement** based on the person's cleansing from impurity, resulting in restoration of fellowship with God (→ 14:15-18).

■ **21-32** Alternative offerings are stipulated for the **poor** who **cannot afford** the regular set of offerings for cleansing from skin disease. Concessions for the poor are common in the sacrificial system (see 5:7, 11; 12:8; → 2:1, 4-9; 3:1; and From the Text for 1:1—3:17). The **grain offering** is reduced from "three-tenths of an ephah of fine flour" (14:10) to **one-tenth of an ephah of fine flour**. The *purification* offering is reduced from a "ewe lamb" (see v 10) to one of **two doves or two young pigeons**. The **burnt offering** is reduced from one of "two male lambs" (see v 10) to one of **two doves or two young pigeons**. The **guilt offering** is the one sacrifice that cannot be reduced; it remains a **male lamb** (see v 12). Likewise, the **log of oil** remains the same volume. This is because the rite involving the blood of the guilt offering and the anointing oil is central to the cleansing and restoration of the skin diseased person (vv 12-18; Noth 1977, 110). Otherwise, the ritual for the poor person repeats the same procedures as described in vv 10-20.

5. Skin Disease on a House (14:33-53)

■ **33-35** The same term for an "infectious skin disease" (*ṣāra'at*) is here applied to houses (→ 13:1-2, 47-58). The NIV relates the practical sense of the issue with the phrase, **spreading mildew in a house** (compare the more literal NASB, "mark of leprosy on a house"). Houses do not become infected with skin disease, but mildew, lichen, or other types of fungus in a house may present the appearance of skin disease, prompting the use of the term *ṣāra'at* (Noth 1977, 110; Wenham 1979, 211). Fungus may result in dry rot in wood; and in stone, mineral efflorescence may cause scaly deposits (Harrison 1980, 155). Such manifestations once again reflect the concept of death (→ 13:45-46, 47-58).

The LORD claims responsibility by stating **I put** the disease **in a house in that land**. This does not mean that *all* disease-stricken homes are God's punishment for some sin on the part of the owner (→ 14:15-18). Wesley proposes the possibility that a stricken home may simply represent the "mischievous nature of sin" (1765, 393). This may be understood as a manifestation of the fallen and broken character of our world, due to the pervasiveness of evil. The strong monotheistic philosophy of the OT recognizes God as the source of all things, the ground of all existence, and the authority behind all events. Accordingly, even disasters are often directly attributed to God (Isa 45:7; Amos 3:6; Porter 1976, 116; Harrison 1980, 155; Hartley 1992, 198).

God Takes Responsibility for Creation

Though houses do not sin, God takes responsibility for inflicting disease upon their walls, as if a punishment for some wrongdoing (→ 14:33-35). This illustrates OT mentality in relation to the authority of God. Old Testament theology does not recognize any equal rival or power next to God (Exod 8:10 [8:6 HB]; 9:14; Deut 4:35, 39; Isa 45:5-7, 14, 21-22; 46:9; Joel 2:27). There is no duality in the OT. Accordingly, all things are under God's authority, and nothing can take place without at least God's permission, if not God's expressed will. Even Satan cannot make a move without God's consent. The dialogue in the opening of the book of Job illustrates this point. God grants permission for Satan to afflict Job, and God sets the limits on the extent of the affliction (Job 1:12; 2:6). Though Satan is the instrument of affliction (Job 2:7), it is God who receives the ultimate blame (Job 1:16 ["fire of God"], 21 ["the LORD has taken away"]; 2:9-10).

Likewise, God takes responsibility for the hardening of Pharaoh's heart in the account of the plagues. The text portrays a progression of the hardening of Pharaoh's heart as the plagues advance. In the earlier plagues, Pharaoh's heart is hardened by an unnamed source ("heart was hardened" [passive], Exod 7:13, 22; 8:19 [8:15 HB]; 9:7 NASB, NRSV), or by Pharaoh himself (Exod 8:15 [8:11 HB], 32 [v 28 HB]; 9:34). In the later plagues, the text switches to God as the subject who hardens Pharaoh's heart (Exod 9:12; 10:20, 27; 11:10; see also 14:4, 8). This is not an indication that the Lord manipulated Pharaoh's brain and forced him to rebel by hardening his heart. Pharaoh clearly is responsible for challenging God and trying to manipulate the circumstances to get his own way. He promises to let the people go until he sees God's mercy in halting a plague. Pharaoh takes advantage of God's mercy by hardening his heart and retracting his promise. It has been suggested that God actually hardens Pharaoh's heart through mercy! Fretheim states that Pharaoh's stubbornness is *intensified* by God's actions (1996, 104). If the Lord would have merely held a plague in force until *after* the people were set free, then perhaps Pharaoh would never have had the chance to change his mind. However, God mercifully stops each plague, giving Pharaoh the opportunity to keep his word. By responding with a hard heart, Pharaoh engages in a power struggle with God. However, the message becomes increasingly clear that God is sovereign, and God's plan will triumph.

One of the most striking examples of this OT mentality appears in relation to the demise of King Saul. The biblical text indicates that "an evil spirit from the LORD tormented" Saul (1 Sam 16:14; see also 16:15, 16, 23; 18:10; 19:9). It seems scandalous to consider that God is ever in the business of distributing evil spirits. The earlier accounts of Saul's relationship with God make it clear that Saul actually brought this upon himself through repeated acts of disobedience and self-reliance. Nevertheless, in the OT, "all things in the end are caused by the one God" (Hertzberg 1976, 140-41).

The same dynamic is expressed in God's response to the sin in the garden of Eden. The Lord proclaims, "*I will greatly increase your pains in childbearing*" (Gen 3:16, emphasis added). Clearly the guilt of the couple's disobedience has introduced brokenness and mistrust into their relationship. As a result, without the caring support and companionship of a spouse, the woman will endure childbirth alone, thereby *greatly increasing* the anguish of an already painful procedure. Though they have brought this upon themselves, God takes responsibility for the actions of his creatures, and initiates the gracious work of reconciliation, beginning with Gen 3:21 and extending throughout the rest of salvation history!

As the inspiration behind the biblical text, God accepts the assignment of responsibility for all things. While God's creatures blame each other (avoiding responsibility; Gen 3:12-13), God takes up responsibility. A scene from the film *Star Trek VI* illustrates this point. Captain James Kirk and Dr. McCoy are put on trial in a Klingon court for the murder of the Klingon ambassador. It is clear to the film's audience that Kirk and McCoy are victims of an elaborate conspiracy in which they have been framed for the crime. False accusations and circumstantial evidence suggest that the unjust trial should not succeed in convicting the two heroes. However, the Klingon prosecutor cleverly asks Kirk, "Are you aware that as the captain of a starship you are required to be responsible for the actions of your men?" Kirk stoically responds, "As captain I am responsible for the conduct of the crew under my command" (Meyer and Flinn 1991, Scene 7). As a result, Kirk and McCoy are convicted of a crime committed by others. In a much more profound way, God graciously and lovingly takes responsibility for the actions of his creatures. Ultimately in Jesus Christ, God even suffers death on behalf of his sinful people.

■ **36** The priest orders **the house to be emptied** prior to examining it for mildew. In this way, **nothing in the house will be pronounced unclean**. Clearly the state of impurity is based on the declaration of the priest and is entirely symbolic (Milgrom 1991, 869). The rigor of the impurity laws are mitigated by a concession to practical need. Valuable household items are rescued from the possible declaration of impurity, before the priestly inspection (Noth 1977, 111).

■ **37-42** The inspection of a house suspected of ṣāra'at ("mildew") contamination corresponds closely to that of ṣāra'at ("skin disease") suspected on a person or in clothing. Like mildew in clothing, a **greenish or reddish** color is a sign of possible infection (13:49). A mark **deeper than the surface of the wall** recalls the symptom of a spot that "appears to be more than skin deep" on a person (→ 13:3). These indications require a quarantine of **seven days** (13:4, 21, 26, 31, 50). After the seven days, the main symptom of concern is whether the mildew has **spread on the walls** (13:5-7, 22-23, 27-28, 32, 34-36, 51, 53, 55). If spreading is evident, then the **contaminated stones** must be removed, and **the inside walls of the house scraped.** This recalls the shaving of a person with skin disease (13:33; 14:8-9; see Levine 1989, 89). Replacing the contaminated stones with **other stones** and using **new clay** to **plaster the house** corresponds to patching cloth that had to be torn due to mildew (→ 13:47-58).

■ **43-47** If the mildew reappears and **has spread in the house,** the house is declared **unclean** and **must be torn down.** This implies a waiting period of "another seven days" (13:5, 33, 54; see 14:38; Rashi in Herczeg 1999, 173). During the times of quarantine, **anyone who goes into the house** becomes **unclean** and must *wait* **till evening** to be clean again. **Anyone who sleeps or eats in the house** incurs greater impurity and **must wash his *or her* clothes.** In each case (entering, sleeping, eating) bathing is also presumed (→ 11:8, 24-25, 26-28, 29-38, 39-40; 13:4-8, 29-37; 14:8-9; Milgrom 1991, 876-77).

■ **48-52 If the priest comes to examine** the house **and the mildew has not spread** (after the second week, → vv 43-47), the house shall be pronounced **clean.** The rite **to purify the house** is the same as the initial rite for purifying a person healed of skin disease (→ vv 3b-4, 5, 6-7). The only noticeable difference is that **the cedar wood, the hyssop, the scarlet yarn and the live bird** are to be dipped <u>into the blood of the dead bird</u> and the fresh water (as opposed to "into the blood of the bird that was killed *over* the fresh water"). This implies that either the liquids were mixed (blood *and* water in one pot), or the elements were dipped twice (once in blood *and* once in water; → v 5). The latter seems to be implied since **bird's blood** and **the fresh water** are listed separately among the elements used to **purify the house.**

The sacrifices of the eighth day rite for a person healed of skin disease (vv 10-20) are not required, because the house only needs to be cleansed, not restored to fellowship with God (Wenham 1979, 211).

■ **53** The **live bird** is released **in the open fields.** This represents returning the home to profitable use for life and well-being (→ vv 6-7). Clearly, **atonement for the house** is not concerned with sin and reconciliation. Rather, atonement here refers to cleansing and restoring the house for beneficial use (see Gorman 1997, 88; Gane 2004, 249).

6. Summation (14:54-57)

■ **54-57** The formula **these are the regulations** opens and closes this concluding statement (→ Behind the Text above). The summation recapitulates and participates in enveloping chs 13—14, the entire unit regarding skin disease (Milgrom 1991, 885; Milgrom explains the triple inclusio encapsulated by these verses).

Rationale for Impurity of Skin Disease

Like the sacrificial regulations, the impurity laws are part of a symbolic, or representative, system (→ 14:36 and sidebar, "The Representative Nature of Sacrifice" at From the Text for 4:1—6:7). Ancient Israel may have literally carried out these rites, but their enduring significance lies in the theological message and intent they represent. If hygiene and infection were really the primary concerns, then the priestly material would surely include a much larger catalog of diseases needing to be addressed. In contrast, the focus is clearly on ritual, not medicine. The central concern is representing and managing impurity (see Milgrom 1991, 817-18).

In relation to ṣāra'at ("skin disease"), impurity is represented with images of death (→ 13:45-46). Skin disease reflects the same destruction of life in the corporeal realm as sin does in the spiritual arena (Keil and Delitzsch n.d., 384). Milgrom marshals the evidence that associates skin disease with death. The person with skin disease is treated like a corpse. When Miriam was stricken with ṣāra'at ("skin disease"), Aaron cried out, "Oh, do not let her be like one dead, whose flesh is half eaten away" (Num 12:12 NASB). The purification rites for skin disease and for touching a corpse have striking similarities (Lev 14:4-7; Num 19:1-13). Skin disease is identified with death in Job 18:13. The scaly/flaky character of skin disease (→ 13:1-2) reflects the disintegration of a corpse and the onset of death (see Milgrom 1991, 819).

In opposition to the representative death of skin disease, the elements of the purification rite for the person healed of skin disease represent life: the *live* bird, the *living* water, the *life-giving* blood, the red cedar wood, and scarlet yarn (→ 14:3b-4, 5, 6-7). The person healed and cleansed of skin disease moves from isolation to community, from impurity to holiness, and from death to life (Milgrom 1991, 889). The impurity regulations participate in a symbolic system that serves to remind "Israel of its imperative to cleave to life and reject death" (Milgrom 1991, 1003). This is a message of hope in which life overcomes death, and God's children are exhorted to embrace life!

Gane highlights the significance of water and blood as foundational elements of purification (14:6-7, 51). The writer of the Johannine Epistles saw water and blood as elements identifying Jesus Christ as the Son of God, the Messiah (1 John 5:5-6). Christ as one risen from the dead overcame *death* and offers eternal *life* through new birth (John 3:3-16; Gane 2004, 252). Gane asserts, "Christ fulfills the Israelite system of ritual purification, providing us with the elements we need to be victorious over the mortal state that characterizes our present sinful world so we can have eternal life that transcends the present era" (2004, 252).

D. Sexual Discharges (15:1-33)

1. Male Discharges (15:1-18)

■ **1-2** This chapter on sexual discharges is organized chiastically in relation to four cases: abnormal (diseased) male discharge (vv 2-15), normal male discharge (seminal emission, vv 16-17), normal female discharge (menstrual flow, vv 19-24), and abnormal (diseased) female discharge (vv 25-30). Verse 18 constitutes the center of the inverted structure and addresses impurity regulations related to marital intercourse (see Keil and Delitzsch n.d., 391; Wenham 1979, 216-17; Milgrom 1991, 905).

The **bodily discharge** (*zāb mibbĕśārô*, lit. "discharge from his flesh/body," NASB, NET, NKJV; see BDB 1952, 142) should not be understood as a discharge from *any* orifice of the body. The context of the chapter makes it clear that "flesh" (*bāśār*) here serves as a euphemism for a man's private part (Ezek 16:26; 23:20; see Ibn Ezra in Carasik 2009, 110; Porter 1976, 119). This diseased discharge is commonly identified as a form of gonorrhea (Wenham 1979, 217-18; Harrison 1980, 160). Alternatively, it has been associated with inflammation of the urinary tract (urethritis; Keil and Delitzsch n.d., 392; Kaiser 1994, 1104) or any number of related infections (Levine 1989, 92). Walton and Matthews specify "infectious urinary bilharzia" as the possible ailment. Excavations have detected bilharzia as a known menace in the ancient world, caused by a parasite related to snails in the water system (1997, 158).

■ **3** A man is **unclean** even if the flow of discharge **is blocked**. This likely refers to blockage caused by a thick discharge resulting in a reduced flow (Milgrom 1991, 908).

■ **4-10** **The man with a discharge** transmits impurity mainly when he **lies on**, or **sits on**, anything (including **any bed** and anything he **sits on when riding**). Such things become unclean, and **anyone who touches** them or **sits on** them becomes unclean. Of course, **whoever touches the man who has a discharge** becomes unclean.

A person who becomes unclean through such contact must carry out the standard three elements of cleansing: **wash his *or her*** clothes, bathe **with water**, and wait **till evening** (→ 11:39-40). The same is true for anyone on whom **the man with a discharge spits**. Spittle transports disease and uncleanness but does not seem to be unclean itself (Levine 1989, 94; Hartley 1992, 209; see Frymer-Kensky 1983, 401).

In the case of one who **touches any of the things that were under** a man with a discharge (i.e., whatever he sits on); such a person is **unclean till evening** (bathing is understood; Milgrom 1991, 919). In contrast, a person who **picks up those things must wash his *or her* clothes and bathe with water**, as well as wait **till evening** (→ 11:24-25).

The emphasis on things that the man lies on, sits on, or rides on (things under him) is due to the proximity of such things to the infected organ as the source of uncleanness (Wenham 1979, 218; see Milgrom 1991, 910-11).

■ **11 The man with a discharge** may avoid polluting another person via touch by **rinsing his hands with water**. Interestingly, Wesley applies the washing of hands to "the person touched." If they wash their hands right away, they will remain clean (1765, 395).

■ **12** If the man with a discharge touches **a clay pot, it must be broken, and any wooden article is to be rinsed with water** (→ 6:27-28 [6:20-21 HB]). In light of the previous verse (15:11), it seems that the man will not pollute these items if he first washes his hands (Milgrom 1991, 920).

■ **13 When a man is cleansed from his discharge** refers to the healing or cessation of the discharge (Wesley 1765, 395; Levine 1989, 95). Rashi explains that the **seven days** of waiting must be consecutive and without further discharge (in Herczeg 1999, 184). Then the man must **wash his clothes and bathe himself** (→ vv 4-10).

In this instance, *běśārô* refers to ***his body*** (NIV = himself), as opposed to just the man's private part (→ vv 1-2). This corresponds with the cleansing instructions for a man with a discharge in the *Temple Scroll* from Qumran (11QT 45:16) and the instructions for a man with an emission in v 16, which read *'t kôl bśrô/ 'et-kol-běśārô* respectively ("his whole body"; Milgrom 1991, 923; see Martínez and Tigchelaar 1997, 2:1262).

Bathing must take place **with *living* water** (→ 14:5). Impurity, which is symbolic of death, is cleansed through elements of life (→ 14:3b-4; Milgrom 1991, 924).

■ **14-15** As with the person healed of skin disease (ch 14), the man "cleansed from his discharge" (15:13) must undergo a two-step process. In this case, the initial cleansing (v 13) purifies the man in relation to "common objects and persons" (Milgrom 1991, 924). Then, **on the eighth day** sacrifices are brought in order to cleanse the man in relation to the tabernacle (→ 14:1-3a).

Two doves or two young pigeons represent inexpensive sacrifices. This may suggest that uncleanness from a discharge is viewed as less serious than other forms of impurity (Wenham 1979, 219). Alternatively, it may reflect an economic concession, especially for a woman with a discharge who offers the same types of animals for sacrifice (15:28-29). Being more susceptible to discharges due to hormonal imbalances, a woman would benefit from a less expensive sacrificial requirement (Milgrom 1991, 926).

In regard to the significance of the **purification** offering and the **burnt offering** pertaining to impurity, and their relation to **atonement,** see comments on 14:19-20. A "guilt offering" is not required for the person cleansed from a discharge (→ 14:12-13).

■ **16-17** The second case of impurity from a discharge is that of a normal male **emission of semen** (→ 15:1-2). This does not refer to intercourse, which is the subject of v 18. Rather, this refers to involuntary nocturnal emission (Levine 1989, 96; Gorman 1997, 91). The man with such a discharge **must bathe his whole body** and wait **till evening. Any clothing** on which the semen has landed **must be washed** and will also be **unclean till evening** (→ vv 4-10). The mention of **leather** likely refers to the man's bedding (Milgrom 1991, 928).

Nahmanides reasons that **semen** pollutes because it is comparable to the uncleanness of a corpse. That is, wasted semen suggests the loss of potential life, thereby reflecting death (in Carasik 2009, 113). This corresponds with the general recognition of impurity as representative of death (→ 11:8, 39-40; 13:45-46, 47-58; 14:33-35; 15:13).

Normal discharges (vv 16-18, 19-24) do not require sacrifices and atonement, as do the abnormal discharges (vv 2-15, 25-30; Budd 1996, 219). This suggests that normal discharges reflect a lesser impurity that does not defile the tabernacle, unless intensified by neglecting to wash (see Milgrom 1991, 928).

■ **18** This verse constitutes a separate case enveloped by the discussion of male and female discharges (→ vv 1-2; Milgrom 1991, 931). Though the focus is impurity (as opposed to sexual ethics), *marital* intercourse is understood. This is reflected in the Samaritan Pentateuch, which reads 'yšh ("her husband") as opposed to **a man** (see Milgrom 1991, 934; and Gall 1918, 237). Marital intercourse itself is not what defiles, rather the presence of **an emission of semen** causes the pollution (→ vv 16-17; Keil and Delitzsch n.d., 393). As a result, both husband and wife **must bathe** and wait **till evening.**

2. Female Discharges (15:19-30)

■ **19-22** A woman's **regular flow of blood** (menstrual cycle) corresponds to a man's normal "emission of semen" in the structure of the chapter (→ vv 1-2). Once again, *bāśār* (*zōbāh bibśārāh*, **discharge from her body**) serves as a euphemism for one's private parts (in this case, a woman's; → vv 1-2; Ibn Ezra in Carasik 2009, 114; Wesley 1765, 396).

The woman's **impurity** will last **seven days.** It is uncertain whether the impurity corresponds to the typical period of menstruation itself (see Frymer-Kensky 1983, 401), or whether it extends to seven days after the cessation of bleeding (therefore fourteen days total; Gerstenberger 1996, 204).

Due to the nature of a woman's regular flow, impurity is imparted to things she **lies on** or **sits on,** similar to that of a man with an abnormal discharge (→ vv 4-10; Levine 1989, 97).

Anyone who touches her will be unclean till evening. The requirement of bathing, but not washing clothes, is understood (Milgrom 1991, 935). In contrast, one who touches that which she lies on or sits on must **wash his *or her* clothes, bathe with water,** and wait **till evening** (→ vv 4-10). Milgrom explains that touching the body of a menstruant is not as polluting as touching that upon which she lies or sits. This is because the exposed parts of the menstruant that a person might touch are not in direct contact with her flow, as are objects upon which she lies or sits. Accordingly, a woman's normal discharge is not as severe as a man's abnormal discharge (v 7; Milgrom 1991, 935-37).

As with a man who has a normal "emission of semen," a woman's "regular flow of blood" does not require any sacrifice or atonement (→ vv 16-17; Nahmanides in Carasik 2009, 114).

■ **23** This verse is awkward for translators. It does not refer to touching the furniture itself (**bed or anything she was sitting on**) but rather to any object on the furniture. Touching such an object incurs a lesser impurity that only requires bathing (understood) and waiting **till evening** (Porter 1976, 122; Milgrom 1991, 938-40).

■ **24 If a man lies with her** refers to having intercourse (Keil and Delitzsch n.d., 393). This verse likely applies to the situation in which the man is not aware of the woman's period, or it commences unexpectedly during intercourse (Wesley 1765, 396; Keil and Delitzsch n.d., 393-94). Intentional intercourse during menstruation is strongly condemned elsewhere (Lev 18:19; 20:18; Ezek 18:6).

If **her monthly flow touches him,** the resultant uncleanness will last **seven days.** In contrast, touching a menstruant or anything she lies on or sits on only pollutes "till evening" (Lev 15:19, 21-23).

The severe restriction and greater impurity ascribed to intercourse during menstruation further reflects the basis of impurity in terms of avoiding death and promoting life (→ vv 16-17). Intercourse during menstruation involves "the loss of both life-giving semen and genital blood," thereby evoking such strong regulation (Milgrom 1991, 941).

■ **25-27** A **discharge of blood for many days at a time other than her monthly period** or one **that continues beyond her period** indicates an abnormal female discharge. This is the final category of sexual discharges addressed in the impurity regulations (→ vv 1-2). Such discharges likely stem from uterine disorders, such as menostaxis (Levine 1989, 92-93; Walton and Matthews 1997, 158). This type of discharge appears to be reflected in the account of the woman with a hemorrhage whom Jesus healed (Matt 9:20; Mark 5:25; Luke 8:43; Wenham 1979, 221).

She will be unclean as long as she has the discharge, just as in the days of her period. This implies that the impurity only lasts during the time of the discharge itself (in the case of a normal period, seven days). However, Lev 15:28 indicates that the woman is not clean until seven days after the cessation of bleeding (→ vv 19-22). This suggests that the cleansing process takes place in stages (→ 14:8-9).

Verses 26-27 of ch 15 abbreviate the parallel instructions for a man with an abnormal discharge. The focus of impurity transmission rests on things the woman **lies on** or **sits on**. Anyone who contacts her impurity must **wash his *or her* clothes, bathe with water**, and wait **till evening** (→ vv 4-10).

■ **28-30** The cleansing procedure for the woman with an abnormal discharge is the same as that for the man with an abnormal discharge (→ vv 13, 14-15). Washing clothes and bathing in *living* water is implicit (v 13; Nahmanides in Carasik 2009, 115).

3. Summation (15:31-33)

■ **31** Moses, Aaron, and the priests are charged to **keep the Israelites separate from things that make them unclean** (v 1; 10:10-11). This serves as a conclusion to all the impurity regulations in chs 11—15 (Gorman 1997, 93). Separation does not always mean avoiding uncleanness, because some sources of impurity cannot be prevented (e.g., skin disease, nocturnal emission, menstrual period). Thus, separation mainly refers to undergoing purification when uncleanness does occur.

The concern is to restrain the effects of impurity from **defiling** the **dwelling place** of God (i.e., the tabernacle; see Wenham 1979, 221; Gane 2004, 260). If the tabernacle becomes overly polluted, God who cannot abide the compromise of the sacred with the profane (→ 6:10-11 [6:3-4 HB]; 6:16-18 [6:9-11 HB]; 6:27-28 [6:20-21 HB]; 7:19-21; see also Hartley 1992, 213) will abandon God's **dwelling place, which is among them** (→ From the Text for 4:1—6:7 [4:1—5:26 HB]). Such rejection can only result in the death of the sacred community. Accordingly, Israel must remain pure, **so they will not die in their uncleanness.**

Maintaining purity contributes to the fulfillment of Israel's call to be "set apart" (holy) for the Lord (see Wesley 1765, 397).

■ **32-33** These verses conclude and summarize the regulations concerning sexual discharges in ch 15 (Gorman 1997, 93; → vv 1-2).

FROM THE TEXT

The impurity laws (chs 11—15), like the sacrificial system, are often considered wearisome and irrelevant for the contemporary church. Carefully monitoring diet, childbirth, certain skin diseases, and sexual discharges including seminal emissions and menstruation, and undergoing purification rites in response to each, seem excessive and somewhat peculiar. Nevertheless, recognizing the representative (symbolic) nature of the impurity laws reveals the biblical intent behind their transmission.

Chapters 11—15 are concerned with *ritual* impurity, distinct from the impurity/defilement generated by sin. Klawans explains that ritual impurity is often part of normal life and unavoidable. It is not a sin to contract ritual impurity, and it is normally a temporary condition (2000, 23-25). The concern is to eliminate the symbolic effects of ritual impurity through acts of purification.

In the context of ancient Israel, the laws regarding sexual discharges had implications for morality and religious practice. Cult prostitution and fertility rites were prohibited by these laws, because intercourse made one unclean and therefore unable to worship in relation to the sanctuary (Wenham 1979, 223). "A ritual 'watch' is placed on the blessing" from God that humans be fruitful and multiply (Gen 1:28; Gorman 1997, 89). While God certainly intends for sexuality to be a vital part of holy living (Song of Songs), the regulations on sexuality separate human mortality/impurity from the sacred. The intention is to generate a high respect for God's holiness (Gane 2004, 261-64).

The intent of the impurity regulations becomes further evident when their common denominator is identified. Milgrom summarizes the particular sources of impurity as follows:

> The only permitted four-legged animals that may be eaten must have cloven hoofs and chew their cud. Some benign skin diseases are diagnosed and quarantined, passing by the spate of known contagious diseases. Genital discharges are declared impure but not issues from other orifices. These are the subjects of the impurity laws of animals and humans. They sound bizarre. But as symbols they reveal deeper, basically ethical values that remain relevant to this day. (2004, 101)

Impurity is limited by the priests to only three main sources: a corpse or carcass, genital discharges, and scale disease. It is striking that other bodily secretions such as mucus, perspiration, urine, and feces are not considered unclean (see Frymer-Kensky 1983, 401). The specific sources of impurity in Leviticus share the feature of representing death in some manner. Obviously, a corpse/carcass reflects death. Genital discharges (semen and vaginal blood) represent forces of life, and therefore their loss represents death. The wasting away of the body, characteristic of scale disease, displays the process of death. Accordingly when Miriam is afflicted with scale disease, Aaron prays, "Oh, do not let her be like one dead, whose flesh is half eaten away when he comes from his mother's womb!" (Num 12:12 NASB). Leviticus 13—14 includes moldy fabrics and fungous houses as impure, not because they have scale disease, but because they give the appearance of it. Milgrom concludes that the impurity laws symbolically call Israel to *choose life* by means of obedience to these commands (1991, 45-47, 767-68, 1002-3). Impurity, associated with death, stands in opposition to holiness, which represents life. In this symbolic system, holiness and life can be seen as overcoming impurity and death. The system represents the victory of life over death! The impurity laws provide an expression of God's commitment to resurrection and life! Consequently, they serve to promote "a foundational concern for a genuine reverence for life" (King 2009, 73).

The impurity legislation also serves as a constant reminder of relationship with God. Even the most private, mundane, irritating, and embarrassing aspects of being human (e.g., seminal emissions, menstrual cycles) are subject to relationship with God, the Creator. The impurity laws remind us to stop in the midst of the most tedious elements of life, acknowledge God, and recognize God's grace even in places where, and at times when, we would rather be left alone. "In the light of the life the blood carries steps must be taken to acknowledge it as a gift which God has given" (Budd 1996, 214). The impurity laws might be considered a radical expression of praying "without ceasing" (1 Thess 5:17 KJV).

IV. THE DAY OF ATONEMENT (16:1-34)

BEHIND THE TEXT

Leviticus 16 represents the height of the sacrificial system. It contains the instructions for the great annual Day of Atonement (*yôm hakkipūrîm*). The term commonly translated "holy" (*qdš*) appears fourteen times in this chapter, in various related forms, accentuating the concern for holiness and purity. In this chapter, the innermost sanctum ("holy of holies") is called *haqqōdeš* (NIV = "the Most Holy Place," vv 2, 3 [NIV = "sanctuary area"], 16, 17, 20, 23, 27). The high priest's garments for this day are labeled *qōdeš* (lit. "holy," NIV = "sacred," vv 4 [twice], 32). Blood is sprinkled on the altar in order to *qiddĕšô* (lit. "make it holy," NIV = "consecrate it," v 19). The high priest is instructed to bathe in a *qādôš* (NIV = "holy," v 24) place. Finally, "the Most Holy Place" is referenced once again, only this time with the unique phrase *miqdaš haqqōdeš* (lit. "the holiest part of the sanctuary," v 33 [twice in same phrase]; see Milgrom 1991, 1058).

The chapter is introduced with a focus on the proper way to approach the Lord. First, there is a reminder of "the death of the two sons of Aaron who died" (v 1), because it appears they did not approach the Lord in a proper manner (→ 10:1). Next, Aaron is instructed on exactly "how" he "is to enter the sanctuary area" (16:3) and thereby properly approach the Lord. Approaching God in the sanctuary recalls God's approach near to the people of Israel at Mount Sinai. On that occasion, the people, the priests, and the mountain were all to be "made holy" (*qdš*, "consecrated," Exod 19:10, 22, 23). The people were to "wash their clothes" (Exod 19:10; compare Lev 16:4, 23-24 in which Aaron must change clothes and bathe). There were warnings of possible death (Exod 19:12, 21; compare Lev 16:2, 13). Finally, the Lord descended on the mountain in smoke (Exod 19:18; compare Lev 16:2, 13).

Even more than approaching God, Lev 16 is ultimately concerned with maintaining God's presence in the midst of the community (see Wenham 1979, 228). The sin and impurities of the people defile the tabernacle, the place of God's presence. If such defilement becomes too great, God will abandon the community (→ From the Text for 4:1—6:7 [4:1—5:26 HB]; also Levine 1989, 99; and Gane 2004, 270). The Day of Atonement addresses this concern by providing an annual overall cleansing of the tabernacle and God's people, so that sin and impurity are eliminated and relationship with God is maintained. Accordingly, this day provided a general and complete atonement for sins and impurities that may have remained unacknowledged through the year (Keil and Delitzsch n.d., 395).

The opening reference back to the deaths of Nadab and Abihu (16:1; see 10:1-2), ties ch 16 to ch 10. The notion that ch 16 should directly follow ch 10 is further prompted by considering the Day of Atonement as the climax of the sacrificial system, following the instructions for the various sacrifices (chs 1—7), and the ordination of the priests with the inauguration of the sacrificial system (chs 8—10). Accordingly, chs 11—15, which focus on the impurity laws, appear to be an interruption. However, the priestly task of distinguishing "between the holy and the common, between the unclean and clean" (10:10), provides in ch 10 the point of departure for chs 11—15. Moreover, since a major concern of ch 16 includes cleansing the sanctuary from impurities, it is appropriate that the impurity regulations of chs 11—15 precede the instructions for the Day of Atonement (Driver 1910, 46; Wenham 1979, 227-28). Finally, the impurity laws anticipate the cleansing of the tabernacle in ch 16 by means of the summary statement requiring Israel to separate from uncleanness lest they die for defiling the tabernacle in which God dwells (15:31; see Möller 1956, 325).

Following the opening warning (vv 1-2), ch 16 begins with instructions regarding the high priest's garments for the day and the identification of the appropriate animals for the ceremony (vv 3-5). The next two sections (vv 6-10 and vv 11-28) are commonly recognized as repetitive, with the latter section including greater detail. The parallel between the two sections is evident, not only by similar general content, but also by repeated terminology. The Hebrew wording in all of v 6 is exactly repeated in the first half of v 11 (unfortunately the NIV translation does not reflect this). Furthermore, the opening terms in vv 6, 7, and 8 are also the opening terms in vv 11, 12, and 13 (*wĕhiqrîb* in vv 6, 11; *wĕlāqaḥ* in vv 7, 12; and *wĕnātan* in vv 8, 13). The two sections should be understood as: an initial outline for the ceremony (vv 6-10), followed by a more detailed account (vv 11-28). A similar pattern is evident in Deut 27, in which vv 2-3 provide an outline, while vv 4-8 follow with a detailed account (Wenham 1979, 228; see Möller 1956, 325-26, who sees a similar pattern of preparation followed by details in 8:1-2 and 9:2-4). The final section of ch 16 designates the date for the ceremony, identifies it as an annual "Sabbath" observance, and provides a brief summation of the ritual (vv 29-34).

IN THE TEXT

A. Overview and Preparation (16:1-10)

1. Introductory Warning (16:1-2)

■ **1-2** The chapter begins with a reminder of **the death of the two sons of Aaron** (→ 10:1, 2). Ibn Ezra understands the phrase **when they approached the LORD** as an indication that Nadab and Abihu actually entered the holy of holies (in Carasik 2009, 117). This reminder prompts the introductory warning that Aaron should not enter **whenever he chooses into the Most Holy Place**. Uniquely, here in ch 16, the holy of holies is called *haqqōdeš* (lit. "the holy place," **the Most Holy Place**, vv 2, 3 [NIV = "sanctuary area"], 16, 17, 20, 23, 27; see Ibn Ezra in Carasik 2009, 117; Noth 1977, 120; and Milgrom 1991, 1013). This is made clear by the qualification that *haqqōdeš* is **behind the curtain** (i.e., the veil separating the holy place from the holy of holies). Haran explains that, in the Priestly source, the term *haqqōdeš* is not a definitive technical term. In some instances, it denotes the holy of holies (as here in ch 16). In other passages the same term is applied to part of the sanctuary courtyard (10:17) and the outer altar (Num 28:7; Haran 1985, 172 n. 50). It can also refer to the holy place itself, that is, the outer sanctum within the sanctuary containing the incense altar, lamp, and table of showbread. Interestingly, *haqqōdeš* ("the holy place") and *qōdeš haqqŏdāšîm* ("the holy of holies") are clearly distinguished in Exod 26:33 where they are divided by the curtain in the sanctuary.

Aaron is not to enter the holy of holies **whenever he chooses,** because God appears **in the cloud over the atonement cover.** In the ancient world, access to holy places was often limited; the more sacred a location, the more restricted the access. This was to prevent defilement, as well as to protect the life of humans who encroached on sacred space (Walton and Matthews 1997, 159). In this case, the space includes the very presence of God! The **cloud** in which God appears may refer to the cloud associated with the glory of God seen in the wilderness (Exod 16:10) and that covered and filled the tabernacle (Exod 40:34-38; Budd 1996, 225; → Lev 1:1; 9:2-6). Alternatively, the cloud in the holy of holies may refer to that created by the incense smoke that Aaron is to produce as a screen to keep him from directly viewing God (16:13; see Milgrom 1991, 1014-15). The cloud of God's presence appears **over the atonement cover** (*kappōret*). The term *kappōret* is commonly translated "mercy seat" (e.g., KJV, NASB, NRSV). It derives from the same root as the verb *kipper*, which in the priestly literature generally carries the meaning "atonement" and more specifically refers to "purging" or "cleansing" (→ 4:20; 8:33-36; 9:7). The **mercy seat** sits on top of the ark of the covenant with two winged cherubim affixed above it. God appears above the mercy seat between the cherubim (Exod 25:17-22; Ps 99:1).

2. Priestly Garments and Assembly of Offerings (16:3-5)

■ **3-5** In light of the previous warning (vv 1-2), the passage now explains, this is how Aaron is to enter the *holy of holies* (NIV = sanctuary area; → vv 1-2). Immediately following is a list of the animals that must be gathered for the ceremony, and a description of the garments Aaron must wear. For himself, Aaron secures a **young bull for a *purification* offering and a ram for a burnt offering.** For the people, **he is to take two male goats for a *purification* offering and a ram for a burnt offering.** Technically, only one of the goats will be sacrificed as a purification offering (vv 9-10). Levine suggests that both goats are potentially a purification offering at this point, because the lot had not yet been cast that will determine which one would actually be sacrificed (1989, 101). Instead of a "young bull" for the community's purification offering (4:13-14), this annual ceremony, like the inauguration ceremony (9:3), uses a **male goat.** Perhaps this serves to clearly distinguish between the purification offering for the priest (bull) and that for the people (goat) during these unique ceremonies that incorporate sacrifices for each.

Aaron must change his clothing and **bathe himself with water** before (v 4) and after (vv 23-24) the purification rites that make up the central feature of this ceremony (vv 6-22). **He is to put on the sacred linen tunic, with linen undergarments . . . the linen sash . . . and . . . the linen turban.** These four garments are similar to, but not the same as, the four garments of the regular priests (see Haran 1985, 174; Milgrom 1991, 1016). Moreover, they are certainly distinct from the elaborate golden garments that the high priest normally wears (→ 8:7-9). The common linen garments for this day likely represent humility and identify the high priest as a servant and representative of the people (see Gersonides in Carasik 2009, 119; Wenham 1979, 230; Gorman 1997, 95). The linen garments may also represent a holiness that transcends that of all other priestly attire (Keil and Delitzsch n.d., 397; Haran 1985, 174). Twice in v 4, the garments are labeled *qōdeš* ("holy"; NIV = **sacred**).

3. Designation of Bull and Goats (16:6-10)

■ **6** Verses 6-10 provide an overview of the ceremony for the Day of Atonement. The details of the ceremony are described in vv 11-28 (→ Behind the Text above). Aaron will offer a **bull for his own *purification* offering.** This corresponds with the purification offering instructions for when a priest sins (4:3). This sacrifice serves **to make atonement for himself and his household** (re *kipper,* to make atonement, → 4:20; 8:33-36; 9:7). The Aramaic Bible adds to this verse, "by means of a confession of sin" (*Tg. Ps.-J*). A similar addition occurs at 16:11, 16, 18, 20, 30, 33. The Hebrew Bible only mentions confession in relation to the sending out of the live goat (v 21). Nevertheless, the Aramaic translation, heavily influenced by rabbinic literature (Maher 1994, 115), demonstrates the rabbinic recognition that confession is necessary, especially in relation to rebellious sins that are included in the purification rites of this day (→ vv 16, 21, and 5:5-6; 6:4-7 [5:23-26 HB]; also Rashi in Carasik 2009, 119).

His household includes the ordinary priests who are descended from Aaron (Gersonides in Carasik 2009, 119; also Rashi in Herczeg 1999, 197-98).
■ **7** As the bull serves for the purification of the high priest (v 6), **the two goats** will serve for the community (v 5).

Before the LORD at the entrance to the Tent of Meeting (→ 1:5-9).
■ **8** Aaron is to **cast lots for the two goats.** The text literally reads, "Aaron shall put lots upon the two goats" (*wěnātan 'ahărōn 'al-šěnê haśśě'îrîm gôrālôt*). Rashi's explanation follows this rendering. He states that Aaron

places one goat to his right and one to his left. Then he draws from an urn a lot in his right hand and one in his left. Finally, he puts the lots on the goats (in Carasik 2009, 120; Herczeg 1999, 196). The goat upon which is placed the lot inscribed **for the LORD** will be sacrificed as a purification offering (v 15). The goat upon which is placed the lot inscribed for *Azazel* (NIV = **for the scapegoat**) will be sent out into the wilderness (vv 10, 21). *Azazel* likely refers to a goat-like demon that inhabits the wilderness (→ sidebar, "Azazel: Wilderness Satyr" below).

Azazel: Wilderness Satyr

Rashi interprets the term *'ăzā'zēl* (Azazel, **scapegoat**) as a severe and harsh mountain to which the live goat of ch 16 is sent (in Herczeg 1999, 196). The Greek (LXX) and Latin (Vulgate) Bibles call Azazel the "goat sent out," sometimes rendered the "goat which departs" or the "go away goat" (de Vaux 1997, 509; Hartley 1992, 237). This view identifies Azazel as the goat itself, in terms of its function, and provides the basis for the common concept of the scapegoat (Levine 1989, 102). Mary Douglas has developed an intriguing argument suggesting that the "go-away goat" serves in a rite of reconciliation aimed at restoring peace between postexilic Judah and the other descendants of Jacob living in the surrounding region (Douglas 2003, 121-41; idem 2004, 45-60). However, the goat is "for Azazel" and "sent to Azazel." It is difficult to understand the goat as designated "for itself" or "sent to itself" (Hartley 1992, 237).

The parallel construction of 16:8 indicates that Azazel must be a proper name, as a counterpart to YHWH (**the Lord;** de Vaux 1997, 509). This suggests that Azazel is a personal being who inhabits the wilderness and to whom the goat is sent. Nahmanides calls Azazel a prince who rules over the waste places (in Carasik 2009, 120). Others see Azazel as the leader of demons (Keil and Delitzsch n.d., 398; Rylaarsdam 1962, 315). The wilderness is often identified as the abode of evil spirits (Isa 13:21; 34:14; Matt 12:43; Luke 11:24; Rev 18:2). Azazel does not appear anywhere else in the Bible beyond four occurrences in Lev 16 (vv 8, 10 [twice], 26). In later Jewish literature (OT Pseudepigrapha), Azazel is identified as a fallen angel who taught people how to make weapons and to adorn themselves with jewelry and makeup. He led people in corruption and was judged for showing people injustice and sin (*1 En.* 8:1-2; 9:6; 13:1-2). He was bound and cast into a hole in the desert, with rugged and sharp rocks thrown on top of him (*1 En.* 10:4-6; Isaac 1983, 16-17, 19; see Feinberg 1958, 328; Rylaarsdam 1962, 315).

The term *śā'îr* is often translated "goat" (as in 16:7-10, 15, 18, 20-22, 26-27), but in some contexts it refers to a satyr, goat-like demon, or goat idol (Lev 17:7; 2 Chr 11:15; Isa 13:21; 34:14; see BDB 1952, 972, defs. II and III [also 2 Kgs 23:8, see NAB and NET translations]). Offering sacrifices to such creatures is forbidden (Lev 17:7). Accordingly, it is clear that the live goat is not sent as an offering to Azazel (see Nahmanides in Carasik 2009, 120). On the contrary, it is loaded with sins and is impure (de Vaux 1997, 509). What may have been the reflection of a pagan rite to a wilderness demon has been transformed into a rite that afflicts the evil spirit with the sins of the nation. The demon Azazel "has been eviscerated of his erstwhile demonic powers by the Priestly legislators" (Milgrom 1991, 1021). Azazel is denied any active role in the rite; he does not receive the goat or attack it. The goat is not treated as a sacrifice with any performance of slaughter or blood manipulation. The goat is merely a vehicle to expel the sins of the people into the wilderness (Milgrom 1991, 1021). The sins of Israel were removed from the community and returned to their representative source, in order to break the power and effect of sin (Hartley 1992, 238; see Keil and Delitzsch n.d., 404). The repeated statement that the goat is presented "before the LORD" (16:7, 10) emphasizes that the offering is God's and not dedicated to Azazel (it is only "sent" to Azazel; Milgrom 1991, 1023). This emphasis also serves to facilitate the transformation of what may have originally been a pagan custom (see Gerstenberger 1996, 220).

■ **9** The rite regarding **the goat whose lot falls to the** LORD (→ v 8) is described in v 15. It is to be sacrificed **for a *purification*** offering (see 4:13-21).

■ **10** The rite regarding **the goat *whose lot falls to Azazel*** (this wording is parallel to the corresponding phrase in v 9, contrary to the change in the NIV; → v 8) is described in vv 20-22. Presenting the goat **before the** LORD emphasizes that, even though it is "sent" to Azazel, it is offered to the Lord (see sidebar, "Azazel: Wilderness Satyr" above). The goat is **to be used for making atonement**. This refers to the general sense of *kipper* ("atonement"), attained in this case **by sending it** [the goat] **to Azazel** into the desert. Sins are dispatched on the back of the goat (v 21) so they no longer interfere with relationship to God. As a result the people are "at one" with the Lord (→ 4:20; 8:33-36; 9:7; see Milgrom 1991, 1083).

B. The Ceremony (16:11-28)

1. The Blood Rite (16:11-19)

■ **11** The first half of this verse is identical to v 6 (→ v 6, and Behind the Text above). Laying a hand on the head of the animal in order to designate the **bull as the high priest's own *purification*** offering is taken for granted (→ 1:4 and 9:8; also Milgrom 1991, 1024).

■ **12-13** The high priest must **take a censer full of burning coals from the altar.** This refers to the outer altar of burnt offering that must be kept burning at all times (→ 6:12-13 [6:5-6 HB]; Rashi in Herczeg 1999, 198; Milgrom 1991, 1025). The phrase **before the** LORD in v 12 applies to the outer altar, as it does in 1:11 and 2 Chr 1:6 (→ Lev 1:5-9). Along with the censer of coals, the high priest is to take **two handfuls of . . . incense.** In order to manage the censer and **two handfuls** of incense, the high priest would have to use something like a ladle to hold the incense (Gersonides in Carasik 2009, 121). Rashi explains that, for the Day of Atonement, the

finely ground fragrant incense was ground even more finely than usual (in Carasik 2009, 121; see Exod 30:34-38).

Aaron is instructed to take these elements **behind the curtain.** The curtain (*pārōket*) is the veil that separates the holy place from the holy of holies. At this point, Aaron enters the holy of holies and must **put the incense on the fire.** Here in v 13, **before the Lord** obviously refers to the space within the holy of holies (→ 1:5-9). When Aaron places the incense on the coals, **the smoke of the incense will conceal the *mercy seat.*** Aaron must create the smoke in the holy of holies **so that he will not die.** God appears in the holy of holies, above the mercy seat, between the cherubim (→ 16:1-2). The incense smoke prevents Aaron from looking upon God and dying, as implied here and by the statement in v 2, "or else he will die, because I appear in the cloud over the *mercy seat*" (see Exod 33:20). Though he survives the encounter, Jacob expresses the same principle when he exclaims, "I saw God face to face, and yet my life was spared" (Gen 32:30). The mortal danger of seeing God directly suggests that the overwhelming majesty and magnificence of God is too much for humans to bear. Accordingly even Moses, with whom God spoke "face to face" (Exod 33:11), only "sees the *form* of the Lord" (Num 12:8, emphasis added).

The mercy seat is **above the Testimony,** which refers to the stone tablets on which are inscribed the Ten Commandments. The tablets are kept inside the ark of the covenant (Exod 31:18; 32:15; 34:29; 40:20; Deut 4:13; 10:4; Budd 1996, 229). The longer phrase "ark of the Testimony" (Exod 25:22; 26:33-34; 30:6, 26; 31:7; and elsewhere) is synonymous with "ark of the covenant" (see Milgrom 1991, 1031).

■ **14** Aaron is instructed to **take some of the bull's blood** and **sprinkle** [*hizzâ*] **it.** The bull serves to make atonement for Aaron and his household (Lev 16:6, 11). Since the blood is sprinkled in relationship to the **atonement cover (*mercy seat*)**, it is clear that the action of this verse takes place inside the holy of holies. The sprinkling of the blood represents cleansing the holy of holies from the defilement caused by the sins and impurities of the priests and also represents the commitment of the priests to offer their lives in service to God (→ 4:5-7 and From the Text for 4:1—6:7 [4:1—5:26 HB]).

Two blood manipulations are described. First the blood is sprinkled **on the surface of the mercy seat.** In parallel with the next verse, *'al pěnê* ("upon the face of" or "on the surface of"; BDB 1952, 819) is understood as equivalent to the shorter form, *'al* ("upon," 16:15; BDB 1952, 752). Thus, the first sprinkling is directed *onto* the mercy seat itself (see Milgrom 1991, 1031-32). The Hebrew text further stipulates that this sprinkling is to occur *qēdmâ* ("toward the East"; BDB 1952, 870). This likely refers to the east side of the mercy seat, or **the front of** the mercy seat (given its orientation facing the priest; see Milgrom 1991, 1032). The second blood application calls for sprinkling the blood **seven times before** (*lipnê*; both vv 14 and 15) **the mercy seat.** The number seven suggests completeness (Hartley 1992, 239; → 4:5-7). The two manipulations likely represent the cleansing of the priests and the sanctuary respectively (Keil and Delitzsch n.d., 399).

■ **15** Aaron shall then slaughter the goat for the *purification* offering (see 16:9). As the bull was sacrificed on behalf of Aaron and his household (v 11), so now the goat is sacrificed **for the people.** The goat's blood is taken **behind the curtain** (→ vv 12-13), indicating that, as with the bull's blood, Aaron enters the holy of holies. He must apply the goat's blood **as he did with the bull's blood.** Thus, he will **sprinkle** [*hizzâ*] it **upon** [*'al*] the **mercy seat and before** [*lipnê*] **it.** The same two blood manipulations are carried out with goat's blood as was done with the bull's blood (v 14). This time, the blood rite serves to cleanse *the people* and the sanctuary respectively, from the defilement of *their* sins and impurities. In addition, the offering of blood (= life; see 17:11) represents the commitment of the people to offer their lives in obedience to God (→ 16:14).

■ **16** The blood rite described in vv 14-15 serves to **purge** [cleanse] **the holy of holies** (re translating *kipper* as "purge," → 4:20; re recognizing *haqqōdeš* as the holy of holies, → 16:1-2). Sins and impurities pollute the sanctuary (→ 4:1-2 and From the Text for 4:1—6:7 [4:1—5:26 HB]). Wesley recognized that, though the people did not enter the sanctuary themselves, their sins did (1765, 400). Thus, it must be cleansed *from* **the impurities of the children of Israel.** Three nouns are identified as the objects of purgation. Impurities (*ṭum'ōt*) include both ritual and moral uncleanness. Ritual impurities recall the pollution that results from uncleanness as related in the impurity laws of chs 11—15. These are not sins or moral faults (→ 4:3). In contrast, moral impurities are generated by sin. The sanctuary is also cleansed *from their rebellious sins.* Deliberate sins (*pěšā'îm*) can only be atoned by confession (16:21) and repentance (→ 4:1-2; 5:5-6; 6:4-7 [5:23-26 HB]). Pollution from these sins penetrates all the way into the holy of holies, thereby requiring this annual cleansing (Milgrom 1991, 1034; → From the Text for 4:1—6:7 [4:1—5:26 HB]). Finally, the blood rite purges the holy of holies *for all their sins.* The noun *ḥaṭṭā't*, related to the verb previously qualified as sinning "unintentionally" (*bišěgāgâ*; 4:2, 22, 27; 5:5), sums up Israel's sins. Accordingly, the sanctuary is cleansed from ritual impurities (chs 11—15) and moral impurities resulting from both unintentional (*ḥaṭṭā't*) and rebellious sins (*pěšāʿîm*; Rashi in Herczeg 1999, 200; Milgrom 1991, 1033, 1035).

The same blood rite is to be carried out **for the Tent of Meeting**. In this case the tent of meeting refers to the holy place (→ 4:4). This abbreviated statement indicates that Aaron is to purge the holy place with the blood from the bull of his own purification offering and the goat of the people's purification offering. The blood is to be sprinkled before the curtain and put on the horns of the incense altar as described in the purification rites for the priest and the congregation (4:5-7, 16-18).

■ **17** The solemnity of this annual blood rite requires that **no one is to be in the Tent of Meeting from the time Aaron goes in to make atonement in the *holy of holies* until he comes out**. Obviously this applies to the priests, for the common people were never allowed inside the holy place (Milgrom 1991, 1035). The purpose of the ceremony is summarized as Aaron making **atonement for himself, his household and the whole community of Israel** (→ 16:14, 15).

■ **18** Aaron **shall come out to the altar**. This is clearly the outer altar of burnt offering (Ibn Ezra in Carasik 2009, 122). Atonement was already made in relation to the inner altar of incense (→ v 16). The phrase **before the LORD** applies to the outer altar, as in v 12 (→ vv 12-13). After making atonement in relation to the holy of holies and the holy place (vv 14-17), Aaron will now **make atonement** in relation to the outer altar. **He shall take some of the bull's blood and some of the goat's blood and put it on all the horns of the altar**. Rashi explains that at this point the blood from the bull and the goat are intermingled (in Herczeg 1999, 202). Aaron shall **put** (*nātan*) the blood on the horns of the altar, consistent with the blood rite for the purification offering for the "leader" (4:25), and the "member of the community" (4:30; → 4:5-7). In this case, Aaron completes the purification of the sanctuary (from holy of holies, through the holy place, and out to the altar of burnt offering) in relation to the sins and impurities of the priests and all the people.

■ **19** Aaron **shall sprinkle** [*hizzâ*] **some of the blood on it with his finger seven times**. Seven signifies completion and perfection (Wesley 1765, 400; → 4:5-7). This second manipulation reflects the previous blood applications in the holy of holies and holy place (→ 16:14, 15, 16). In this case, however, the purpose is **to cleanse** (*ṭihar*) and **to consecrate** (*qiddaš*) the altar **from the impurities** [*ṭumʾōt*] **of the children of Israel** (→ v 16). The outer altar was previously consecrated with oil (→ 8:10-11) and with blood (→ 8:15) during the ordination ceremony. This annual *reconsecra-*

tion serves to cleanse the altar from past impurities and sanctify it for future use (Rashi in Herczeg 1999, 202).

Christ as the Mercy Seat of God

The sacrificial system depicts the presence of God as virtually inaccessible. The mercy seat (NIV = "atonement cover") sits on top of the ark of the covenant, with two winged cherubim affixed above it. God appears above the mercy seat between the cherubim (Exod 25:17-22; Ps 99:1). The ark is kept behind the curtain, inside the holy of holies, within the tabernacle. No one is allowed access to the holy of holies, except the high priest on this one day each year (Day of Atonement), and then he must fill the room with smoke lest he die from looking upon the glory of God. Only priests are allowed access to the holy place outside the curtain from the holy of holies. All other Israelites are only allowed as near as the outer altar in the courtyard of the sanctuary. Once a year, before the mercy seat, within the hidden, innermost region of the sanctuary, the high priest secures atonement for Israel and offers life to God representing the commitment and obedience of the people. Accordingly, the mercy seat serves as *the place of God's presence* and *the place where atonement is secured*.

Jesus Christ brings a profound sense of fulfillment to the function of the mercy seat. In the book of Romans, Paul explains that "righteousness from God is revealed" in the gospel (Rom 1:17). He argues that various attempts at attaining the righteousness of God have failed (righteousness through self-fulfillment [Rom 1:18-32]; righteousness based on a pretense of law and ritual [Rom 2:1-29]). Paul underscores this point with a collection of quotes from Psalms, and Isaiah, which exclaim a history of human failure in relation to attaining righteousness (Rom 3:10-18). After decrying the abysmal human record of reaching God's righteousness, Paul finally announces that "a righteousness from God . . . has been made known" (Rom 3:21). It is "apart from law," yet "the Law and the Prophets testify" to it (Rom 3:21).

In expounding this righteousness from God, Paul points to Jesus Christ. He states that "God presented him as a *hilastērion*" (Rom 3:25). The term *hilastērion* (NIV = "sacrifice of atonement") appears twenty-nine times (in twenty-two verses) in the Bible (twenty-seven times in the OT [LXX, Greek Bible]; two times in the NT). Twenty-two of the twenty-seven occurrences in the OT translate the Hebrew term *kappōret* (Exod 25:17-22; 31:7; 35:12; 37:6, 8-9 [LXX 38:5, 7-8]; Lev 16:2, 13, 14-15; Num 7:89; Amos 9:1 [*kaptôr* read as *kappōret*]). The remaining five OT occurrences all appear in Ezek 43 (vv 14, 17, 20) and translate the term *'ăzārâ*, which refers to a ledge on the altar (BDB 1952, 741). In all of these texts (except Ezekiel), the term *kappōret* refers to the lid on the ark of the covenant (i.e., "mercy seat," → 16:1-2). There is only one other occurrence of the term *hilastērion* in the Bible, at Heb 9:5. Here, too, the term refers to the lid on the ark of the covenant. Thus, every instance of *hilastērion* in the Bible refers to a physical object related to the tabernacle, namely, the lid on the ark of the covenant (or in the case of Ezekiel, a ledge on the altar).

Modern translations commonly translate *hilastērion* in Rom 3:25 as "sacrifice of atonement" (NIV, NRSV), "propitiation" (KJV, NASB, NKJV), or "expiation" (NAB,

RSV). Nevertheless, the consistent use of the term elsewhere in the Bible as a reference to temple furniture (100 percent of the time referring to the mercy seat or a ledge on the altar) strongly suggests that Rom 3:25 should also be translated "mercy seat" (with NET, YLT). Yet, does it make sense to refer to Christ as a piece of temple furniture (the lid to the ark of the covenant)? Recognizing Christ as the incarnation of God (*the place of God's presence*) and Savior of humanity (*the place where atonement is secured*) suggests the answer is yes! The function of the mercy seat finds fulfillment in the life, death, and resurrection of Jesus Christ. This is further affirmed by the preceding phrase in Rom 3:25, which qualifies *hilastērion*. Paul asserts that Christ is one "whom God *displayed publicly*" (NASB, emphasis added; *hon proetheto ho theos*) as a *hilastērion*. Such a qualification makes a bold and profound statement. The mercy seat of the tabernacle is *never* publicly displayed. Rather, it is completely inaccessible, except to the high priest, only once a year, after hiding it in a cloud of smoke.

In Rom 3:25, Paul is making the powerful statement that, in Christ, the mercy seat of God is now available to all people at all times! The Gospel writers reflect the same powerful message by describing the tearing of the temple curtain (which hides the mercy seat within the holy of holies) at the moment of Christ's death (Matt 27:51; Mark 15:38; Luke 23:45; see Wenham 1979, 237). In Christ, *the place of God's presence* and *the place where atonement is secured* (i.e., functions of the mercy seat) is exposed for all time and made accessible to everyone (see Hartley 1992, 245).

2. The Live Goat (16:20-22)

■ **20-22** After making atonement [*kipper*; → 4:20] for the **holy of holies** [vv 14-16a], the **holy place** [v 16b] and the altar (v 18), Aaron is instructed to bring forward **the live goat** (→ vv 8, 10 and 16:8 sidebar, "Azazel: Wilderness Satyr"). **Aaron is to lay both hands on the head of the live goat.** By this act, Aaron will take the sins of the people **and put them on the goat's head.** This signifies transference of sin, but not substitution (→ 1:4). The sins are placed on the goat; however, the goat is not punished in place of the sinners. Rather, the goat serves as a means of transporting the sins away from the community. **The goat will carry on itself all their sins to a solitary place.**

Aaron must **confess over** the goat all the sins of the people. Confession makes it possible for even their deliberate sins to be atoned (→ 5:1-4, 5-6; 6:4-7 [5:23-26 HB]). Three terms are used to identify the sins **of the Israelites.** Gane states that in chs 1—16, the term *ăwōnōt* ("iniquities"; NIV = **wickedness**) refers to blame or culpability that arises from an act of *ḥaṭṭā't* ("expiable sin"; 2004, 282). This prompts the comparable meaning of "guilt," which also arises from acts of sin. The term *ăwōnōt* replaces *ṭum'ōt* ("impurities") in the corresponding list of offenses in v 16. The recognition that moral impurities result from acts of sin parallels the thought that "guilt" arises from acts of sin. The second term for sin is the same as that in v 16, that is, *pěšāʿîm* (***rebellious sins***). Also, as in v 16, the transgressions of Israel are summed up with the phrase, ***for all their sins*** (*ḥaṭṭāʾt*). In v 16, the focus is on cleansing the sanctuary and people from impurity (ritual and moral) and sins that generate impurity (i.e., moral impurity); while here the emphasis is on ridding the community of guilt and sins that generate guilt (→ v 16).

The goat, laden with the sins and guilt of the community, is sent **away into the desert . . . to a solitary place.** The text literally refers to "a land of cutting off." Thus, the goat is cut off from the community in a place from which it cannot return (Wenham 1979, 233; Budd 1996, 232-33). Rabbinic literature relates that the goat was chased up a cliff and pushed over (Ibn Ezra in Carasik 2009, 120). Tradition holds that a strip of crimson cloth was tied to the goat and another to the temple door. At the moment the goat was pushed off a cliff and died, the cloth turned white, symbolizing the return of innocence (Nahmanides in Carasik 2009, 123). The concern here is not so much to do harm to the animal as it is to ensure that the sins are not able to return to the community.

3. Remaining Offerings and Closing Procedures (16:23-28)

■ **23-25** Aaron must now **take off the linen garments.** These garments had been **put on before he entered the *holy of holies*** (→ vv 3-5). This statement serves as a reminder that the high priest had put on the linen garments specifically for the purpose of entering the holy of holies (Milgrom 1991, 1048).

Aaron must **leave** the linen garments in the ***holy place*** (Tent of Meeting; → 4:4), and **bathe himself with water.** There is no discussion of bathing facilities inside the tent of meeting. Thus, the high priest must have bathed in the laver in the courtyard. However, if his garments are left inside the tent of meeting, how did he avoid being seen naked on his way out to the laver? Rabbinic tradition explains that a sheet or improvised curtain must have been held up to shield the high priest from view (Ibn Ezra in Carasik 2009, 124; Milgrom 1991, 1049).

Various reasons are given for why Aaron must bathe again at this point in the ceremony (he bathed previously as indicated in v 4). Some argue that he became impure while transferring sins to the head of the live goat (v 21; Budd 1996, 234; Gorman 1997, 99). Others claim that Aaron must wash off the super holiness he contracted from entering the holy of holies (Milgrom 1991, 1048-49; Hartley 1992, 242). Such holiness must not be allowed to mix with the profane. This reflects the concern to maintain strict separation between that which is holy and that which is common (→ 6:10-11 [6:3-4 HB]; 6:16-18 [6:9-11 HB]; 6:27-28 [6:20-21 HB]; Gerstenberger 1996, 223). Gane suggests the reason for washing is based on the requirement that the priests must always bathe *before* performing any sacrificial service (Exod 30:20; Lev 16:4). Since the live goat ceremony interrupted his service at the altar, Aaron must wash again before sacrificing the burnt offerings (v 24; Gane 2004, 275). After bathing, Aaron must **put on his regular garments** (→ 8:7-9).

Next, Aaron shall **sacrifice the burnt offering for himself and the burnt offering for the people** (16:3, 5). These offerings also participate in making **atonement for himself** [the high priest] **and for the people** (→ 1:3; 4:20; 9:7). Finally, Aaron **shall also burn the fat of the** *purification* **offering on the altar**. This refers to both the bull for the high priest and the goat for the people (Rashi in Carasik 2009, 125).

■ **26** The man who releases the goat *to Azazel* [→ 16:8 and sidebar, "Azazel: Wilderness Satyr"] **must wash his clothes and bathe himself**. This is necessary because this layman has become defiled by handling the goat that carried the sins of the community. The sins, having been transferred onto the goat (v 21), cause the man to become impure by contact (Levine 1989, 107).

■ **27** The bull and the goat for the *purification* offerings (vv 6, 15) must be burned up. The flesh of these offerings cannot be eaten by the priests because their **blood was brought into the** **holy of holies** (6:30 [6:23 HB]; re *haqqōdeš* in ch 16 as holy of holies, see 16:1-2). More significantly, the priest may not benefit (eat) from purification offerings presented on his own behalf or that of the congregation of which he is part (→ 4:11-12; 6:29-30 [6:22-23 HB]; → 10:16-18 with related sidebar, "Why Priests Eat the Meat of the Purification Offering"; also Budd 1996, 235).

■ **28** The man who burns them [the bull and goat, 16:27] **must wash his clothes and bathe himself.** In this case, washing is required because this man has become impure through contact with the dead corpses of the animals he burned (11:25; for a different view of defilement by contact with death, see Kiuchi 1987, 138-42).

C. Final Instructions (16:29-34)

1. Designation of Date and Sabbath Instruction (16:29-31)

■ **29-31** **This is to be a lasting ordinance for you.** The audience is plural (*lākem*, **you**), indicating that the Lord is now addressing the people (see v

2; Milgrom 1991, 1053). The annual rite of the Day of Atonement is assigned **the tenth day of the seventh month** (see 23:26). On this day the people are told, **you must deny yourselves.** The verb *'ānâ* in the intensive form (*piel*) carries the meaning "to humble," "afflict," or "weaken" (BDB 1952, 776). It is commonly understood as a reference to fasting (see Ibn Ezra in Carasik 2009, 126; Porter 1976, 133; Harrison 1980, 175; Gane 2004, 271). Caesarius of Arles included fasting among those afflictions that purify hearts and facilitate redemption (Lienhard 2001, 186). The stipulations of this verse apply to both the one who is **native-born** and the ***resident* alien** (*gēr*). The inclusion of the resident alien is a characteristic of H (→ Behind the Text for ch 17) and suggests that these final instructions (vv 29-34) are a later addition (Knohl 1995, 27-28; King 2009, 139-40; see Milgrom 1991, 1064-65).

The people are told that as a result of this day, **you will be clean from all your sins.** The Day of Atonement provides an annual cleansing from all sin, and the opportunity to continue relationship with God with a clean slate.

The Day of Atonement is designated a *šabbat šabbātôn* (lit. "a sabbath of sabbatic observance"; BDB 1952, 992; NIV = **sabbath of rest**). This phrase has superlative force suggesting a stricter observance than the *šabbātôn* required on the first and eighth day of a festival (23:39; Levine 1989, 109-10). This corresponds with the instruction that the people shall **not do any work** (*kol-mĕlā'kâ*). In contrast, on the festivals, the work prohibition is expressed as *kol-mĕle'ket 'ăbōdâ* (i.e., you shall not do any *laborious work*; Num 28; Lev 23). The difference is that on the festivals, light work is permitted; while on the regular Sabbath and Day of Atonement, not even the slightest exertion is allowed (Milgrom 1991, 1054-55).

2. Summation (16:32-34)

■ **32-34** These final verses provide a brief summary related to the Day of Atonement ceremony. The officiant for the day is explicitly designated as **the priest who is anointed and ordained to succeed his father as high priest.** Aaron initially serves in this role, as he is named throughout the instructions for this day (vv 2, 3, 6, 8, 9, 11, 21, 23). In the generations to follow, Aaron's ordained descendants shall perform the ceremony. The officiant shall wear the **sacred linen garments** (→ vv 3-5). The purpose of the ceremony is reviewed in terms of making **atonement for the *holy of holies*, for the *holy place*** and the altar, and for the priests and all the people of the community (vv 6, 15-18, 20, 24). The general and overall cleansing character of the ceremony is expressed by the closing statement, **atonement is to be made once a year for all the sins of the Israelites.**

FROM THE TEXT

The annual Day of Atonement provides a comprehensive cleansing from sin and impurity for the congregation of Israel. Individual and community purification offerings may be presented throughout the year as needed (ch 4). However, on the annual Day of Atonement all remaining or overlooked sins and impurities are atoned and removed. In addition on this day, even deliberate sins, which penetrate and pollute all the way into the holy of holies, are atoned (→ 5:1-4, 5-6; 6:4-7 [5:23-26 HB]). The priest and his household are dealt with first, in keeping with the principle that the priest must be cleansed before he can facilitate the cleansing of others. The blood rite for the ceremony represents the purification of the sanctuary (holy of holies, holy place, and outer altar) and purification of the people. Such cleansing is necessary so that God may continue to abide in the midst of the community. In addition, the presentation of blood before the mercy seat represents the offering of life to God, not as substitutionary death, but as a commitment to obedient living (→ From the Text for 1:1—3:17 and for 4:1—6:7 [4:1—5:26 HB]).

The sending out of the live goat to Azazel represents the removal of all the sins of the community, so that past sins and guilt no longer influence or demoralize the people. The transformation of what may have been a pagan rite is consistent with the renovation of other ancient practices and beliefs through the biblical sacrificial system (→ sidebars, "Azazel: Wilderness Satyr" at 16:8 and "Agricultural Origins of Festivals" at 23:5-8). For example, when priests eat the flesh of purification offerings, it serves to refute the pagan belief that there is magical power in the blood of the sacrifice (→ 10:16-18 sidebar, "Why Priests Eat the Meat of the Purification Offering"). The biblical sacrificial system affirms that only the action and mercy of God are able to cleanse sin (Rylaarsdam 1962, 316). Also, consistent with the prophetic tendency to mock foreign idols (Isa 44:9-20; 45:20; Jer 10:3-5, 8, 14-15), representatively banishing sins back to a wilderness demon demonstrates the impotence and nonexistence of such a being.

Jesus Christ brings fulfillment to multiple aspects of the Day of Atonement. As the *mercy seat* of God, Christ represents the place of God's presence and the place where atonement is secured (→ 16:19 sidebar, "Christ as the Mercy Seat of God"). Christ truly demonstrated *offering life to God* (as represented by the presentation of blood [life; 17:11] before the mercy seat). He did so, not only by *living* in daily obedience to God, but also by literally surrendering his *life* (shedding his blood) on a cross. Similar to the live goat, Jesus is identified as the "Lamb of God, *who takes away the sin* of the world" (John 1:29, emphasis added). Through the live goat, and later through Christ, sins are removed "as far as the east is from the west" (Ps 103:12; see Kaiser 1994, 1112). Rather than portraying a substitutionary role, Christ calls his followers to take up their own cross and follow him (Matt 16:24; Mark 8:34; Luke 9:23). The Apostle Paul reflects the same notion using sacrificial terminology, with the exhortation, "I urge you, brothers [and sisters], in view of God's mercy, to *offer your bodies as living sacrifices*, holy and pleasing to God" (Rom 12:1, emphasis added). Accordingly, through Christ, and with the power of the Holy Spirit, God calls people to remove sin from their communities and live holy lives in obedience to the Lord.

V. THE HOLINESS CODE (17:1—27:34)

A. Slaughter and the Blood Prohibition (17:1-16)

BEHIND THE TEXT

Leviticus 17—26 is commonly referred to as the Holiness Code. This label derives from Klostermann's term, *"das Heiligkeitsgesetz"* (1893, 368-85, esp. 385). Source theory assigns this material to H (Holiness source) and traditionally considers it an early component of the priestly literature. Knohl attributes the material to an independent priestly school (i.e., the Holiness School [HS]), and along with Milgrom recognizes the work of H as later than P (Knohl 1995, 6; Milgrom 1991, 13).

The thematic emphasis on "holiness" begins with a call to holiness addressed to the people of Israel. The call is primarily expressed through two clauses: *qĕdōšîm tihyû* (alternatively, *wihyîtem qĕdōšîm;* "you shall be holy," 19:2; 20:7, 26 NRSV), and *'ănî YHWH mĕqaddiškem* ("I am the LORD, who makes you holy," 20:8; 21:8; 22:32). The second clause is echoed in "the characteristic signature of HS," that is, the formula *'ănî YHWH ĕlōhêkem* ("I am the LORD your God"), and "the distinguishing concluding formula of HS," that is, *ănî YHWH* ("I am the LORD"; Knohl 1995, 16, 38). These formulas appear fifty times within chs 18—26 (in one instance the longer version appears as *ănî YHWH ĕlōhêhem* ["I am the LORD *their* God," emphasis added]; see King 2009, 126-27).

The Holiness Code extends the call to holiness beyond the tabernacle and the priests, to all Israel. For H, the land is holy and all who dwell in it must be holy (Milgrom 1992, 457). H extends P's conception of God's presence in the tabernacle to a broader image of God dwelling among the people. This is expressed clearly in 26:11-12: "I will put my dwelling place among you, and I will not abhor you. I will walk among you and be your God, and you will be my people."

Leviticus 17 opens the Holiness Code with instructions regarding animals for food, including sacrificial animals, wild game, and animals found dead. Central to these instructions is the prohibition against ingesting blood and its rationale. Schwartz explains that the chapter is made up of five laws dealing with the proper disposal of the blood of animals that may be eaten (1991, 36-43). Gorman identifies the first four of the five units of the chapter by means of the introductory phrase, "if anyone from the house of Israel . . ." (*'iš 'iš mibbêt yiśrā'ēl*; vv 3, 8, 10, 13). The fifth unit begins with "all persons who eat . . ." (*kol-nepeš 'ăšer tō'kal*; v 15; 1997, 101).

IN THE TEXT

1. Ban on Common Slaughter of Sawcrificial Animals (17:1-9)

■ **1-2** The Lord commands Moses to address the priests and **all the Israelites.** This reflects H's theological concern to include the Israelites in matters of the sanctuary and holiness (Milgrom 2000, 1451).

■ **3-7** The initial instruction here relates to **any Israelite who sacrifices an ox, a lamb or a goat.** These are domestic animals acceptable for use on the altar as sacrifices. It is uncertain whether the law refers only to occasions when such animals are slaughtered specifically to perform a sacrificial rite or whether the ruling includes common slaughter of such animals for food. The NIV's use of the verb **sacrifices** implies the former, but the term *yišḥaṭ* refers to slaughter that may apply to sacrifice or to nonsacrificial slaughter for food (Milgrom 2000, 1453).

If sacrificial slaughter is in mind, then the prohibition seeks to centralize sacrificial practice at **the Tent of Meeting** and not allow sacrifice to be performed elsewhere **in the camp or outside of it** (Rashi in Herczeg 1999, 209; Wesley 1765, 403; Levine 1989, 112-13). This corresponds with the concern to eliminate a form of idolatry in which Israelites were slaughtering animals **in the open fields** and offering **sacrifices to the goat idols** (Wesley 1765, 403). Rashi explains that *śě'îrîm* ("he-goat," "satyr," "demon"; BDB 1952, 972) here refers to "demons" (in Herczeg 1999, 210). It seems these demons were thought to take the shape of goats, like satyrs of mythology (Wenham 1979, 243). Israel may have been influenced by such goat worship through contact with Egyptians (Josh 24:14) who appear to have worshiped goats as gods (Josephus, *Ag. Ap.* 2.7; Keil and Delitzsch n.d., 409; Harrison 1980, 180; Kaiser 1994, 1118). King Josiah's reform may have included the destruction of high places dedicated to goat demons (2 Kgs 23:8; reading *hš'rym* ["gates"] as *hś'rym* ["goats," "demons"]; Porter 1976, 140; Hartley 1992, 272). Accordingly, this law would still allow for common or profane slaughter of domestic animals when the purpose is merely to provide meat for the table (Levine 1989, 112-13; Kaiser 1994, 1118).

If common slaughter is the focus of the prohibition, then the ruling seeks to ban the eating of meat from domestic animals except when sacrificed as ***well-being*** **offerings** (Nahmanides in Carasik 2009, 127; Pedersen 1940, 341; Milgrom 2000, 1453-54). This understanding of the Law reflects the principle of reverence for life (→ 11:46-47 sidebar, "Rationale for the Dietary Restrictions," and From the Text for 11:1—15:33). One who kills an animal for food, without first dedicating a portion of it to God on the altar, is considered equivalent to a murderer. Such a person is **considered guilty of bloodshed** (Rashi in Herczeg 1999, 209; Porter 1976, 139).

Milgrom asserts that the noun *zebaḥ* ("sacrifice") and the verb *zābaḥ* ("to sacrifice"), found in 17:5 and 7, are used exclusively in relation to the well-being offering. This indicates that the focus of the pericope (vv 3-7) is on the proper means of providing meat for the table (2000, 1459). The proper means is stipulated as bringing sacrifices **to the Tent of Meeting . . . as fellowship offerings,** and no longer **in the open fields . . . to the goat idols.** This serves as a second rationale for the ban on common slaughter.

Cut off from his people (→ 7:19-21).

Question of Common Slaughter and Centralization

A ban on common slaughter is only feasible if there is reasonable access to the sanctuary. Nahmanides explains that in the wilderness setting, it would not be difficult for every animal meant for food to be brought to the tabernacle and turned into a well-being offering. However, this ruling does not apply after the Israelites enter the promised land. Deuteronomy clarifies that "when the LORD your God has enlarged your territory," and the sanctuary is "too far away from you," you may slaughter domestic animals and eat them "in your own towns" (Deut 12:20-21; see also vv 13-15; in Carasik 2009, 127; also Gane 2004, 302).

Some hold that the original form of the law in Lev 17:3-7 presupposed multiple sanctuaries, whereby those who live far from the main tabernacle would still be able to eat domestic meat by traveling to a regional altar (as illustrated by the events in 1 Sam 14:32-35). This original law was later accommodated to the single sanctuary when incorporated by P (depicting P as later than H). Yet, a ban on common slaughter is not strictly consistent with P, which does seem to allow common slaughter of domestic animals for food (Lev 7:22-27; Driver 1910, 51).

Milgrom maintains that P (seen as earlier than H) indeed espouses common slaughter *and* multiple sanctuaries. While H also allows for multiple sanctuaries, the innovation of H, here in 17:3-7, is the ban on common slaughter. Given the reversal of this ban in Deuteronomy (D), it does not seem to have lasted very long (H may be associated with the reform of Hezekiah, while D is associated with the reform of Josiah, see King 2009, 152-53). D must reverse H's ban on common slaughter because of D's insistence on centralization (Milgrom 2000, 1452-55, 1503-4). The ban on common slaughter only applies to domestic animals eligible for sacrifice. Game animals are only subject to the prohibition against ingesting blood (Lev 17:13-14; see Milgrom 2000, 1457).

■ **8-9** These verses expand the preceding ruling (vv 3-7) to include the **burnt offering,** and indeed any **sacrifice,** in the demand that slaughtered animals be brought **to the Tent of Meeting.** In addition, this ruling is applied to **any alien living among** the Israelites (Noth 1977, 131; Porter 1976, 140). The foundational concern here is that every sacrifice be offered exclusively **to the LORD.**

The **alien,** often translated "sojourner" (RSV, YLT), is required to abide by the main laws of Israel; for example, Sabbath (Exod 20:10), the Day of Atonement (Lev 16:29), abstaining from heathen worship (20:2), and refraining from blasphemy (24:16; Wenham 1979, 244). In this case, though sojourners might be allowed common slaughter for food (see 17:3-7), they are not allowed to sacrifice to other gods (see Milgrom 2000, 1463).

Cut off from his people (→ 7:19-21).

The *Gēr*, "Sojourner," "Resident Alien"

The population of ancient Israel included some who were designated *gērîm*, or resident foreigners (sometimes simply translated "strangers"). The *gēr* is considered similar to the Arabic *jâr*, a refugee seeking protection from another tribe. The *gēr* was a foreigner living within another community in which he or she is accepted and able to enjoy certain rights. Resident aliens did not own land in Israel, and therefore served as hired laborers (Deut 24:14). They were often associated with the poor, orphans, and widows (Lev 19:10; 23:22). Israelites were exhorted to care for aliens, while recalling that they too were once *gērîm* in the land of Egypt (Exod 22:21 [v 20 HB]; 23:9; de Vaux 1997, 74-75). Knohl refers to a "principle of the equality of stranger and citizen," which is characteristic of the Holiness Code (1995, 21). Beginning with Lev 16:29 (→ 16:29-31), the inclusion of the resident alien as subject to the laws of Israel is found throughout the Holiness Code (1995, 21). Milgrom clarifies that the gēr was obligated to obey the prohibitive commands, but not the performative ones. For example, aliens must never consume blood (17:10), but they are not required to participate in the festivals (2000, 1496, see also 1470).

2. Prohibition against Ingesting Blood (17:10-12)

■ **10-12** This pericope seems to interrupt the flow of the chapter that otherwise addresses the consumption of domestic animals eligible for sacrifice (vv 3-9), wild game (vv 13-14), and animals found dead (vv 15-16). The blood prohibition, stated twice in this pericope (vv 10, 12) and repeated in v 14, is prompted by the overall focus of the chapter on the consumption of animal flesh. Its mention further prompts the statement of its rationale, which is enveloped within the two occurrences of the prohibition in vv 10-12 (Schwartz 1991, 45-46). The rationale for the blood prohibition speaks to the overall importance of blood in the sacrificial system.

H clarifies and extends the priestly understanding that blood must be returned to God (→ 1:5-9). H draws on distinct priestly material (P^N, see Introduction, "C. Composition") reflected in Genesis to develop its prohibition against eating blood. Initially, only plants are designated as food sources (Gen 1:29-30), effectively restricting the shedding of animal blood. After the flood, the consumption of meat is allowed; however, the blood representing the life of the creature must be drained and not eaten (Gen 9:3-4; King 2009, 147). Preserving the blood promotes respect for life (→ Lev 17:3-7; Wenham 1979, 244-45). From this foundation, H applies the blood prohibition to the sacrificial system and dietary laws. Priestly passages outside of Genesis that explicitly express the prohibition against eating blood can all be attributed to H (Lev 3:17; 7:26; 17:14; 19:26; King 2009, 147). Here in 17:10-12, H provides the rationale for the prohibition by emphasizing blood as life (see Gen 9:4) and highlighting the role of blood in atonement.

The significance of blood in the sacrificial system is expressed through three clauses in Lev 17:11 (Schwartz 1991, 46). The first clause indicates that the blood is significant because it carries within it (represents) **the life of a creature** ("the life of the flesh is in the blood," NASB, NRSV; Levine 1989, 115). The second clause relates that God has **given it** ["assigned it"; Milgrom 2000, 1473] **to you to make atonement for yourselves on the altar.** Thus, blood is assigned a significant role in the process of making atonement (Schwartz 1991, 50-51). The third clause clarifies that blood is able to make atonement because of its identification with life. The blood is a symbol of life, not death. Atonement occurs, not by means of death, but through life! (Füglister 1977, 147). The phrase *kî-haddām hû' bannepeš yĕkappēr* should be translated "for it is the blood by reason of [*by means of*] the life that makes atonement" (NASB; see de Vaux 1997, 419; Milgrom 2000, 1478). Blood serves to atone as it represents an offering of the life of the offerer (→ 4:5-7 and 4:32-35 sidebar, "The Offering of Life in the Sacrificial System").

It should be noted that 17:11 does not indicate that blood is the only means of atonement. Atonement is also attested as a result of a grain offering (5:11-12), the oil rite for a person recovering from skin disease (14:15-18), payment of a coin (Exod 30:15-16), the intercession of Moses (Exod 32:30), and direct concession from God (Pss 65:3 [v 4 HB]; 78:38; 79:9; Hartley 1992, 273-74). Furthermore, blood by itself is not able to atone, but it must be activated by God (Milgrom 2000, 1479).

Use of *Nepeš* in Lev 17:10-15

The usual term for "person" in ch 17 is *'îš*, while *nepeš* is used for "life." However, in vv 10-15 *nepeš* is used for "person" (Milgrom 2000, 1471). Verses 10-15 actually reflect a play on words in which *nepeš* alternates between the meaning of "person" and "life." In five instances *nepeš* refers to the "life" in the flesh of an animal, which is equated with blood and which atones (vv 11, 14). In three instances *nepeš* is used in reference to a "person" who eats the flesh or blood of an animal (vv 10, 12, 15). The final use of *nepeš* in these verses refers to "persons" as the object of atonement (**yourselves**/"your persons," v 11). The passage communicates that the *nepeš* in the blood of an animal must not be eaten and serves to atone (vv 11, 14). Eating the blood of an animal, which contains its *nepeš*, will result in being "cut off" (vv 10, 14; see v 12). Thus, the prohibition forbids any *nepeš* (person) from eating *nepeš* (life that is in the blood) in order to preserve *nepeš* (life in the blood), which serves to atone *nepeš* (persons; King 2009, 131-32).

3. Wild Game and Animals Found Dead (17:13-16)

■ **13-14** The focus of the chapter proceeds from the consumption of domestic animals to wild game. The only restriction here is the blood prohibition (→ vv 10-12). One **who hunts any animal or bird** for food **must drain out the blood.** This reflects the principle that life (blood) must be returned to God. Draining the blood is an act of respect for God and reverence for life (Gorman 1997, 104). Game is not eligible for sacrifice upon the altar, but its life (blood) still belongs to God, the Creator. Just as the blood of a sacrifice must be poured out at the altar (→ 1:5-9), so the blood of wild game must be drained and the hunter must **cover it with earth.** The blood must be covered so that no other creature might consume it (Noth 1977, 132; Schwartz 1991, 62).

■ **15-16** The chapter concludes by addressing the consumption of animals **found dead or torn by wild animals.** It is striking that the thrice-repeated blood prohibition (vv 10, 12, 14) is not mentioned here in relation to the consumption of animal carcasses. Some claim that it is assumed that the blood must be drained and buried (Porter 1976, 142; Milgrom 2000, 1484). Others maintain that ingesting blood is unavoidable when consuming carrion (Schwartz 1991, 42, 64). Milgrom explains that the blood of an animal torn by beasts would likely drain by itself. In the case of animals that die on their own, the blood would coagulate, becoming indistinguishable from the flesh and thereby lose its symbolic association with the life of the animal. Accordingly, the blood prohibition is "nowhere expressed in this law" (2000, 1486).

Persons are not prohibited from eating carcasses, but they are warned that doing so will cause them to become **ceremonially unclean.** Such a person **must wash his *or her* clothes and bathe with water** and wait **till evening** (→ 11:8, 39-40 and 15:4-10). Failure to do so results in the person being **held responsible.** The concern here is to keep a person from eating that which is holy or approaching the sanctuary *while in a state of impurity* (7:20; Rashi in Herczeg 1999, 213; → 11:8). Once again, this reflects the strong concern to maintain separation between that which is holy and that which is common (→ 10:8-11).

FROM THE TEXT

Requiring that animals eligible for sacrifice be brought to the sanctuary (17:3-7), even when slaughtered just for food, highlights two important biblical themes: the sacredness of life and the abomination of idolatry. Killing a sacrificial animal without first dedicating a portion of it to God is considered an act of bloodshed. Such acknowledgment contributes to the priestly emphasis on reverence for all life (→ 11:46-47 sidebar, "Rationale for the Dietary Restrictions").

Requiring that sacrificial animals be brought to the sanctuary also keeps Israel from making offerings to the goat idols to whom they prostitute themselves. The terminology of 17:7 (*znh;* "prostitute," "harlotry") portrays idolatry as equivalent to the disloyalty and betrayal of marital infidelity (Levine 1989, 114). Accordingly, offering worship to any besides God breaks the covenantal relationship of love between the worshiper and the Lord.

The prohibition against eating blood (v 11) reinforces the principle of reverence for life. Douglas affirms that "this solemn injunction teaches the sanctity of life (the life is in the blood). In religious terms, the mosaic dietary code is an invitation to Israel to join in the divine work of creation by living a life that honours the way God made the world and the covenants God has made with his people" (1999, 137).

In the NT it is shocking, even scandalous, that Christ associates his blood with the cup of the Eucharist and commands his followers to drink from it (Matt 26:27-28). Yet, in this case, a life has not been taken, but rather it has been freely offered. Christ boldly proclaims that partaking of the elements commemorates his sacrificial death and establishes a deep communion in which believers abide in Christ, and Christ abides in them (John 6:54-56; Hartley 1992, 279-80).

Relationship to God remains the foundational concern of the Holiness Code. Sacrifices are not to be offered to any other being. It is God who designates blood as sacred and assigns it as a central element in the process of atonement. Atonement itself does not magically transpire when blood is applied to the altar but is only efficacious by the will and grace of God.

The inclusion of the *gēr* ("resident alien," "stranger") within the community of Israel contributes to the larger theme of God's concern for the disadvantaged and the foreigner. It serves as a reminder that Israel's election was not to be self-serving. The *chosen* position of Isaac and Jacob in relation to covenant has often prompted the misconception that Ishmael and Esau were rejected by God. In the same way, Israel's covenant position is sometimes mistakenly understood as a sign of God's exclusive love for Israel and hatred for all other nations. However, the accounts of Ishmael and Esau make it clear that God also loved and blessed them (Gen 17:20; 33:9). God loved and blessed Ishmael, but established covenant with Isaac (Gen 17:21). The purpose of covenant election is not to designate those whom God favors above all others. Rather, the covenant functions as a foundation for pouring out God's blessing upon *all* nations. This is expressed in God's initial call to Abraham: "all peoples on earth will be blessed through you" (Gen 12:3). It is further implicit in the Sinai covenant in which Israel is called to become "a kingdom of priests" (Exod 19:6). If the entire nation is to be made up of priests, the congregation is surely made up of all other nations. Israel's election is intended to be a vehicle for reaching the nations, not rejecting them. Isaiah provides a vision reflecting the fulfillment of this calling, as God's glory is proclaimed "among the nations," and "all mankind" comes to bow down before the Lord in worship (Isa 66:19, 23). Welcoming the *gēr* into the community of Israel and caring for the stranger in their midst serves as a subtle reminder of this purpose underlying Israel's election.

B. Prohibited Sexual Relations (18:1-30)

BEHIND THE TEXT

Chapter 18 is framed by an introduction (vv 1-5) and a conclusion (vv 24-30) made up of exhortations urging the Israelites to obey God's laws and refrain from the customs of other nations (see Driver 1910, 51). The characteristic formulas of the Holiness Code appear six times in this chapter, with four occurrences in the introduction and conclusion. Verses 2, 4, and 30 include the formula "I am the LORD your God" (*'ănî YHWH 'ĕlōhêkem*), while verse 5 concludes with the shortened version, "I am the LORD" (*'ănî YHWH*; → Behind the Text for ch 17). The formula "I am the LORD" also appears in vv 6 and 21, suggesting their unique character within the body of the chapter. The exhortation to abstain from the behavior of other nations is repeated seven times in the opening and closing framework (vv 3 [twice], 24, 26, 27, 29, 30). The contrast between the laws of the Lord (signed with the formula *'ănî YHWH*, "I am the LORD") and the behavior of the nations highlights the purpose of this chapter in terms of distinguishing Israel through standards of sexual morality (Wenham 1979, 249).

The body of the chapter (vv 6-23) is made up of sexual prohibitions that can be divided into two lists. The first list forbids sexual encounters with close relatives (vv 6-18). The second list addresses adultery, homosexuality, and bestiality (vv 19-23). The second list also prohibits sexual intercourse with a woman during her monthly period (v 19) and sacrificing a child to Molech (v 21).

IN THE TEXT

1. Introductory Exhortation (18:1-5)

■ 1-2 God's identification formula, **I am the LORD your God** (*'ănî YHWH 'ĕlōhêkem*), recalls God's revelation of the divine name (YHWH) to Moses in the context of Israel's deliverance from Egypt (Exod 6:2-8). The formula serves as a reminder of what God has done for Israel and calls Israel to imitate God as holy (Lev 11:44; 19:2; 20:7; Wenham 1979, 251).

This long version of the formula (→ Behind the Text above) appears here at the head of a legal list, instead of its usual place at the end as a characteristic signature (see 18:30). It is equivalent to God's declaration at the head of the Ten Commandments (Exod 20:2; Deut 5:6). This may indicate an intentional attempt to recall the covenant at Sinai and suggest that the laws of ch 18 are equal in importance to the Ten Commandments (Milgrom 2000, 1517-18).

■ **3-4** The formula **I am the LORD your God** envelops Lev 18:3-4 (appearing at vv 2*b* and 4*b*), thereby highlighting Israel's call to be set apart from the nations, by **not** doing **as they do in Egypt** or **as they do in the land of Canaan.** In contrast to the nations, God commands Israel to **obey my laws** and **follow my decrees.** In this chapter, the behavior to be shunned and the laws to be obeyed relate to sexual morality. It is implied that the sexual offenses addressed are characteristic of Egyptian and Canaanite practices (Porter 1976, 143). Many ancient societies rejected incest. A Hittite treaty prohibited sexual relations with sisters-in-law and cousins on pain of death. Egypt, however, was known for incest, especially among the royalty, perhaps to consolidate authority (Walton and Matthews 1997, 161). Furthermore, marriages between father-daughter, brother-sister, aunt-nephew, uncle-niece, and others were prevalent in Egypt even outside the royalty (Milgrom 2000, 1518-19). Egyptian and Canaanite mythology reflects bestiality. Rameses II claimed to have been born from the relationship between his mother and the goat-god Ptah. Canaanite Ugaritic texts included references to gods and goddesses having intercourse with one another and with animals (Kaiser 1994, 1124-25).

Egypt and Canaan are specified due to the wilderness setting of Leviticus. Accordingly, these exhortations look to the past in Egypt and also to the anticipated future in Canaan (Gorman 1997, 106).

■ **5** The one who obeys God's laws **will live by them.** This can be understood in two ways. It may simply mean that an obedient person's life will be lived in accordance with God's laws (Levine 1989, 119; Kaiser 1994, 1125). More commonly, the expression is understood as a result clause. Rashi claims that the reward of obedience is life in the world to come (in Herczeg 1999, 216). In contrast, Rashbam asserts that this verse promises a long life in this world (in Lockshin 2001, 95). Ibn Ezra combines the two views by stating that obedience to God's laws results in life in *both* worlds (in Carasik 2009, 133-34). Bekhor Shor highlights the relational aspect of this verse. He observes that those who do not follow God's laws shorten their lives, because the jealous husband kills the man who sleeps with his wife (in Carasik 2009, 133). This reminds us that God's laws promote healthy and right relationships, thereby extending life.

Modern commentators often interpret this verse as a promise of blessing and prosperity in the present; specifically, for Israel, in the promised land (Porter 1976, 143; Wenham 1979, 253; Kaiser 1994, 1125; Gane

2004, 322). Obedience and the promise of life were linked in the liturgy of Israel from early times. Hearing God's commandments placed Israel in the position of choosing life or death (Deut 30:15-16; von Rad 1962, 194).

The Ancient Israelite Family Unit and Sexual Prohibitions

Society in ancient Israel was structured around patrilineal (tracing descent through males) and patriarchal lines. Family was identified in terms of relationship to the *father*. The male perspective provided the normative point of view (Gorman 1997, 106). Milgrom describes family associations as follows:

> The basic sociological unit was the *bêt 'āb* "father's house." It included three to five generations consisting of fifty to a hundred people living in close proximity. Although the average Israelite house could accommodate four persons (father, mother, two children), the kin-related group, numbering about twenty persons, lived in close quarters around a common courtyard. Such compounds are evidenced at Raddana and Ai and at the later Iron Age settlements Tell Beit Mirsim, Tell Far'ah, and Tell en-Naṣbeh (Stager 1985: 18-23; van der Toorn 1996b: 195-97). When this family grew too large, the younger sons would break away to form their own "father's house," but familial bonds would still unite them into a *bêt 'ābôt / mišpāḥâ* "family association" (popularly called a clan). (2000, 1526)

Sexual prohibitions aided in the definition and clarification of family lines. In accordance with the patriarchal norm, one's father's wife, father's brother's wife, and brother's wife were prohibited because the "nakedness" of a wife was equivalent to that of her husband (see Lev 18:7). Since a wife is bonded to her husband, her bloodlines became parallel to his own and were thereby also prohibited. Sexual relations within the family would blur family lines and cause family relations to collapse (Frymer-Kensky 1989, 95). Consequently, one purpose of the sexual prohibitions was to maintain harmony and order within the family group. Preserving the clear social order and long-practiced relationships defended the community against social and psychological chaos (Schenker 2003, 166-67).

2. Sexual Prohibitions (18:6-23)

■ **6** **No one is to approach**, literally, ***any flesh of his flesh*** (Keil and Delitzsch n.d., 412; Milgrom 2000, 1533). The NIV rightly translates this superlative as **close relative** (see Milgrom 2000, 1533). A close relative should not be approached **to have sexual relations**. The Hebrew text literally reads ***to uncover nakedness***, which serves as a euphemism for sexual intercourse (Keil and Delitzsch n.d., 412; Wenham 1979, 253).

The signature phrase **I am the LORD** (*'ănî YHWH*; → Behind the Text above) appears here and at the end of v 21, thereby enveloping this set of prohibited sexual relations. The prohibition against sacrificing to Molech (v 21) is included in this set because of the severity of the sin (Milgrom 2000, 1536). In addition, Milgrom argues that the laws in this list (vv

6-21) fall under the authority and control of the patriarchal head of the household to whom these laws are addressed. Consequently, there is no one else in the household who could bring this one to justice, except the Lord. Thus, the enveloping proclamation, **I am the Lord**, asserts that God indeed will be the One who will punish (2000, 1536).

Who Is Included in the Laws against Incest?

Leviticus 18:6 is commonly understood as a general prohibition against incest, which is then detailed in the following verses (Noth 1977, 135; Wenham 1979, 253; Levine 1989, 120). The problem with this view, however, is that the verses that follow omit some close relatives that one would expect to find in the list. Most strikingly, one's daughter and full sister (depending on how v 9 is understood) are not mentioned among the laws against incest (Gorman 1997, 107). This is normally resolved with a variety of explanations. Some claim that these laws are not concerned with prohibiting sexual relations with blood relatives. Rather, the aim is to regulate sexual intercourse and forbid promiscuity among large family units living together in proximity in tent encampments. The goal therefore is to secure peace and harmony in the community (Noth 1977, 135; Porter 1976, 145; Gerstenberger 1996, 248-49).

The most striking of the omissions, one's daughter, can be explained as simply having been *understood* as an illicit union (Gen 19:30-38). Such a union is forbidden in the laws of Hammurabi and in Hittite law. Thus, the regulations in Lev 18:6-18 serve to extend incest prohibitions beyond those that were already accepted in other parts of the ancient Near East (Wenham 1979, 254). Similarly, some assert that these laws are not intended to exhaust all possible illicit combinations but are only representative (Harrison 1980, 186; Kaiser 1994, 1124). Levine argues that since one's granddaughter is forbidden (v 10), then surely the closer relation of one's daughter is *assumed* as forbidden for sexual relations (1989, 120).

Susan Rattray affirms that the omitted incestuous relationships are indeed assumed, but she provides a textual basis for the argument. They are assumed in the phrase *šĕ'ēr bĕśārô* ("close relative," v 6). A related phrase in 21:2 defines the expression as including mother, father, son, daughter, brother, and unmarried sister. Thus, 18:6 automatically includes mother, sister (full), and daughter in the list of forbidden sexual relationships. Therefore, 18:6 is not a general introduction but rather specifies basic forbidden incestuous relationships, after which vv 7-18 indicate *who else* is forbidden. The reason that mother appears redundantly specified in v 7 is for the purpose of establishing a principle based on the case that is least likely to occur and which is most universally abhorred. That is to say, just as one would certainly not have sexual relations with one's mother, so one must not have sexual relations with one's stepmother, half sister, etc. (1987, 542).

■ **7** This verse literally begins, **you shall not uncover the nakedness of your father, that is, the nakedness of your mother.** The connecting *wāw* is "circumstantial" (Levine 1989, 120), or "explicative" (Milgrom 2000,

1537) and should be translated "that is." Rashi clarifies that having sexual relations with one's mother is signified by the expression "uncovering the nakedness of one's father" (in Herczeg 1999, 217). This is because by so dishonoring a wife, the honor of the husband is violated (Keil and Delitzsch n.d., 413). This reflects the unity of the married couple, for they have become one flesh (Gen 2:24; Hartley 1992, 294; see Wenham 1979, 255). To violate the one is to violate the other.

The focus of the prohibition is made explicit by the seemingly redundant command, **she is your mother; do not have relations with her.**

■ **8** At first glance this verse appears completely redundant in relation to the previous verse. This verse literally reads, **you shall not uncover the nakedness of your father's wife, it is the nakedness of your father.** Once again, the unity of the married couple is highlighted as the father's honor is connected to that of his wife (→ v 7). In contrast to v 7, one's "mother" is not explicitly identified in v 8. Rather, the object of concern here is one's father's wife. Rashi understands this as an extension of the prohibition in v 7 in order to include the woman even after the father has died (his widow [in Herczeg 1999, 217; Carasik 2009, 135]). Ibn Ezra specifies that v 8 refers to one's father's wife, who is not one's mother (i.e., one's *stepmother*; in Carasik 2009, 135; see Levine 1989, 120).

■ **9** This verse appears to forbid **sexual relations** with one's **sister,** whether full sister or half sister (stepsister is the concern of v 11). However, if full sister is specified by the wording of v 6 (→ 18:6 sidebar, "Who Is Included in the Laws against Incest?"), then the focus of this verse would be one's half sister. Accordingly, the phrase **either your father's daughter or your mother's daughter** specifies one's paternal or maternal half sister.

A sister born **elsewhere** is commonly understood as a half sister born to one's mother in a previous marriage (Hartley 1992, 295). Milgrom argues that the distinction here is not between a half sister born at home (father's daughter) or born outside (mother's daughter). Rather, the entire distinction applies only to the mother's daughter in relation to whether she derives from a household *clan* or an outside *clan* (*môledet* is rendered "clan" as opposed to "one born" or "offspring"). As a result, even if one's half sister comes from a different clan, she is still one's mother's daughter, and one is prohibited from having sexual relations with her (2000, 1540).

■ **10** One is forbidden to have **sexual relations** with his granddaughter, whether born of his son or his daughter. The concluding phrase literally reads **they are your nakedness.** Grandchildren were considered to belong to the grandfather who was deemed head of household. Therefore, the granddaughter's nakedness was the grandfather's own nakedness, the uncovering of which (sexual relations) brought **dishonor** to the grandfather (→ vv 6 and 7; Keil and Delitzsch n.d., 414; Porter 1976, 146; Hartley 1992, 295).

■ **11** The phrase **your father's wife** (as opposed to "your mother") refers to one's stepmother (→ v 8; Milgrom 2000, 1541). In this context, **born to your father** implies one's half sister. However, that would make this verse redundant to v 9. This affirms Milgrom's rendering of *môledet* as "clan" (→ v 9). Accordingly, the prohibition here is in regard to one's stepsister, *of your father's clan* (Milgrom 2000, 1541-42; see Wenham 1979, 256-57). The assertion that **she is your sister** signifies that she must be treated as a full or half sister (Hartley 1992, 295-96).

■ **12-13** Sexual relations are forbidden with one's aunt, whether **father's sister** or **mother's sister**. The phrases *šěʾēr ʾābîkā* (**father's close relative**) and *šěʾēr ʾimměkā* (**mother's close relative**) reflect *šěʾēr běśārô* ("close relative," v 6). Thus, as an extension of the opening prohibition in v 6, one must not have sexual relations with the close relatives of one's parents (→ 18:6 sidebar, "Who Is Included in the Laws against Incest?").

■ **14-16** These verses prohibit **sexual relations** with the wives of one's uncle (v 14), one's son (v 15), and one's brother (v 16) respectively. In the case of one's uncle's wife and one's brother's wife, having sexual relations would **dishonor your father's brother** and **dishonor your brother**. This follows the principle that the nakedness of a wife reflects the nakedness of her husband (→ vv 7 and 8). The same is not said of the son in v 15; instead we find the statement **she is your son's wife**. This was necessary because the term for **daughter-in-law** (*kallâ*) also means "bride." Thus, it must be specified that **she is your son's wife** (Rattray 1987, 540; Milgrom 2000, 1545).

The prohibition against having sexual relations with one's sister-in-law (v 16) appears to contradict the law of levirate marriage, which requires a brother to marry his sister-in-law if she is widowed without a son (Deut 25:5-6). Some argue that this prohibition (Lev 18:16) assumes that one's brother is still alive (Noth 1977, 136; Keil and Delitzsch n.d., 415; Levine 1989, 121). Others consider Deut 25 as an exception to the rule. Wenham explains that the law of Lev 18:16 does not address sexual relations with one's sister-in-law while the brother is still alive. That would constitute adultery, which is forbidden in v 20. Thus, v 16 prohibits relations with one's sister-in-law after the brother's death or divorce. Deuteronomy 25 is the one exception to this rule if the widowed sister-in-law had no son (1979, 254, 257).

■ **17** Rashi argues that this verse assumes the one addressed is already married to the woman. In such case, he cannot have **sexual relations** with **her daughter** (in Herczeg 1999, 219-20). On the other hand, Porter asserts that the aim of the verse is to prohibit sexual relations with one's mother-in-law (thereby assuming the man is already married to the daughter; 1976, 147).

The prohibition is extended to the woman's **son's daughter** and the woman's **daughter's daughter.** This suggests that the man addressed is initially married to the woman. Since previous verses have already prohibited sexual relations with one's daughter (v 6; → 18:6 sidebar, "Who Is Included in the Laws against Incest?") and one's granddaughter (v 10), this verse must refer to one's stepdaughter and step-granddaughter (see Gorman 1997, 107; and Milgrom 2000, 1547).

■ **18** In keeping with the principle of unity between husband and wife (→ vv 7 and 8), a woman's sisters become her husband's sisters, and therefore he may not **take** his **wife's sister** as a **wife** (see vv 9, 11; Wenham 1979, 257-58). A concern for harmony in the household becomes evident in that the prohibition forbids establishing a **rival wife** at the same time **your wife is living.** It has been suggested that the term **sister** is being used in an idiomatic sense here, referring to any two women. If so, then this verse prohibits polygamy in general (Gane 2004, 319).

■ **19** This verse shifts from sexual relations related to incest, and begins a focus on other types of sexual activity (Keil and Delitzsch n.d., 416; Levine 1989, 122). Gorman suggests that the common concern of vv 19-23 is wasted seed. The activities forbidden in these verses are activities that cannot produce and maintain children within the socially approved family structure (1997, 108).

One is forbidden from having **sexual relations** with a woman **during the uncleanness of her monthly period** (→ 15:24). Gane points out that a menstruant is described as *dāwâ* ("faint," "state of malaise") in 20:18 (see 12:2; Lam 1:13; 5:17). Accordingly, this prohibition may reflect a concern to protect women during a period of frailty. The Law protects a woman from unwanted advances from her husband during a time of her weakness (2004, 325).

■ **20** This verse is commonly recognized as a prohibition against adultery (Keil and Delitzsch n.d., 416; Porter 1976, 148; Wenham 1979, 258). One who commits adultery becomes defiled. Ibn Ezra claims defilement from adultery is forever and cannot be cleansed (in Carasik 2009, 138). Milgrom explains there is no antidotal purification rite for adultery; it is a nonritual, moral impurity (2000, 1551). In contrast, the Day of Atonement includes purification for both ritual and moral uncleanness (→ 16:16).

■ **21** The medieval Jewish exegetes assemble the arguments for the identification of **Molech** and what it means to **give any of your children to be sacrificed to Molech.** Ibn Ezra notes that the sages understood "Molech" as a general term referring to any god that one makes into his or her *melek* ("king"). He then suggests that perhaps Molech is an alternate name for Milcom, the pagan god of the Ammonites (1 Kgs 11:5; the NIV uniquely translates *milkōm* as "Molech" in this verse). Nahmanides points out that the verse here (18:21) literally reads "the *Molech*." Thus, like "Baal," it is not a proper name but rather a noun referring to lordship ("baal" ["master]"; "molech"/"melek" ["king"]). Therefore, Nahmanides associates Molech with Baal worship and also the worship of Adrammelech and Anammelech, gods of the Sepharvaim (2 Kgs 17:31; in Carasik 2009, 138-39).

The prohibition here literally reads **you shall not give your offspring to pass through to Molech.** Rashi states that a child offered to Molech was made to walk between two great bonfires. Ibn Ezra explains that the method of Molech worship was burning and that some say children were made to "pass through" the fire with some surviving and some dying. Nahmanides declares that children were slaughtered by being passed through the fire repeatedly until completed consumed (Ezek 23:37-39). The Judean Kings Manasseh and Ahaz were guilty of performing this type of ritual (2 Kgs 21:6; 2 Chr 33:6; 2 Kgs 16:3; 2 Chr 28:3). The Sepharvites burned their children as offerings to their gods Adrammelech and Anammelech (2 Kgs 17:31). Jeremiah condemns the practice of burning children as offerings to Baal (Jer 19:5). Jeremiah further seems to equate Baal and Molech worship with the accusation that *"they built high places of Baal . . . to cause their sons and their daughters to pass through . . . to Molech"* (Jer 32:35 KJV, NASB, emphasis added; in Carasik 2009, 138-39). In light of the association with Baal, it has been contended that Molech actually refers to a type of infant sacrifice, rather than the name of a deity (Vainstub 2011). Though the term "fire" (*'ēš*) is missing from this verse (18:21), the complete expression *"cause his son or daughter to pass through the fire to Molech"* appears in relation to a practice that Josiah sought to eliminate (see 2 Kgs 23:10).

Clearly, this verse (Lev 18:21) prohibits what appears to be an egregious practice involving the dedication of children to a pagan deity, possibly through burning. Accordingly, such a practice served to **profane the name of your God.** The name of God (YHWH) was entrusted to Israel and represented God's nearness and holiness. The name served as the presence of God in the same way cultic images served for other religious groups. Thus, whenever Israel looked toward other gods, the name of the Lord was profaned (von Rad 1962, 182-84). Perhaps this is the reason why this verse concludes with the signature phrase **I am the Lord** (*'ănî YHWH*), as a reminder of the covenant name and the one true God (→ v 6). Milgrom suggests that God's name may have been profaned because the name YHWH was actually invoked as part of the forbidden Molech ritual, and Molech was erroneously considered an agent of YHWH carrying out God's will (2000, 1560-65).

The prohibition against Molech worship seems out of place in the context of laws regarding sexual relations. However, Gane highlights a connection between this verse and the immediately preceding verse forbidding adultery. Both adultery and Molech worship violate the covenant by giving precious seed (*zeraʿ*, "semen/offspring") to parties forbidden to receive it. Both adultery and the practice of sacrificing children (as with Molech worship) are explicitly linked in Ezek 23:37 (2004, 321).

■ **22** Homosexuality is proscribed by the command, **do not lie with a man as one lies with a woman.** Ibn Ezra states "the meaning of the verse is quite straightforward: a man is not to have sex with another man" (in Carasik 2009, 140). It reflects the sin of Sodom (Gen 19:5; Judg 19:22-24; Rom 1:27; Keil and Delitzsch n.d., 417). The homosexual acts of the Sodomites (Gen 19:5) and the men of Gibeah (Judg 19:22-24) led to their destruction and interdiction (of the whole tribe) respectively (Milgrom 2000, 1565).

The explanation for this prohibition varies. It is viewed as a violation against nature (Porter 1976, 148) and is associated with the abominations of the Canaanites (Levine 1989, 123). Frymer-Kensky asserts that homosexuality blurs the distinctions between male and female, a condition that cannot be tolerated in the biblical system of discrete categories (1989, 96-97; Deut 22:5; see Deut 22:9-11; Lev 19:19). Biblical cosmology requires that the lines of distinction between categories of human existence be kept neat, or "the foundations of the earth totter" (Frymer-Kensky 1989, 98). The cosmic force of sexuality is reflected in the Song of Songs: "For love is fierce as death, passion is mighty as Sheol; its darts are darts of fire, a blazing flame. Vast floods cannot quench love, nor rivers drown it" (8:6-7 NJPS; Frymer-Kensky 1989, 98).

Milgrom argues that the theme binding together all the prohibitions of this chapter is "procreation within a stable family" (2000, 1568). Furthermore, he claims that the *plural* phrase *miškĕbê ʾiššâ* ("as the *lyings down* of a woman") in this verse refers to *illicit* carnal relations, as opposed to the singular *miškāb*, which implies *licit* relations. Milgrom concludes, "It may be plausibly suggested that homosexuality is herewith forbidden for only the equivalent degree of forbidden heterosexual relations, namely, those enumerated in the preceding verses (D. Stewart). However, sexual liaisons occurring with males outside these relations would not be forbidden" (Milgrom 2000, 1569). The limited number of occurrences of this term (singular and plural) in the context of sexual relations in the OT raises doubt regarding the strength and "plausibility" of Milgrom's conclusion. Nevertheless, the sentiment serves as a caution against a xenophobia, which raises homosexual sin above all other sins and treats it as if beyond the grace and mercy of our loving Creator.

■ **23** This verse begins with the general prohibition, **do not have sexual relations with an animal.** This is followed by the more specific ruling that **a woman must not present herself to an animal to have sexual relations with it.** Levine explains that, in the context of such a patriarchal society, women had little access to men on their own initiative. However, they would have had opportunity to engage in bestiality (1989, 123). An Egyptian cult at Mendes included rites in which women lay down before he-goats (Keil and Delitzsch n.d., 418). More generally, Hittite laws forbid lying down with some animals but not with others, and Ugaritic myths describe sexual relations between gods and animals (Hartley 1992, 297).

Israel is called to be distinct from the nations by not practicing such acts by which one may **defile yourself with it** (→ vv 3-4). Bestiality not only results in uncleanness (*ṭom'â*) but is also called **a perversion.** The term *tebel* denotes "confusion" and identifies a violation of nature (see BDB 1952, 117; also Porter 1976, 148). As with homosexuality, bestiality creates a wrongful blurring of distinctions. In the case of bestiality, an improper mixing of human and animal realms threatens human existence and generates a return to chaos (Frymer-Kensky 1989, 96; → v 22). This aligns with other biblical laws condemning certain mixtures (19:19; Deut 22:5, 9-11). Such fusion violates purity and holiness (Wenham 1979, 260; Hartley 1992, 298).

3. Concluding Exhortation (18:24-30)

■ **24-28** The chapter is summed up with the admonition, **do not defile yourselves in any of these ways.** The Lord explains that **this is how the nations that I am going to drive out before you became defiled.** This statement provides a rationale for the expulsion of the inhabitants of the land of Canaan, which God had promised to the children of Israel (Gen 17:8; Deut 20:16-18). The Israelites are told that **all these things were done by the people who lived in the land before you.**

H extends P's concept of the presence of God located in the tabernacle to a divine presence that is evident throughout the land and among the people (→ Behind the Text for ch 17). Consequently, just as in P the pollution of sin and impurity defiles *the tabernacle*, so in H impurity from moral sin defiles *the land*. Given that God cannot abide sin and impurity, God will abandon the tabernacle if it remains defiled (→ From the Text for

4:1—6:7 [4:1—5:26 HB]). However, for H it is the inhabitants who will leave (be expelled) if the land becomes overly defiled (see Milgrom 2000, 1577-78, 1580). So when the inhabitants of Canaan practiced such immorality, **even the land was defiled** and **vomited out its inhabitants**. All of Israel is warned **not to do any of these detestable things**. The Israelites are told that otherwise the land **will vomit you out as it vomited out the nations that were before you**. The image of the land vomiting, or spewing out, its inhabitants serves as a metaphor, not only for the expulsion of the Canaanites, but also for the future exile of the children of Israel due to their own immorality. The metaphor reflects eviction by means that include famine and war (see Levine 1989, 123; Hartley 1992, 298).

The Lord exhorts the Israelites to **keep my decrees and my laws** in order to distinguish themselves from the other nations. This chapter is enveloped by this theme, which reflects the separation of Israel from the nations as a rationale for the laws on sexual morality (→ 18:3-4).

■ **29-30** The punishment for **everyone who does any of these detestable things** is that **such persons must be cut off from their people** (→ 7:19-21). Israel is exhorted by God to **keep my requirements** and avoid the **detestable customs** that are practiced by other nations, specifically those who were in the land of Canaan before the Israelites (→ 18:24-28). The chapter closes with the signature phrase, **I am the LORD your God** (→ vv 1-2 and also Behind the Text here and for ch 17).

FROM THE TEXT

The two rationales that stand out in relation to the laws on sexual morality are: (1) a desire for harmony and order within the family structure, and (2) the exhortation for Israel to be set apart from the immoral practices of other nations, especially Egypt and Canaan. The biblical laws against incest recognize the marital bond and unity between a husband and a wife ("one flesh"; → vv 7 and 8). They also suggest a sense of respect and honor for relationships that are often disdained (half siblings, stepsiblings, stepmother, etc.; e.g., → vv 9 and 11). The prohibitions of ch 18 extend concerns for harmony and order in the family (incest) to that of the community (adultery), the larger creation (bestiality), and even nature and the cosmos (→ vv 22 and 23). Practically speaking, these laws promote right and healthy relationships among people. As Bekhor Shor implied, neighbors will get along better (and live longer) if they refrain from sleeping with each other's spouses (→ v 5).

As Israel distinguishes itself (by being "set apart" ["holy"]) from the immoral practices of the nations, it reflects God's holiness. Abstaining from incest, adultery, homosexuality, and bestiality contributes to the maintenance of purity and promotes holiness in life. The pursuit of holiness and purity is pictured as critical to the sustenance of life. Just as in relation to the sacrificial system, the defilement of the tabernacle through sin and impurity threatens the presence of God in the community, so also the defilement of the land through the sexual immorality of its inhabitants threatens the presence of the people in the home promised by their God (→ vv 24-28).

Laws against sexual immorality should serve, not only to prohibit wrongful actions, but also to highlight the good and righteous gift of marital pleasure. Within the proper context of marriage, sexuality is not only permitted, but encouraged. Deuteronomy includes the provision of exemption from military duty for new bridegrooms who are called "to stay at home and bring happiness to the wife he has married" (Deut 24:5; see also Deut 20:7). The joy of marriage is intended to be sexual as well as social (Prov 5:16-19; Frymer-Kensky 1989, 91-92).

When interpreting the Bible one must keep in mind that God has chosen to reveal God's written revelation through the context of the ancient Near East. Some presume that God's written word always communicates directly in relation to the current twenty-first-century context. As a result, confusion and frustration erupts when one is confronted with biblical texts that reflect a strong patriarchal mentality with its poor view of women. The interpreter must bear in mind that this patriarchal bias is not a reflection of God's will for humanity but is rather a reflection of the ancient context through which God is communicating. Accordingly, laws that appear to express limited advancements with too many concessions, are actually bold statements of progress in the midst of ancient society. For example, consider Ziskind's description of the impact of biblical incest laws:

> These changes clearly benefited the women of a household. Women could no longer be handed around to the other men in the family as wives or concubines. A widow could now marry anyone she wished outside the family or could be free not to remarry at all. These were especially beneficial options to a widow whose husband had died childless and who was obligated by custom or Deuteronomic law to marry the deceased's father or brother (Gen. xxxviii; Dt. xxv 5-10)....
>
> The rules forbidding a man to marry a woman and then to marry or make a concubine of her mother, daughter or sister prevented the unseemliness of a man moving about from one member of a woman's family to another, and thus ended an abuse in the practice of polygamy (Lev. xviii 17-18). P did not wish any dilution of affec-

tion to take place among sisters or between mother and daughter by reason of a circumstance in which these women were forced to compete for the attention of the same husband. (1996, 128-29)

In moving from the ancient context to the contemporary setting of the modern church, one must continue to apply the *intention* reflected in God's written revelation. One expression of such application can be found in the statement on human sexuality produced by the Board of General Superintendents of the Church of the Nazarene:

> We further wish to reemphasize our call to Nazarenes around the globe to recommit themselves to a life of holiness, characterized by holy love and expressed through the most rigorous and consistent lifestyle of sexual purity. We stand firmly on the belief that the biblical concept of marriage, always between one man and one woman in a committed, lifelong relationship, is the only relationship within which the gift of sexual intimacy is properly expressed. (ICN Online, 2011)

C. Commands for Holiness (19:1-37)

BEHIND THE TEXT

Leviticus 19 is framed by the focus on idolatry and sexual offenses that appears in both chs 18 and 20. Laws pertaining to righteousness and honesty in ch 19 are at the center, while laws regarding sexual sins appear on the periphery (chs 18 and 20; see Douglas 1999, 234-40). As a result, the three "chapters contrast the pure and noble character of the Hebrew God with the libidinous customs of the very strange false gods" (Douglas 1999, 238). In relation to this structure Douglas draws the following conclusion regarding ch 19: "As the elaborate rhetorical framing suggests, it is in fact the most important chapter of the whole book, the chapter on the meaning of righteousness" (1999, 239).

Echoes of the Ten Commandments have long been recognized in Lev 19. Ibn Ezra lists the following connections: v 4 corresponds to Exod 20:3-5 (idolatry), v 12 corresponds to Exod 20:7 (misuse of God's name), v 3*a* corresponds to Exod 20:12 (honor father and mother), v 3*b* corresponds to Exod 20:8 (Sabbath), v 16*b* corresponds to Exod 20:13 (endangering a life), v 20 corresponds to Exod 20:14 (adultery), and vv 11 and 13 correspond to Exod 20:15-17 (steal, lie, deceive/defraud; in Carasik 2009, 143-44). Accordingly, Porter acknowledges that Lev 19 may be referred to as "the priestly Decalogue" (1976, 151).

Leviticus 19 expresses the call to holiness more than any other chapter in the Holiness Code. It begins with the explicit exhortation to "be holy because I, the LORD your God, am holy" (v 2). This is followed by fifteen instances of the characteristic formulas that appear as an abbreviation of this exhortation (*ănî YHWH 'ĕlōhêkem* ["I am the LORD your God"] and *ănî YHWH* ["I am the LORD"]; → Behind the Text for ch 17; one or the other of these two formulas appear at vv 3, 4, 10, 12, 14, 16, 18, 25, 28, 30, 31, 32, 34, 36, 37). These abbreviated formulas serve to recall the fuller expression in v 2 summoning God's people to holiness. Gerstenberger goes so far as to refer to God's self-identification formula as a "formula of sanctification" and affirms that its appearance throughout the chapter reflects the demand to be holy in v 2 (1996, 281). Leviticus 19 includes an assortment of laws that has prompted scholars to organize the chapter by means of a variety of divisions and units (see Milgrom 2000, 1596-1600). Nevertheless, it is commonly held that the overall purpose of the chapter "is to set the people of Israel on the road to holiness" (Milgrom 2000, 1596; see Levine 1989, 125; Hartley 1992, 308).

IN THE TEXT

1. Parents, Sabbath, Idols, Well-Being Offering (19:1-8)

■ **1-2** The word from the Lord to Moses in ch 19 begins with an exhortation **to the entire assembly of Israel**. The exhortation gives full expression to the foundational theme of the Holiness Code (Lev 17—26; → Behind the Text for ch 17). God's call to **be holy because I, the LORD your God, am holy** is developed in the rest of the chapter through ethical and ritual laws (see Driver 1910, 52; Wenham 1979, 265). This summons to holiness recalls Israel's foundational calling to be "a kingdom of priests and a holy nation" (Exod 19:6; Wenham 1979, 264; Gorman 1997, 111).

The Call to Holiness!

Christians often struggle with God's call to holiness due to the fallen state of humanity in contrast with the perfect all-powerful character of God. The struggle is driven by common understandings of the doctrine of sin. An overemphasis on the sinful condition of humanity (e.g., biologically or genetically inherited depravity) implies that God has asked the impossible in calling for holiness among corrupt human creatures. Is God ignorant of the human condition in asking such a thing? Underlying this dilemma is the question of whether human freedom (free will) is as much a reality as is depravity. Is a person capable of consistently choosing holiness over wickedness? God's call to holiness presumes such is indeed possible. The call of the Creator imploring humans to live holy lives suggests that humanity is indeed intended to be righteous. The word from the Lord here does not allow room for compromise, for the standard held before Israel is the Lord God ("... because I, the LORD your God, am holy," 19:2).

Lest one err in the opposite direction (underemphasis on the sinful condition), it must be acknowledged that the human capacity for holiness is severely impeded by the global milieu of brokenness and alienation due to the proliferation of sin. In the face of this reality, humanity finds empowerment in the divine provisions of sanctification and the gift of God's Holy Spirit. The capability to obey God's call to holiness is not a matter of independent accomplishment, as if a person becomes his or her own God. God does not call persons to become God, but rather to become holy as God is holy. By definition, holiness begins in relationship to God (set apart from all that defiles), not apart from God. Indeed, the key to understanding holiness and righteousness is relationship. The call to holiness is a call to close relationship with God by means of emulating God (see Levine 1989, 125). While even the Bible makes use of legal (courtroom) metaphors, genuine and loving personal and corporate *relationships* are what truly define God's desire for humanity. The Ten Commandments, including their "priestly" expression here in ch 19 (→ Behind the Text above), are readily encapsulated within the two categories of loving God and loving neighbor. Christ makes this explicit by stating that "all the Law and the Prophets hang on these two commandments" (Matt 22:40; see Gerstenberger 1996, 267). The call to holiness expressed in ch 19 is expounded through ethical and ritual regulations intended to promote right relationships with God and neighbor.

■ **3** The NIV helpfully translates the first regulation in this verse by stating that each one **must respect his mother and father.** The verb here is literally "fear" (*yārē'*) but includes the meaning of reverence and respect (Wesley 1765, 408; Hartley 1992, 312-13). The same verb appears in vv 14 and 32 in relation to *fearing* God. By respecting parents who themselves are faithful, children can learn about God and what God requires (Wenham 1979, 265).

In my own experience as a child, I recall being *afraid* of disobeying my father and receiving punishment. At the same time, I held him in the greatest *respect* because of his consistency and integrity. He always followed punishment with explanation, forgiveness, and loving embraces. That experience has shaped my relationship to God for whom I likewise carry a great fear and respect, informed by mercy and love.

It is striking that **mother** is listed before **father** in the context of a highly patriarchal ancient environment (in contrast to the order reflected in the Ten Commandments; Exod 20:12; Deut 5:16). Levine suggests that the two statements taken together (Lev 19:3 and Exod 20:12) provide an equitable estimation of both parents (1989, 125). This aligns with Bekhor Shor's statement that the reversal of order indicates equal stature between mother and father (in Carasik 2009, 144). This appears as one of the significant occurrences of God's revelation subtly, yet intentionally, working against the grain of the patriarchal norms evident in ancient Israelite society.

Israel is instructed to **observe** the Lord's **Sabbaths**. Harrison notes that the seventh-day Sabbath is replaced by the first day of the week in Christian practice (Matt 28:1; Mark 16:1; Luke 24:1; John 20:1). He explains that honoring the Sabbath provides regular opportunity for believers to worship God in the company of others (1980, 196).

I am the LORD your God (→ Behind the Text above).

Observing the Sabbath

Christians regularly question the relevance of OT ritual and laws in relation to contemporary practice. Certainly most believers today do not participate in the sacrifice of animals, concern themselves with Hebrew dietary restrictions, or worry about mixing different types of cloth. The assertion reflected in this work is that contemporary faith and practice should focus on the *intention* behind such regulations, rather than the literal *letter* of the law as practiced in its ancient context. This does not allow Christians to ignore OT legislation, but calls them to carefully investigate the rationale behind it. Christ already began such application of the Law as reflected in the NT. When confronted by Pharisees who accused Christ and his disciples of breaking the law of the Sabbath, Jesus responded by pointing out how David and his companions also broke the Law when they ate consecrated bread meant only for the priests (Mark 2:23-26). At first glance, such a defense seems bizarre. Is Jesus justifying violation of the Law by identifying others who have violated the Law? How often parents confront the similar defense that exclaims "everyone else is doing it!" In regard to Christ and his disciples, however, Jesus concludes with the statements that "The Sabbath was made for man, and not man for the Sabbath," and "the Son of Man is Lord even of the Sabbath" (Mark 2:27, 28). Thereby, Jesus presses the discussion to the point of *intention* with regard to the Sabbath, as well as highlighting that one greater than the Sabbath is present. The Sabbath was not instituted for the purpose of enslaving humanity to its regulations. Rather, the Sabbath is intended to serve humanity for the purpose of enhancing relationship to God.

In Exod 20:11 the reason given for keeping the Sabbath is because God created the heavens and the earth and rested on the seventh day. In Deut 5:15 the reason for celebrating the Sabbath is because God delivered Israel from slavery in Egypt "with a mighty hand and an outstretched arm." Consequently, it might be concluded that the purpose of the Sabbath is to cease labor in order to worship God and honor the Lord for God's mighty acts (e.g., creation and deliverance). In the NT, one might think that God had forgotten what day of the week it was when God performed another mighty act to be commemorated. Christ was resurrected on the first day of the week, instead of the seventh (Matt 28:1; Mark 16:1-2, 9; Luke 24:1; John 20:1). Consequently, followers of Christ are found meeting on the first day of the week (John 20:19; Acts 20:7; 1 Cor 16:2). Historical Christianity has maintained the practice of meeting on the first day of the week. Keeping Sabbath is not really concerned with which day of the week it is. While the *letter* of the Law stipulates the seventh day, the *intent* of the Law calls for regular assembly for the purpose of glorifying God for God's mighty acts!

■ **4** Among the biblical terms for **idols,** ʾĕlîlîm is a derogatory label conveying the sense of weakness or nothingness (i.e., nonbeings; Wenham 1979, 266; Harrison 1980, 196). The sound of the Hebrew term is in assonance with the term for God (ʾĕlōhîm). This creates an appropriate contrast between idols who are nothing and God who is all-powerful (Noth 1977, 140; see Milgrom 2000, 1613).

The prohibition against making **gods of cast metal** expands the ban against idolatry to include images intended to signify the Lord God. Such images can only be inadequate and false representations of YHWH's true and full identity (Hartley 1992, 313).

■ **5-8** The inclusion of instructions regarding the ***well-being*** **offering** seems intrusive and out of place in the midst of material that so clearly reflects the Ten Commandments (→ Behind the Text above). Furthermore, these instructions are mostly redundant with the discussion of the same offering in 7:16-18. Wenham suggests that the instructions here are intended for laypersons, as opposed to the more complicated version in ch 7, intended for priests (1979, 266). Medieval Jewish exegetes see the concern here as one of intention. They understand the phrase **that it will be accepted on your behalf** to mean that the offerer must sacrifice with the intention of pleasing God, in an attitude of goodwill, generously and not grudgingly (see Rashi, Nahmanides, and Bekhor Shor in Carasik 2009, 145).

Noordtzij suggests that the reference to sacrifice appears here among laws on holy living in order to express that holiness must embrace every dimension of life, including ethical and ritual practice (1982, 191; see Hartley 1992, 313). Milgrom proposes the novel idea that the concern of this legislation is related to the sanctity of the home. The offerer must be sure he has not **desecrated what is holy to the Lord.** The sacred meat of this particular type of offering may be brought home and shared with one's family, so long as they are all in a state of purity. In this sense, the home replaces the temple! The juxtaposition of Sabbath and *home* sanctuary here (19:3 and 5-8) is again reflected in v 30 where Sabbath and sanctuary are explicitly coupled. Milgrom concludes that Israel is being taught that in order to pursue holiness, precautions must be taken to avoid desecrating the one sanctum a layperson has the right to possess, that is, the *well-being* offering that may be eaten at home. Such desecration would negate all other efforts to maintain holiness through observance of the commands that follow (2000, 1615-16).

The legislation here describes only two of the three types of *well-being* offerings. Only the votive and freewill offerings can be **left over until the third day** (see 7:16-18). The thanksgiving offering can only be eaten on the day it is offered (7:15). This has led some to conclude that H treats the thanksgiving offering as a separate category of sacrifice, while P treats it as a subset of the *well-being* offering (Driver 1910, 52). Milgrom explains that H intentionally saved its treatment of the thanksgiving offering until 22:29-30 in order to create a literary inclusio for chs 19—22. Chapter 22 marks the last time that *qādôs/qōdeš* ("holy," "holiness") is applied to an Israelite. As a result chs 19—22 form a "little Book of Holiness" specifically in relation to the holiness of persons (2000, 1616-17).

Cut off from his people (→ 7:19-21).

2. Laws Regarding Treatment of Neighbor (19:9-18)

■ **9-10** Leaving the **gleanings of your harvest** and **grapes that have fallen** may reflect originally pagan practices intended to offer portions of one's crop to spirits of the soil or deities of the ground (Noth 1977, 141; Porter 1976, 153; Walton and Matthews 1997, 162). Here these practices have been reinterpreted and expanded as a means of providing for the poor. This illustrates the tendency to transform some ancient Near Eastern pagan rites into rituals and practices that honor and glorify God (→ 16:8 sidebar, "Azazel: Wilderness Satyr"). In this case, not only is dropped produce left behind, but in addition portions of a crop are not to be harvested by the owner. Farmers are instructed not to **reap to the very edges of your field,** and vinedressers are told not to **go over your vineyard a second time.** Produce that falls, is dropped by reapers, and is intentionally left unharvested is all designated **for the poor and the alien** (re "alien," → 17:8-9 sidebar, "The *Gēr,* 'Sojourner,' 'Resident Alien'"). This further demonstrates God's strong concern for the poor and disadvantaged as evident throughout Scripture. A popular illustration of this law can be found in the story of Ruth (Ruth 2:2-17).

■ **11-12 Do not steal** repeats the same injunction in the Ten Commandments (Exod 20:15). **Do not lie** and **do not deceive one another** loosely, though not directly, reflect the commands in Exod 20:16-17 (→ Behind the Text above). By including such commands within the context of Lev 19, H subsumes ethics along with ritual under the rubric of holiness (Milgrom 2000, 1629-30; → Behind the Text above and 19:1-2 sidebar, "The Call to Holiness!").

Ibn Ezra claims that v 12 naturally follows v 11 because one who is suspected of deceit will be compelled to swear his or her innocence (in

Carasik 2009, 147). Since oaths were normally accompanied by invocation of the deity, one was prohibited from using God's name to **swear falsely** (von Rad 1962, 183-84). Utilizing God's name in relation to deception or falsehood indicts God in the falsehood as well (Porter 1976, 154). Thereby the Lord's name is profaned. This understanding links this prohibition with the command in the Decalogue that prohibits misusing the name of the Lord. In fact, the NJPS translates Exod 20:7 as equivalent to this verse: "You shall not swear falsely by the name of the LORD your God" (see Milgrom 2000, 1633).

■ **13** The verb *'āšaq* carries the sense of "oppress, extort" (Milgrom 2000, 1636; NIV = **defraud**). The NIV implies that the second phrase should be understood in relation to the first, by supplying the pronoun; that is, **or rob him**. The Hebrew text, however, does not include the pronoun and does include the conjunction *waw*. As a result the NRSV reads the second phrase as, "you shall not steal," making this admonition equivalent to the first line of v 11. The NJPS renders the second phrase as an independent statement: "You shall not commit robbery."

A practical and contemporaneous example of the law in this verse is expressed by the command, **do not hold back the wages of a hired man overnight**. A day laborer would be vulnerable to such exploitation. If the hireling's wages were not paid at the completion of the day's work, that person may be forced to go without food until the next day, or when payment is finally made (see Matt 20:8; Porter 1976, 154). Such a situation would create severe hardship for a poor man and his family (Wenham 1979, 268; see Deut 24:14; Prov 3:28; Milgrom 2000, 1638).

■ **14** Nahmanides explains that one who curses a **deaf** person or causes **the blind** to stumble may think they can do so without fear, because they will not be heard or seen. However, God hears and sees what may be hidden from others, and God will punish the wrongdoer (in Carasik 2009, 148). Thus, the Israelite is commanded to **fear your God**. Levine asserts that though the verb *qillēl* has the connotation "to **curse**, blaspheme," it literally means "to treat lightly." It reflects the opposite of how one should behave, that is, with honor, respect, and blessing (1989, 128). Accordingly, a holy life reflects a high regard for others and expresses compassion for the disadvantaged (Hartley 1992, 315).

■ **15** True **justice** requires that one **not show partiality**, either toward **the poor** or **the great**. The common temptation is to exhibit **favoritism** to the famous and wealthy (see Jas 2:1-4). Judging **fairly** demands equal treatment for both rich and poor. Thus neither compassion for the needy nor preference for the affluent must be allowed to influence sound judgment. The term *ṣedeq* may literally be rendered "in righteousness," thus **judge your neighbor *in righteousness*** (see KJV, NKJV, RSV, YLT; Milgrom 2000, 1643).

■ **16** The term *rākîl* (**slander**) is related to the noun *rōkēl* (a "merchant," one who has access to secret dealings and gossip). The concern here may be that a person should not focus solely on "business" and profit when dealing with others. Instead, one should behave in a considerate and friendly manner (Levine 1989, 129). Accordingly, one should **not go about spreading slander among your people**.

The second portion of the verse literally reads, **you shall not stand over the blood of your neighbor** (see KJV, RSV, YLT). This has been interpreted in a variety of ways. It may mean that a person should not stand idly by when another is in danger. Alternatively, it may be rendered, "do not rise up against your neighbor" (see the LXX). Others have understood the verb in the sense of not *profiting* by the blood of your fellow. Considering the verse as a whole, the first portion prohibits slandering another, which may place that one in danger. The second portion of the verse suggests that slander may lead to death, and the slanderer should not stand "aloof" as his or her false words cause harm to another (see Exod 23:7; Milgrom 2000, 1645). In relation to the metaphor of a merchant, one should not pursue their business in a manner that endangers another or at the expense of another person's well-being (Levine 1989, 129).

■ **17-18** These verses complete the section on the treatment of one's neighbor (vv 9-18) with a short series of commands beginning with the verb **hate** and ending with the verb **love**. One is instructed not to hate your brother **in your heart**. It has long been recognized that the heart in ancient Israel was understood as the center of the intellect and rational function (see Wolff 1974, 46-51). Accordingly, the hate to be avoided here is not just emotion but includes mental activity (Milgrom 2000, 1646). Hateful feelings toward another can grow to the point of bearing a **grudge** and desiring to **seek revenge**. Instead, one is instructed to **rebuke your neighbor frankly** with the aim of correcting the neighbor's wrong and also averting any buildup of hatred toward that neighbor (see Levine 1989, 129; Gane 2004, 337). Stopping another, as well as yourself, from sin brings release **so you will not share in his guilt**.

This section on how to treat your neighbor concludes with the well-known command to **love your neighbor as yourself**. This is one of the two greatest commandments that together subsume all the Law (Matt 22:36-40; → 19:1-2 sidebar, "The Call to Holiness!"). Love must be active, not just the improbable conjuring up of positive emotion toward another (→ From the Text below). This is what makes it possible to *command* love, that is, love can be generated by deeds. Milgrom demonstrates that the Bible often treats love as a term that implies deeds as well as attitude. This includes Jesus' statement, "*Do* unto others as you *would do* unto yourselves" (Matt 7:12; Luke 6:31; Rom 13:8-10; Milgrom 2000, 1653). Here again, Jesus states that this maxim "sums up the Law and the Prophets" (Matt 7:12).

3. Various Laws (19:19-37)

■ **19** This section begins with the general command from the Lord, **keep my decrees**. This is followed by three prohibitions regarding mixtures: mating **different kinds of animals,** planting **with two kinds of seed,** and wearing **clothing woven of two kinds of material.** Such restrictions seem odd in our contemporary society of cross-breeding, mixed fabric, and hybrid cars (consider the delicious Oregon marionberry, the result of complex agricultural crossbreeding). As with many of these laws, revealed in the context of ancient practices and perceptions, present-day believers must look behind the laws to their purpose and intention (→ 19:3 sidebar, "Observing the Sabbath"). Prohibitions against mixtures reflect a strong concern for order and harmony. The blurring of distinctions and categories is viewed as a threat to divinely established order (→ 18:22, 23). The creation account in Genesis repeatedly describes the elements of creation as being "according to their kinds/according to its kind" (Gen 1:11, 12, 21, 24, 25), illustrating discrete categories in creation that must remain separate (Rashbam in Lockshin 2001, 107-8; Kaiser 1994, 1134). The parallel passage in Deut 22:9-11 changes the restriction from mating different types of animals, to plowing with them. This suggests a practical outgrowth of the law as mules became commonly utilized (2 Sam 13:29; 1 Kgs 1:33; 10:25; 18:5; 1 Chr 12:40; Ezra 2:66; Isa 66:20; see Porter 1976, 157).

Milgrom points out that portions of the tabernacle and of the priests' garments are composed of mixed fabrics. He concludes that mixtures belong exclusively to the realm of the sacred. Thus, the prohibition against mixtures, outside the sacred sphere, serves to remind Israel to maintain the critical separation between that which is holy and that which is common (2000, 1660-62; → 10:8-11).

■ **20-22** The penalty for adultery in the OT is normally death (Lev 20:10; Deut 22:22). However, in a case involving **a slave girl,** she and the man **are not to be put to death.** The reason is **because she had not been freed.** The slave was seen as the *property* of her master and not considered a legal person (Porter 1976, 157; Milgrom 2000, 1665, 1675). The term *biqqōret* (NIV = **due punishment**) may refer to damages that are to be paid to the girl's owner. After the affair, the girl's owner would not be able to ask as much money for her from a future marriage partner. On the other hand, if betrothal is implied here (now a broken engagement), then the damages would be paid to the fiancé, who would have already paid bride-money to the owner (Wenham 1979, 270-71). Alternatively, Milgrom argues that *biqqōret* refers to an *inquest* that must be held to determine whether adultery was committed, and to verify that the slave girl is indeed **promised to another,** though not yet **ransomed or given her freedom** (placing her in the position of "half-free half-slave"; 2000, 1670, 1672, 1675). Such status would revoke the death penalty and require the man to offer **the ram of the guilt offering.**

The **guilt offering** is required especially for violations against God (→ 5:14-16). Adultery is particularly identified as a crime not only against husband and wife but against God (Gen 20:6; 39:9; see Milgrom 2000, 1665-75). Perhaps this is why adultery is so often used by the prophets as a metaphor of Israel's unfaithfulness to God (Jer 3:8-9; Ezek 16:32-38; Hos 2:2-23). The sacrilege that requires the guilt offering in this case is a violation against the sanctity of marriage. Even marriage proposed to a slave woman in the ancient Near East carries a sacred dimension, and its infringement constitutes **sin** that must **be forgiven** (Gane 2004, 339).

■ **23-25** The Hebrew text literally reads **any** *tree for food* (see KJV, NASB, NJPS, NKJV, NRSV, RSV). For the first **three years** the **fruit** (produce) of newly planted trees is to be considered *uncircumcised* (*'ărēlîm;* NIV = **forbidden**). This term is commonly used to refer to persons and groups who are outside of the covenant God made with Abraham and his descendants. The sign of that covenant is circumcision (Gen 17:7-14). The term is often used in a reproachful manner in reference to ungodly heathens, such as the Philistines (Judg 14:3; 1 Sam 14:6; 17:26), and other nations, including Israel (metaphorically) when the nation acts unfaithfully (Jer 9:26 [v 25 HB]). "Uncircumcised" is used figuratively in regard to ineffective speech (Exod 6:12, 30). Here it is obviously figurative in relation to the early produce of trees that should be considered forbidden; **it must not be eaten.**

The phrase *wa'ăraltem 'orlātô* can be literally rendered "you shall trim (treat) its foreskin as foreskin." Levine argues that the sense of this metaphor relates to trimming trees and vines (1989, 131-32). Similarly, Gorman suggests that this ruling may reflect practical effective horticulture (1997, 115). Nahmanides asserts that the first three years of produce from trees is small and tasteless. In some cases, trees will not even bring forth fruit until the fourth year (Carasik 2009, 153; see Wenham 1979, 271). **In the fourth year all its fruit will be holy.** This reflects the law of firstfruits, in which the first of everything is offered to God (crops, animals, even people; Exod 13:2; 23:19; 34:19-20; Lev 23:10; Num 8:15-19; Deut 15:19; 26:1-10). Accordingly, the fourth year produce of trees is to be dedicated to God, as **an offering of praise to the** LORD (Wenham 1979, 271). The fourth year produce that is designated as sacred is presumably given to the priests to eat (Gane 2004, 340). Finally, **in the fifth year,** Israel is instructed, **you may eat its fruit.** Faithful adherence to the law of firstfruits comes with the assurance that **your harvest will be increased,** and God will provide during the years of waiting (see Lev 25:18-22).

■ **26 Do not eat any meat with the blood still in it** (→ 17:10-12). The LXX reads "do not eat on the mountains," paralleling Ezek 18:6, 11, 15; 22:9. Such a reading serves as a warning against high places (Gerstenberger 1996, 275). High places were associated with idolatrous worship and were forbidden (Deut 12:2). The Hebrew text may be rendered "you shall not eat *on* the blood." This may reflect an ancient rite of divination in which the meat of a sacrifice was consumed over an area in which its blood had been poured onto the ground in order to feed the spirits of the earth who would then be inclined to reveal the future. This understanding matches the concern of the rest of the verse, which prohibits such divination (Grintz 1972, 80-90).

Israel is strictly commanded **not to practice divination or sorcery.** God revealed the Law and God's will through Moses and the prophets, and indirectly through the Urim and Thummim (→ 8:7-9). However, no other means for discerning God's will, or influencing the future, were allowed (Deut 18:10; 2 Kgs 17:17; 21:6). In the ancient world in which gross superstition led to multiple avenues of communicating with gods and the dead, Israel was instructed to aim its inquiries for divine guidance toward the Lord God alone (see Harrison 1980, 201).

■ **27-28** The prohibitions in these verses contribute to the ubiquitous warnings in the OT against idolatrous rites. The practice of cutting **hair at the sides of your head** or clipping **off the edges of your beard** is likely associated with a cult of the dead and its related rites (von Rad 1962, 208 n. 42). Canaanite practice included offerings of hair to propitiate spirits of the dead (see Deut 14:1; see Porter 1976, 158). Along with blood, hair was considered representative of one's life essence and was often used in sympathetic magic. This is illustrated by the practice in Mesopotamia of sending a lock of a prophet's hair along with prophecies that were sent to the king of Mari. The hair was used in divination to determine the validity of the prophet's words (Walton and Matthews 1997, 163).

Similarly, Israel was instructed not to **cut your bodies for the dead.** Such disfigurement was associated with pagan mourning rites. The connection between such rites and the worship of Baal certainly affirms such practice as idolatrous (1 Kgs 18:28; see Milgrom 2000, 1693). Altering God's creation of the human body dishonors the divine image and compromises the reflection of God's holiness (Wenham 1979, 272; Harrison 1980, 201). **Tattoo marks** on the skin likely included emblems of pagan deities and demonstrated devotion to other gods (Porter 1976, 158; Harrison 1980, 201). Such markings may have reflected belief in a form of protection from malevolent spirits of the dead (Walton and Matthews 1997, 164). Since slaves were marked by their owners, Milgrom suggests that this ban against tattooing may have also been aimed "at the abolition of slavery in Israel" (2000, 1694-95).

■ **29** Further sustaining the message against idolatrous practices is the command **not** to **degrade your daughter by making her a prostitute**. Cultic prostitution intended to promote agricultural fertility was a startling feature of Canaanite worship that was strongly denounced (Deut 23:17 [v 18 HB]; Hos 4:13-14; Porter 1976, 158-59; Wenham 1979, 272). Recent investigations, however, conclude that *cultic* prostitution for the sake of increasing fertility did not really exist in the ancient Near East. Nevertheless, temple prostitutes did exist for economic, rather than cultic, reasons. This too was condemned in Israel (Deut 23:18 [v 19 HB]; Milgrom 2000, 1695-96). Harrison argues that this prohibition is too general to represent a decree specifically against cult (or temple) prostitution. Rather, this ruling condemns hiring out one's daughter as a prostitute for the sake of one's own gain. This would certainly **degrade** the sacredness of the daughter's womanhood and deny her control of her own body (1980, 201-2).

■ **30** To observe the **Sabbaths** of the Lord was a foundational means of honoring God and maintaining regular devotion and commitment in relationship to God (→ v 3 and sidebar, "Observing the Sabbath"). The Lord's instruction here includes upholding **reverence for my sanctuary**. The sanctuary (tabernacle) of God represents the central place of God's presence within the community. It must be kept pure and revered as holy (→ 15:31).

■ **31** The prohibition against turning to **mediums** or seeking out **spiritists** recalls the injunction against divination and sorcery in v 26 and relates to the condemnation of practices associated with rites involving the dead in vv 27-28 (see von Rad 1962, 208). Such activities are allied and mutually denounced in the OT (Deut 18:10-13; 2 Kgs 21:6). They are recognized as typical Canaanite practices (Porter 1976, 159). Rabbinic literature indicates that consultation of the dead is yet another form of idolatry: "'If you contaminate yourself by them, take note of what you are exchanging, what [i.e., the Lord] for what [i.e., the dead]' (*Sipra* Qedoshim 7:11)" (Milgrom 2000, 1702).

■ 32 Showing **respect for the elderly,** demonstrated in part by rising **in the presence of the aged,** reflects a reverence for the accumulation of wisdom and experience associated with maturity in old age. It is juxtaposed here with the command to **revere your God,** who is identified in Daniel's vision as "the Ancient of Days" (Dan 7:9). This exhortation extends a similar concern to the elderly as that for the deaf and the blind in Lev 19:14, where it is likewise stated, you shall **revere your God** (in v 14 the NIV renders this phrase "fear your God," though the Hebrew terminology is identical to that here in v 32). That is, the elderly and disadvantaged should be treated with honor, respect, and blessing (→ v 14).

■ 33-34 This ruling extends the command to "love your neighbor" (v 18) to include the **alien** who **lives with you in your land** (→ 17:8-9 sidebar, "The *Gēr*, 'Sojourner,' 'Resident Alien'"). Israel is instructed **not to mistreat him,** but rather the alien **must be treated as one of your native-born.** Like your neighbor, the alien should be loved **as yourself** (see v 18). The rationale provided is that **you were aliens in Egypt** (see Deut 10:17-19). "It is a tribute unparalleled in early Jewish congregational theology that, contrary to all tendencies toward delimitation and purity (cf. Ezra 10; Neh 13), this commandment for integration, along with its historical justification, was able to maintain itself" (Gerstenberger 1996, 280). In the midst of the foundational emphasis on holiness and separation from the pagan practices of the nations, Israel is yet exhorted to embrace the foreigner who seeks to reside amid the covenant community. This distinguishes between foreigners who in themselves were not a threat to Israel's holiness, and their idolatrous practices that were the real danger for Israel.

■ 35-36*a* The final decree in this speech (see v 1) forbids **dishonest standards** and requires **honest scales and honest weights, an honest ephah and an honest hin.** These indicate measures that were used in commerce and the marketplace in relation to buying and selling. The prophets consistently condemned cheating related to dishonest measures (Hos 12:7 [v 8 HB]; Amos 8:5; Mic 6:10-11).

■ 36*b*-37 These verses form an inclusio with the opening verses of ch 18. The statement **I am the LORD your God, who brought you out of Egypt** reflects the opening words of ch 18: "I am the LORD your God. You must not do as they do in Egypt, where you used to live." Verse 36*b* here provides the rationale for 18:3*a* (and all of ch 18). That is, Israel is instructed not to follow the ways of Egypt, because God brought Israel *out of Egypt* in order to serve the Lord God by obeying God's commands (Milgrom 2000,

1710). Similarly, v 37 here echoes the substance of 18:4-5. More specifically, the phrase **keep all my decrees and all my laws** repeats the opening phrase of 18:5. However, the wording here in v 37 adds two occurrences of the term **all**, thereby indicating that *all* the commands of both chs 18 and 19 should be observed (Hoffmann 1906, 61; see Milgrom 2000, 1710).

I am the Lord (→ Behind the Text above).

FROM THE TEXT

This chapter emphasizing practical holiness is grounded in Israel's intimate relationship with God based on having been chosen as God's holy covenant people (Exod 19:4-6; Gerstenberger 1996, 281). Accordingly, the unifying theme of ch 19 is the concept of becoming "a kingdom of priests and a holy nation" (Exod 19:6; Levine 1989, 125). Ancient Israel appears to have on occasion interpreted their election as a sign of God's exclusive love for Israel and hatred for all others. However, the implication of being a kingdom of priests suggests that the congregation consists of the other nations. Thus, Israel's election does not reflect their superior character in God's eyes, but rather speaks to the function of their calling as a light to the nations. The ultimate aim of the covenant with Israel is to model right relationship with God and others, as part of God's overarching plan to reconcile the world to God. The role of the children of God is to pursue holiness, by emulating God.

Leviticus 19 describes holiness in terms of ethical and ritual exhortations. Hartley observes that the laws of this chapter cluster around three topics: faithfulness in worship (vv 3-8, 21-22, 27-28, 30-31), love and respect in interpersonal relationships (vv 11, 13-14, 17-18, 19-20, 29, 32-34), and justice in business and at court (vv 15-16, 35-36). "All these laws reveal God's desire that Israel bring every area of her life into conformity with his holy character" (1992, 308). Leviticus 19 expands the concept of holiness beyond just a quality or power of God and defines it in relational and experiential terms. Holiness is enacted and actualized through the life of the community. It is "manifest in relationships characterized by integrity, honesty, faithfulness, and love" (Gorman 1997, 111-12). For the sake of contemporary application "in Leviticus, if you want to be holy, don't pass out a tract; love your neighbor, show hospitality to the stranger, and be a person of justice" (Kaiser 1994, 1136).

In relation to the patriarchal bias against women, the OT does not abolish all of the offenses in ancient Near Eastern society (see From the Text for ch 18). Similarly, the status of slaves in the OT is less than that of a legal person (→ 19:20-22). Nevertheless, within the context of ancient

Near Eastern norms, the word of God to Israel commands that even slaves be treated with dignity, as reflected in the sacred character of Israel's relational commitments.

Contemporary application of the laws in the Holiness Code consistently calls for recognition of the *intent* behind the laws. Too often, the church today gets caught up in debates about whether modern hairstyles or skin art (tattoos) are an abomination to God. One must recall that the original intent of the biblical text in these instances was to address expressions of idolatry and related rites (rites related to the spirits of the dead and expressions of devotion to other gods). Accordingly, present-day concern should be to ensure that current actions and expressions reflect devotion to the Lord God alone.

Loving others, which Christ identified as the second greatest commandment (Matt 22:39; Mark 12:31), encapsulates most of these laws. Recognizing the human inability to consistently control emotions, we decry our ability to follow such a command. Yet the statutes in Lev 19 speak of actions and commitments, not just attitudes. Love can be commanded because it can be generated by deeds. C. S. Lewis explains:

> The rule for all of us is perfectly simple. Do not waste time bothering whether you "love" your neighbor; act as if you did. As soon as we do this we find one of the great secrets. When you are behaving as if you loved someone, you will presently come to love him. . . . whenever we do good to another self, just because it is a self, made (like us) by God, and desiring its own happiness as we desire ours, we shall have learned to love it a little more or, at least, to dislike it less. (1952, 110-11)

Loving God, which Christ identified as the greatest commandment (Matt 22:37-38; Mark 12:29-30), is expressed in this chapter by keeping all God's decrees and all God's laws and following them. This includes rejecting all forms of idolatry, observing God's Sabbaths, and reverencing God's sanctuary. I am reminded of growing up in relation to the churches where my father served as pastor. My brothers and I were taught to refrain from running or acting up in the sanctuary of the church. The sacred character of the house of God was impressed upon us. Accordingly behavior, attitude, and even manner of dress were important concerns when approaching what we understood to be the place of the presence of God. This should never be applied in a manner that excludes those who seek fellowship with the Lord, but rather in a manner that recognizes the holy character of God.

Kaiser concludes that, while the formal expression of some of its principles has changed, the "spirit" of the law remains unchanged. The call to holiness encounters us in the field, at home, in business, with friends, with foreigners, in worship, and in family (1994, 1136). Holiness as expressed in Lev 19 is well summarized in the following words:

> Holiness is thus not so much an abstract or a mystic idea, as a regulative principle in the everyday lives of men and women. The words, "ye shall be holy," are the keynote of the *whole* chapter, and must be read in connection with its various precepts; reverence for parents, consideration for the needy, prompt wages for reasonable hours, honourable dealing, no talebearing or malice, love of one's neighbor and cordiality to the alien, equal justice to rich and poor, just measures and balances—together with abhorrence of everything unclean, irrational, or heathen. Holiness is thus attained not by flight from the world, nor by monk-like renunciation of human relationships of family or station, but by the spirit in which we fulfil the obligations of life in its simplest and commonest details: in this way—by doing justly, loving mercy, and walking humbly with our God—is everyday life transfigured. (Hertz 1960, 497-98)

D. Molech Worship and Sexual Prohibitions (20:1-27)

BEHIND THE TEXT

Leviticus 20 echoes much of the legislation in chs 18 and 19. It is commonly held that ch 18 lists the prohibitions, and ch 20 stipulates the penalties for disobeying those prohibitions. However, the correspondence between the two chapters is not exact. The order of some of the laws varies, and four cases that appear in ch 18 are not treated in ch 20 (i.e., 18:7, 10, 17*b*, 18; Driver 1910, 53). Wenham outlines the content of ch 20 as follows:

Introduction (vv 1-2*a*)
Sins against Religion (vv 2*b*-6)
Exhortation to Holiness (vv 7-8)
Sins against Family (vv 9-21)
Exhortation to Holiness (vv 22-26)
Sins against Religion (v 27; Wenham 1979, 276)

Leviticus 20, in conjunction with ch 18, serves to frame ch 19 as the central discussion on righteousness and holiness in the book of Leviticus (→ Behind the Text for ch 19). Laws regarding sexual relations (20:10-21; similar to ch 18) appear to make up the original core of ch 20. They begin with a warning against cursing mother or father (v 9) and are framed by the exhortation to keep God's decrees and follow them (vv 8, 22*a*). Following this framework is appended the rationale for keeping God's commands (v 22*b*, "so that the land" will "not vomit you out"; see 18:25, 28), an exhortation to remain separate from the nations (20:23-24; see 18:3, 24, 27, 30), and a reminder of the dietary restrictions (20:25-26). The core of vv 10-21 with this appendix (vv 22*b*-26) is then further framed by prohibitions related to mediums and spiritists (vv 6, 27). Finally, appended to the *beginning* of the chapter is a prohibition against offering children to Molech (vv 2-5).

The material appended to the core of ch 20 (vv 10-21) may seem unrelated and out of place. Nevertheless, Schenker asserts that the redactor of Lev 20 considered the sacrifice of children to Molech by the hand of their own parents (vv 2-5), illegal divination (v 6), and the cursing of parents (v 9) as analogous to the confusion of social relationships represented by the laws on sexual relations in vv 10-21 (2003, 171-72). In addition, the motive of the land vomiting out its inhabitants, found in both 18:24-28 and 20:22-24, serves to bind chs 18—20 together as a literary unit. As a result, all the commands in these three chapters convey the conditions required to maintain possession of the promised land. The stimulus for combining the laws regarding family relations (20:10-21; see 18:6-23) with possession of the land (20:22-24; see 18:24-28) may have been the commandment to honor parents in the Ten Commandments, which promises long life in the land (Exod 20:12; Deut 5:16; see Lev 20:9 and 19:3; Schenker 2003, 176-78).

IN THE TEXT

1. Molech Worship Forbidden (20:1-5)

■ **1-5** All those **living in Israel (Israelite or alien)** are prohibited from giving their **children to Molech** (→ 18:21). Those who do so are to be **put to death** by means of stoning. The sentence is to be carried out by **the people of the community.** Noth expresses that this is in tension with the following statement that *God* will set God's **face against that man** and **will cut him off from his people.** However, Noth asserts that 20:4-5 resolves the tension by explaining that if the people **fail to put him to death,** *then* God will undertake to **cut off** the guilty parties (1977, 148; see Levine 1989, 136-37). In contrast, Wenham regards stoning by the people and being **cut off** by God as two distinct punishments. If so, then cutting off involves more than death (→ 7:19-21). In this case, 20:4-5 indicates that if the people fail to punish the guilty, then God's greater punishment still remains (1979, 278). Hartley suggests that sacrificing a child to Molech is so egregious that God will exclude the guilty party from the covenant community, thereby cutting that one off from the benefits of the community in the age to come (1992, 337-38). Milgrom asserts that "cutting off" could mean depriving one of life after death altogether (2000, 1734; see idem 1991, 460).

The gravity of this idolatrous sin is expressed by God's statement that one who commits such an act **has defiled my sanctuary** (→ 15:31 and From the Text for 4:1—6:7 [4:1—5:26 HB]) and **profaned my holy name** (→ 18:21).

2. Sorcery, Call to Holiness, Dishonoring Parents (20:6-9)

■ **6** The one who turns to **mediums and spiritists** will **prostitute himself or herself** by doing so. This reflects the idolatrous nature of consulting the dead (→ 19:31; also comments on 19:26 and 19:27-28). Harlotry, adultery, and prostitution are commonly used in the OT as metaphors for idolatry (Exod 34:15-16; Lev 17:7; Deut 31:16; Judg 2:17; Jer 3:6; Ezek 6:9).

Cut him off from his people (→ 7:19-21 and 20:1-5).

■ **7-8** The verb **consecrate** (*wĕhitqaddištem*) and the adjective **holy** (*qĕdōšîm*) derive from the same root. The sense of the opening line might be rendered ***make yourselves holy and thereby you shall be holy.*** For H, the people make themselves holy by observing God's commandments (→ 19:1-2 and sidebar, "The Call to Holiness!"; also Wright 1999, 353; Milgrom 2000, 1739-40). "Unswerving obedience to God's commands is one indication of a sanctified life in both the Old and New Testaments" (Harrison 1980, 205). Hartley affirms that "sanctification involves affirmative action," and "consciously avoiding any activity that defiles" (1992, 338). The means of attaining holiness is made explicit by God's instruction in v 8: **keep my decrees and follow them.**

Israel's pursuit of holiness through obedience may seem to be contrasted by God's declaration, **I am the LORD, who makes you holy.** However, rather than a competition, the attainment of holiness is a cooperative, relational effort. God is the One who provides the means of holiness, that is, the commandments (Milgrom 2000, 1739). The process of sanctification is reciprocal. "By keeping the law and by worship, the people sanctify themselves and revere Yahweh as holy in the congregation (22:32). Yahweh himself also sanctifies them through his holy power working in their lives, affirming the noble and purging out the corrupt" (Hartley 1992, lxi). "Yahweh and the people share in the construction of a holy community: 'I am the one who sanctifies you; sanctify yourselves!'" (Gorman 1997,

118). "Thus, God and God's people come into dialectical interplay: when the people live a life in accordance with divine holiness, they are, in turn, sanctified by God" (Wright 1999, 353).

I am the LORD your God (→ Behind the Text for chs 17 and 19).

▪ **9** Anyone who **curses his *or her* father or mother** is subject to the death penalty. This concern relates to the similar exhortations to "respect" (→ 19:3) and "honor" (Exod 20:12) one's parents. The term here, *yĕqallēl* (NIV = **curses**), is the very opposite of *honoring*. It literally means "to make light of, despicable" (Wenham 1979, 279; see Milgrom 2000, 1745). The strong commands regarding parents reflect a determination to sustain the structure of family and to portray parents as representative of God's authority to the child. Thus, cursing parents is nearly equivalent to blasphemy (Wenham 1979, 279; Harrison 1980, 205-6). The breakdown of relationship to one's parents leads to the breakdown of relationships with other family members, including infringement of the sexual prohibitions. That is why this law heads the following commands regarding sexual relations (Milgrom 2000, 1744-45). Dishonoring parents tears down the basic unit of the family and ultimately "has the effect of destroying the fiber of society itself" (Kaiser 1994, 1141).

The statement that **his blood will be on his own head** affirms that the guilty party is worthy of death and also releases those who inflict the punishment from bloodguilt (Hartley 1992, 339).

3. Penalties for Sexual Transgressions (20:10-21)

▪ **10** The law prohibiting **adultery** stipulates that **both the adulterer and the adulteress must be put to death** (→ 18:20). The phrase *'îš 'ăšer yin'ap 'et-'ēšet* (**if a man commits adultery with *the wife of*) appears twice back-to-back at the beginning of the verse. This seeming dittography may actually be an intentional stylistic device to draw attention to the importance of the legislation (Harrison 1980, 206). The significant addition to the second appearance of the phrase is the term **neighbor**. Milgrom understands this addition as a means of restricting the original wording of the law to the wife of a fellow Israelite (2000, 1747).

▪ **11** If a man sleeps with his father's wife, he has dishonored his father (→ 18:7 and 18:8). The latter part of the sentence can literally be rendered, **he has revealed the nakedness of his father** (see NASB, NJPS, NRSV; → 18:6). Since **both the man and the woman must be put to death**, it is assumed that the woman consented to the advances of her husband's son (Hartley 1992, 339).

Their blood will be on their own heads (→ v 9).

■ **12** **If a man sleeps with his daughter-in-law** (→ 18:14-16). This act is referred to as **a perversion** (*tebel;* → 18:23). Wesley explains that this *confusion* of the natural order results because the man has made "the same off-spring both his own child and his grandchild" (1765, 414).

■ **13** **If a man lies with a man as one lies with a woman** (→ 18:22). Wesley suggests that both **must be put to death,** unless one forced the other, based on the analogous ruling of Deut 22:25 (1765, 414; see Milgrom 2000, 1749).

■ **14** **If a man marries both a woman and her mother** (→ 18:17). Note the inversion between these two verses: "woman and her daughter" (18:17) and **woman and her mother** (20:14). Together the two verses address the question of whether the man is already married to the mother (thus prohibited from also marrying her daughter), or the man is already married to the daughter (thus prohibited from also marrying his mother-in-law).

In this instance, the punishment is designated as being **burned in the fire.** This includes **both he and they.** Wesley asserts that "they" would only involve those who consented to it (1765, 414; see Milgrom 2000, 1750). Hartley suggests that both women may have been held accountable because, as mother and daughter, it is presumed some scheming must have taken place for such living arrangements (1992, 339-40). The severe punishment of death by fire may be due to the identification of this act as **wicked** (*zimmâ*). This term carries the meaning of "scheme, plot" and suggests the two women may have conspired with the man (Milgrom 2000, 1751). The term *zimmâ* is also applied in the situation of degrading one's daughter by "making her a prostitute" (19:29), and punishment by fire is applied to a priest's daughter who "defiles herself by becoming a prostitute" (21:9). This suggests that the prohibited act here (20:14) may have been considered a form of harlotry (see Milgrom 2000, 1751).

■ **15-16** These verses stipulate the death penalty for bestiality (→ 18:23). In the case of either a **man** or a **woman** who **has sexual relations with an animal,** both the person and the animal **must be put to death.** This results from the notion that animals also bear guilt (Gen 6:7; 9:5; Jonah 3:7-8; Levine 1989, 138). There may also have been the fear that the animal might produce a monstrous birth (Wesley 1765, 414; see Milgrom 2000, 1752).

Their blood will be on their own heads (→ v 9).

■ **17** It is called **a disgrace** (*ḥesed*) if **a man marries his sister** (→ 18:9 and 18:11). The term *ḥesed* is normally translated "great love, lovingkindness, steadfast love" (e.g., Lam 3:22, NASB, NIV, NRSV). However, in this and one other biblical verse, the term carries the very different meaning of "shame, reproach" (Prov 14:34; BDB 1952, 340). This unusual use of the term may have been intentional in order to express the gross distortion of godly love into hedonistic sexual passion (Wenham 1979, 280; Kaiser 1994, 1142). Saalschütz explains that proper love degenerates to disgrace when it is unleashed in the form of uncontrolled lustful desire. The term *ḥesed* is used to express both original proper love and its corruption in the form of shameful passion (1853, 792-93). Alternatively, Levine asserts that these two meanings (lovingkindness and reproach) stem from two unrelated homonyms (1989, 138; an example of a *verb* form of the *ḥesed* that means "reproach" can be found in Prov 25:10).

The text literally reads, **and he sees her nakedness and she sees his nakedness.** This serves as a euphemism for the statement, **they have sexual relations** (→ 18:6), indicating that they "consummate the marriage" (Porter 1976, 165). At this point punishment shifts from death in regard to offenses addressed in the previous verses, to being **cut off** in this and the following verse (see Milgrom 2000, 1742; re "cut off," → 7:19-21 and 20:1-5). It appears that the greater burden falls upon the brother who **will be held responsible** for failing to guard his sister's honor (Hartley 1992, 340). The Hebrew phrase literally reads, **he shall bear his iniquity** (see NASB, NJPS, RSV). This is not an additional punishment but a declaration that a person is liable for punishment that is sure to come (Milgrom 2000, 1488-90, 1754, 1757).

■ **18** This verse expresses the prohibition against having **sexual relations** with a woman **during her monthly period** (→ 18:19). Emphasis is placed on exposure of **the source of her flow** (lit., **he has laid bare her flow, and she has uncovered the flow of her blood;** see NASB, NRSV). This reflects the symbolic importance of blood (→ 17:10-12; see also Hartley 1992, 340) and the impurity attached to a woman's menstrual cycle (→ 15:19-22 and 15:24).

Both of them must be cut off from their people (→ 7:19-21 and 20:1-5). This presumes the compliance of the woman, so that both are guilty (Milgrom 2000, 1755).

■ **19-20** These verses prohibit **sexual relations** with one's **aunt,** whether the **sister of** one's **mother** or **father,** or the wife of one's **uncle** (→ 18:12-13 and 18:14-16). Sexual relations with the sister of one's mother or father **would dishonor a close relative.** This likely refers to one's mother or father as those who would be dishonored (→ 18:6 sidebar, "Who Is Included in the Laws against Incest?"). In the case of sexual relations with one's uncle's wife, the uncle would be **dishonored,** because dishonoring someone's wife violates the honor of the corresponding husband (→ 18:7). The statements **both of you would be held responsible/they will be held responsible** refer to the man and the consenting aunt with whom he had sexual relations (re **held responsible,** → 20:17; in the case of v 20, *ḥēṭ'* ["sin"] is treated as synonymous with *'āwōn* ["iniquity"]; see Milgrom 2000, 1757; → 16:20-22).

The punishment for sexual relations with an aunt is stipulated in 20:20 as becoming **childless**. The threat here is the elimination of one's posterity (see 2 Sam 18:18).

■ **21** If a man marries his brother's wife (→ 18:14-16).

It is an act of impurity. The term *niddâ* in this context is extended to mean "disgrace, indecency" (Levine 1989, 139). Hartley explains that outside of the proper conditions of levirate marriage (Deut 25:5-6), this situation may reflect a brother's attempt to appropriate his deceased brother's estate, thereby putting to an end the deceased brother's legacy. The union creating such a condition was repugnant and therefore labeled *niddâ*, "odious, foul, impure" (1992, 340). In this case, the punishment of being **childless** turns the crime back upon the guilty party by eliminating his own posterity (→ Lev 20:19-20).

4. Concluding Exhortation, Distinguishing Clean and Unclean, Appendix on Sorcery (20:22-27)

■ **22** The command to **keep all my decrees and *all my* laws and follow them** exactly repeats 19:37a, which echoes 18:4-5, serving to draw together chs 18—20 (→ 19:36b-37 and Behind the Text for chs 19 and 20). This phrase also reflects the opening portion of 20:8, "Keep my decrees and follow them," forming an inclusio encompassing the laws on sexual relations in vv 10-21 (→ Behind the Text above). The rationale for keeping God's commands, **so that the land where I am bringing you to live may not vomit you out,** echoes the closing of ch 18, which likewise addresses laws on sexual relations (see 18:25, 28).

■ **23-24** These verses express a similar message as that communicated in 18:24-30 (see also 18:3). This message concludes the laws on sexual relations that appear in both chapters (→ Behind the Text above). Emphasis is placed on avoiding **the customs of the nations.** God explains that because of **these things,** God will **drive out** the nations before Israel. In their place, God will allow Israel to **possess their land** (→ 18:24-28). The land is described as fertile and abundant by means of the popular phrase **flowing with milk and honey** (Exod 3:8, 17; 13:5; 33:3; Num 13:27; 14:8; 16:14; Deut 6:3; 11:9; 26:9, 15; 27:3; 31:20; Josh 5:6; Jer 11:5; 32:22; Ezek 20:6, 15). The phrase depicts Canaan as a land "with plentiful, milk-producing herds and flocks and abounding in fruit trees" (Levine 1989, 139).

The characteristic signature of H, **I am the LORD your God** (→ Behind the Text for chs 17 and 19), appears in this instance with the appended phrase, **who has set you apart from the nations.** The admonitions reflected in 18:3-4, 24-30 clearly call for Israel to *separate themselves* from the ways of the nations around them (→ 18:24-28). At the same time it is God **who has set** them **apart from the nations.** This reflects the same relational focus evident in 20:7-8, in which both God and Israel work together in order to nurture holiness among God's people (→ vv 7-8). Separation is an intrinsic aspect of holiness (see Milgrom 2000, 1762).

■ **25-26** The concept of separation links v 25 to the previous verse. As God "set apart" (*bādal*) Israel from the nations, now Israel must **make a distinction [*bādal*] between clean and unclean animals** (see Porter 1976, 165; Wenham 1979, 280; Milgrom 2000, 1762). Just as Israel must avoid defilement from the practices of the nations as reflected in the laws on sexual relations (18:3-30; 20:10-24), so also Israel must not **defile** itself **by any animal or bird.** The term *těšaqqěṣû* (NIV = defile; related to *šeqeṣ*) refers to that which is "detestable," which can cause one to become defiled (*ṭāmēʾ* ["unclean"]; → 11:9-12 and 11:41-43). The animals and birds that God has **set apart as unclean** (*ṭāmēʾ*) are delineated in ch 11. The editorial hand of H can be seen in 11:44-45, which echoes 20:26 here (→ 11:44-45). The call **to be holy to me because I, the** LORD, **am holy** is echoed in the same exhortation that concludes the dietary restrictions at 11:44*a*, 45*b*. In addition, the assertion from God that **I have set you apart from the nations to be my own** is reflected in the statement that God is the One "who brought you up out of Egypt to be your God," in 11:45*a*. Thereby, the dietary restrictions are drawn into ch 20, to be included among the laws of separation that make Israel holy unto the Lord. The concept of cleanness is joined to holiness (Kaiser 1994, 1143). The dietary laws were a symbolic means by which Israel separated itself from the nations and their pagan practices, thereby maintaining order and preventing chaos with regard to Israel's all-important covenant relationship to God (see Milgrom 2000, 1762-63). "It is now for Israel to live a holy life by distinguishing every day at mealtime between impure and pure animals and thereby remind itself to make distinctions between practices that enhance holiness and those that desecrate it" (Milgrom 2000, 1764).

■ **27** This unit concludes with a statute relating the punishment for **a man or a woman who is a medium or spiritist.** This forms an inclusio with the injunction against anyone "who turns to mediums and spiritists" in v 6 (→ Behind the Text and comments on v 6 and 19:31; → 19:26 and 19:27-28). As a result, separation from forms of idolatry (→ 19:31) is appended to separation by means of observing laws on sexual relations (20:10-24) and separation by means of dietary restrictions (vv 25-26) as a channel for pursuing holiness.

The medium or spiritist **must be put to death** by stoning. This recalls the punishment stipulated for the person "who gives any of his children to Molech" (v 2).

Their blood will be on their own heads (→ v 9).

FROM THE TEXT

Chapter 20 continues the focus on the holiness of the people that began in ch 18 ("speak to the Israelites," 18:2; "speak to the entire assembly of Israel," 19:2; "say to the Israelites," 20:2). This unit (chs 18—20) is preceded by a chapter that includes "Aaron and his sons" (17:2) in the address and is followed by a chapter that is exclusively addressed to the priests ("speak to the priests, the sons of Aaron," 21:1). The content of ch 20 repeats topics already addressed in chs 18 and 19 and expands them mainly by adding punishments. The three main themes included in ch 20 are: idolatry (vv 1-6, 27), sexual relations (vv 10-21), and dietary restrictions (v 25). Framing the laws on sexual relations is the call to holiness and the command to keep God's decrees (vv 7-8, 22-24, 26).

As with many of the laws in Leviticus, application in the contemporary church requires recognition of the *intent* behind God's commands (→ 19:3 sidebar, "Observing the Sabbath"). We rarely, if ever, encounter child sacrifices in the fire to Molech or cases of bestiality; nor do we restrict our diets based on ancient regulations of what is clean and unclean. Nevertheless, we should be concerned to live in ways that separate us from contemporary expressions of idolatry, sexual immorality, and impurity (→ 11:46-47 sidebar, "Rationale for the Dietary Restrictions"). As a contemporary example illustrating the intent behind the prohibition against Molech worship (child sacrifice and idolatry), Gane points to sacrifice for personal gain.

> What about passively sacrificing children on the altar of greed by neglecting them in order to climb the ladder of the god we call "Success"? Are we giving them the physical, mental, social, and spiritual care they need and deserve as gifts of God entrusted to us? Or do we let them fend for themselves year after year with junk food, TV, and whatever friends they can find to keep them company? (2004, 369)

The penalties for crimes addressed in ch 20 may come across as cruel and harsh. They are a further expression of God's revelation made known in the context of ancient society (→ From the Text for ch 18). Wenham compares Israel's law with other legal codes from the ancient Near East. In doing so, he highlights the unique features and intent of biblical law. While OT laws do not demonstrate the kinds of advancement and humanitarian compassion for which we might strive in contemporary society, they do reflect significant values consistent with the rest of God's revelation. For example, biblical law places noticeable emphasis on *human* ideals, compared to a greater *economic* concern reflected in other ancient Near Eastern law codes. That is, Israel's laws tend to exact more severe punishments in response to offenses against life and family, as opposed to other law codes that consider financial loss as more serious. Wenham extracts five principles he sees illustrated in the laws of the Pentateuch: (1) the guilty must receive their legal due (not revenge), which must correspond with the crime; (2) evil must be purged from the midst of the community/land; (3) punishment should deter others from committing the same offense; (4) punishment makes way for atonement and reconciliation with society; and (5) punishment allows the offender to recompense the victim. Wenham also concludes that penalties in the Pentateuch were *maximum penalties*. Various circumstances allowed for lesser penalties to be enforced (1979, 281-85).

Relational Aspect of Sanctification

Chapter 20 includes clear indication of the cooperative relationships God desires with God's children. The *people* are explicitly called to *act* in order to cultivate holiness ("consecrate yourselves," v 7; "be holy," v 7; "keep my decrees and follow them," v 8; "keep all my decrees and laws and follow them," v 22; "you must not live according to the customs of the nations," v 23; "you must therefore make a distinction between clean and unclean," v 25; "do not defile yourselves," v 25). At the same time, *God acts* to secure Israel's holiness ("I am the LORD, who makes you holy," v 8; "I am the LORD your God, who has set you apart from the nations," v 24; "I, the LORD, am holy, and I have set you apart from the nations to be my own," v 26). Sanctification, like salvation, is a participatory process involving relationship with the divine. The church often struggles with this concept. It rightly rejects expressions of arrogance and hubris that claim exclusively human accomplishment (Deut 8:11-20). However, the church often goes too far and denies all human participation in the call and work of the divine. This is normally driven by the NT emphasis that rightly asserts that people are "justified by faith apart from works of the Law" (Rom 3:28 NASB). Nevertheless, just as in Leviticus both God and the people act to nurture holiness, so in the NT faith in God and the works of God's people together establish justification ("you see that a man is justified by works and not by faith alone," Jas 2:24 NASB, RSV). The NT call requiring human participation in the realization of salvation and sanctification is just as loud as that in the OT (see Matt 25:31-46; John 5:28-29; Rom 2:5-11; 2 Cor 11:15; Phil 2:12; Col 1:22-24; Rev 20:12-13). The point is not a competition between human and divine ability to save. It is already clear that almighty God far exceeds any and all human power and that without God there is absolutely no hope for the salvation or holiness of humanity. The point is that God has chosen to establish salvation and sanctification *in relationship* with humanity. So long as this is God's determination, then one cannot save without the participation of the other. Human attempts to achieve holiness *without God* fail according to the very first and greatest commandment, which already demands that holiness begin in relationship to God (Exod 20:2-3; Deut 6:5; Matt 22:37-38). Likewise, any attempt by God to sanctify God's children without their participation compromises God's expressed desire for free and genuine relationships of love.

E. Priestly Holiness and Acceptable Sacrifices (21:1—22:33)

BEHIND THE TEXT

The call to holiness is here applied to the *priesthood*. Holiness in relation to the *people* was previously addressed in chs 18—20. The content of chs 21—22 can be divided into five sections: (1) ceremonial restrictions incumbent on the priests (21:1-9) and the high priest (21:10-15); (2) restrictions regarding physical defects among priests (21:16-24); (3) conditions for consuming sacrificial food (22:1-16); (4) restrictions regarding physical defects among sacrificial animals (22:17-25); and (5) three additional regulations regarding sacrifices (22:26-30), with a concluding exhortation (22:31-33; Driver 1910, 53). Each section is introduced by the heading, "the LORD said to Moses" (21:1, 16; 22:1, 17, 26; see Noth 1977, 153, 159). Alternatively, these chapters may be divided into six sections, based on the *concluding* formula, "I am the LORD, who makes you/him/them holy" (21:8, 15, 23; 22:9, 16, 32; Wenham 1979, 289).

The discussion of defects among sacrificial animals (22:17-25) appears to parallel that of defects among priests (21:16-24). That is, many of the defects that prohibit a priest from offering sacrifices are the same defects that exclude animals from being sacrificed on the altar (Wenham 1979, 290; see Levine 1989, 140-41). These chapters are bound to the previous chapters addressing the holiness of the people (chs 18—20) by means of the repeated call to holiness that emphasizes obedience to God's commands (22:31-33; see 18:24-30; 19:36-37; and 20:22-26; Wenham 1979, 290; → 20:22 and 20:23-24).

IN THE TEXT

1. Restrictions for the Priests (21:1-9)

■ 1 The Lord instructs Moses to **speak to the priests** (→ From the Text for ch 20). The Hebrew text literally reads, **he shall not defile himself** *for a person among his people* (see NASB). There is no explicit reference to the dead in this verse. The term *nepeš* normally refers to a living person (see BDB 1952, 659). The full expression assumed here is found in 21:11: *napšōt mēt* ("dead body/*person*"; Levine 1989, 142). Accordingly, it is understood that the source of defilement in this context is a corpse (→ 11:8, and From the Text for ch 15). As a result, a priest must abstain from attending funerals. Wesley asserts that the reason for this restriction is to facilitate a priest's entire devotement to God. "Yea, to renounce all expressions of natural affection, and all worldly employments, so far as they are impediments to the discharge of their holy services" (1765, 416). However, the impact of defilement and preservation of the holiness of the sanctuary are more likely the primary concerns here (see Hartley 1992, 347). A priest must be especially cautious to avoid any form of impurity because of his service in proximity to the sanctuary (→ 15:31 and From the Text for 4:1—6:7 [4:1—5:26 HB]). In addition, Israel must avoid any appearance of the idolatrous practice of veneration for the dead (→ 19:26; 19:27-28; 19:31; and 20:6; see also Hartley 1992, 347).

■ **2-3** Exceptions to the ruling in v 1 are listed here. That is, a priest may allow himself to become "ceremonially unclean" for the sake of **a close relative.** Thus, a priest could attend and participate in the funeral of **his mother or father, his son or daughter, his brother, or an unmarried sister.** In such cases, the priest would still incur the same impurity as a layperson (Porter 1976, 167). After undergoing the required purification rite, the priest may return to his appointed functions (Num 19:16-19; Milgrom 2000, 1796). The priest's sister for whom **he may make himself unclean** is qualified as **unmarried.** She would be **dependent on him** to bury her, **since she has no husband.** A *married* sister would be the responsibility of her husband and family (Wesley 1765, 416). It is striking that the priest's wife is omitted from the list of exceptions. Gerstenberger suggests that the wife is omitted because she belongs to the clan of her parents and is a "close relative" of her children. These would be the ones to bear the obligation for burying her at her death (1996, 310). In contrast, some argue that the wife is assumed in the expression **close relative,** in relation to her husband (Wesley 1765, 416). Similarly, since they are "one flesh," the Law would indeed assume that a priest may defile himself for his wife (Keil and Delitzsch n.d., 429-30; Wenham 1979, 290).

■ **4** Verse 4 is difficult to translate as evident by comparing various English translations (see KJV, NAB, NRSV, YLT). Noth renders the verse as a supplement to v 3, distinguishing between a married and unmarried sister (as with the NAB; 1977, 155). Porter lists two additional possibilities for the sense of v 4: (1) any relative by marriage (in-laws) is excluded from those for whom a priest may become unclean (as with the NIV), or (2) a "husband" (*baʿal*) who is a priest must not become unclean for his own dead wife (see NRSV; 1976, 168). A fourth possibility takes *baʿal* to mean chief or master and understands v 4 as a general statement indicating that as a leader among his people, a priest shall not defile himself (as with KJV, see YLT; Harrison 1980, 209; see Keil and Delitzsch n.d., 430). Finally, Paran suggests that *baʿal* may be a partial dittography (scribe copies letters from a previous word in the text and accidently inserts a new word into the text) of *běʿammāyw*. Thus, *baʿal* was not part of the original text, and the verse should be read **he shall not defile himself among his people, and so profane himself.** This reading repeats the sense of v 1, forming an inclusio around vv 2-3 (1983, 152-53, cited in Milgrom 2000, 1800).

■ **5** The prohibition that does not allow priests to **shave their heads or shave off the edges of their beards or cut their bodies** relates to pagan mourning rites for the dead. Such activities are forbidden due to their association with idolatry (Milgrom 2000, 1801-2). Such rites are banned for laypersons and all the more for the priests (→ 19:27-28; Wesley 1765, 416).

■ **6** Priests **must be holy to their God,** just as, if not more than, the laity (→ 19:1-2 and 20:7-8). Priests **must not profane the name of their God** (→ 18:21). These exhortations refer back to the preceding injunctions regarding ceremonial uncleanness (which compromises holiness, 21:1-4) and idolatrous rites that profane the name of God (v 5).

Priests are especially called to be holy **because they present the offerings made to the LORD by fire.** That is, they approach the altar of God and present the offerings of Israel to the Lord. The phrase **the food of their God** is a general phrase designating portions burnt on the altar that are committed to God. It should not be reckoned as an indication that sacrifices are intended to feed God (→ 3:11).

■ **7 Priests must not marry women defiled by prostitution or divorced from their husbands.** Ministerial leaders in the early church were given exhortations reflecting similar concerns related to family order (1 Tim 3:2-4; Titus 1:6). Of course, a primary concern here is the purity of the priests who **are holy to their God.** Holiness would be especially compromised if the priest's wife was a cultic prostitute (Porter 1976, 168; Harrison 1980, 210; → 19:29). This injunction also suggests interest in the character and reputation of a priest's wife, as opposed to sexual experience. This is evident by the recognition that the ordinary priest was allowed to marry a widow (in contrast to the high priest, see v 14). A divorcée, regardless of how innocent, would have a stained reputation due to the stigma of divorce (Wenham 1979, 291). Levine adds force to this argument by pointing out that divorce in ancient Israel likely required proof of marital infidelity. The ground for divorce in Deut 24:1 is stipulated by the phrase *'erwat dābār* (NIV = "something indecent"). The phrase literally refers to something sexually improper. Accordingly, it was taken to mean that only marital infidelity constituted grounds for divorce. If proof of such was not provided, then a husband presenting a false accusation is punished and not allowed to divorce his wife (Deut 22:13-19). However, if the charge against the wife is true, then the woman is charged with a disgraceful act and punished (Deut 22:20-21; Levine 1989, 143-44). Thus, a divorced woman was likely guilty of infidelity and would compromise the holy character of a priest who sought to marry her. The ruling of this verse may also reflect a concern for the purity of the priestly lineage. If a priest married a sexually active woman he could not be sure that his initial offspring was his (Hartley 1992, 348; Gorman 1997, 122).

■ **8** This verse basically repeats the message of v 6. It appears to be secondary because Israel is suddenly addressed (second person) in the midst of a speech addressed to the priests (→ v 1; Noth 1977, 156). Wesley understands this verse as an aside to Moses (see v 1) who is instructed to ensure that the priests be holy (1765, 417). However, the addition of v 24, which explains that Moses "told this to Aaron and his sons *and to all the Israelites*" (emphasis added), affirms that it was intended that Israel be listening as well (see Hartley 1992, 348). Israel is reminded to **regard the priests as holy** and **consider them holy**, treating them with the respect due their position and function (Harrison 1980, 210). In addition, the people are given the responsibility to make sure that the priests behave according to these instructions (Hartley 1992, 348). This understanding reckons *wĕqiddaštô* (**regard them as holy**) more in the sense of *consecrate* or *sanctify* (see NASB).

Food of your God (→ v 6).

I who make you holy (→ 20:7-8).

■ **9** The verb *ḥālal* appears twice in this verse, though the NIV renders it differently in each case (**defiles, disgraces**). Given a context that is highly concerned with purity, a more consistent rendering might be, **if a priest's daughter defiles herself by becoming a prostitute, she *defiles* her father** (see NJPS; re the defiling impact of prostitution, → v 7 and 19:29). The punishment for such an act is that the daughter **must be burned in the fire** (→ 20:14 and From the Text for ch 20). Consistent with the emphasis of this chapter, the concern here is to protect the holiness of the priest who serves near the presence of God who is holy.

2. Restrictions for the High Priest (21:10-15)

■ **10-12** Focus now shifts from the ordinary priest to the **high priest**. The high priest is identified as **the one among his brothers who has had the anointing oil poured on his head and who has been ordained to wear the priestly garments** (→ 8:12-13 and 8:7-9). It is assumed that the high priest must abide by the same regulations as the ordinary priests (21:1-9; see Gerstenberger 1996, 311). Additional, and stricter, rules exclusively for the high priest are included here (vv 10-15), indicating his greater position and responsibility. The levels of responsibility in relation to guarding holiness (people, priest, high priest) recall the gradations reflected in the tabernacle and the sacrificial system (→ From the Text for 4:1—6:7 [4:1—5:26 HB]). The high priest is the one person who approaches closest to the Lord, even into the holy of holies (→ 16:3-5, 12-13). As a result, the high priest must abide by the highest standard of holiness (Hartley 1992, 349).

While the ordinary priests are not allowed to "shave their heads or shave off the edges of their beards or cut their bodies" (v 5), the high priest **must not** even **let his hair become unkempt**. The term *yiprāʿ* includes the meaning "unbind, uncover," resulting in translations that state that the high priest must not "*dishevel* his hair" (NRSV, emphasis added; similar to NIV) or "*uncover* his head" (NASB, emphasis added). Either rendering is tied to acts of mourning, as is the prohibition that does not allow the high priest to **tear his clothes** (Wesley 1765, 417; Porter 1976, 169). What may appear to be the most innocent mourning customs are forbidden for the high priest, due to their possible association with idolatrous rites for the dead (→ v 5). Wenham, however, implies that merely disturbing his anointed hair or specially designed clothes might nullify the high priest's consecration (1979, 291; see Gerstenberger 1996, 312). With regard to tearing his clothes, Milgrom suggests that this specifically applies to the high priest's special garments worn only at the sanctuary. Accordingly, when the high priest tore his clothes in response to Jesus (Mark 14:63), they were not his sacred garments because this took place at the high priest's home (Mark 14:53; Milgrom 2000, 1814).

Defiling contact with the dead is so restricted that the high priest **must not enter a place where there is a dead body**, or **make himself unclean, even for his father or mother** (→ Lev 21:1). Thereby, he is not even allowed the funeral exceptions granted the ordinary priest (→ vv 2-3). In fact, the high priest is not to **leave the sanctuary of his God,** implying that he lived within the sacred precincts of the tabernacle. Such strict boundaries nearly guaranteed that the high priest would have no contact with anything unclean (Noth 1977, 156). In contrast, Porter asserts that the high priest was only restricted from leaving the sanctuary to participate in a funeral (1976, 170). Similarly, Wenham explains that the high priest did not live on the sanctuary grounds but is taught here that his sacred duties take precedence over even family ties (1979, 291).

■ **13-15** In addition to the prohibition against marrying **a woman defiled by prostitution** or **a divorced woman,** the high priest is also restricted from marrying **a widow** (re "woman defiled by prostitution" and "divorced woman," → v 7). These restrictions seem to reflect a concern to maintain the purity of the priestly lineage, as further implied by the emphasis on marrying **only a virgin** (mentioned twice in these verses), and the rationale, **so he will not defile his offspring.** The virgin he marries must be **from his own people,** understood to mean his kinsfolk (Porter 1976, 170; Wenham 1979, 292). Levine affirms that in this context, *mē'ammāyw* "refers specifically to the priestly clan"; thus the high priest can only marry a virgin from a priestly family (1989, 145; see Philo, *Spec. Laws* 1.110). All these restrictions seek to ensure that the children of the high priest will be of priestly heritage (Wenham 1979, 292).

I am the LORD, who makes him holy (→ 20:7-8).

3. Priests with Physical Defects (21:16-24)

■ **16-23** Any priest **who has a defect** is prohibited from **coming near to offer the food of his God.** This means that priests with defects are not allowed to present sacrifices at the altar (re **food of his God,** → v 6 and 3:11). This is clarified by the synonymous expression, **come near to present the offerings made to the LORD by fire.** Physical defects were considered defiling because they marred the wholeness and perfection that the priesthood represented (Porter 1976, 171; see Wenham 1979, 292). Consequently, a priest with defects would **desecrate** the **sanctuary.** It is striking that the term *miqdāšay* (**sanctuary**) is plural. Porter concludes that this verse stems from a period when multiple shrines were acceptable in Israel (1976, 171; → 17:3-7 sidebar, "Question of Common Slaughter and Centralization"). In contrast, the term may be rendered "holy localities, furnishings" (Noth 1977, 157) or "sacred precincts, sanctums" (Milgrom 2000, 1832). Nevertheless, the sacred courtyard must have remained accessible to the blemished priest, because the sacred food he is allowed could only be eaten in a holy place (see 6:16 [6:9 HB]; 6:26 [6:19 HB]; 7:6; Milgrom 2000, 1825).

Out of concern for keeping the sanctuary pure, a priest with defects could not **go near the curtain or approach the altar.** Noth claims that since the curtain is mentioned before approaching the altar, it must not refer to the curtain that divides the holy place from the holy of holies, but must refer to some curtain that stood "at the entrance to an inner part of the holy precincts" (1977, 157). The term *yābō'* is commonly translated "go in, enter" (see KJV, NASB, NET, NJPS, YLT; BDB 1952, 97). If entering the veil before the holy of holies is meant, then this particular restriction can only refer to the high priest, who is the only one allowed to enter the holy of holies, and only on the Day of Atonement (ch 16). Indeed, this is how Haran understands the passage. He asserts that "he shall not go behind the *pārōket*—veil" refers to the high priest, and "he shall not approach the altar" refers to the ordinary priest (1985, 206 n. 1). Milgrom argues that these two phrases express the technical meaning of *officiating* in the holy place (*before* the curtain, not in the holy of holies) and at the outer altar, as opposed to merely entering or approaching. Thus, the blemished high priest was not allowed to *officiate* but was allowed to *enter* the holy place for the sake of cleaning, repairing, or assisting (2000, 1830-31).

Priests with defects were still free to eat the **most holy food** (→ 2:3), **as well as the holy food** (e.g., well-being offering; → 7:11-38). This implies that priests with defects were still considered holy (Wright 1999, 354). This recognition suggests that defects were perhaps not so defiling, as they were physical limitations to effective service at the sanctuary (see Harrison 1980, 211-12; Walton and Matthews 1997, 166).

■ **24** And to all the Israelites (→ v 8). Though the information in this chapter is addressed to the priests (v 1), the addition of all Israelites reflects H's emphasis on inclusiveness in regard to the people (Levine 1989, 146-47; → Behind the Text for ch 17).

4. Sacred Donations (22:1-16)

■ **1-3** This unit is introduced with the general command calling for the priests to **treat with respect the sacred offerings.** This phrase literally reads that the priests **should separate themselves from** ("hold sacredly aloof from"; BDB 1952, 634) **the holy things of the children of Israel.** The following verses delineate ways in which the priests can fulfill this injunction. Wesley explains that the priests should separate themselves and refrain from eating the portions of the offerings assigned to them, *if* they are unclean as described in the following verses (1765, 419; re portions assigned to the priests, see 6:14—7:36 [6:7—7:36 HB]). By doing so, **they will not profane** the **holy name** of the Lord (→ 18:21).

I am the LORD (→ Behind the Text for ch 17).

If a priest officiates in the sanctuary while **ceremonially unclean**, he will pollute the sacred area and thereby profane the name of the Lord (Harrison 1980, 212). The Lord stipulates that such a priest **must be cut off from**

my presence. Normally this phrase appears in relation to laypersons as "cut off from his people" (→ 7:19-21). In the case of the priest, who serves in proximity to the place of God's presence (→ From the Text for 4:1—6:7 [4:1—5:26 HB]), the phrase appears to mean being removed from priestly service (see Wesley 1765, 420; Porter 1976, 173; Hartley 1992, 355). However, in light of H's expanded emphasis regarding the presence of God (→ Behind the Text for ch 17), being cut off from God's presence could include excommunication from the entire community of Israel.

■ **4-9** The following are listed among those things that will make a priest unclean: **infectious skin disease** (chs 13—14), **bodily discharge** (ch 15), **something defiled by a corpse** (→ 11:8 and 11:29-38; re *nepeš* as "corpse," → 21:1), **anyone who has an emission of semen** (15:16-17), and **any crawling thing** (*šereṣ*; → 11:9-12). The list is concluded with the general statement that the priest must avoid contact with **any person who makes him unclean, whatever the uncleanness may be.** Verse 8 of ch 22 adds that the priest **must not eat anything found dead or torn by wild animals** (17:15), which would also make him **unclean.**

In the case of a priest with an infectious skin disease or bodily discharge, he must **not eat the sacred offerings until he is cleansed** (22:4a). This presumably requires the seven-day rituals described previously (chs 13—14 and 15; Gorman 1997, 124). In the case of touching something unclean (22:4b-6), the priest must undergo the standard procedures of waiting **till evening** and bathing **himself with water,** and then **he may eat the sacred offerings.** Missing is the requirement to wash one's clothes (→ 11:39-40; 15:4-10; and 17:15-16). This is apparently assumed (Gorman 1997, 124; though Milgrom argues that no laundering is required for merely *touching* these items [2000, 1855]; → 11:24-25).

In this unit (22:2-8) the **sacred offerings** (*qŏdāšîm*) include both the *less sacred,* "holy" offerings, and the "most holy" (*qodšê qŏdāšîm*) offerings (→ 21:16-23; Porter 1976, 173; Milgrom 2000, 1852, 1865). The concern of these regulations is to maintain a strict separation between the holy and the unclean (Wenham 1979, 294; → 10:8-11). Failure to **keep God's requirements** will cause the priests to **become guilty and die.** This severe penalty reflects the critical importance of the priestly role in mediating between God and the people (a matter of life and death) and maintaining the integrity of the holy place (Gorman 1997, 124).

I am the Lord, who makes them holy (→ 20:7-8).

■ **10-13** These instructions supplement the regulations regarding the portions of the sacrifices that are allotted to the priests to eat (6:16-18 [6:9-11 HB], 26-29 [19-22 HB]; 7:6-7, 9-10, 14, 31-36). The text simply uses the term *zār* ("stranger") to refer to, in this case, anyone who is **outside a priest's family**. **A slave** bought by a priest or **born in his household** is considered part of the family and is allowed to **eat his food** (see Noth 1977, 161). **A priest's daughter** loses her right to **eat any of the sacred contributions** if she **marries anyone other than a priest**. However, if she **becomes a widow or is divorced**, with **no children**, and **returns to live in her father's house**, then **she may eat of her father's food**.

Porter claims that this instruction represents a later period when all members of a priest's family were allowed to eat the sacred contributions (see Num 18:11). Earlier priestly instruction stipulated only that "any *male* in a priest's family" is eligible for the priestly food portions of the sacrifices (6:29 [6:22 HB]; 7:6; see 6:18 [6:11 HB]; Porter 1976, 173). Levine, however, distinguishes *tĕrûmat haqqŏdāšîm* (**sacred contributions**), designated in relation to what a priest's daughter may eat (v 12), as *levied* contributions of lesser sanctity (Num 18:19 affirms this type of contribution as that which daughters of priests may eat). In contrast most offerings had to be eaten in sacred precincts and could not be shared with an entire priestly family (1989, 149-50, 210 n. 22:11). This may explain the discrepancy between the earlier instructions (6:18 [6:11 HB]; 6:29 [6:22 HB]; 7:6), and those here (the same discrepancy appears between Num 18:8-10 and 18:11). Similarly, the discrepancy can be clarified by recognizing that this unit (Lev 22:10-16) only involves the *lesser* "sacred offering" (*qōdeš* [v 10], equivalent to *qŏdāšîm*), which may be shared by the priest's entire family (see Milgrom 2000, 1861, 1865). This would include the priestly portions of the well-being offering (→ 10:12-15 and 21:16-23). In contrast, the "most holy" offerings (*qōdšê qŏdāšîm*) are those that must be eaten in sacred precincts and only by the priests themselves (see Gerstenberger 1996, 325-26).

■ **14-16** A person who **eats a sacred offering by mistake** has acted unfaithfully "in regard to *one* of the LORD's holy things" (5:15). That person **must make restitution to the priest and add a fifth of the value to it**. In addition, this type of offense requires a "guilt offering" (→ 5:14-16; Wesley 1765, 421).

I am the LORD, who makes them holy (→ 20:7-8). In this case, this phrase could be interpreted to mean that God ordains the priests as holy, or God declares the offerings as holy (Levine 1989, 150).

5. Rules for Acceptable Offerings (22:17-33)

■ **17-18 Alien living in Israel** (→ 17:8-9 sidebar, "The *Gēr*, 'Sojourner,' 'Resident Alien'").

Verse 18 refers to any **Israelite** or resident **alien** who **presents *his offering for any of their votive offerings or any of their* freewill *offerings which they present* to the** LORD ***as* a burnt offering.** The priestly legislation (P) distinguishes between the **burnt offering** (*ʿōlâ;* → 1:3) and the ***votive*** (*neder*) and **freewill** (*nĕdābâ*) offerings, which are both types of well-being offerings (→ 3:1 and 7:16-18). Thus, it appears confusing that here H refers to votive and freewill offerings as **a burnt offering.** Porter suggests that votive and freewill offerings could be presented as either whole offerings (burnt offerings, vv 18-19) or as shared offerings (well-being offerings, v 21; Porter 1976, 175). Hartley explains that the different types of burnt offerings (such as votive and freewill) were not discussed in ch 1, just as the different types of well-being offerings were not identified in ch 3 (they are only distinguished in ch 7; 1992, 359-60). Likewise, Milgrom asserts that H adds to P's instruction regarding the burnt offering. Just as ch 7 supplements ch 3 by adding three types of well-being offerings (thanksgiving, votive, and freewill), so here H adds two purposes (votive and freewill) for the burnt offering, which was originally described in ch 1 (2000, 1872).

■ **19-25** These verses specify the types of defects that make animals ineligible for sacrifice. These defects mostly parallel those that also make a priest ineligible to officiate in the sanctuary (21:17-21; Porter 1976, 175). The requirement of a **male without defect** corresponds with a burnt offering (22:18-19; see 1:3, 10). Well-being offerings could be "male or female" (22:21; see 3:1, 6; Wesley 1765, 421; Porter 1976, 175). Since the freewill offering is an optional sacrifice, minor blemishes were acceptable (v 23). However, the votive offering did not allow such exceptions due to the prior commitment (a vow) attached to this sacrifice (Porter 1976, 176; Levine 1989, 152). Alternatively, Milgrom, following Abravanel, suggests that the concession for the freewill offering is based on the spontaneous nature of the sacrifice. The offering is made using the best animal available at the time. In contrast, a votive offering awaits the future fulfillment of a vow, allowing time to provide the highest quality animal (Milgrom 2000, 1878-79).

The prohibition against **testicles** that are **bruised, crushed, torn or cut** (forms of castration) reflects the ancient concern that such conditions nullify God's *good* creation and contradict God's blessing for creatures to be fruitful and multiply (Gen 1:22, 28; 8:17; Wenham 1979, 296). Any animal with a defect fails to fully reflect divine holiness, the overall emphasis of these chapters (→ Behind the Text for chs 17, 19, and 21—22; see Harrison 1980, 213). The command stating that **you must not do this in your own land** (v 24*b*) refers specifically to v 24*a* stipulating what should not be *done to* animals. In contrast, the defects described in vv 22-23 are likely congenital or the result of injury (Levine 1989, 152).

Whereas the eighth-century prophets decried the hypocritical abuse of the sacrificial system in the form of proper ritual followed by unrighteous behavior (Isa 1:11-19; Hos 6:6; Amos 5:21-24; Mic 6:6-8), Malachi ridicules the opposite abuse in the form of improper ritual using blemished and unworthy animals (Mal 1:8-14). These regulations promote respect and the proper attitude of *sacrifice,* in terms of giving one's best in relation to offerings presented to the Lord. Inferior offerings are an insult to the Lord and fail to bring honor to God (Gerstenberger 1996, 327-28). Milgrom asserts that this principle explains why God preferred Abel's offering. Abel honored God by giving "the choicest of the firstlings of his flock" (Gen 4:4; re "fat" as "choicest," → 3:2-4; Milgrom 2000, 1875).

Food of your God (→ 21:6 and 3:11).

■ **26-28** These two regulations reflect the concern for the humane treatment of animals and further promote "reverence for life" (→ 11:46-47 sidebar, "Rationale for the Dietary Restrictions"; also Gane 2004, 382). A newborn **calf, a lamb or a goat** must **remain with its mother for seven days. From the eighth day on, it will be acceptable as an offering.** Clement of Alexandria affirms that "in taking the offspring away from the providential endowment of the milk, a person is doing violence to nature" (Lienhard 2001, 193). He further asserts that this serves as a lesson from the Law that promotes honor for life. While the Law is generous in regard to irrational beasts, there are those who "expose human offspring to abortive death . . . For if the law refuses to allow the offspring of irrational creatures to be separated from their mother before taking milk, it is far more forceful in preparing human beings against that cruel, uncivilized view [exposure to death of infants]" (2001, 193). Porter argues that this ruling is *not* concerned with kindness to animals. He relates it to the seven-day period of impurity prior to the eighth day circumcision of a human boy (12:2-3; Porter 1976, 177). This would suggest that the newborn animal was considered impure from its mother's blood for the first seven days, and therefore must not be allowed to defile the altar of sacrifice (see Hizkuni in Carasik 2009, 177). Gorman views the seven-day period as a time of separation between the act of birth and the act of death, thereby maintaining an appropriate boundary between life and death (1997, 126). Finally, Kaiser suggests that an animal is simply not fit for eating before the eighth day (1994, 1152).

Likewise, Israel was instructed that one must **not slaughter a cow or a sheep and its young on the same day.** Bekhor Shor asserts that this is a matter of compassion similar to Deut 22:6 (in Carasik 2009, 178). The Aramaic Bible adds to this verse, "My people, children of Israel, just as I am merciful in heaven, so shall you be merciful on earth" (*Tg. Ps.-J.*, v 28). Similarly, Wesley recognized such same-day slaughter as an act of cruelty (1765, 422). Wenham sees this law as a call to Israelites to avoid "wanton destruction of the God-given creation" (1979, 296). With regard to concern for the offerer with a small herd, it may be that this law protects an overzealous worshiper from endangering their livelihood by sacrificing both "a bearer and her offspring" at the same time (Hartley 1992, 362; see Gerstenberger 1996, 331). Alternatively, some regard this injunction as a prohibition against some unknown pagan practice (Noth 1977, 163; Porter 1976, 177).

■ **29-30** The thanksgiving offering is treated here, separately from the other well-being offerings that were discussed in a similar manner at 19:5-6. In both instances, the Israelites are told to **sacrifice it in such a way that it will be accepted on your behalf.** This is followed by instruction on how soon the offering must be eaten. In the case of votive and freewill offerings, they must be consumed by the third day (19:5-7; see 7:16-18). In the case of the thanksgiving offering, it **must be eaten that same day** (see 7:15; → 19:5-8).

■ **31-33** This concluding exhortation echoes similar exhortations that appear throughout chs 18—21, thereby binding together these chapters centered on aspects of holiness (see Wenham 1979, 296; Gane 2004, 382-83; also → From the Text for ch 20 and Behind the Text for chs 21—22). **Keep my commands and follow them** (see 18:4, 26; 19:37; 20:8, 22). **I am the LORD/I am the LORD, who makes you holy** (→ Behind the Text for ch 17; also → 20:8). **Do not profane my holy name** (see 18:21; 19:12; 21:6; 22:2). **Who brought you out of Egypt to be your God** (→ 19:36*b*-37).

FROM THE TEXT

All of Israel is called to be holy. However, chs 21—22 demonstrate that the priesthood is held to higher standards of holiness. Furthermore, within the priesthood, the high priest is held to even more stringent requirements than ordinary priests (21:10-15; Noth 1977, 153). This is due to the responsibility and accountability attached to the priests as representatives of God and representatives of the community (Luke 12:48; Jas 3:1; Harrison 1980, 208; → 4:3). Human reflections of holiness are held to increasingly stricter criteria as one moves through the divisions of people, priesthood, and high priest. At the apex of Israel's sanctity stands the high priest on whose forehead an inscription reads "HOLY TO THE LORD" (Exod 28:36; 39:30; Kaiser 1994, 1147; → 8:7-9).

The instructions prohibiting priests with physical defects from officiating in the sanctuary appear as discriminatory and narrow-minded. Contemporary society has come a long way in promoting respect for, and addressing the needs of, those who are disabled or disfigured (certainly more advancements need to be made). In the context of ancient Israel, Hartley clarifies that, though a priest with defects was barred from officiating at the altar, he was "not reduced to poverty or forced to earn his living by another profession" (1992, 350). The regulations allowed him to continue to benefit from the priestly food (Lev 21:22). The Holiness Code, however, is focused on a different concern. Similar to the representative nature of the sacrificial system (→ sidebar, "The Representative Nature of Sacrifice" at From the Text for 4:1—6:7), the regulations regarding physical defects are representative of holiness and purity. "The wholeness of the body is seen as a reflection of the integrity of the holy" (Gorman 1997, 123). The holiness regulations seek to instill within Israel an overwhelming realization of the sacred and holy nature of the Lord God and invite the community to participate in that divine character. In the NT physical defects give way to moral faults, as children of God are exhorted to "become blameless and pure" and "spotless," through *obedience* and godly *living* (Phil 2:15; 2 Pet 3:14; Harrison 1980, 213).

The regulations requiring that sacrificial animals be without defect likewise seem overly concerned with form over function. While the eighth-century prophets ridiculed Israel's failure to *function* morally and ethically in light of what the sacrifices represented, Malachi criticized Israel's negligence and apathy in relation to the *form* of its sacrificial practice ("blind, . . . crippled or diseased animals," Mal 1:8). The emphasis on forms of sacrifice and worship remind us of the importance of respect and reverence due the holy God of the universe (→ 22:19-25).

F. Appointed Times of the Lord (23:1-44)

BEHIND THE TEXT

Regulations regarding holiness in relation to the people are presented in chs 18—20, and regulations regarding holiness in relation to the priests are presented in chs 21—22. Here, in ch 23, holiness is addressed in relation to the *appointed times* for "sacred [*holy*] assemblies." The priestly festival calendar is found here in ch 23 (H's rendition) and in Num 28—29 (P's version; see Driver 1910, 67-68). The priestly calendars reflect the agricultural roots of the major festivals but introduce distinctive priestly concerns (see Porter 1976, 177). Specifically, the festivals and related occasions are presented as liturgical events and are fixed within a regular annual cycle. As a result, the list of community agricultural celebrations becomes an enumeration of *mô'ădê YHWH* ("the appointed times of the LORD"). Kalisch describes the focus of the priestly calendar as an upgrading of the calendar to the ethical sphere.

> An advance had been made from the cosmic and historical to the ethical sphere: the festivals were no longer understood merely as days of thanksgiving for the bounty of *nature*, nor as occasions for tracing, with awe and reverence, in past and present events, the rule of a *Divine Providence*, but as seasons for self-examination and contrition, for the improvement and purification of the *soul* and the *heart*. (1872, 487)

The composite nature of this chapter is evident by its dual titles and conclusions. Nahmanides recognized that the Sabbath instruction (v 3) was sandwiched between two headings for the list of "appointed times" (vv 2, 4; in Carasik 2009, 180). Following the closing subscription (vv 37-38), additional instructions regarding the Festival of Tabernacles (previously addressed in vv 33-36) form an appendix (Driver 1910, 55). Consequently, "there are two titles (vv 2 and 4), two conclusions (vv 37 and 44), two rulings for the feast of Tents (vv 34-36 and 39-43) and the latter ruling is not homogeneous" (de Vaux 1997, 472). The Sabbath instruction (v 3) seems to be a later addition to the original list because it appears *outside* (added prior to) the original heading (v 4) and is explicitly excluded from the original list of appointed times according to v 38 (see Noth 1977, 166). De Vaux concludes there must be at least two strata represented in ch 23. He identifies one as the original law of holiness dating from the preexilic period, and the second strata as later additions from the exilic and postexilic periods. He attributes the Sabbath instruction (v 3), the appended ritual for the Festival of Tabernacles (vv 39-43), and the second conclusion (v 44) to the second, exilic/postexilic, strata in the chapter (1997, 472-73). Milgrom sees four strands related to H in this chapter. His final strand, which he labels H_R represents an exilic source. Milgrom explains that the addition of the Sabbath as an "appointed time" and the appended instructions regarding the Festival of Tabernacles are innovations of H. The purpose of these innovations was to provide means by which Israel could retain its ethnic and religious identity while in exile (2001, 2055-56).

The initial list of appointed times (vv 4-38) is clearly marked by the original heading (v 4) and conclusion (vv 37-38), which form "a chiastically related inclusio" (Milgrom 2001, 2033). That is, v 37a repeats v 4, though it inverts the phrase "the sacred assemblies you are to proclaim" (*miqrā'ê qōdeš 'ăšer-tiqrě'û 'ōtām*, v 4; compare, "which you are to proclaim as sacred assemblies" [*'ăšer-tiqrĕ'û 'ōtām miqrā'ê qōdeš*], v 37a). Thus, vv 4-38 constitute an original festival calendar. To this list of appointed times, an exilic strand of H has affixed up front, the Sabbath (v 3) with a new introductory heading (v 2) serving to include the Sabbath among the "sacred assemblies." This strand of H also added to the end of the original list, new instructions for the Festival of Tabernacles with a new final conclusion (vv 39-44).

Within the original list (vv 4-38), de Vaux also assigns the instructions regarding the Day of Atonement (vv 27-32) to the exilic/postexilic strand (1997, 473; re vv 26-31 as a later addition, see also Elliger 1966, 311). This addition might also be explained as a means of maintaining religious identity through the period of the exile (→ vv 26-32).

IN THE TEXT

1. Introduction and Sabbath (23:1-4)

■ **1-2** Verse 2 appears to be a secondary introduction that repeats the information in v 4. This added introduction serves to include the Sabbath (v 3) among the **appointed *times*** of the LORD (→ Behind the Text above). This chapter lists and briefly describes the *mô'ădîm* (**appointed feasts** or **appointed *times*,** see BDB 1952, 417), which the Lord instructs Israel to **proclaim as sacred assemblies.** The phrase *miqrā'ê qōdeš* (**sacred occasions**) appears eleven times in this chapter (vv 2, 3, 4, 7, 8, 21, 24, 27, 35, 36, 37) and only eight times elsewhere in the Bible (Exod 12:16 [twice]; Num 28:18, 25, 26; 29:1, 7, 12). Every occurrence appears in one of the two priestly calendars (→ Behind the Text above), except for the Exodus passage. Nevertheless, Exod 12:1-20 is traditionally attributed to P (though Knohl assigns it to H [1995, 19, 52]). Thus, the phrase appears to be a uniquely priestly idiom. The term *miqrā'* is related to the verb "to call, summons" (see Wenham 1979, 301). Accordingly, *miqrā'ê qōdeš* has been understood as a *call* for Israel to gather and sanctify these occasions (Nahmanides in Carasik 2009, 179). It seems doubtful that H intended that all of Israel should gather for every *miqrā'ê qōdeš* including the weekly Sabbath, as was expected for the three annual pilgrimage festivals (Exod 23:14-17; 34:18-23). Thus, rather than the calling of national assemblies, *miqrā'ê qōdeš* likely refers to designating and announcing the arrival of festival days, or **sacred *occasions*** (see Noordtzij 1982, 227-28; Milgrom 2001, 1957-58). Gerstenberger notes that each day designated a sacred occasion in ch 23 includes a strict mandate prohibiting any work. He suggests that these special occasions are elevated to the status of "most holy" days.

Excluding the Sabbath, the original calendar (vv 4-36; → Behind the Text above) designates exactly seven of these "most holy" occasions (*miqrā'ê qōdeš*). As a result, secular time is undergirded with a "Lord's week" of holy occasions placed within the calendar year (1996, 339).

■ **3** By affixing the **Sabbath** at the head of the calendar (vv 4-36), and adding a new introduction (v 2), H includes the Sabbath among the days designated as *miqrā' qōdeš* (**sacred *occasion*;** → vv 1-2 and Behind the Text above). This reflects the exilic strata of H (→ Behind the Text above). Emphasizing the work prohibition as the central feature of the Sabbath provides a means of practicing Sabbath even in exile, apart from the temple and sacrificial system (see Milgrom 2001, 1956). The Sabbath is designated as a *šabbat šabbātôn* (**Sabbath of rest**). This label is only applied to the Sabbath (Exod 31:15; 35:2), the Day of Atonement (Lev 16:31; 23:32), and the Sabbatical Year for the land (25:4). In relation to the Sabbath and the Day of Atonement, this designation appears in conjunction with the strict work prohibition, *kol-mĕlā'kâ lō' ta'ăśû* (**you are not to do any work;** see vv 28, 31-32). These two days stand out among the "sacred occasions" as days in which absolutely no work was to be done. Thus, an appropriate translation for *šabbat šabbātôn* might be **Sabbath of *complete* rest** (see NASB, NJPS, NRSV). This is contrasted by the lesser work prohibition *kol-mĕle'ket 'ăbōdâ lō' ta'ăśû* ("do no *regular* work," emphasis added) applied to the other "sacred occasions" (vv 7, 8, 21, 25, 35, 36; see Wesley 1765, 422-23; Milgrom 2001, 1959, 1977-78).

There are six days when you may work (→ 19:3 sidebar, "Observing the Sabbath").

■ **4** This verse records the original introduction to the calendar of appointed times (→ vv 1-2 and Behind the Text above).

2. Passover and Festival of Unleavened Bread (23:5-8)

■ **5-8 Passover** (*pesaḥ*) is designated **on the fourteenth day of the first month** (see Exod 12:1-13). The priestly writings employ a numbered-month calendar. The use of this system may reflect the rejection of ancient month-names associated with pagan gods and their worship (de Vaux 1997, 185; Hartley 1992, 383-84). Ancient Israel followed a lunar month, with the new moon indicating the first of the month, and the full moon indicating the middle of the month (Noth 1977, 169; see de Vaux 1997, 183; and Noordtzij 1982, 231). The Psalmist notes that "He made the moon to (mark) the fixed times" (Ps 104:19; see Gen 1:14; Milgrom 2001, 1965). Psalm 104:19 uses the same term (*mô'ădîm*, "fixed times") as that employed in this chapter of Leviticus to designate "appointed times" in the priestly calendar (→ vv 1-2).

The Festival of **Unleavened Bread** (*maṣṣôt*) begins **on the fifteenth day** of the first month and lasts **for seven days**. This occasion is called a *ḥag* (**Feast**). The term *ḥag* may literally mean "pilgrimage" and is applied to the three *pilgrimage* festivals: Unleavened Bread, Weeks, and Tabernacles (Exod 23:14-17; 34:18-23; Lev 23:34). These three occasions were eventually celebrated at the temple in Jerusalem and involved a pilgrimage for those who lived out of town (Wenham 1979, 303; see Levine 1989, 156; re Weeks as an exception, → vv 15-21). The pilgrimage for Unleavened Bread only involved one day (Milgrom 2001, 1976; → vv 33-36).

For each of the seven days of Unleavened Bread Israel is to **present an offering made to the LORD by fire**. The phrase *wĕhiqrabtem 'iššeh laYHWH* ("you shall present an offering by fire to the LORD") is used throughout this chapter as a generalization referring to the sacrificial details recorded in Num 28—29 (Milgrom 1991, 193; see Knohl 1995, 11). Accordingly, Num 28:3 begins with the introductory statement, "these are the offerings by fire that you are to present to the LORD" (NJPS; Levine 1989, 157). The **first day** and the **seventh day** of Unleavened Bread are designated *miqrā'ê qōdeš* (**sacred occasions**; → Lev 23:1-2). On these two days Israel is instructed to **do no regular work** (*kol-mĕle'ket 'ăbōdâ lō' ta'ăśû*). The term *'ăbōdâ* qualifies "work" as that which is "laborious" (Milgrom 2001, 1978), that is, the **regular** work of a normal weekday. This designates a lesser restriction than that required for the Sabbath and for the Day of Atonement (→ v 3). It is commonly held that the prohibition restricting **laborious work** does not forbid the preparation of food (Exod 12:16; Nahmanides in Carasik 2009, 181; Hertz 1960, 520).

Agricultural Origins of Festivals

The brief calendars in Exodus reveal the early agricultural contexts of the three major festivals (Exod 23:14-19; 34:18-26). The second festival listed in these texts ("Weeks") is identified as **the festival of the harvest of the first fruits of your labor which you sow in the field** (Exod 23:16; see NJPS, NRSV; see also Exod 34:22). The third festival listed in these calendars ("Tabernacles") is labeled "the festival of ingathering" (Exod 23:16; 34:22 NRSV). This third festival is further described with the temporal clause, "when you gather in your crops from the field" (Exod 23:16). The first festival mentioned in these calendars ("Unleavened Bread") is not so explicitly linked to agricultural events. Nevertheless, it is tied specifically to the month of Abib (Exod 23:15; 34:18). The term *'ābîb* ("Abib") includes the meaning "fresh, young ears of barley" and might be called the "month of ear-forming, or of growing green" (BDB 1952, 1). Milgrom affirms that scholarly consensus views both Passover and Unleavened Bread as originally firstfruit festivals (1990, 371). Unleavened Bread in the spring celebrated the firstfruits of the barley crop, Weeks in the summer celebrated the firstfruits of the wheat harvest, and Tabernacles in the fall celebrated the harvest of grapes and olives (MacRae 1960, 251). Each of these three main festivals that required Israel to gather before the Lord (make pilgrimage; Exod 23:14, 17; 34:23-24) were invested with historical commemorations honoring God. Unleavened Bread, along with Passover, is associated with God's mighty act of deliverance from slavery in Egypt. Weeks is later associated with the giving of God's law. Tabernacles is linked to God's provision through the wilderness sojourn (Queen-Sutherland 1991, 76; see MacRae 1960, 251). The transformation of merely agricultural festivals into ritual celebrations aimed at commemorating God's wondrous provisions and mighty acts is another example of the way in which God makes use of that which is already familiar in the ancient Near East and invests it with God's own purposes (→ 16:8 sidebar, "Azazel: Wilderness Satyr," and From the Text for ch 16; see also Gorman 1997, 131). Over time, the early church further spiritualized and adopted these festivals in the form of Passover, Pentecost, and Epiphany (see Milgrom 2001, 2028).

3. Offering of the First Sheaf (23:9-14)

■ **9-14** The **first grain** of the **harvest** is to be presented **before the LORD**. The priest is instructed to **wave** the *'ōmer* (**sheaf**) from the first of the harvest, before the Lord. Rashi states that *'ōmer* refers to a measure of flour made from the grain (Exod 16:18, 36; in Carasik 2009, 182; see Milgrom 2001, 1983). However, the translation **sheaf** suggests a bundle of the first ears of grain to be reaped (Noth 1977, 170; see Deut 24:19; and Noordtzij 1982, 234). The context implies that this must be an offering of *barley*, the first of the grains to be harvested (→ sidebar, "Agricultural Origins of Festivals" above; Noth 1977, 170; also Rashi in Carasik 2009, 185). The *'ōmer* (**sheaf**) is to be symbolically *waved* (*wĕhēnîp*) before the Lord, in the same manner as a "wave offering" (*tĕnûpâ*), thereby dedicating the firstfruits of the harvest to the Lord (→ 7:28-34).

The *'ōmer* (**sheaf**) must be waved **on the day after the Sabbath**. Exactly which Sabbath is intended here is uncertain. Rashi asserts that the "day after the Sabbath" refers to the day following the first festival day of Passover. Nahmanides clarifies that this must be the 16th day of the first month. A *day of rest* is prescribed for the first day of Unleavened Bread (15th day of first month), as indicated in 23:7. Therefore, the following day (16th day of first month) is the day meant by "the day after the Sabbath" (in Carasik 2009, 182-83; see Wesley 1765, 423; → vv 5-8). It seems the same argument might be made in regard to the seventh day of Unleavened Bread, which is also designated as a *day of rest* (v 8; thus the *'ōmer* would be presented on the 22nd day of the first month; see Gerstenberger 1996, 344). A third possibility is that "the day after the Sabbath" refers to the first ordinary Sabbath (Saturday) after the *beginning* of the Festival of Unleavened Bread (falling sometime in the midst of the seven-day festival; Wenham 1979, 304; see Noordtzij 1982, 234). Alternatively, Levine implies that the Sabbath in question may be the first ordinary Sabbath following the *completion* of the seven-day Festival of Unleavened Bread (1989, 157). Finally, the offering of the 'ōmer (**sheaf**) may be independent of the Festival of Unleavened Bread. Since this offering is dependent on the harvest, "the day after the Sabbath" would vary each year and refers to the first Sabbath after the grain has ripened (Noth 1977, 170-71). Thus, whenever the barley becomes ripe, the first sheaf harvested must be brought to the priest who will present it before the Lord on the day after the very next Sabbath (Gorman 1997, 129; see Gane 2004, 389).

On the same day, a **burnt offering** must be sacrificed, along with its accompanying **grain offering** and **drink offering** (chs 1—2; → Behind the Text for 1:1—3:17). Normally, H would simply refer to the sacrificial details in Num 28—29 by means of the phrase *wĕhiqrabtem 'iššeh laYHWH* ("you shall present an offering by fire to the Lord," NASB; → Lev 23:5-8). In this case, however, Num 28—29 does not include a discussion of the 'ōmer. Thus, H must provide the sacrificial details that accompany this day. The waving of the 'ōmer (**sheaf**), with these accompanying offerings, serves to acknowledge God as the provider of all produce, and consecrate the crops by offering a representative portion to the Lord (Harrison 1980, 217). Proverbs highlights God's blessing in response to the offering of firstfruits: "Honor the Lord with your wealth, with the firstfruits of all your crops; then your barns will be filled to overflowing, and your vats will brim over with new wine" (Prov 3:9-10). Israel is prohibited from consuming any **bread, or roasted or new grain** until the 'ōmer (**sheaf**) and its accompanying offerings have been presented to the Lord. This indicates that nothing should be eaten from the *new* crop until a portion has first been dedicated to God, in thanksgiving and consecration.

4. Festival of Weeks (23:15-22)

■ **15-21** **From the day after the Sabbath** refers to the same Sabbath following which Israel presented **the sheaf of the wave offering** (→ vv 9-14). From that day Israel is instructed to **count off seven full weeks** (lit. **seven sabbaths**); that is, **fifty days,** which brings one to **the day after the seventh Sabbath.** At that time, Israel is to present **an offering of new grain to the Lord.** Following the **wave offering** of the 'ōmer (**sheaf**) from the *barley* harvest (vv 9-14), this **new grain** must refer to the *wheat* harvest. The Dead Sea Scrolls make this explicit in their version of this biblical instruction by specifying that the loaves here are *wheat* bread (11QT^a 18:14; see Martínez 1996, 158). This occasion is commonly called the Festival of Weeks.

Other sources designate Weeks as one of the three pilgrimage festivals (*ḥag*; Exod 34:22; Deut 16:10, 16; → Lev 23:5-8, and sidebar, "Agricultural Origins of Festivals"). However, it is not designated a *ḥag* ("pilgrimage festival") in this passage. Milgrom explains that the priestly texts do not consider this day a *ḥag* requiring pilgrimage, due to the demands of the harvest (2001, 1991-92, 2009). Ginsberg points to the concluding phrase of this pericope as confirmation that no pilgrimage is required: **this is to be a lasting ordinance for the generations to come, wherever you live.** The phrase **wherever you live** (lit. "in all your dwelling places," see NASB) indicates that this occasion can be celebrated locally (1982, 72; → 17:3-7 sidebar, "Question of Common Slaughter and Centralization"). The phrase appears in conjunction with the statement "this is to be a lasting ordinance for the generations to come" to form the conclusion to pericopes involving major occasions that do not require a pilgrimage (vv 14 [*'ōmer;* waving of the sheaf], 21 [Weeks], 31 [Day of Atonement]). In contrast, the H appendix comprising the second Tabernacles pericope (→ Behind the Text above) repeats this concluding statement but leaves off the phrase "wherever you live" (v 41). This is because Tabernacles is indeed designated a *ḥag* ("pilgrimage festival," vv 34, 39, 41).

The Festival of Weeks is also referred to as *Pentecost* (Greek meaning *fiftieth* [day]; BDAG 2000, 796; Hertz 1960, 521; see LXX of Lev 25:10, *pentēkoston*, "fiftieth"). This day is proclaimed a *miqrā' qōdeš* (**sacred occasion;** → 23:1-2 and Behind the Text above), in which **no regular work** (*kol-mĕle'ket 'ăbōdâ lō' ta'ăśû*) is to be done (→ v 3 and vv 5-8).

The sacrifices enumerated here do not precisely match those listed in the corresponding instructions in Num 28:26-31. Normally, H would simply refer to the sacrificial details in Num 28—29 by means of the phrase *wĕhiqrabtem 'iššeh laYHWH* ("you shall present an offering by fire to the LORD," NASB; → Lev 23:5-8). In this case, however, the sacrifices for the day are addressed here. These instructions may be considered as additional to those revealed in Num 28 (Hertz 1960, 522). Alternatively, Milgrom explains the discrepancy between the two texts as the result of H's attempt to convert private individual firstfruits offerings into collective public sacrifices (2001, 1992-96, 2005).

As with the *'ōmer* (**sheaf**) of the *barley* harvest (→ vv 9-14), the Festival of Weeks centers around the presentation of **new grain** (in this case *wheat*) as a **firstfruits** (*bikkûrîm*) offering (→ 2:12; here H has reversed P's use of *rē'šît* [first *processed* grain] and *bikkûrîm* [first-ripe, *raw* grain];

Milgrom 2001, 2004). **Two loaves** are to be presented as a **wave offering** (*těnûpâ;* → 7:28-34). Since they are leavened **(with yeast)**, these loaves cannot be burned on the altar (→ 2:11). They must be given to the priests to eat (Porter 1976, 185). A **burnt offering** is to be presented, consisting of **seven male lambs, . . . one young bull and two rams.** These are to be brought **together with their grain offerings and drink offerings.** The **two lambs** that make up the ***well-being*** offering would normally be shared by the Lord (portions on the altar), the priests, and the offerer (→ 7:28-34). In this case, however, since the offering represents the entire community, the meat of the lambs along with the **bread of the firstfruits** form a **wave offering** and are given to the priests (Noordtzij 1982, 236-37). The reason for a ***purification*** offering (→ 4:1—5:13) during the festivals is unclear (see Num 28:22; 29:16). It may reflect the periodic need to restore the people to a state of purity (Levine 1989, 159; → 12:6-7a; 14:19-20). As with the presentation of the *'ōmer* **(sheaf)** from the barley harvest, the offering of the firstfruits **(new grain)** of the wheat harvest serves to acknowledge God as provider and dedicate the first portion of the crop to God with thanksgiving and consecration (→ 23:9-14).

■ **22** The immediately preceding instructions related to the barley and wheat harvests (vv 9-14, 15-21), prompt this reminder for the Israelites: **When you reap the harvest of your land, do not reap to the very edges of your field or gather the gleanings of your harvest. Leave them for the poor and the alien.** This is repeated from 19:9, though it excludes the related statement regarding the harvesting of grapes. This is likely because the grape harvest is later in the year, associated with the Festival of Tabernacles (vv 33-36; → vv 5-8 sidebar, "Agricultural Origins of Festivals"). As the community honors God for the harvest and celebrates the promise of a bountiful crop, Israel is exhorted not to forget the needs of the poor and the stranger.

5. First Day of the Seventh Month (23:23-25)

■ **23-25** As opposed to *šabbat šabbātôn* ("Sabbath of ***complete*** rest"; → v 3), **the first day of the seventh month** is simply designated as *šabbātôn* **(day of rest).** Accordingly, Israel is instructed to **do no regular work** (→ vv 5-8). This day is also designated a *miqrā' qōdeš* (**sacred** *occasion;* → vv 1-2 and Behind the Text above).

The distinguishing feature of this occasion is that it is **commemorated with trumpet blasts** (lit. "a reminder by means of alarm blasts"; see Milgrom 2001, 2014). Various types of trumpet calls and alarms are addressed in Num 10:1-10. The use of the verb *tāqa'* ("blow") with the noun ḥăṣōṣĕrâ ("trumpet") appears to designate signals intended to gather the community or its leaders (Num 10:2-4, 8), and to announce "appointed times" (môʿădîm; → vv 1-2 and Behind the Text above) and the beginning of each month ("New Moon"; Num 10:10). In contrast, the use of the verb rûʿa ("blast") or its related noun tĕrûʿâ ("alarm"), sometimes in conjunction with tāqaʿ ("blow") or ḥăṣōṣĕrâ ("trumpet"), indicates a signal for the camps to move out (Num 10:5-6), or a call to battle (Num 10:9; see Num 31:6). This distinction is affirmed in Num 10:7, which specifies that gathering the community requires *blowing* the trumpets (tāqaʿ) but not *blasting* an alarm (rûʿa). In the case of **the first day of the seventh month (23:24)**, the commemoration **with trumpet blasts** is expressed with the noun tĕrûʿâ ("alarm"). Thus, the **trumpet blasts** for this day are not the same as that normally used to announce the "appointed times" or the beginning of other months. Ibn Ezra describes this distinction by claiming that all other months require the sounding of trumpets, but this seventh month calls for the sounding of the ram's horn. Likewise, the Day of Atonement is announced by means of the ram's horn (šôpār [popularly, "shofar"]; 25:9; in Carasik 2009, 187). The reason an *alarm* is sounded on this day may be explained by the rabbinic tradition that it is a day of judgment. This day introduces the month in which the Day of Atonement falls. Thus, it is fitting that the month should open with God's judgment regarding sins to be atoned (see Nahmanides in Carasik 2009, 187-88). Knohl explains that the commemorative blasts reflect an appeal to God that God might remember the people with kindness as they anticipate salvation (1987, 93). As the Day of Atonement approaches, the trumpet blasts also remind the people of the importance of repentance and reformation (Gane 2004, 402). At the same time, the people are called to remember God's great mercies that sustain them through the year (see Harrison 1980, 219).

Later tradition celebrates the New Year (rōʾš haššānâ) on this first day of the seventh month. However, there is little or no indication of this in the biblical text. The only biblical passage in which the expression rōʾš haššānâ is found is Ezek 40:1. Strangely, it is applied there to the tenth day of a month (de Vaux 1997, 502). Nevertheless, Noth suggests that the liturgical calendar held this day of **trumpet blasts** to be the beginning of the New Year, from early times. The old Feast of Ingathering (later Tabernacles, in the seventh month) was celebrated in the fall and described as taking place "at the end of the year" (Exod 23:16; 34:22 ["at the turn of the year"]; 1977, 172-73). Porter asserts that initially the "appointed times" in the seventh month were all parts of a single great festival that celebrated the grape harvest and the New Year. This included early elements of the

Day of Atonement, which provided the nation with a clean start for the New Year. This is paralleled in the ancient Near East by the Babylonian New Year Festival that likewise celebrated the New Year with purification rites (1976, 124-25, 187). For Israel, the seventh month contributes to the Sabbatical character of the liturgical calendar. Just as the seventh day (Sabbath), seventh year (Sabbatical Year), and the Jubilee (end of seven weeks of years) are set apart as holy; so also the seventh month is set apart (Noordtzij 1982, 237; see Wesley 1765, 426).

Present an offering made to the LORD by fire (→ vv 5-8).

6. Day of Atonement (23:26-32)

■ **26-32** The Day of Atonement is addressed with greater detail in ch 16. The title *yôm hakkippūrîm* (lit. Day of *Atonements*) is plural. This is likely a "plural of amplification" indicating complete or full purgation (GKC 1910, 397-98; see Milgrom 2001, 2011). The Day of Atonement is designated a *miqrā' qōdeš* (**sacred** *occasion*; → 23:1-2 and Behind the Text above). It is also designated a *šabbat šabbātôn* (**Sabbath of** *complete* **rest**; → v 3), with the corresponding strict prohibition insisting that the Israelites **do no work** (*kol-mělā'kâ lō' ta'ăśû*; → v 3 and vv 5-8). The strict work prohibition is stated twice (vv 28, 31), surrounding a threat of *destruction* for **anyone who does any work on that day** (v 30). This appears in conjunction with the twice-stated command to **deny yourselves** (vv 27, 32), likewise surrounding a threat of *cutting off* for **anyone who does not deny himself** (v 29). The verb *'ānâ* (**deny**) in the intensive form (*piel*) carries the meaning "to humble," "afflict," or "weaken" and is commonly understood as a reference to fasting (→ 16:29-31). Wesley explains the term as a call to fasting and repentance (1765, 426; see also Wenham 1979, 305). The connection between self-denial ("affliction") and fasting is further evident in Ps 35:13; Isa 58:3, 5, 10; and Dan 10:3, 12 (see Milgrom 1990, 246).

The emphasis on Sabbath rest and fasting likely stems from a later strata of H for the purpose of providing Israelites during the exilic period with a means of implementing the Day of Atonement at a time when the temple and sacrificial system were not available (→ Behind the Text above). The parallel instruction to "do no work" in Num 29:7 reflects the lesser work restriction ("do no regular work"; *kol-mĕle'ket 'ăbōdâ lō' ta'ăśû*; → Lev 23:3 and 23:5-8) in a number of manuscripts (Medieval Hebrew, Greek, Syriac, Aramaic, Latin; see BHS 1983, 268). This suggests the possibility that the later strata of H upgraded the work restriction for the Day of Atonement in order to compensate for the lack of any temple ritual in the context of the exilic period.

Present an offering made to the LORD by fire (→ vv 5-8).
Cut off from his people (→ 7:19-21).

7. Festival of Tabernacles (23:33-36)

■ **33-36** The *Festival* of Tabernacles is the third "appointed *time*" (→ vv 1-2) in the **seventh month**, along with the day of trumpet blasts and the Day of Atonement. It is identified as a *ḥag* (**Feast**) and comprises one of the three original pilgrimage festivals (→ vv 5-8 and sidebar, "Agricultural Origins of Festivals"). Tabernacles was originally called the *"Festival of Ingathering"* (Exod 23:16; 34:22) and was associated with the harvest of grapes and olives. It is a time of great rejoicing in celebration of the culmination of the harvest season (Deut 16:13-14; Porter 1976, 188). Gane suggests that Tabernacles celebrates God's goodness in providing the harvest, with a purpose similar to that of the American Thanksgiving holiday inspired by the first successful harvest of the early Pilgrim settlers (2004, 402). The festival takes place from the **fifteenth day** until the twenty-first day of the month. The **first day** and the **eighth day** are each designated a *miqrā' qōdeš* (sacred ***occasion;*** → vv 1-2 and Behind the Text above), in which **no regular work** (*kol-mĕle'ket 'ăbōdâ lō' ta'ăśû*) is to be done (→ v 3 and vv 5-8).

The term *sukkôt* (**Tabernacles**) literally refers to "booths" (see v 42; BDB 1952, 697). Ehrlich explains that Tabernacles was the one time of the year in which farmers would have been able to attend an extended pilgrimage festival. Passover and Weeks were at the beginning and middle of the demanding work season of the harvest and therefore would not permit pilgrimage for an extended period (→ vv 5-8 and vv 15-21). However, since Tabernacles marked the end of the harvest season, more leisure time was available. When Israel's celebrations shifted from local to regional sanctuaries, and eventually to the one central temple, all pilgrimage participants would have gathered in Jerusalem. The increased population would have been more than the city could handle. As a result, participants were forced to set up temporary shelters in the form of booths (1968, 85; see also Levine 1989, 265; and Milgrom 2001, 2049-50). This activity likely became a featured characteristic of the festival and may explain the name change from *"Festival* of Ingathering" to **Festival of Tabernacles**. Alternatively, some argue that camping in booths reflects an older practice in which agricultural laborers dwelt in temporary shelters in the midst of orchards and vineyards during harvesttime (Noth 1977, 176; Porter 1976, 189; Hartley 1992, 389).

Unlike the Festival of Unleavened Bread (vv 6-8), this festival has its concluding *miqrā' qōdeš* (**sacred *occasion***) on the **eighth day** instead of the "seventh day" (see v 8). This final day is designated *'ăṣeret* (**closing assembly**). The NIV rendering of this term follows the Greek translation (LXX), which reads *exodion*, meaning "finale" (see Levine 1989, 162). This likely stems from the application of this term to the concluding day of an extended festival (Deut 16:8; see Hertz 1960, 524; and Levine 1989, 162). Alternatively, Noordtzij defines the term as "festive assembly" (1982, 239), while Milgrom argues that "solemn assembly" is the most likely meaning (2001, 2029-30). The Aramaic Bible adds to v 36 the statement, "You shall be assembled to pray for rain before the Lord" (*Tg. Ps.-J.*). Milgrom sees this as an indication of the purpose of the *'ăṣeret* assemblies; that is, to pray for successful harvest, or in this case for a good rainy season for the next harvest (2001, 2030-31). In time, the eighth day of Tabernacles took on the character of a separate festival celebrating the law of God. On this day the annual reading of the Torah (Law) was completed and restarted (Hertz 1960, 524; see Neh 8:18).

Present offerings made to the LORD by fire (→ Lev 23:5-8).

8. Summation (23:37-38)

■ **37-38** These verses express the original conclusion to the priestly calendar (Porter 1976, 188). The opening line of this summation repeats v 4 to envelop the list of *môʿădîm* (**appointed times**), which are to be proclaimed *miqrāʾê qōdeš* (**sacred *occasions;*** → vv 1-2 and Behind the Text above). The **offerings made to the LORD by fire** for each occasion are detailed in Num 28—29 (→ Lev 23:5-8). The statement that **these offerings are in addition to those for the LORD's Sabbaths** indicates that the ordinary Sabbath was not originally considered among the *miqrāʾê qōdeš* (**sacred *occasions;*** → v 3).

9. Supplement Regarding Tabernacles (23:39-44)

■ **39-43** At this point, there is an addendum to the chapter providing additional treatment of the Festival of Tabernacles (→ vv 33-36 and Behind the Text above). That this **festival to the LORD** refers to Tabernacles is made clear because it begins **with the fifteenth day of the seventh month** and includes a *šabbātôn* (**day of rest**) on the **first day . . . and the eighth day** of the festival (see vv 34-36). Also, the indication that this occasion takes place **after you have gathered the crops of the land** affirms that it corresponds to the Festival of Tabernacles (→ vv 33-36).

This appendix adds two new instructions regarding the Festival of Tabernacles. The Israelites are instructed to **take choice fruit from the**

trees, and palm fronds, leafy branches and poplars. Milgrom explains that Neh 8:13-17 represents a misunderstanding of Lev 23, in which Ezra conflated the two separate stipulations in vv 40 and 42. Ezra understood the branches to be the materials for building booths (2001, 2050, 2063-67). Abarbanel asserted that these items were not intended to make booths, in contrast to Neh 8:15. Rather, as the text states, their purpose is to **rejoice before the LORD** (in Carasik 2009, 193). This likely entails a joyful procession carrying and waving fruits and branches (Noth 1977, 175).

In addition, the Israelites are instructed to **live in booths for seven days.** Originally this practice may have been due to overcrowding in Jerusalem during the extended pilgrimage festival (→ Lev 23:33-36). Here, a historical commemoration is provided for the practice (→ vv 5-8 sidebar, "Agricultural Origins of Festivals"). The Lord reminds Israel that **I had the Israelites live in booths [sukkôt] when I brought them out of Egypt.** Levine points out a possible double entendre in that the first stop in the wilderness journey from Egypt was Succoth (Exod 12:37). Thus, God brought them to *Sukkot* and made them dwell in *sukkot* (1989, 163). Not only does this recall God's mighty deliverance from Egypt and provision through the wilderness, but it also serves as a call for humility. Rashbam cites Deut 8:7-18 and explains that Israel must not grow haughty when the harvest has been gathered and their homes are full of every good thing. Instead, they are instructed to go out of their homes and live in booths, to recall that in the wilderness they had no property and no houses in which to live. As a result, in response to an abundant harvest they will avoid thinking, "My power and the strength of my hands have produced this wealth for me," and instead they will give glory to God (Deut 8:17; in Carasik 2009, 194; also Wenham 1979, 305-6).

This addendum reflects the exilic strata of H. It makes no mention of sacrifices or temple ritual associated with the festival. Instead, it reemphasizes an original aspect of the festival (living in booths; → vv 33-36) and prescribes a joyful celebration with branches and fruit. This provides a means by which Israel, during the crisis of the exile, could still meaningfully celebrate relationship with God in a context devoid of the temple and its related sacrificial system (→ Behind the Text and comments on v 3 and vv 26-32; also Milgrom 2001, 2050-51).

I am the LORD your God (→ Behind the Text for ch 17).

■ **44** Verses 37-38 constitute the original conclusion to the priestly calendar and form an inclusio with its original beginning at v 4 (→ vv 37-38). This verse (v 44) provides a secondary conclusion and forms an inclusio with the added opening at v 2 (→ Behind the Text and vv 1-2). The envelope effect is generated by the simple repetition of the phrase, **the appointed *times* of the** LORD (*mōʿădê YHWH*), here and in v 2 (see Milgrom 2001, 2053).

FROM THE TEXT

The calendar of "appointed times" and "sacred ***occasions***" serves to structure the life of the people, and provides "a temporal order" and "context for the life of the community" (Gorman 1997, 132). Accordingly, life is organized around liturgical celebrations that acknowledge God's provision throughout the year and provide opportunity for expressing relationship with God.

The dedication of the firstfruits of the harvest is an acknowledgment that all produce comes from God. As a token of thanksgiving, the very first of the crop is committed back to the Lord. The contemporary practice of tithing in the church reflects a similar expression of thanksgiving and consecration.

Historical commemorations attached to the festivals afford a means of reliving salvation history (see Noth 1977, 176). Passover, Unleavened Bread, and Tabernacles are ritual events that recall and actualize sacred history. God's activity becomes an experienced reality for each new generation (Gorman 1997, 129). Similarly, Moses sought to bring history into current reality for the new generation of Israelites coming out of the wilderness. His speech in Deut 5:1-22 was directed to the second generation of the slaves delivered from Egypt (see Deut 2:14-15). The generation that stood at Sinai (Horeb) had all died previously. Thus, it is striking that Moses addresses the crowd with these words: "It was *not* with our fathers that the LORD made this covenant, but with *us*, with *all of us who are alive here today.* The LORD spoke to *you* face to face out of the fire on the mountain" (Deut 5:3-4, emphasis added). Moses' intent is clear; he desires to bring the past vividly before the new generation and relate them directly to the saving event at Sinai (von Rad 1966, 55).

Growing up in the church as the child of a pastor gave me the naive impression that I was born with faith in Christ and the commitment of a disciple. I was raised within the influential environment of my parents' strong belief in God. Nevertheless, there came a time at which I realized I could no longer live on my parents' faith. I had to make a decision for my own life in regard to following Christ. My relationship with God had to become real and genuine in my own life. That is what Moses sought to create for the second generation of those coming out of the wilderness from Egypt. Their relationship with God had to become as real as if they stood at the foot of Mount Sinai and received the law of God themselves. In the same way, contemporary Christians affirm their living relationship with God each time they reenact the Lord's Supper. Rather than merely reading the account from the Gospels or Paul's Letter to the Corinthians, Christians actually eat pieces of bread and drink cups of juice to reenact the Last Supper. Such "ritual 'remembering' provides an occasion to reconstruct, actualize, and concretize events" from sacred history (Gorman 1997, 131). The historical commemorations attached to the festival calendar generate such ritual enactments that thereby bring to life salvation history for each new generation.

Evidence of editing and expanding God's word can be disconcerting if we presume that each biblical book was revealed all at once to the same individual. However, signs of editing are no threat to the authority of Scripture once we acknowledge the oversight of the Spirit of God across time and in the lives of numerous inspired authors. Leviticus 23 provides a clear example of God's revelation being updated and reapplied to the new circumstances in which God's children find themselves. The additions to ch 23 that reflect an editor from the time of the Babylonian exile demonstrate God's ongoing concern to provide means by which God's people can express their relationship to God through time (→ Behind the Text above). In a context in which the temple had been destroyed and sacrificial ritual suspended, the exilic additions to ch 23 provided renewed ritual activities by which Israel could continue to practice its faith and relive its sacred history (→ v 3 [Sabbath], vv 26-32 [Day of Atonement], and vv 39-43 [Festival of Tabernacles]).

Recognizing the intent of the festivals reveals the significance of the priestly calendar for the church today. Contemporary liturgical occasions (e.g., Christmas, Easter, Pentecost) likewise bring Christians into contact with the saving acts of God (see Hartley 1992, 394). They provide opportunities to relive sacred history and express relationship to God with thanksgiving and praise.

G. Oil and Bread for the Tabernacle; Blasphemy (24:1-23)

BEHIND THE TEXT

Chapter 24 contains two accounts. The first includes instructions regarding the care of the lamps in the tabernacle and the bread displayed in the tabernacle. The second account relates the story of a man who blasphemed the name of the Lord, and provides legislation regarding restitution in response to death or injury. These passages seem out of place and interrupt the flow of material addressing holiness in relation to people (chs 18—20), priests (chs 21—22), and sacred times (ch 23). More specifically ch 24 appears to disrupt the calendar theme that continues from ch 23 into ch 25, which provides instructions regarding the Sabbatical Year and Year of Jubilee (see Noordtzij 1982, 242; also Gorman 1997, 132).

The discussion of the lamps and bread in the tabernacle do relate to the overall treatment of the sacrificial system in relation to the tabernacle in chs 1—7. The bread as a regular share for the priests to eat corresponds with the larger discussion of priestly portions in chs 6—7. In a broad sense, any discussion related to the tabernacle of God's presence relates to conversations regarding holiness. Along such lines, Keil and Delitzsch maintain that the oil for the lamps and the bread were regular offerings the Israelites were commanded to provide, not only during festivals, but also on ordinary days as part of the sanctification of life (Keil and Delitzsch n.d., 451). Nevertheless, especially with regard to the story of the blasphemer, direct thematic relations between this chapter and those surrounding it remain elusive. It has been suggested that the sequence of events here reflects the character of Leviticus as mainly a narrative work (see chs 8—10) in which laws are dispensed at particular times in order to address specific circumstances (Wenham 1979, 308-9). Accordingly, perhaps the account of the blasphemer is placed here simply because the historical incident took place at the time these laws were given (Keil and Delitzsch n.d., 453).

Trevaskis proposes a symbolic meaning for the light and bread of ch 24 and thereby reveals a possible purpose for the placement of ch 24 in its literary context within the Holiness Code. He suggests that the light (*mā'ôr*) of the lamps in the tabernacle (v 2) recall the heavenly lights (*mě'ōrōt*) God created in Gen 1:14-16. The heavenly lights serve to "mark seasons and days and years" (Gen 1:14). That is, the heavenly lights govern Israel's calendar (Lev 23 and 25). In addition, this term for light evokes the presence of God (Ps 90:8). Thus, the command in Lev 24:2-4 to keep the light continually burning represents a call for Israel to continue living holy lives under God's rule through the sacred calendar (2009, 300-302).

It has long been recognized that the "twelve loaves of bread" (Lev 24:5) may represent the twelve tribes of Israel (Ibn Ezra in Carasik 2009, 196; Wesley 1765, 429). Regularly positioning them on the table under the light of God's presence (just outside the curtain before the holy of holies) serves as a reminder to Israel to remain faithful to God's rule and reflect God's holiness (Trevaskis 2009, 303-5). In relation to the blasphemer account, the phrase "among the Israelites" (v 10) "occurs once more in Leviticus," at 22:32 (310; Trevaskis apparently overlooks a third occurrence in 25:33). That verse (22:32) is tied to the account of the blasphemer (24:10-23) because it too is concerned with profaning the *name* of God. Accordingly, the blasphemer in ch 24 threatens the sanctity of Israel as depicted in ch 22. The account of the blasphemer impresses upon Israel the critical need to remove any such threat to the sanctity of the community. As a result this passage extends the abstract ideal of Israel's holiness to practical, everyday life within the community by adhering to God's laws (Trevaskis 2009, 310-12).

The account of the blasphemer illustrates the command-fulfillment pattern characteristic of priestly literature (Driver 1910, 130; McEvenue 1971, 14-18; see King 2009, 21). God gives the command to "take" and "stone" the blasphemer (24:14), and the Israelites fulfilled the command when they "took" and "stoned" the blasphemer (v 23; Wenham 1979, 309). Inserted in the midst of the account of the blasphemer is legislation regarding retribution for injury or death. Wenham demonstrates the careful symmetry of the legislation as follows:

A	"alien or native-born" (v 16)
B	"takes the life of a human being" (v 17)
C	"takes the life of someone's animal" (v 18)
D	"whatever he has done must be done to him" (v 19)
D'	"as he has injured the other, so he is to be injured" (v 20b)
C'	"kills an animal" (v 21a)
B'	"kills a man" (v 21b)
A'	"the alien and the native-born" (v 22)

At the very center of this concentric pattern is highlighted the principle of making the punishment fit the crime: "fracture for fracture, eye for eye, tooth for tooth" (v 20a; Wenham 1979, 311-12).

IN THE TEXT

1. Lamp and Bread of the Tabernacle (24:1-9)

■ **1-4** The **light** (*mā'ôr*) in the tabernacle recalls the heavenly lights (*mĕ'ōrōt*) God created in Gen 1:14-16. The term for light here also suggests the presence of God (Ps 90:8; Trevaskis 2009, 300-302). The rabbis understood the **Testimony** to be the western lamp in the lampstand, testifying to all that God's divine presence rests upon Israel (Rashi in Herczeg 1999, 306). The presence of God is considered especially near, on the other side of the curtain in the holy of holies (16:2). Consistent with H's tendency to expand the presence of God within the community (→ Behind the Text for ch 17), the light of the tabernacle suggests a strong manifestation of God's presence in the holy place, as well as the holy of holies, within the tabernacle. Gerstenberger sees the background for the light of the tabernacle in Gen 1:3-5 and the creation of light (*'ôr*) from chaotic darkness. The light in the holy place represents God's power "enduring from the daylight hours into the night and until morning" (1996, 356). God's power does not diminish when the sun goes down. Thus, the light in the tabernacle signifies God's "unbroken life" (356).

The **lamps** in the tabernacle are to be **kept burning continually** (see Exod 27:20-21). The Hebrew text in Lev 24:2 mentions only one lamp (*nēr*), while v 4 refers to multiple lamps (*nērôt*). Wesley explains that seven lamps made up one lamp (1765, 428). That is, seven lamps were placed into a single candelabrum (**lampstand,** *měnōrâ;* popularly, the menorah; see Exod 25:31-37). Haran states that *nēr* can be used collectively, and therefore Lev 24:2 (singular) and v 4 (plural) refer to the same object (1985, 208 n. 4). Alternatively, Porter suggests that v 2 reflects an original single lamp in the Jerusalem temple, while v 4 reflects the later "lamps on a lampstand" of the *Second* Temple built after the exile (1976, 190-91; see Milgrom 2001, 2088). **Continually** (*tāmîd*) does not mean that the lamps burned "continuously." Rather they must be *regularly* lit and tended in order to burn **from evening till morning** (Rashi in Carasik 2009, 195; see Haran 1985, 207-8).

The lamps are placed **outside the curtain of the Testimony in the Tent of Meeting** (re **Tent of Meeting,** → 1:1). The **Testimony** (*'ēdūt*) is an abbreviation of "ark of the Testimony" (*'ărōn hā'ēdūt;* also known as "ark of the covenant," Exod 30:6 NRSV). The **Testimony** refers to the Ten Commandments held inside the ark (in contrast to the early rabbis [see above]; Milgrom 2001, 2089). Thus, the lamps are in the holy place outside the curtain that hides the ark (see Noth 1977, 177).

■ **5-9** **Twelve loaves of bread** were to be placed **in two rows, six in each row, on the table of pure gold before the** LORD. These loaves are sometimes referred to as the *showbread* or "bread of the Presence" (Exod 25:30; 35:13; 39:36; 1 Sam 21:6; 1 Kgs 7:48; 2 Chr 4:19). Moses is the one being addressed (Lev 24:1), but rather than baking the bread himself, he is responsible for having it done. Wesley asserts that the priests were responsible for preparing the bread, which was purchased from money contributed by the people (1 Chr 9:32; Wesley 1765, 429). However, the immediate context suggests that the Israelites were responsible for offering the ingredients for the bread, just as they were responsible for supplying the oil for the lampstand (Lev 24:2; Ibn Ezra in Carasik 2009, 196). Verse 8 affirms this with the statement that the bread was to be set out **on behalf of the Israelites** (Milgrom 2001, 2095; Trevaskis 2009, 303; both argue that Moses *initiates* the rite). The bread represents the tribes of Israel (Ibn Ezra in Carasik 2009, 196; Wesley 1765, 429). Trevaskis suggests that positioning the bread that represents Israel under the light of the lamps that represent God's presence (→ vv 1-4) symbolically encourages Israel to remain loyal to God's sovereign rule (2009, 303-4).

Pure incense was placed **along each row** to serve **as a memorial portion** (*'azkārâ*). The incense was likely held in bowls or containers next to the bread. In this case, the memorial portion serves as a *token* **to represent the bread** (see Porter 1976, 191). The early church fathers saw the incense as a symbol of prayer (Bede in Lienhard 2001, 196). Accordingly, the *azkārâ* would remind God of the petitions of the people (→ 2:2; also Harrison 1980, 221). The memorial portion is to be **an offering made to the Lord by fire**. It was likely burned on the incense altar inside the holy place (Milgrom 2001, 2094-95).

This bread is to be set out before the Lord regularly. The term translated **regularly** here is the same as that translated "continually" in vv 2, 3, and 4 (*tāmîd;* → vv 1-4). Accordingly, the bread was to be set out *regularly* every Sabbath (**Sabbath after Sabbath**), **as a lasting covenant.** The bread with its **memorial portion** (*'azkārâ*; "reminder"), always set out before the Lord, serves to remind God of God's covenant with Israel (Milgrom 2001, 2094-95). At the same time, Israel's obligation to supply the ingredients for the bread is a ritual demonstration of Israel's ongoing commitment to abide by the covenant (2100).

The bread is designated for the priests **to eat** as **part of their regular share of the offerings** (see 6:14—7:36 [6:7—7:36 HB]). Thus, the incense for the memorial portion was burned on the altar, while the bread was eaten by the priests. This occurred each Sabbath when the bread was replaced with fresh loaves (Rashi in Carasik 2009, 196). The explicit notice that the priests eat the bread reinforces the notion that for Israel the bread is *not* intended as food to sustain God (→ 3:11).

2. Case of the Blasphemer (24:10-23)

■ **10-12** These verses introduce a narrative about **the son of an Israelite mother and an Egyptian father.** This man of mixed heritage engaged in **a fight** with **an Israelite.** The man of mixed heritage **blasphemed the**

Name. That the **Name** refers to "the name of the LORD" is made explicit in v 16. The **Name** refers to the divine name YHWH, which is not to be pronounced, out of reverence for God. The term *'ădōnāy*, which means "Lord," is read in place of the name (Hertz 1960, 526). Out of respect for this tradition, most English translations use "LORD" wherever YHWH is found in the OT text. The man is accused of having *wayyiqqōb* (**blasphemed**) and having *wayĕqallēl* (***cursed***). The first term, *wayyiqqōb*, stems from the verb *nāqab*, which can mean "pierce, bore" or "curse" (BDB 1952, 666, see entries I and II). However, in conjunction with *šēm* ("name"), *nāqab* means "utter, pronounce, designate" (Milgrom 2001, 2107-8; see Porter 1976, 192-93; also BDB 1952, entry I). The second term is literally a verb (***and he cursed;*** contrary to a noun as in the NIV) with God as the assumed object (see vv 15-16; Milgrom 2001, 2108; see also Wesley 1765, 430). Thus, the man both ***pronounced*** God's name and ***cursed*** God (see Rashi and Rashbam in Carasik 2009, 197). That is, the man used God's name in a curse. Both misusing God's name and cursing God are forbidden (Exod 20:7; 22:28 [22:27 HB; see NASB]; Wenham 1979, 311).

The man who cursed was placed **in custody until the will of the LORD should be made clear to them.** This is an illustration of the *living* aspect of OT law as it addresses new situations (see Gorman 1997, 135). In this context, it seems there had been no clear legislation to follow for this case. Thus, Israel inquires of the Lord, a verdict is rendered (vv 13-16), and new legislation is decreed (vv 17-22).

■ **13-16** The punishment decreed by the Lord regarding the **blasphemer** (vv 10-12) is death. The blasphemer is to be taken **outside the camp.** Executions are held outside the camp in order to avoid defiling the holiness of the camp (Hertz 1960, 527; Noordtzij 1982, 245).

All those who heard the blasphemer are instructed to **lay their hands on his head.** Those who heard the blasphemy are defiled by having a curse against God penetrate their thoughts. The ritual of laying hands on the guilty party serves to symbolically transfer the pollution back onto the blasphemer (Noth 1977, 180; Péter 1977, 53; Milgrom 2001, 2113-14; → 1:4). Alternatively, Hartley suggests that the hand gesture was a means of designating the guilty party and releasing the hearers from guilt in taking his life (1992, 410). This view, however, seems to be contradicted by the following instruction, which dictates that **the entire assembly is to stone him,** not just the hearers.

In the midst of the judgment against the blasphemer, related legislation is made explicit. **If anyone curses his God, he will be held responsible; anyone who blasphemes the name of the LORD must be put to death.** The same two verbs from 24:11 are found here, but in reverse order: *yĕqallēl* (**curses**) and *wĕnōqēb* (***pronounces*** [NIV = **blasphemes**]). It appears that the two verbs represent two distinct actions, each of which is prohibited: cursing God and pronouncing the name of the Lord (→ vv 10-12). Some hold that the first act relates to the case of a foreigner in the midst of Israel who may "curse his god," and therefore be subject to whatever punishment that god may be able to render. The second act refers to the more serious offense of *anyone* blaspheming the name of the Lord, the one true God of the universe (Noordtzij 1982, 246-47; see Philo, *Moses* 2.204-6). Others, however, view the two actions as parallel, describing the same sin (see Wesley 1765, 430). Lee suggests that the first verb is part of a general statement (v 15) that is developed more specifically by the statement containing the second verb (v 16). That is, the general act of insulting the deity in v 15 is developed by means of the more specific detail of pronouncing God's name in v 16. The general object **his God** (*'ĕlōhāyw*; v 15) is specified by **the name of the** Lord (*šēm-YHWH*; v 16). Finally the general penalty of being **held responsible** (*wĕnāśā' ḥeṭ'ô*; v 15) is specified as **death** (*môt*; v 16). Thus, the two laws of vv 15 and 16 depict a literary movement from the general to the specific while addressing the circumstances of a single case (2006, 348-49).

The second verb/act is repeated in the final phrase of v 16: **whether an alien or native-born, when he *pronounces* the Name, he must be put to death.** While some argue that pronouncing God's name for any reason is prohibited, others clarify that merely pronouncing the name of the Lord is not forbidden. Rather, pronouncing God's name is prohibited only when done in conjunction with cursing. Accordingly, the NJPS translates the opening of v 16 with "if he *also* pronounces the name Lord" (emphasis added; Milgrom 2001, 2117-19; see Rashbam in Carasik 2009, 198).

■ **17-22** The case of the blasphemer is interrupted by a short series of laws regarding retribution for death or injury. These laws are enveloped by the account of the blasphemer, which concludes with v 23. These laws are intertwined with the case of the blasphemer as evident by the literary pattern that begins at v 16 and concludes with v 22. This pattern highlights the central statement, which expresses the principle known as *lex talionis* (Latin; "law of reciprocal punishment, retaliation"): **fracture for fracture, eye for eye, tooth for tooth** (→ Behind the Text above). The concept is first expressed in this pericope as **life for life.** The expression of this principle in the Bible is not to be taken literally in terms of physical mutilation (re fractures, eyes, teeth), except in the case of capital punishment. In the case of the murder of a human life, capital punishment was called for because of the image of God in humanity (Gen 9:5-6; see Wenham 1979, 312) and the resultant pollution of the land in which God dwells (Num 35:31-34; de Vaux 1997, 150). Otherwise, **life for life** and the related phrases are to be understood as legal terms for *fair compensation*. The demand here is for "adequate and equitable" reparation, following "due and judicial appraisement of the injury inflicted" (Hertz 1960, 527). The intent of the principle here is financial recompense, not physical vengeance (Rashi and Ibn Ezra in Carasik 2009, 199). Accordingly, immediately following an expression of *lex talionis* in Exod 21:23-25, there follows a law requiring a slave to be liberated in compensation for the loss of an eye or a tooth (Exod 21:26-27). Likewise, preceding the same expression of *lex talionis* appears a law requiring payment of compensation and medical expenses in the case of one who injures another in a fight (Exod 21:18-19; de Vaux 1997, 150). The principle also applies in the case of animals: **anyone who takes the life of someone's animal must make restitution.** Thus, the offender must pay the owner enough money for him to buy another animal (Wenham 1979, 312). Such recompense would be especially important for a farmer who lost a valuable bull or goat.

Alternatively, the application of *lex talionis* in ancient Israel may have been meant to dictate the *maximum* amount of retaliation allowed. Such limits served to restrain vengeance from accelerating violence beyond what was proportionate to the original offense (Harrison 1980, 222; Noordtzij 1982, 248-49). This implies, in the case of human injury, not just monetary compensation, but literal physical retaliation penalties. This is suggested by the wording of the phrases in vv 19 and 20: **whatever he has done must be done to him** and as **he has injured** the other, so **he is to be injured** (emphasis added; Gane 2004, 420; see Milgrom 2001, 2126).

Alien (→ 17:8-9 and sidebar, "The *Gēr*, 'Sojourner,' 'Resident Alien'").

I am the LORD your God (→ 18:1-2 and Behind the Text for ch 17).

■ **23** The case of the blasphemer is closed by means of the fulfillment statement indicating that **the Israelites did as the LORD commanded** (→ Behind the Text above).

FROM THE TEXT

The light of the lamps in the tabernacle, representing both God's creation of light and the presence of God, depicts a powerful image of hope and assurance. God's light dispels the darkness and is not overcome as it burns continually. God's gracious presence watching over those who submit themselves to God's sovereignty (as the loaves arranged under the lamps) generates confidence and peace in the pursuit of holy living. A significant threat to such well-being in the community of God's people is the direct assault against God represented by the misuse of God's name in relation to cursing God. Merely hearing such an assault defiles the listener. So egregious is this act that those who hear it must transfer its pollution back to the blasphemer, and the blasphemer must be put to death. This ruling, like so many in OT law, seems antiquated and excessively harsh. Contemporary society often tolerates, protects, and at times celebrates the freedom to speak openly in opposition to authority. As humans we often place ourselves as the ultimate authority for our lives, proudly rejecting those who would seek to rule over us. Misusing God's name in the form of a curse against God represents a blatant denunciation of God's sovereignty. The Creator of the universe whose very breath sustains our being (Gen 2:7) is truly the only One who has the authority to give and take life. Blatant rejection of God, whether through turning to other gods or cursing God, leads to death. Like a potter who wields the clay that she brings to life (through form and function), God has the authority to destroy or prosper God's creatures (Jer 18:3-17). This may be seen as capricious on God's part or as a vindictive outbreak of wrath in reaction to rejection. In contrast, God's revelation repeatedly expresses God's desire to bless and prosper people in the context of loving relationships. Accordingly, another vantage point suggests that those who blatantly reject God *place themselves in a position of death*, not due to God's wrathful reaction, but due to having separated themselves from the source of life. So strong is God's desire for restoring relationship that, in Christ, God absorbs blatant rejection from humanity, even to the point of God's own death. In response God graciously returns forgiveness and love. With God's miracle of resurrection, even death is finally disabled for those who return and submit to God's sovereign love.

The particular application of the principle of *lex talionis* ("law of retaliation") in ancient Israel further demonstrates the progression of values God seeks to instill in God's people (→ From the Text for ch 20). In a society that tends to accelerate violence by means of retaliatory assaults with ever-increasing destructive results, the requirement for equity in punishment is a significant advance. Israel is instructed to restrict its penalties to the types of recompense that reflect justice and aim at reparation, rather than appeasing a lust for vengeance. In the process, God directs Israel's values toward life and humanity, above property and prejudice.

In contrast to other ancient Near Eastern law codes, Israel's instruction stands out by the humaneness of its punishments (de Vaux 1997, 149). While surrounding nations exact harsher penalties (reflecting higher value) in regard to property offenses, Israel is called to place higher value upon matters of family and religion (Wenham 1979, 311). Other nations applied principles of equity only to their *free* citizens, while God directed Israel to provide proper justice for native and stranger, rich or poor (see 19:15; Noordtzij 1982, 248; Hartley 1992, lxii). In Christ, God presses beyond justice and equity, to mercy and sacrifice. Instead of requiring equitable compensation, Christ calls followers to rise to a higher plane in the realm of love: "You have heard that it was said, 'Eye for eye, and tooth for tooth.' But I tell you, Do not resist an evil person. If someone strikes you on the right cheek, turn to him the other also" (Matt 5:38-39; see Harrison 1980, 223). Christ calls for a dramatic advance in the progression of ethics and values among God's people. Accordingly, Christians are called, not to judge equitably, but to give generously even as Christ gave as one innocent on behalf of the guilty.

H. Laws Regarding Sabbatical and Jubilee Years (25:1-55)

BEHIND THE TEXT

The sacred calendar begun in ch 23 continues in ch 25. Chapter 25 extends the concept of Sabbath by means of the Sabbatical Year and the Year of Jubilee. Chapter 23 identified the ordinary Sabbath at the end of every seven days, the Festival of Weeks at the end of seven weeks, and the seventh month as the month containing more sacred occasions than any other. This chapter now treats the Sabbatical Year at the end of seven years and the Year of Jubilee at the end of seven times seven years (see Hertz 1960, 531). The long treatment of the Year of Jubilee (25:8-55), compared to the treatment of the Sabbatical Year (vv 1-7), is due to the need for more detail in relation to the complicated arrangements attached to the Year of Jubilee (Noth 1977, 184). Chapter 25 is bound to the following chapter (ch 26), and together they constitute a unified speech from the Lord to Moses. This is evident in that ch 26 is missing the introductory statement, "The LORD said to Moses," which begins all the other chapters in the Holiness Code (chs 17—27). This speech begins and ends with the somewhat rare (for Leviticus) mention of this instruction coming from the Lord "on Mount Sinai" (25:1; 26:46; see 7:38; 27:34). The two chapters share the theme of the *land* and mention of the Sabbatical Year (Milgrom 2001, 2150-51; Gane 2004, 432).

The instructions for the Sabbatical Year focus on leaving the land fallow every seventh year (see Exod 23:10-11). There is little direct evidence that a Sabbatical Year was regularly practiced before the time of the Babylonian exile. Upon return from Babylon, the exiles promised to observe the Sabbatical Year as part of a larger commitment to keep God's laws (Neh 10:28-31 [10:29-32 HB]). Josephus writes that in the time of Alexander the Great, the Jews were released from paying tribute in the seventh year "because they did not now sow thereon" (*Ant.* 11.8.5-6). Likewise Julius Caesar waived annual tribute from the Jews during the seventh year "because thereon they neither receive the fruits of their trees, nor do they sow their land" (*Ant.* 14.10.6; see Hertz 1960, 531). Also, in the period of the Maccabees, it appears that the Sabbatical Year was observed (1 Macc 6:49, 53; see Noth 1977, 183).

The Year of Jubilee deals mainly with the return of family property to its original owner every fifty years. Laws similar to those attached to the Year of Jubilee are found in other biblical texts, but they call for the cancelation of slavery and debts every seventh year (Exod 21:2; Deut 15:1-15; Neh 10:31 [10:32 HB]; Jer 34:13-16). Porter suggests that the related legislation for the Year of Jubilee was crafted after the exile during a more developed economic period in which such debt cancellation would be too disruptive on a seven-year cycle (1976, 197; for a more detailed discussion of the possible origins and viability of the Year of Jubilee in early Israel, see Hartley 1992, 427-30).

The significance of these laws is best understood in light of ancient Israel's historical situation as an agrarian society. Nearly all indebtedness was related to the land. Loans were secured for the purpose of securing seed, tools, work animals, and the cost of laborers. Repayment was to be made after the harvest, by means of profits from the harvest. If adverse circumstances prevented paying off loans, then mortgaging or selling the land was required. Those who no longer owned land were often forced to sell themselves or their children as servants to work off debt. The laws related to the Year of Jubilee functioned to address such circumstances and bring a measure of relief in times of hardship and loss (Levine 1989, 169).

The centrality of *land* in this chapter is further evident by its prevalent occurrence. The term 'āreṣ ("land") occurs twenty times in ch 25 and is nearly the first and last word in the chapter. Land appears as the basis of life, and the primary entity upon which everything else depends (Gerstenberger 1996, 374). Two main statements express the supporting rationale for the instructions in this chapter. First, the *land* belongs to the Lord, and the Israelites live on it as God's tenants (vv 23-24). Second, the Israelites are God's servants who previously had been released from the *land* of Egypt (v 55).

These declarations provide the foundation for the regulations regarding land tenure and the redemption of indentured servants (Gorman 1997, 137).

IN THE TEXT

1. The Sabbatical Year (25:1-7)

■ 1-7 Holiness is extended to the land, which **itself must observe a sabbath to the** LORD (→ Behind the Text for ch 17). The text literally reads ***the land shall rest,*** **a Sabbath to the** LORD (see Milgrom 2001, 2152). For **six years** the land is to be sown and harvested as usual in relation to **fields, vineyards,** and **crops.** But every **seventh year** shall be designated *šabbat šabbātôn* (**sabbath of *complete* rest;** → 23:3) *for the land* (see NRSV). To give the land its rest, Israel is given the instruction: **Do not sow your fields or prune your vineyards. Do not reap what grows of itself or harvest the grapes of your untended vines.** Kalisch explains that the spontaneous growth of fertile fields may yield two or three harvests from a single sowing (1872, 544). Similarly, grapevines and fruit trees provide plenty of produce during a fallow year without requiring any labor (Milgrom 2001, 2159). The prohibition against reaping **what grows of itself** seems to contradict the provision that **whatever the land yields during the sabbath year will be food for you . . . whatever the land produces may be eaten.** The medieval Jewish exegetes explain the sense of the verses to mean that one should not reap even that which grows on its own *as if* it were his or her own possession to gather and store. That which the land yields on its own should be considered free to all. Thus, along with the rest of the community, an owner may reap what the land produces on its own (Rashi, Ibn Ezra, and Nahmanides in Carasik 2009, 203). Gersonides clarifies, "You shall not reap as the reapers do, all at once; you may only reap and gather little by little, as necessary, and so that others will also have the opportunity to do so" (in Carasik 2009, 203). Alternatively, the command not to reap even that which grows of itself may refer to cultivated land from which nothing may be eaten whatsoever, while that which may be eaten during the Sabbatical Year must only be taken from uncultivated *wild* lands (i.e., *living off the land,* as in the wilderness years; Porter 1976, 198; Harrison 1980, 224-25).

The Sabbatical Year teaches the Israelites to trust and depend on God for their sustenance (Wesley 1765, 431). It also develops a sense of community and sharing, as the fields, vineyards, and orchards belong to none but God (v 23), who makes them available to all, including the poor (Exod 23:11). Clement of Alexandria suggests that the law "educates us in piety, sharing, justice, and humanity" as the fallow land invites the poor "to use any crops that grow by God's grace, nature acting as farmer for any who will" (Lienhard 2001, 197). Similarly, Philo asserts that the Sabbatical Year provides dignity for the poor, and teaches liberality to the rich (*Spec. Laws* 2.105-7). Porter asserts that originally the practice of leaving the land fallow for a year was intended to "leave a year's produce for the spirits of the soil" (1976, 198). If so, this provides another example of how God's revelation transforms pagan ritual by investing it with God's own purposes (→ 3:11 and 19:9-10; also → sidebars, "Azazel: Wilderness Satyr" at 16:8 and "Agricultural Origins of Festivals" at 23:5-8, and From the Text for ch 16).

2. The Year of Jubilee (25:8-55)

■ **8-13** This regulation makes clear that **seven sabbaths of years** means seven *weeks* of years, that is **seven times seven years—so that the seven sabbaths of years amount to a period of forty-nine years**. After counting forty-nine years, the **trumpet** should be **sounded everywhere on the tenth day of the seventh month**, that is **on the Day of Atonement**. Like the first day of this seventh month during an ordinary year, *tĕrû'â* ("alarm") is to be sounded by means of a ram's horn (*šôpār* [popularly, "shofar"]). The alarm serves to announce the opening of the **jubilee** year and to call Israel to reflect on judgment and salvation (in relation to the Day of Atonement) and the mercies of God that sustain the nation throughout the year (→ 23:23-25). The Jubilee Year begins in the fall to coincide with sowing the new crop for the following harvest (see Ibn Ezra in Carasik 2009, 205).

Wesley explains that the Day of Atonement is an appropriate start date because as people seek forgiveness from God, they might also consider forgiving others' debts (1765, 432). Hertz adds that the message of both the Day of Atonement and the Year of Jubilee is one of *new birth*. The Day of Atonement frees people from sin and enables them to start life anew. Likewise, the Year of Jubilee sets people free from poverty and allows them a fresh start in relation to the social and economic strata within the community (1960, 532). Milgrom adds that the Day of Atonement is chosen to begin the Jubilee so that the *shofar* call (trumpet blast) would not be confused with the same call on the first day of the seventh month (23:24; Milgrom 2001, 2164). In addition, since the Jubilee Year **is to be holy,** it must begin only after the tabernacle and the people have been cleansed of impurity on the Day of Atonement (Gaster 1953, 183-84).

Israel is to **consecrate the fiftieth year.** As with the Festival of Weeks, which takes place on the *fiftieth* day ("day after the seventh Sabbath," see

23:15-16), the Year of Jubilee takes place in **the fiftieth year,** the year after **seven sabbaths of years** (see Milgrom 2001, 2163, 2169). Alternatively, some argue that the Year of Jubilee takes place during the forty-ninth year and corresponds with every *seventh* Sabbatical Year (North 1954, 109-34; Noth 1977, 186-87). Otherwise, a Jubilee Year during the following year (fiftieth year) would create two fallow years in a row (see vv 11-12; see Hertz 1960, 532). This would mean two years without a harvest, which some scholars argue is unrealistic. Noordtzij explains that the first year of the fifty years mentioned here must be a Sabbatical Year. Beginning the following year, counting seven Sabbaths (forty-nine years) would culminate in a Year of Jubilee, the same year as the seventh Sabbatical Year (1982, 251). Nevertheless, the sense of the text suggests that the Year of Jubilee is in the fiftieth year, distinct from the previous forty-ninth year, which would be a Sabbatical Year (thus, two successive fallow years; → vv 18-22).

The term *yôbēl* refers to a "ram" or "ram's horn" blown to announce the beginning of the *yôbēl* (**jubilee**) year (BDB 1952, 385; see Wesley 1765, 433). In the Year of Jubilee, **liberty** is to be proclaimed so that each person **is to return to his family property and each to his own clan.** The proclamation of **liberty** here includes both the release of slaves (sold into servitude to pay a debt) and the forgiveness of property debt (Rashi in Carasik 2009, 205-6; Basil the Great in Lienhard 2001, 198; Hertz 1960, 533). The release of indentured slaves returns people to their families, that is, **each to his own clan** (Wenham 1979, 319). Returning family property to original owners restores the initial division of the land among the tribes of Israel. This serves as a reminder that God is owner of all the land, and the people are God's tenants (v 23). In addition it prevents a few from accumulating land and swallowing up the inheritances of their brothers and sisters, and it prevents others from falling into poverty due to misfortune or mismanagement of resources (see Wesley 1765, 433; and Hertz 1960, 533).

The Hebrew term *děrôr* (**liberty**) corresponds to an Akkadian term that refers to an edict of release issued by Old Babylonian kings. Such an edict was sometimes issued when a king ascended the throne, as part of a suspension of debts and servitude (Levine 1989, 171-72). Milgrom asserts that this concept of debt release was not limited to Mesopotamia but is also evident to the north (Hittites), west (area of present-day Syria), and south (Egypt) in the ancient Near East (2001, 2168).

The fiftieth year is also to be treated like a Sabbatical Year in which the land must rest and lie fallow. Thus, Israel is instructed: **Do not sow and do not reap what grows of itself or harvest the untended vines . . . eat only what is taken directly from the fields.** As in the case of the Sabbatical Year, some argue that natural aftergrowth in the cultivated fields may not be eaten (i.e., **what grows of itself**). Rather, only that which grows in the "open, noncultivated ground may be consumed" (Noordtzij 1982, 379; → vv 1-7).

■ **14-17** These verses explain how to handle the purchase of land in relation to the law regarding the Year of Jubilee. **You are to buy from your countryman on the basis of the number of years since the Jubilee.** This statement seems irrelevant based on what follows. However, Kalisch explains that one must count the years that have passed since the *last* Jubilee in order to calculate how many years remain until the *next* Jubilee (1872, 556). Then the sale can be negotiated **on the basis of the number of years left for harvesting crops.** The price should **increase** or **decrease** relative to whether the remaining years until the next Jubilee are **many** or **few.** Thus, instead of land, what is really being sold is **the number of crops.** The calculation of the years impacting the price should exclude any Sabbatical Years (vv 2-7) remaining before the next Jubilee (Kalisch 1872, 556; see Wesley 1765, 433).

These verses begin and end with the admonition that the Israelites should **not take advantage of each other.** God's watchful concern to ensure that people are not oppressed or abused when negotiating over God's land (v 23) is evident in the command to **fear your God** (see 19:13-14; see also Noordtzij 1982, 254; and Levine 1989, 173).

I am the LORD your God (→ 18:1-2 and Behind the Text for ch 17).

■ **18-22** Verses 18-19 express God's declaration that those who **follow my decrees and** are **careful to obey my laws . . . will live safely in the land.** The Israelites are assured that if they obey, **the land will yield its fruit, and you will eat your fill and live there in safety.** Naturally, in light of the fallow years required during the Sabbatical Year and the Year of Jubilee, the question arises, **What will we eat in the seventh year if we do not plant or harvest our crops?** The Lord responds with the assurance that the harvest **in the sixth year** will be so abundant that it **will yield enough for three years.** This divine provision recalls the double portion of manna supplied on the sixth day in the wilderness, in order to provide for the weekly Sabbath (Exod 16:21-26; Hertz 1960, 534).

A number of scholars understand these verses as an explanation related specifically to the Sabbatical Year, which occurs every seven years. For some this pericope also applies to the Year of Jubilee because they hold that the Jubilee takes place concurrently on a Sabbatical Year (i.e., every seventh Sabbatical Year; → Lev 25:8-13; North 1954, 110-21; see also Noth 1977, 186-87; Porter 1976, 200; Wenham 1979, 319; Noordtzij 1982, 254-55; Levine 1989, 174; and Hartley 1992, 437). In contrast, these verses can be understood in their literary context in relation to the Year of Jubilee as the fiftieth year that follows a Sabbatical Year in the forty-ninth year (thus, two fallow years in a row; Harrison 1980, 225-26). Rashi argues that vv 21-22 refer to the Sabbatical Year but acknowledges that when a Jubilee occurs, then the yield of the sixth year must supply enough produce to last *four* years (Carasik 2009, 209).

The key, however, to recognizing that the text as it stands addresses both the fallow year of the Sabbatical Year and the following fallow year of the Year of Jubilee, lies in the overlap of religious (spring start) and agricultural (fall start) calendars. The agricultural calendar begins in the fall when planting/sowing takes place. This is followed by the harvest (reaping) in spring, which continues through the summer (→ 23:5-8 sidebar, "Agricultural Origins of Festivals"). Verses 21-22 of ch 25 speak in terms of the numbered-month (religious) calendar that begins with *month one* in the spring (Exod 12:2). At the same time, however, the Sabbatical Year and Year of Jubilee begin in the fall ("seventh month," Lev 25:9) after harvest and before sowing a new crop for the new *agricultural* year (→ vv 8-13 and 23:23-25). Thus, the reference to *planting* **during the eighth year** (25:22) refers to the fall segment of a year that began in the spring (religious calendar). At the same time, *planting* **during the eighth year** aligns with the new year that just began in the fall (agricultural calendar), following the end of the Year of Jubilee (thus sowing could commence). **The harvest of the ninth year** refers to the beginning of a new year in the spring (religious calendar), while at the same time aligning with the latter half of an agricultural year that began the previous fall (following the Year of Jubilee). The following table illustrates the sense of vv 21-22:

Fall		Spring
Fifth Year (plant)		Sixth Year (harvest)
Sixth Year (fallow) →	Sabbatical Year →	Seventh Year (fallow)
Seventh Year (fallow) →	Year of Jubilee →	Eighth Year (fallow)
Eighth Year (plant)		Ninth Year (harvest)

The Sabbatical Year begins in the fall of the sixth year and concludes in the spring of the seventh year, analogous to the Sabbath rest attached to the Day of Atonement that begins on "the evening of the ninth day" of the seventh month, and continues "until the following evening" of the tenth day (23:32). The same is true for the Year of Jubilee. According to this scheme, the harvest of the sixth year must yield enough for three calendar years (religious *spring* calendar); the sixth, seventh, and eighth years of the sabbatical cycle, until the harvest of the ninth year comes in (Gane 2004, 434-35; see Milgrom 2001, 2182-83; and Nahmanides in Carasik 2009, 209).

■ **23-24** At this point, the Lord expresses the supporting rationale behind the laws regarding land tenure. God states, **the land is mine**. Therefore, it is never **to be sold permanently**. The Israelites must keep in mind that they are God's **tenants**. The Israelites are designated *gērîm* (resident **aliens** who do not own land) in relation to God (→ 17:8-9 sidebar, "The *Gēr*, 'Sojourner,' 'Resident Alien'"). Nevertheless, the Lord refers to the land as that which Israel holds **as a possession** (granted by God as God's tenants).

In accordance with the regulations that follow, Israel must **provide for the redemption of the land.** Levine explains that the law of redemption is preferable to waiting for the Year of Jubilee. Land should be restored to the original *owner* as soon as financially possible (1989, 175). The Jubilee serves as a guarantee for restoring land to its originally assigned tribes (Num 33:50-56; Josh 13—19), in case the law of redemption is not carried out (see Milgrom 2001, 2185, 2189). More specifically, the Jubilee restores property to the appropriate "family" (Lev 25:10). A redeemer (near relative within the same clan as the original landowner) can only hold the land until the next Jubilee, at which time the redeemer must return the land to the original owner on behalf of whom the land was redeemed (2192). Wright explains that the Jubilee functioned as a further corrective beyond the practice of redemption. Over the years, land redemption may result in the entire territory of a clan being held by a few wealthy families in the clan, with other families in the clan living as indebted tenants of the wealthy. The Year of Jubilee prevents such from happening by restoring each individual "to his family property" (v 10; 1992, 1027).

■ **25-28** This is the first of several cases or stages of poverty for which *redemption* procedures are described. Each case is introduced with the phrase *kî-yāmûk ʾāḥîkā* (**if one of your countrymen becomes poor;** lit. *your brother;* vv 25, 35, 39, 47 [*ûmāk ʾāḥîkā*]). In this case, a poor countryman is forced to sell **some of his property**. In an attempt to keep the property within the same clan, it is to be redeemed by **his nearest relative**. The phrase *gōʾălô haqqārōb* includes the noun form of the verb **redeem** (*gāʾal*). Thus, the phrase might be translated **his nearest *redeemer*** (see Milgrom 2001, 2194). This is the source of the popular term "kinsman-redeemer" (see NIV at Ruth 3:12; 4:1). A second means of restoring the land to the clan is possible if the original owner **himself prospers** and is able **to redeem it**. Redemption occurs by means of payment based on the original selling price minus **the years since he sold it** (value of crops for those years, Lev 25:16; see Levine 1989, 176; Milgrom 2001, 2197). The original sale would have been based on the number of years from the original purchase date until the next Jubilee (vv 14-17; see Wesley 1765, 435). The final means of redemption, if the first two fail, is to wait **until the Year of Jubilee. At that time the land will be returned.**

Some hold that a redeemer immediately returns the property redeemed back to the original owner and never possesses the land himself (Noth 1977, 189; Levine 1989, 175). However, Milgrom argues that the redeemer does retain control over the redeemed land, until the Year of Jubilee. The first concern is for the land to be restored to the tribe of Israel to which it was originally allotted. Since the redeemer is a close relative, this concern is satisfied. However, the Holiness Code seeks to prevent tribal land from being gathered into the hands of only the wealthy tribal families (→ vv 23-24). Thus, at the Year of Jubilee, the redeemer must surrender the land back to the original owner in the tribe. This allows the redeemer the opportunity to regain the cost of redemption through the value of the crops remaining until the Jubilee (Milgrom 2001, 2195; see Pedersen 1926, 88-89).

■ **29-31** A **house in a walled city** creates a special circumstance in relation to the laws regarding redemption of property (v 29 indicates a **walled** city; the Hebrew text of v 30 indicates a city that has *no* wall, likely reflecting an error in the manuscripts). Such homes may be redeemed (purchased back by the original owner) within the first year of being sold. Otherwise, the house **shall belong permanently to the buyer and his descendants. It is not to be returned** even **in the Jubilee.** This exception does not apply to **houses in villages without walls.** Village homes are considered as if in **open country** and **can be redeemed** or **returned in the Jubilee.** Village homes are more closely tied to the land and are necessary for the management of the land (Wesley 1765, 435; see Harrison 1980, 226-27).

■ **32-34** The **Levites** constitute another exception to the regular rules regarding property redemption (→ vv 29-31). They **always have the right to redeem their houses in the Levitical towns.** Kaiser suggests that this special consideration for Levitical priests is reflected in *contemporary* housing allowances made for the clergy (1994, 1173). The tribe of Levi did not receive a regular inheritance of land as did the other tribes (Num 18:23-24; Josh 13:14, 33; 18:7). However, they were assigned towns in which to live, with pasturelands for their livestock (Num 35:1-5). These **Levitical towns** were allotted in all the tribes of Israel, so that every tribal territory had Levites living among them (Josh 21:1-8).

The homes of Levites were always **redeemable** and subject to being **returned in the Jubilee.** The opening phrase of v 33 is problematic: *waʾăšer yigʾal min-halĕwiyyim.* It can be read *that which one redeems from* *the Levites* (Levites as object) or **who of the Levites redeems** (Levites as subject). The first option, if understood as an Israelite redeeming his home back from a Levite, does not fit the context of the rest of the verse, which presumes that a Levite's home is the subject of redemption here. If understood as a Levite redeeming his home back from another Israelite or Levite, the reading becomes redundant with v 32. Furthermore, this view actually treats the Levite as subject, not object, of the phrase. The second reading implies the situation in which a Levite redeems a home on behalf of a fellow Levite. Even though it may be a home in a walled city, it is still subject to redemption because it is a Levitical home. The Levite redeemer may be tempted to think that he may forever keep the home he has redeemed since it remains a Levitical property (now in his hands). He may also think that, like a normal Israelite house in a walled city, it can be held forever (after the first year). However, the Law refutes both thoughts and clarifies that the Levitical home must be returned to the original Levite owner **in the Jubilee** (Milgrom 2001, 2202-3; see Nahmanides in Carasik 2009, 212; also Harrison 1980, 227).

Levitical **pastureland belonging to their towns must not be sold.** These lands are a **permanent possession** for the Levites. Such land could not be sold because it did not belong to an individual but to the community of Levites who resided there (Noordtzij 1982, 257; see Porter 1976, 203).

■ **35-38** These verses address for Israel a second case in which **one of your countrymen becomes poor** (→ vv 25-28). This case generally includes any circumstance resulting in the poor person being **unable to support himself among you.** The Israelites are instructed to **help him** in order to enable the person to **continue to live among you.** The foundational concern is to provide for every fellow Israelite so that they can continue to live among the people of Israel, as expressed twice in this pericope (vv 35, 36). The regulation includes practical means of supporting a fellow countryman through the following commands: **Do not take interest of any kind from him,** and **you must not lend him money at interest or sell him food at a profit.** Interest in the ancient Near East could be thirty percent or more (Noordtzij 1982, 258; Kaiser 1994, 1173). Milgrom cites evidence suggesting interest was as high as sixty percent in Elephantine (2001, 2209).

This exhortation to support a countryman in need is reinforced by the reminder to **fear your God** and by the expression of who is speaking, that is, **I am the LORD your God** (→ vv 14-17). In addition, referring to the poor person as equivalent to **an alien or a temporary resident** in conjunction with the reminder that God **brought you out of Egypt,** where *all* Israelites were once aliens, suggests that the poor person is to be considered no different from the rest of those in Israel (see Exod 23:9; Deut 10:17-19). God's generous treatment of the Israelites, to whom God gave **the land of Canaan,** serves as a model for how the Israelites should treat each other (Matt 18:23-35; 1 John 4:11; Wenham 1979, 322).

■ **39-43** Another case in which **one of your countrymen becomes poor** is addressed here (→ vv 25-28). In this instance, the poor person reaches a state in which he **sells himself to you.** Nehemiah 5:1-5 provides a vivid illustration of conditions that press people to sell their land, themselves, and even their children into servitude (Gerstenberger 1996, 383). The person who does so is not to be treated **as a slave.** Instead, **he is to be treated as a hired worker.** The person will work as if a hired laborer **until the Year of Jubilee** (see v 10). This situation appears to reflect that of a paid servant whose family resides with the employer, although the servant is not actually paid (Porter 1976, 205). That is, his labor serves as compensation to pay off his debt, without additional financial remuneration to the servant. In contrast, v 49 implies a servant may somehow "prosper" financially. Gerstenberger describes the situation as one in which the debtor surrenders his land (sells it), hires out as a day laborer, and works what was previously his own land for a meager wage. If the debtor could not save enough to pay off his debt, then he must wait for the Jubilee (1996, 384).

Milgrom clarifies that *for Israelites,* slavery is abolished here, including debt-slavery. Similar to what Gerstenberger describes, debt-slavery is transformed into work-for-hire in which the worker's wages are used to pay off his debt (Milgrom 2001, 2212-14). It is striking that no provision is described here regarding redemption for the poor Israelite who sells himself to a fellow Israelite (see vv 25-27, 48-49). The reason is because this person is *not* a slave but rather is a hired worker (2216). Here H has improved upon the laws of Exod 21:2 and Deut 15:12 (releasing slaves after seven years), by *eliminating* the slavery of Israelites. Instead, the indebted Israelite is released to his family property as soon as he pays off his debt or when the Jubilee arrives (2253). At the Year of Jubilee (if the debt has not yet been paid), **he and his children are to be released** in order to **go back to his own clan and to the property of his forefathers.** The contrast with texts that call for the release of fellow Israelite servants every *seven* years (Exod 21:2; Deut 15:12; Jer 34:14; as opposed to fifty years for the Jubilee release) may reflect a change made in the context of postexilic conditions (→ Behind the Text above; in contrast to Milgrom's view that H effectively eliminates the slavery of Israelites).

Employers (masters?) are exhorted to **not rule over them *harshly*** (i.e., over their fellow Israelite servants). This is reinforced with the reminder to **fear your God** (→ Lev 25:14-17 and vv 35-38). In addition, employers are put on the same level as their hired servants when God reminds them that all **the Israelites are my servants** (see Gerstenberger 1996, 389).

■ **44-46** The Israelites are informed, **your male and female slaves are to come from the nations around you.** Slaves can also be purchased if they are non-Israelites **living among** the Israelites. Clearly such slaves are not released at the Jubilee, since they can be willed to **children as inherited property** and made **slaves for life.** This instruction supplements and contrasts vv 39-43, which address the issue of *Israelite* servants, who are not to be treated as slaves. As expressed in the previous pericope, Israel is told **you must not rule over your fellow Israelites ruthlessly** (see v 43).

■ **47-55** These verses address the final case in this list in which **one of your countrymen becomes poor** (→ vv 25-28). In this instance the poor person **sells himself to the alien living among you.** This is a case in which an Israelite sells himself as a slave to a non-Israelite, specifically a *gēr* (alien; → 17:8-9 sidebar, "The *Gēr*, 'Sojourner,' 'Resident Alien'"). This instruction indicates that the poor countryman still **retains the right of redemption.** This is in contrast to the reverse situation (a resident alien enslaved to an Israelite, vv 45-46). It is also in contrast to an Israelite servant working for a fellow Israelite, who is only released at the time of the Jubilee (unless he pays off his debt first; → vv 39-43; also Porter 1976, 206).

The Israelite who has sold himself into servitude to an alien may be redeemed by any one of three methods. **One of his relatives may redeem him.** As in the case of one who redeems land, the redeemer would likely hold on to the redeemed relative as a servant, until the Jubilee, in order to reimburse the cost of redemption (Milgrom 2001, 2237; → vv 25-28). Alternatively, **if he prospers, he may redeem himself.** If both of these possibilities are not realized, then **he and his children are to be released in the Year of Jubilee** (→ vv 25-28).

The cost of redemption is to be determined based on the number of years remaining until the Year of Jubilee. First the amount *per year* of the original sale is calculated **from the year he sold himself up to the Year of Jubilee.** This amount can then be multiplied by the number of years remaining until the Jubilee (see Rashi in Carasik 2009, 216). Accordingly, **if many years remain,** the slave owner is to be reimbursed **a larger share of the price paid** for the slave. **If only a few years remain until the Year of Jubilee,** when the slave will be released anyway, then the cost of redemption will be less. In effect, the servant **is to be treated as a man hired from year to year.** Thus, just as crops are sold rather than land (v 16), so labor is sold rather than persons (see Rashi in Carasik 2009, 216; Wesley 1765, 437).

In regard to an Israelite enslaved to an alien, Israel is exhorted to **see to it that his owner does not rule over him ruthlessly** (see vv 43, 46). God proclaims that the reason Israelites may not be kept as permanent slaves is because **the Israelites belong to me as servants. They are my servants, whom I brought out of Egypt** (→ vv 39-43).

I am the Lord your God (→ 18:1-2 and Behind the Text for ch 17).

FROM THE TEXT

The land of Israel is personified as the Lord requires that the land "*observe* a Sabbath to the Lord" (emphasis added). The concept of Sabbath is extended through time (→ Behind the Text above) and in relation to physical space (land). The agricultural practice of leaving land fallow on a regular cycle is enfolded into the framework of Sabbath. Sabbath *rest* is applied to everyone and everything. When the land takes its rest during the Sabbatical Year, the people must be satisfied with whatever grows of itself in the fields and vineyards. No individual can make personal claim to what is produced. All are allowed to partake freely, while there is no official *harvest* and no particular *owner* besides God (see Noordtzij 1982, 250).

Psalm 24:1 well expresses the foundation underlying the laws of both the Sabbatical Year and the Year of Jubilee ("the earth is the Lord's, and everything in it"; see Lev 25:23). God ordains that the land must have its rest. In so doing, God promises to provide for the nutritional needs of God's children (vv 20-22). This arrangement serves to generate trust and dependence upon God in relation to human sustenance. The Israelites depended on God for food and protection through the wilderness, and likewise they must depend on God's provision for ongoing life in the promised land. This highlights a significant characteristic of holiness in relationship to God. God's children through all of history must learn to trust the Lord in all circumstances of life. This goes hand in hand with the realization that ultimately, as humans, we own nothing. As the Israelites learned that the land belongs to God and they are only God's tenants, so we must learn that all we have comes from the Lord and belongs to God, and we are merely stewards of the resources God grants to us. Dependence upon the Lord not only sustains God's people through *fallow* years but also keeps God's people from wrongful overdependence upon, and greedy pursuit of, material goods. Philo conveys the character-building benefits of embracing a *fallow* year:

> Do not, he says, be entirely under the power of lucre, but submit voluntarily to some loss, so that you may find it easy to bear some involuntary injury, if ever it should occur, instead of resenting it as some strange and alien misfortune and falling into despair. For some of the rich are so poor-spirited that when adversity overtakes them, they are

as mournful and depressed as if they had been robbed of their whole substance. But among the followers of Moses all who have been his true disciples, trained in his excellent institutions from their earliest years, by allowing even rich territory to lie idle inure themselves to bear privations calmly and by the lesson of magnanimity thus learned voluntarily and deliberately to let even undoubted sources of wealth fall almost from their very hands. (*Spec. Laws* 2.87-88)

Similarly, Harrison expresses the importance of observing God's Sabbaths in order to avoid obsession with the accumulation of material wealth to the exclusion of all else. This same principle is evident in Christ's instruction to seek first God's kingdom and trust God for necessary provisions (Matt 6:33; Harrison 1980, 225).

As a personal commitment to developing a character of dependence upon God and charity toward others, a radio preacher once described how he and his wife divested their home every five years of all their possessions and started afresh without worldly attachments. Stewardship of possessions extends even to the point of self. As is true for the Israelites, all those who seek after holiness must recognize that we belong to God as God's servants (Lev 25:55; see 1 Cor 6:19).

The purpose of the Year of Jubilee was to restrain poverty and impede social divisions. When a person incurs debt, he may be forced to sell his land or sell himself and family members as servants to work off the debt. Without restraints, such conditions lead to a segregation characterized by wealthy landowners exploiting poor landless tenants. The prophets condemned the types of injustice and oppression that separated the community into classes distinguished by wealth and resource. Isaiah denounces those "who add house to house and join field to field till no space is left and you live alone in the land" (5:8; see also Isa 3:14-15; Amos 2:6-7; 4:1; 8:4-6; Mic 3:1-3). By providing for the redemption of land and eliminating slavery in Israel (in favor of *work-for-hire*), the Year of Jubilee offered the opportunity to eliminate personal debt and regain a fresh start (see Wenham 1979, 317).

As with the presence of patriarchal biases and harsh penalties for certain crimes, the acceptance of slavery in the OT (see Lev 25:44-46) reflects the ancient Near Eastern context within which the laws of Israel are disclosed. In light of God's greater revelation in the Bible, such is not to be taken as God's will for humanity. Consider Paul's bold exhortation to Philemon to treat Onesimus as a brother and no longer a slave, in the face of a similar ancient context (Phlm 15-16). Noordtzij states that OT law regarding slaves already demonstrates progression beyond that of other nations in the ancient Near East (Exod 21:20-26; Deut 23:15-16 [23:16-17 HB]; Noordtzij 1982, 260; → From the Text for Lev 18 and 20). Priestly law takes a large step forward by abolishing the enslavement of Israelites to Israelites (→ 25:39-43). Revelation from God may advance God's people at a pace that we do not understand, but it often does so without compromising God's overall commitment to human freedom (even when that freedom is exercised poorly).

I. Reward, Punishment, and Repentance (26:1-46)

BEHIND THE TEXT

Chapter 26 continues the speech begun in ch 25 (→ Behind the Text for ch 25). The book of Leviticus draws near its close with a series of blessings (26:3-13) and punishments (26:14-39), in response to obedience and disobedience respectively. The chapter then closes with an emphasis on the benefits of repentance in terms of God's remembering the covenant with Israel. The list of blessings and punishments reflect the ancient Near Eastern tradition of concluding treaties with blessings and curses directed toward those who keep or break a contract. The same can be found in Deut 27—28 (see Noth 1977, 195-97; Porter 1976, 208-9). Once again, this attests to how God's revelation makes use of that which is familiar to the ancient context and invests it with God's own purposes (→ sidebars "Azazel: Wilderness Satyr" at 16:8 and "Agricultural Origins of Festivals" at 23:5-8 and From the Text for ch 16).

Wenham identifies the structure of the chapter based on repeated phrases within the material. The blessings are introduced by the phrase *wěnātattî* ("I will give," vv 4, 6, 11; Wenham 1979, 328). Alternatively, one might argue that the blessings are introduced simply by first person singular verbs with God as the subject ("I will . . ."; vv 4, 6, 9, 11, 12; see Hartley 1992, 457). The curses are introduced with phrases similar to, "if you will not listen to me" (vv 14, 18, 21, 23, 27), and "I shall punish you" in conjunction with "seven times for your sins" (vv 16, 18, 21, 24, 28; Wenham 1979, 328). The series of blessings begins with *'im* ("*if* you follow my decrees," v 3, emphasis added), while the series of punishments begins *wě'im* ("*but if* you will not listen to me," v 14, emphasis added).

The repetition of "if" in the series of punishments introduces progressively more severe consequences if disobedience continues (vv 18, 21, 23, 27). A final "but if" reflected in the *sense* of the text (v 40) brings to an end the escalating threat of penalties and seeks to turn around the progression of sin by calling for confession and repentance (Gane 2004, 452). This is consistent with the pattern often found among the eighth-century prophets in which oracles of wrath and punishment are invariably followed by oracles calling for repentance and promising restoration. This is illustrated by the overall structure of Hosea, in which oracles of judgment are followed by words of salvation. Punishment and salvation alternate in the opening chapters of Hosea as follows: judgment (1:2-9); salvation (1:10—2:1 [2:1-3 HB]); judgment (2:2-13 [2:4-15 HB]); salvation (2:14-23 [2:16-25 HB]). Likewise chs 4—11 and 12—14 emphasize words of judgment, yet both sections culminate in oracles of hope and salvation (11:1-11 and 14:1-8; see Mays 1969, 15-16). This suggests that the purpose of judgment and punishment is to drive Israel to repentance and restoration (see Porter 1976, 213; Milgrom 2001, 2289). In the same way, the punishments of ch 26 culminate in a call for confession (vv 40-41) and promise of restoration through God's remembrance of the covenant (vv 42-45).

As occurs with ch 19, ch 26 begins and ends with double appearances of the characteristic signature, "I am the LORD" (vv 1-2, 44-45; Harrison 1980, 231; → Behind the Text for ch 17). Verse 46 of ch 26 serves as a conclusion summarizing the entire Holiness Code (chs 17—26) with all of its "decrees, the laws, and the regulations"; contributing to the thought that ch 27 follows as an appendix (Levine 1989, 182, 192; see Gorman 1997, 142, 148). Balentine suggests that the use of *tôrōt* ("laws") in v 46 may refer to *all* the ritual and ethical regulations in the book of Leviticus (2002, 197; see Hoffmann 1906, 379).

IN THE TEXT

1. Blessings for Obedience (26:1-13)

■ 1-2 The treatment of the Sabbatical Year and Year of Jubilee in ch 25 is followed by the closing blessings and punishments of ch 26 (→ Behind the Text above). However, between the two chapters appear these two verses with a prohibition against **idols** and an exhortation to **observe my Sabbaths and have reverence for my sanctuary** (see 19:30). The rejection of idols is required in order to worship God alone with one's whole heart, soul, and strength (Deut 6:5; see Bonar 1851, 471). Bonar asserts that observing Sabbath and reverencing God's sanctuary serve to guard such wholehearted devotion: "All declension and decay may be said to be begun wherever we see these two ordinances despised—the *Sabbath and the sanctuary*. They are the *outward* fence around the *inward love* commanded by ver. 1" (472; → 19:3 sidebar, "Observing the Sabbath"). Chapter 19 opens with similar statements regarding idols and the Sabbath (19:3-4).

Reverence for my sanctuary may include properly fulfilling all the obligations related to the purification of the tabernacle and carrying out the instructions regarding the entire sacrificial system centered around the tabernacle (see Hertz 1960, 539). This would serve to link this closing section of the Holiness Code to the sacrificial and impurity laws in chs 1—16.

■ **3-5** A series of blessings is introduced based on the conditional statement, **if you follow my decrees and are careful to obey my commands**. In addition to the usual verb *šāmar* ("keep" [NIV = **careful to obey**]; see 18:5, 26; 19:37; 20:22; 22:31), 26:3 includes the term *tēlēkû*, indicating, literally, that Israel should ***walk*** in God's **decrees** (see 18:4). This suggests that God's laws constitute the proper "path of life" (see 18:5; Levine 1989, 182). Agricultural blessings (26:4-5, 10) imply that the **decrees** and **commands** may refer to the immediately preceding instructions regarding the Sabbatical Year and Year of Jubilee (ch 25). However, the additional blessings related to peace, security, and the presence of the Lord (26:6-9, 11-12) suggest that the call for obedience here refers to the entire Holiness Code (chs 17—25).

God's blessing in response to obedience includes **rain in its season** so that **the ground will yield its crops and the trees of the field their fruit**. Rain is especially needed in dry climates like Palestine in order for crops and orchards to survive, not to mention flourish (see Porter 1976, 209-10; Noordtzij 1982, 264). The **threshing** of grain **will continue until grape harvest**, which in turn **will continue until planting** (season of sowing grain). As a result, **you will eat all the food you want**. Normally there was a two-month gap between the grain harvest and the picking of grapes and olives (Wenham 1979, 329). The extension of harvests so that they overlap each other reflects the eschatological promise of the same phenomenon in the age to come: "'The days are coming,' declares the LORD, 'when the reaper will be overtaken by the plowman and the planter by the one treading grapes'" (Amos 9:13; Kaiser 1994, 1179). The blessings of faithfulness to the Lord include the provision of plenty of food for sustenance. The last phrase of Lev 26:5 introduces the following blessings of peace and security (vv 6-9) with the promise that you will **live in safety in your land**. Alternatively, safety here may relate to the preceding agricultural blessings by promising freedom from the fear of famine, as also implied by 25:19 (Hertz 1960, 542).

■ **6-8** Blessings of **peace** and security **in the land** are expressed in terms of the elimination of threats from wild animals and human enemies. Israel is assured that **you will lie down and no one will make you afraid**. In the context of war, when the land is "desolate," "wild animals" become more "numerous" (Exod 23:28-29; Hertz 1960, 542). Thus, God **will remove savage beasts from the land**. Human enemies will also be eradicated. **The sword** [symbol of war; see Wesley 1765, 438] **will not pass through your country** in the form of enemy threat. In contrast, **you will pursue your enemies** who **will fall by the sword before you**. Divine assistance will be evident as **five of you will chase a hundred, and a hundred of you will chase ten thousand**.

■ **9-12** The description of blessings continues with a focus on abundance and God's presence. Forms of the tandem verbs *pārâ* ("be **fruitful**") and *rābâ* ("multiply, **increase**") in v 9 reflect the theme of abundance that H has extended from priestly material found in Genesis (P^N; see Introduction, "C. Composition"; King 2009, 144; also Porter 1976, 210). Verse 12 further reflects the **covenant** in P^N recorded in Gen 17. God's commitment to Israel to **be your God** echoes the same commitment made to Abraham and his descendants in Gen 17:7-8 (see Gorman 1997, 143). In addition, the assertion from God promising that **I will walk among you** depicts P^N's unique description of faithful people who "walk about" with God (Gen 5:22, 24; 6:9; 17:1; these verses share with Lev 26:12 use of the hithpael form of the verb *hālak*; King 2009, 144, also 79-80, 85-87; see also Hartley 1992, 463).

The blessing of abundance extends to agricultural produce. God proclaims that **you will still be eating last year's harvest when you will have to move it out to make room for the new** harvest. The blessings of obedience are climaxed with the promise of God's presence within the community. The expression **I will put my dwelling place among you** may refer to the tabernacle as the place of God's presence in the community (→ From the Text for 4:1—6:7 [4:1—5:26 HB]). However, as characteristic of H, God's presence is extended throughout the community with the more intimate assurance that **I will walk among you** (→ Behind the Text for ch 17; also Levine 1989, 184; Milgrom 2001, 2300-2301).

■ **13** I am the LORD your God (→ 18:1-2 and Behind the Text for ch 17).

The blessings close with a reminder to Israel that God is the One **who brought you out of Egypt so that you would no longer be slaves to the Egyptians**. This recalls the latter portion of the previous chapter, which also makes reference to deliverance from Egypt and emphasizes that the Israelites are no longer to be treated as slaves (25:39-40, 42, 55). In this instance, Israel's freedom is expressed in the context of blessings producing a liberty and security that enable the Israelites **to walk with heads held high** (see Wesley 1765, 439). The metaphor of a **yoke** accentuates the point. The weight of a yoke around the neck causes one to be bent over. Once the yoke is broken and removed, the person can stand upright (Levine 1989, 184). Reference to the great deliverance from Egypt also provides a reminder of God's power, thereby assuring Israel that God is able to bring about the above blessings (Hertz 1960, 543; Harrison 1980, 231).

2. Punishments for Disobedience (26:14-39)

■ **14-17** The list of punishments begins with a condition that contrasts the corresponding condition for the blessings: **But if you will not listen to me** (see v 3). The condition for punishment is expressed with a redundant series of related phrases: **if you will not listen . . . not carry out all these commands . . . if you reject my decrees . . . abhor my laws . . . fail to carry out all my commands . . . violate my covenant.** The instruction seeks to emphasize what will bring on the following punishments from the Lord. The terminology used here expresses deliberate disobedience and a repugnant attitude toward God's law (Hartley 1992, 464). This extended introduction likely serves for the entire list of punishments, in addition to the various sub-introductions (vv 18, 21, 23, 27; Gerstenberger 1996, 412). Divine discipline is exercised out of God's love and God's desire to correct the evil ways of his children (Deut 8:5; Ps 94:12; Prov 3:11-12; Jer 30:11; 31:18; Heb 12:5-11; Wenham 1979, 330-31).

The punishments begin with a broad statement threatening **sudden terror, wasting diseases and fever that will destroy your sight and drain away your life** (see Deut 28:22). The phrase *mĕkallôt ʿênayim* can literally be translated "which exhausts the eyes." It implies the eyes are worn out (with tears) due to anxious expectation (Levine 1989, 185; see 1 Sam 2:33; Lam 4:17). The safety promised in response to obedience is compromised by disobedience as the Lord informs Israel that **you will be defeated by your enemies** (see vv 6-8). Agricultural abundance will be reversed **because your enemies will eat** the crops (see vv 4-5). Instead of a few Israelites chasing many enemies (v 8); the Israelites will run from none, as they are told **you will flee even when no one is pursuing you** (see Kaiser 1994, 1180). Fear and dejection will result in a type of paranoia (see Hertz 1960, 543).

■ **18-20** The punishments for disobedience increase in severity (Hertz 1960, 543), and each step is introduced with a conditional statement; in this case, **if after all this you will not listen to me** (see vv 21, 23, 27). The Lord declares, **I will punish you for your sins seven times over.** The punishments are intended to turn Israel from its sin (Gorman 1997, 145). The reference to sevenfold affliction is repeated with each step increase in the severity of punishments (see vv 21, 24, 28). The number seven is understood to represent wholeness and totality (→ 4:5-7). This suggests that the punishments described will be complete and extensive (Noth 1977, 199). However, since further punishments in later verses include the same statement of wholeness, it appears that for some, one round of discipline is not complete enough. Alternatively, the number seven here may simply represent "very much more" (Hertz 1960, 544).

God's opposition to **stubborn pride** is well documented in the OT (Deut 8:10-20; 1 Sam 2:3; Ps 75:4-7; Prov 16:18; Isa 2:9-17; 13:11). Further punishment is described in terms of agricultural failure. With the **sky above you like iron,** rain will not be able to fall through such a hard surface (Wesley 1765, 440; Porter 1976, 214). As a result, **the ground beneath you like bronze** will be too hard for planting (see Deut 28:23). Gerstenberger suggests that these are poetic expressions depicting the sky with a strong sun as a "glowing iron plate," and the scorched earth "like bronze" (1996, 415). **Your strength will be spent in vain** when attempting to sow seed in such hard and dry ground. The **soil will not yield its crops, nor will the trees of the land yield their fruit.** This contrasts the blessing described in Lev 26:4-5.

■ **21-22** The next stage increase of punishment is introduced with the expanded conditional statement, **if you remain hostile toward me and refuse to listen to me** (see v 18). In addition, Israel is reminded that the punishments are dispensed **as your sins deserve.** Once again, God's instruction makes clear the reason for punishment (i.e., remaining hostility and refusal to listen, as sins deserve; → vv 14-17). In response to *ongoing* sin and disobedience, God will **multiply your afflictions seven times over** (→ vv 18-20). The blessing of safety from "savage beasts" (v 6) is reversed as God **will send wild animals** to devastate Israel. They will threaten **children, cattle,** and adults who will end up **so few in number that your roads will be deserted.** The sense of the verse may also indicate that fear of wild animals will be so great that no one will venture out on the roads (Noordtzij 1982, 268; Hartley 1992, 465).

■ **23-26** A further increase in punishment is promised **if in spite of these things you do not accept my correction but continue to be hostile toward me** (see vv 18, 21). God's punishments are not vindictive expressions of wrath but are intended as **correction** and discipline (Hertz 1960, 544). In response to continued disobedience, God **will be hostile toward you and will afflict you for your sins seven times over** (→ vv 18-20). Hostility toward God, and sins, are equated with **breaking of the covenant.** Levine explains that the term for **avenge** (*nōqemet*) in this context "does not mean 'vengeance,' in the usual sense, but rather the threat of punishment" (1989, 187). The **sword** represents punishment in the form of war (→ vv 6-8). Israel's withdrawal into its **cities** contrasts the blessing in which only a few will be needed to chase numerous enemies (v 8). Furthermore, their cities will not provide refuge or escape, for **plague** will find them, and they will still be delivered **into enemy hands.** This overturns the blessings of peace and success against enemies expressed in vv 6-8. Consistent with a siege of war (**sword**), Israel's food supply will be diminished. **Ten women** will only have enough **to bake your bread in one oven** (see Rashbam in Carasik 2009, 226; Noth 1977, 199). Bread will have to be rationed **by weight** (see Hertz 1960, 544). There will not be enough to eat in order to **be satisfied.**

■ **27-35** A final warning is conveyed to Israel beginning with the conditional statement, **if in spite of this you still do not listen to me but continue to be hostile toward me** (see vv 18, 21, 23). God declares, **I myself will punish you for your sins seven times over** (→ vv 18-20). The conditions resulting from this punishment decline to the point of cannibalism: **you will eat the flesh of your sons and the flesh of your daughters.** Cannibalism reflects the worst stage of famine, which results from a prolonged war siege (Deut 28:53-57; Jer 19:9).

This punishment describes the rejection and destruction of sacred places and objects that have been used in idolatrous worship or in conjunction with hypocritical worship. This includes **high places, incense altars, idols, sanctuaries,** and **offerings.** Even the sacrifices and offerings that are part of legitimate worship are worthless if not accompanied by moral obedience (Hertz 1960, 545; → From the Text for Lev 1:1—3:17; also → sidebar at 4:1—6:7 [4:1—5:26 HB], "The Representative Nature of Sacrifice"; also → 4:5-7). The term used here for **idols** (*gillûlêkem*; **your idols**) derives from *gālāl*, which means "dung, dung balls" (Milgrom 2001, 2319). The term "draws a parallel between human excrement and the form of the idol images and is the most contemptuous term in the Hebrew language" (Noordtzij 1982, 269). This is consistent with the prophetic tendency to mock idols (Isa 44:9-20; 45:20; Jer 10:3-5, 8, 14-15; → Lev 19:4). In addition, the **land will be laid waste,** Israel's **cities will lie in ruins,** and the Israelites will be scattered **among the nations.** This depicts a dramatic contrast to the blessing of God's intimate presence within the community (vv 11-12). Life without God (having rejected God) becomes devoid of meaningful worship and leads to devastating ruin and loss. Nevertheless, even in the midst of tragedy, God's purposes can be advanced through those who repent (vv 40-45). Having been scattered among the nations provides opportunity for the spreading of God's word (Hertz 1960, 545). This does not mean that God requires or desires tragedy to accomplish God's will, but rather it illustrates the gracious miracle of bringing forth good from wrongful circumstances (see Gen 50:20).

In the aftermath, **the land will enjoy its sabbath years** while **it lies desolate**. Verses 34 and 35 redundantly emphasize that **the land will have the rest it did not have during the sabbaths you lived in it**. This expression of divine irony depicts the land finally resting while Israel is expelled from it (Noordtzij 1982, 270). The Sabbath rest for the land that Israel has neglected is associated not only with fallow ground but also with releasing the fields to provide for the poor, restoring inherited property, and canceling indebtedness (see ch 25).

■ **36-39** **As for those of you who are left** likely refers to those who survive the punishment described in vv 27-35. Thus, these verses simply continue the previous pericope (Hertz 1960, 545). Survivors will be made **fearful in the lands of their enemies**. Panic will overtake them as they flee **even though no one is pursuing them** (→ vv 14-17). The ongoing devastation depicts war (**sword;** → vv 6-8) and exile. Israel **will perish among the nations**. Those **who are left will waste away in the lands of their enemies because of their sins**. The punishment is also attributed to **their fathers' sins**. This may suggest God's longsuffering in delaying punishment for more than one generation. Sinful parents will endure the pain of watching their children suffer for following the evil example of their parents (Hertz 1960, 546). Similarly, Rashi contends that with the phrase **because of their fathers' sins** the verse implies the condition, *if they (the children) continue the same evil behavior* (in Carasik 2009, 229). Hartley asserts that though individuals are accountable for themselves before God, the accumulated sins of generations will bring punishment upon the nation (1992, 468-69).

3. Repentance and Remembrance of Covenant (26:40-46)

■ **40-45** Following blessings (vv 3-12) and punishments (vv 14-39), the chapter transitions to repentance. In contrast to continuing in sin, **if they will confess their sins**, humble **their uncircumcised hearts**, and **pay for their sin**, God will **remember** the **covenant** with **their ancestors** and **the land**. Relationship remains foundational as both the people and God must act for reconciliation. "The blend of divine grace and human responsibility is apparent" (Gorman 1997, 147). Humbling uncircumcised hearts recalls God's opposition to pride (→ vv 18-20). **Uncircumcised hearts** evoke the covenant with Abraham in which the sign of circumcision was instituted for Israel (Gen 17:10-11). Uncircumcised hearts represent those who have placed themselves outside the covenant due to disobedience (Deut 30:6; Jer 4:4; → Lev 19:23-25). The **covenant with Jacob** may recall the Sinai covenant addressed to "the house of Jacob" (Exod 19:3). However, reference to the **covenant with Isaac** and especially the **covenant with Abraham** suggests that it is particularly (though not exclusively) the Abrahamic covenant being recalled here (Gen 17). This is affirmed by the promise **to be their God** (Gen 17:7-8), which points to the restoration of God's intimate presence (→ Lev 26:9-12). This is further highlighted by the one instance in which the "the characteristic signature" of the Holiness Code appears with a third person suffix instead of the usual second person suffix (**I am the L**ORD **their God;** → From the Text for ch 17). Remembering **the land** in the context of the **covenant with Abraham** implies restoration from exile (see 26:38-39) in light of God's promise to give "the whole *land* of Canaan . . . as an everlasting possession to you and your descendants after you" (Gen 17:8, emphasis added; see Porter 1976, 217). Of course, the covenant with **Abraham** was renewed and passed on to **Isaac** and **Jacob** (Milgrom 2001, 2334-35).

The repentance described here presumes the context of punishment in exile, **for the land will be deserted by them and will enjoy its sabbaths while it lies desolate without them.** God's promise is *not* **to destroy them completely.** "God desireth not the death of the sinner; and, therefore, every threat of punishment for disobedience is followed by a promise of mercy, if there is repentance and amendment. Divine discipline is for moral ends; and in truth the Exile proved a purifying furnace unto Israel" (Hertz 1960, 546; → Behind the Text above). God is "ever hopeful that his people will repent" (Hartley 1992, 465). In remembering the covenant and land, and opening the door to restoration through repentance, God does not dispense measure-for-measure justice to Israel. Instead, mercy reigns as Israel will continue to be the people of God, and the promises of the covenant will remain (Gerstenberger 1996, 432; Milgrom 2001, 2337). Milgrom asserts that the covenant God promises to remember refers to both the patriarchal covenant (Abrahamic) and the Sinai covenant (2001, 2338-39).

■ **46** Reference to regulations established **on Mount Sinai** serves to enclose the speech begun in ch 25 (see 25:1; → Behind the Text for ch 25). **These are the decrees, the laws and the regulations** may serve as a conclusion to the Holiness Code, or perhaps the entire book of Leviticus (→ Behind the Text; also Hertz 1960, 547).

FROM THE TEXT

The principle that obedience will result in blessing while disobedience will bring punishment is certainly expressed here and throughout the OT. This principle is sometimes referred to as the retribution dogma. It is a *general* principle and should not be considered absolute in this world. The book of Job struggles directly with this doctrine. Job and his friends appear to hold fast to the retribution dogma. However, Job is frustrated because he does not experience it functioning properly. As he undergoes suffering (assumed to be punishment), Job cannot identify any sin or disobedience that would justify such pain. Even God describes Job as "blameless and upright, a man who fears God and shuns evil" (Job 1:8; 2:3). Accordingly, the retribution dogma would dictate that Job should be blessed with great prosperity, but instead he undergoes tremendous loss.

Likewise the Psalmist and writer of Ecclesiastes struggle with the prosperity of the wicked and the suffering of the righteous (Pss 10:1-15; 73:3-16; Eccl 7:15; 8:14). The OT thereby reflects the reality of injustice and unfairness in this broken and sinful world. Nevertheless, in texts like Lev 26 and many others, God continues to affirm the general rule that obedience brings blessing, and rebellion invites punishment from the Lord. Furthermore, hope is expressed from an eternal perspective that *in the end* God will set all things aright (Eccl 8:12-13; Dan 12:1-3 Rev 21—22; see Gane 2004, 459). This same dichotomy of seeing blessings and punishments mercifully distributed in the last judgment, but only provisionally in the contemporary world is expressed also in the NT (Rom 8:18; Wenham 1979, 334).

The description of punishments with increasing severity promised "seven times over" in ch 26 calls to mind the repeated destruction brought about by the ten plagues against Egypt (Exod 7—12), and the waves of devastation following the seven seals, seven trumpet blasts, and seven bowls of wrath in the Apocalypse (Rev 6—16; see Wenham 1979, 331). Such thorough retribution makes one wonder if there are enough *thirds* of creation available for each wave of destruction (Rev 8:7-12; 9:15, 18). Clearly, such multiple rounds of punishment ("seven times over") are meant to symbolize a complete chastisement and cleansing of sin.

Such a list of harsh punishments may seem excessive. In addition, the first person references to God as the one personally administering the punishments might depict God as vengeful and vindictive. However, the representation of God in Lev 26 is consistent with much of the OT. It reflects the OT mentality of the sovereignty and authority of God. Accordingly, even though humans bring upon themselves the consequences of their own wrongful behavior, God takes responsibility for the actions of God's creatures (→ 14:33-35 sidebar, "God Takes Responsibility for Creation"). Another way of viewing punishments directed against Israel is to consider the consequences of life with God, and life without God. When the Israelites reject God and break covenant with God through apostasy and disobedience, they enter into life without God (by their own choosing). When God is pushed aside and discarded, the Israelites lose God's blessing and protection, thereby leaving themselves vulnerable to their enemies (see Hartley 1992, 464-65). Kaiser affirms that God's judgments do not come in a vindictive manner, but rather God speaks "out of the events of life, so that erring believers might all the more quickly be restored to favor" (1994, 1183). Life without God collapses into the kind of meaninglessness and loss described in 26:14-39. This is contrasted by the blessings of life with God described in vv 3-13.

The long list of punishments concludes with a call to repentance and hope for restoration (vv 40-45). In the end, God's mercy overwhelms any supposed need for the type of justice that demands measure-for-measure retribution (see Hos 11:8-9).

God's promise to uphold the covenant is unilateral; it will not be subverted, not even by God's own commitment to the talionic principle for judgment. Even when Israel languishes in exile, convinced that its sins have effectively canceled every conceivable divine incentive for mercy, God will not abandon the covenant that begins with an inviolable divine promise—"I am the Lord your God" (v 1)—and ends with an equally inviolable divine hope—"You shall be my people" (v 12). When the final word of chapter 26 is spoken, the gift of "the statutes and ordinances and laws" at Sinai (v 46) should summon Israel to celebrate, not fear, *God's promise not to be bound by God's own principles of justice.* (Balentine 2002, 203, emphasis added)

J. Consecrations and Redemption (27:1-34)

BEHIND THE TEXT

The book of Leviticus seems to conclude at 26:46 (→ 26:46 and Behind the Text for ch 26). Chapter 27 appears as an appendix addressing contributions to the Lord. It does not directly relate to the preceding material, except for mention of the Year of Jubilee, which is treated with more detail in ch 25. Noth claims ch 27 is a later supplement that should be considered a separate unit, originally distinct from the Holiness Code (1977, 203-4). Hertz claims that ch 27 concludes the book of Leviticus as it began, with a focus on sanctuary regulations (1960, 547). The main topic of ch 27 is gifts dedicated to the Lord. Much of the instruction in this chapter deals with the monetary valuation of such gifts. The first two sections of the chapter deal with the dedication of persons and animals (vv 2-13) and houses and land (vv 14-24). Each of these sections is introduced by the designation for a general category, *'îš kî* ("if anyone," v 2/"if a man," v 14). In each case, subsidiary specific instances are introduced with *wĕ'im* (*and if;* vv 4, 5, 6, 7, 8, 9, 11, 13, *15, 16, 17, 18, 19, 20, 22*). This pattern of organization is also found in the early chapters of Leviticus (→ Behind the Text for 1:1—3:17 and 4:1—6:7 [4:1—5:26 HB]). The final section of the chapter contains miscellaneous regulations regarding dedications (27:25-33; Wenham 1979, 336-37).

The system of monetary equivalents for dedications is reflected in 2 Kgs 12:4-5 (12:5-6 HB). The king of Judah collected funds to repair the temple from various sources, including "the money received from personal vows" (2 Kgs 12:4 [12:5 HB]) such as those described here in Lev 27 (Levine 1989, 193).

IN THE TEXT

I. Vows Regarding Humans and Animals (27:1-13)

■ 1-8 When a special vow to dedicate [*yaplī' neder;* see v 14] persons to the LORD is made, a payment could be rendered instead of actually leaving the person as a servant for the priests (as was done with Samuel; 1 Sam 1:11-28). Ordinary persons so dedicated could not do the work of priests or Levites, but they could function in some type of subservient role to them (i.e., nonceremonial duties; Harrison 1980, 235). However, if the sanctuary was overrun with such helpers, or some other circumstance prevented such service, payment could be made to the priests in order to redeem such persons (Wesley 1765, 443; see Noth 1977, 204).

Alternatively, it is argued that there were no duties related to the tabernacle that non-Levites could perform (Num 18:1-7). Therefore, ordinary people were required to release themselves from any **vow** dedicating themselves or their family to the Lord, by means of a payment to the sanctuary (Wenham 1979, 338). An example of such income being used for the sanctuary can be seen in 2 Kgs 12:4-5 (12:5-6 HB), which describes King Joash collecting funds, including those from "personal vows," in order to repair the temple (see Kaiser 1994, 1187).

These verses in Lev 27 indicate the monetary **value** determined to be **equivalent** to persons when they are dedicated to the Lord. The monetary value for dedicating a person varied depending on age and gender. The valuation of a **male** is set higher than that of a **female**, likely due to the perception of their comparative physical strength and the patriarchal attitude toward women in ancient Israel. The valuation is based on a perception of the productive *ability* of men versus women (Hertz 1960, 547; Levine 1989, 193; → From the Text for ch 18).

Wegner suggests that the discrepancy between the valuation of men and women may be based on the perception of their respective capacity to contribute *economically* to society. "Women occupied with childbearing and nurturing would have less time to devote to their 'economic' labor at spindle or loom" (1992, 43). In terms of age, the greatest value is set for those **between the ages of twenty and sixty**. The next highest value is set for those **between the ages of five and twenty**. Then, the next to the lowest monetary value is placed on those **sixty years old or more**. Finally, the lowest monetary equivalent is placed on those **between one month and five years** of age. If a person is **too poor to pay the specified amount**, the priest will set the value at an amount the person **making the vow can afford**. The **equivalent values** seem to reflect how much a person may have been able to contribute in terms of labor to the work of the Lord (Noordtzij 1982, 275). The greatest value was placed on those whose age reflected the most strength and vitality (see Wesley 1765, 443-44). Once again, concession is made to enable the poor to participate in sanctuary activity (→ 2:1, 4-9; 3:1; 5:7-10 and From the Text for 1:1—3:17).

Payments for dedications are to be made with **shekels of silver** and are to be delivered into the sanctuary treasury (Hertz 1960, 547). To ensure a standard measure of weight for a shekel, dedicatory payments of silver are to be audited **according to the sanctuary shekel** (→ 27:25).

■ **9-13** One who donated animals or property to the sanctuary was held in high esteem (Levine 1989, 194). These verses address the regulations for vows in which **an animal** is dedicated. If the animal is one that is **acceptable as an offering to the Lord**, it will become **holy**. The status of holiness makes the animal eligible for the altar (Wesley 1765, 444). This also restricts the animal as the exclusive property of the sanctuary (Hertz 1960, 548). At this point, redemption of the animal is no longer possible (Levine 1989, 194). This would include domestic animals "from the herd" (cattle; see 1:3), "from the flock" (sheep, goats; see 1:10), and "of birds" (see 1:14). Such an animal dedicated to the Lord in a vow should not be exchanged or substituted with another animal. If a substitution is attempted, then the owner loses both the original and substitute animal as each of them **become holy**. This serves as a penalty against those who may wish to trade out a good animal for a lesser quality animal, thereby compromising the act of reverence in giving one's best to the Lord (see Wesley 1765, 444). Such a substitution is described and condemned by the prophet Malachi: "Cursed is the cheat who has an acceptable male in his flock and vows to give it, but then sacrifices a blemished animal to the Lord" (Mal 1:14; see Milgrom 2001, 2376-77).

If the animal to be dedicated in a vow is **ceremonially unclean,** and therefore **not acceptable as an offering to the** LORD, its **quality** must be judged by the priest, who will establish its **value. If the owner wishes to redeem the animal,** the owner must pay that value and **add a fifth to its value.** Unclean animals are not eligible for sacrifice. Therefore the priests can use such animals for their own purposes or sell them for profit (Wenham 1979, 339). Most domestic animals (cattle, sheep, goats) are eligible for sacrifice on the altar. It is likely that the unclean animals referenced here are *blemished* animals that would otherwise be acceptable for sacrifice (see 22:21-22; Rashi in Carasik 2009, 234). Otherwise, **unclean animal** here refers not to the quality but to the kind of animal (see ch 11; Wesley 1765, 444). An animal of a species that is not eligible for sacrifice on the altar is to be donated based on the value of the animal itself, rather than its benefit as a sacrifice. That is why such animals may be redeemed (Levine 1989, 194-95).

2. Consecrations Regarding Houses and Fields (27:14-25)

■ **14-15** If a person *consecrates* (*yaqdîš;* see v 2) his house as something holy to the LORD, its **quality** will be judged by the priest, who will establish its **value.** If the owner **redeems it,** he must pay that value and **add a fifth to its value.** Thereby, **the house will again become his.** Philo explains that adding twenty percent to the value, for the redemption price, is penalty for thoughtlessness in making the vow and for greed in desiring to regain what was consecrated (*Spec. Laws* 2.37). Houses consecrated to the Lord become property of the sanctuary, and the priests may use or sell them as they determine. It is presumed that such houses are "in a walled city." Otherwise they would revert back to the original owner at the Jubilee (25:29-30; Wenham 1979, 339).

■ **16-21** These verses deal with the consecration (*yaqdîš;* see v 14) of a field that is part of a person's **family land.** The next unit (vv 22-25) addresses the person who wishes to consecrate a field that has been purchased and is "not part of his family land." Family land requires unique handling because it reverts back to the owner in the Year of Jubilee (25:8-24). The monetary **value** of family land **is to be set according to the amount of seed required for it.** The standard rate is **fifty shekels of silver to a homer of barley seed.** Thus the value of the field is initially determined based on the size of land required for properly sowing one homer of barley seed (Kalisch 1872, 625). The value of the field is to be adjusted based on the **number of years that remain until the next Year of Jubilee** (from the year when the field is consecrated). The **set value** of the field is determined by the number of homers of barley seed needed to sow the field over forty-nine years (time between Jubilees; see Hertz 1960, 548). This is reduced by the value of the required seed for the number of years that have passed since the previous Jubilee (→ 25:14-17 and 25:25-28).

If the man who *consecrates* the field wishes to redeem it, he must pay the value of the field and **add a fifth to its value**. Then, **the field will again become his. If, however, he does not redeem the field, or if he has sold it to someone else, it can never be redeemed**. Wesley clarifies that selling the field (after having been consecrated to the Lord) refers to the priests who might sell it after the original owner has refused to redeem it (1765, 445-46; see Rashi in Carasik 2009, 235; also Levine 1989, 196). Thus, if not redeemed or if sold, at the next Jubilee the field **will become holy**. At such time it reverts **to the LORD** and becomes **the property of the priests**.

Alternatively, v 20 can be read, **if, however, he does not redeem the field, but has sold the field to another** (see NASB). This has been interpreted as an act of dishonesty in which the owner sells that which has already been given over to God. In such a case, the dishonest owner loses the land permanently (Porter 1976, 223; see Kalisch 1872, 625; also Noth 1977, 206). Haran explains a third rendering of v 20. He suggests that the phrase **has sold the field to another** can be understood as having taken place *before* the land was consecrated (i.e., it was consecrated *after having sold it*). Consecrating the land after selling it means that the original owner intends for the land to become a permanent gift to the sanctuary at the next Jubilee. In other words, the owner has turned over his right to regain the land in the Jubilee, to the sanctuary (Haran 1971, 394; cited in Milgrom 2001, 2385; and in Gane 2004, 466).

■ **22-24** Instructions regarding the consecration (*yaqdîš*; see vv 14 and 16) of a field continue from the previous verses (16-21). This case involves a person's **field** that has been purchased and is **not part of his family land**. If a man *consecrates* such a field, it must be redeemed (in regard to its consecration, not inheritance), **and the man must pay its value on that day** (see Wenham 1979, 341). Levine adds that the person must also pay the additional fifth of its value (1989, 197). However, that is not stated in the text, and since redemption is mandatory in this case, it does not seem likely that the *penalty* of the extra twenty percent would be applied (see Gerstenberger 1996, 445). The payment becomes **something holy to the LORD**, but not the field itself, which reverts to the original owner in the Jubilee (→ vv 9-13; Hartley 1992, 484). Though it is not part of the current owner's family land, the field is "family land" for **the person from whom he bought it**. Thus, in the **Year of Jubilee the field will revert** to that original owner.

■ **25** In relation to all the transactions described above (vv 2-24), the value of a shekel is determined according to the standard of the **sanctuary shekel**. **Twenty gerahs** refers to the proper weight of a sanctuary shekel (Exod 30:13; Num 3:47; 18:16). The use of *silver* ingots and objects for commerce is evident in Palestine as early as the tenth century B.C. A system for weighing silver appears to have been used in Judah during the seventh century B.C. The system included marked dome-shaped stones as weights. Stone weights for one, two, four, and eight shekels were used. Stones were marked with the sign for "shekel" and the appropriate amount (Mazar 1990, 510-12). Second Samuel 14:26 mentions another unit of measure for shekels called the "royal standard" (lit. "stone of the king" or "king's weight"; see NASB, NRSV; also "the royal 'stone,'" Levine 1989, 197).

3. Firstborn, Devoted Things, and Tithes (27:26-34)

■ **26-27** The remaining verses of this chapter add some clarifying regulations regarding the dedication, redemption, and sale of persons and property. For example, **the firstborn of an animal** *cannot* be dedicated to the Lord, simply because **the firstborn already belongs to the LORD** (Exod 13:1-2, 12-15; 22:29-30; 34:19-20; Num 3:40-51; 8:14-18). If a firstborn is **one of the unclean animals,** the owner may redeem it (i.e., **buy it back**) **at its set value, adding a fifth of the value to it** (see Lev 27:13). If it is not redeemed by the owner, then **it is to be sold at its set value** (as initially determined by the priest; see v 12). **Unclean** firstborn animals are most likely to be redeemed or sold because they are not eligible to be sacrificed on the altar. The proceeds are to be given to the priests or added to the sanctuary treasury (Wesley 1765, 446-47; → vv 9-13). Levine argues that this represents a change in sanctuary administration. According to Exod 13:13 and 34:20, the firstborn of a donkey (example of unclean animal) must be redeemed or killed. Thus the sanctuary could attain no benefit from an impure animal (if not redeemed). The legislation here allows for the sanctuary to dispose of impure animal donations at a profit, by having them sold if they are not redeemed (1989, 198).

■ **28** Distinct from something dedicated with a vow (*yaplîʾ neder;* v 2) or something consecrated (*yaqdîš;* v 14), that which is *devoted* [*yaḥărîm*] to the LORD may *not* be sold or redeemed. Such persons or things are **most holy to the LORD** (*qōdeš-qodāšîm;* a status above that which is merely *qōdeš* ["holy"]; see vv 9, 10, 14, 21, 23). Most-holy persons and objects become the permanent property of the sanctuary. Hertz explains that a purchased field (not inherited "family land") or an Israelite servant could not be **devoted** in this way. This is because the field would revert to the original owner in the Jubilee, and the Israelite servant would regain freedom in the seventh year (1960, 549-50).

■ 29 This verse relates to those who are placed under "the ban" (*ḥērem*) in order to be destroyed. This term and its related verb are normally applied to pagan nations, such as the Canaanites, who are offensive to the Lord because of extreme immorality and idolatry (Num 21:3; Deut 7:1-2; 20:16-18; Josh 6:17). Nevertheless, even those among the Israelites who join in apostasy are subject to being **devoted to destruction** (Deut 13:12-18 [13:13-19 HB]). Such persons may *not* **be ransomed**. As opposed to *yigʾal* ("redeem") used throughout Lev 27 (vv 13, 15, 19, 20, 27, 28, 31, 33), the verb *yippādeh* ("ransom") appears in v 29. This verb also appears in v 27 ("buy back"), seemingly in parallel with *yigʾal* ("redeem"). Persons devoted to destruction **must be put to death** in order to eliminate the spread of unrepentant rebellion against the Lord. The use of "devoted" in v 28 refers to a "priestly devotion" in which such objects or persons become property of the sanctuary. However, the use of **devoted** in v 29 reflects a "judicial devotion" in regard to the violation of God's commandments (Noordtzij 1982, 278-79; similarly, Milgrom refers to a "peace-*ḥērem*" and a "war-*ḥērem*," 2001, 2392-93).

■ 30-33 **A tithe is required of everything from the land.** A *tenth portion* (*maʿśar*; see BDB 1952, 798) of crops and fruit **belongs to the LORD and is holy to the LORD.** Likewise, the **tithe of the herd and flock** is to be designated **holy to the LORD**. This includes **every tenth animal that passes under the shepherd's rod** (see Jer 33:13; Ezek 20:37; see Wesley 1765, 447-48). In choosing the tithe, the owner of the animals **must not pick out the good from the bad or make any substitution.** If a substitution is made, the owner loses both animals, which **become holy and cannot be redeemed** (→ vv 9-13). If a person does redeem any tithe (of that eligible for redemption), **he must add a fifth of the value to it.**

■ 34 The chapter, and effectively the book, closes with the summary statement indicating that **these are the commands the LORD gave Moses on Mount Sinai for the Israelites** (→ 26:46 and Behind the Text for ch 26).

FROM THE TEXT

This chapter provides legislation regarding the dedication and consecration of persons and property to the Lord. Votive dedications, consecrations, tithes, and offerings represent various required and voluntary gifts to the Lord. Such contributions acknowledge God's sovereignty as Creator and ultimately as the owner of all that exists. Such presentations also serve to express devotion, praise, and gratitude to God.

Israel's donations and offerings to the Lord are mostly allotted to the priests and the sanctuary treasury (except for those, such as burnt offerings, that are wholly consumed unto the Lord). This is to provide a livelihood for the priests who have "no inheritance among the Israelites" (Num 18:23-32) and to support the services of the sanctuary. In a similar manner, contemporary offerings serve to provide for those who dedicate their lives as ministers and to support the work of the church.

For those who fear that giving too much to God will bankrupt them, Leviticus includes the assurance of God's provision: "You may ask, 'What will we eat in the seventh year if we do not plant or harvest our crops?' I will send you such a blessing in the sixth year that the land will yield enough for three years" (25:20-21). In light of such promise, the contemporary church should take note that it does not stand in the role of sacred *tax collector*, demanding payments and mandating faith. Rather, as with the priests in Leviticus, the church has opportunity to demonstrate compassion by acknowledging when someone "is too poor to pay the specified amount" (27:8). At the same time, the poor are not to be eliminated from participating in acts of dedication and consecration. As with the rituals of the sacrificial system, economic limitations should not exclude any of God's people from the inspiration and blessing of offering life to God (Mark 12:41-43; → Lev 2:1, 4-9; 3:1 and From the Text for 1:1—3:17).

While it is often tempting to calculate exactly how much one must hand over to God, the book of Leviticus makes it evident that such a calculation has no end. Believers rich and poor have often struggled to comply with the requirement of giving a tithe, on the one hand without endangering their livelihood, and on the other without adopting a legalistic and callous attitude toward giving. However, Leviticus makes it clear that ten percent is only the beginning of a holy heart toward God.

The discussion of the tithe is near the end of a chapter already filled with opportunities for contributing to the sanctuary in terms of animals, houses, and land. Elsewhere in the book, people are exhorted to leave portions of their harvest for the sake of the poor and alien (23:22). The epitome, however, of offerings to God is expressed in the dedication of self and family to the Lord (27:2-8). The purification offering at the height of the sacrificial system includes the representation of offering one's life to God (→ sidebars, "The Offering of Life in the Sacrificial System" at 4:32-35 and "The Representative Nature of Sacrifice" at From the Text for 4:1—6:7). Wenham alludes to the totality of one's giving to the Lord in his description of the theme of holiness in Leviticus:

Those not of priestly stock can still serve God, indeed they must be holy for God is holy (11:44-45; 19:2; 20:7, 26). This theme runs through chs 11-20: the elect people of God must visibly embody the character of God. In their choice of food, in sickness and in health, in their family life, in their honest and upright dealing, and in their love of neighbor, they show the world what God is like. (1979, 342-43)

Gregory the Great recognized the same call for complete consecration to God as expressed in the NT: "What is said by the law is less exacting than what is commanded by the Lord. The law prescribed the giving of a tithe, but our Redeemer ordered those who would follow the way of perfection to give up everything" (Mark 10:21; Lienhard 2001, 204).